Survival by Association
Supply Management Landscapes of the Eastern Caribbean

The establishment of the European Economic Community in 1957 put preferential agreements with non-European trading partners in jeopardy, projecting the spectre of economic ruin for small Caribbean territories dependent on only one or two crops. Yet, surprisingly, almost forty years later certain industries, notably the banana industry, are still vital elements in Eastern Caribbean economics. How have they survived? Barbara Welch answers this question by comparing the banana industries of Dominica, St Lucia, Martinique, and Guadeloupe and the critical role of the banana growers' associations in preserving a precarious status quo.

Although the four islands have similar colonial backgrounds and more-or-less parallel development of the postwar banana industry, Welch finds dramatic variations in land use from island to island. She argues that the most critical factor in differences in land use is not politico-economic affiliation, agrarian structures, or the physical environment but the growers' associations that regulate the banana industries. She provides an account of the origin and development of banana growers' associations in the Eastern Caribbean, assesses the impact and influence of their policies and activities, and examines the way in which both associations and land-use patterns have evolved since the 1960s.

Survival by Association addresses an issue of crucial importance not only for the banana growers of the Eastern Caribbean but for all developing countries whose economies are in jeopardy as a result of major realignments in patterns of world trade.

BARBARA WELCH is research associate in geography, McGill University.

Survival by Association

Supply Management Landscapes of the Eastern Caribbean

BARBARA M. WELCH

McGill-Queen's University Press
Montreal & Kingston • London • Buffalo

ISBN 0-7735-1370-1 (cloth)
ISBN 0-7735-1543-7 (paper)

Legal deposit second quarter 1996
Bibliothèque nationale du Québec

Published simultaneously in the Caribbean by
The Press University of the West Indies
Mona Kingston 7 Jamaica WI

Printed in the United States on acid-free paper

McGill-Queen's University Press is grateful to the Canada Council for support of its publishing program.

Canadian Cataloguing in Publication Data

Welch, Barbara M. (Barbara Marian), 1940–
Survival by Association : supply management landscapes of the eastern Caribbean
Includes bibliographical references and index.
ISBN 0-7735-1370-1 (bnd)
ISBN 0-7735-1543-7 (pbk)
1. Banana trade - Caribbean Area. 2. Caribbean Area - Economic conditions - 1945- I. Title
HD9259.B3C45 1996 338.1'74772'09729 C95-920847-X

Typeset in Baskerville 10/12
by True to Type Inc.

I dedicate this book to my parents, who in 1961 saw me embarked for the West Indies on the *Ascania* on a fifteen-month odyssey to study volcanic landforms. If they did not view this enterprise with wild enthusiasm, at least they accepted it with admirable sang-froid.

Contents

Tables

Figures

Preface

Driving north from Hewanorra Airport in St Lucia in February 1988, it struck me forcefully that the present was a foreign country: they did things differently here, and I was a stranger in this unfamiliar land of straightened roads, bypassed villages, and stuccoed villas with arcaded verandahs. Indeed, it actually was a different country from the one I had first visited twenty-six years before, when it was part of the already faltering Federation of the West Indies, and had last left in 1967, as a British Associated State, a stopgap status contrived to accommodate remnants of Empire unable to balance their budgets. By the 1980s, few countries were prepared to acknowledge an unbalanced budget as a disqualification for nationhood, and St Lucia had become an independent member of the Commonwealth. Could there be any point in trying to pick up the threads of a study begun over twenty years ago in what now seemed to have been an entirely different land? Were the characteristics and activities of banana growers' associations still of any relevance in the Antillean landscapes of 1988?

My reimmersion in the Eastern Caribbean milieu brought swift reassurance. It would be absurd to suggest that nothing had changed since the 1960s, and yet in many respects the predicament of the area's all-important banana industries in the late 1980s evoked a strong sense of déjà vu. Like the Day of Judgement, the full implementation of the Treaty of Rome in the insufficiently distant future was anticipated with varying degrees of dread. Production was expanding, markets were saturated, and in four neighbouring islands, producers' associations were confronting similar problems with four different and independent strategies, each association expressing the conviction that its approach would prove to be the most appropriate.

As I originally conceived it more than twenty years ago, the study on which this book is based was to cover a timespan of two or three years, but circumstances conspired to postpone its completion until two decades had passed. While this delay has permitted me to add a whole new dimension to what was initially a study focusing on spatial rather than temporal variation, it has also subjected conclusions reached tentatively in the early 1970s to the uncompromising test of time.

During the lengthy gestation of this work, I have received inspiration and encouragement from many quarters. It was on my first visit to the Caribbean in 1961–62 that chance remarks by friends about the disparate colonial heritages of Britain and France provoked my curiosity about the real nature and importance of culture as a factor in landscape development. In 1966, supported by the funds of the Centre for Developing-Area Studies and the enthusiasm of the Department of Geography of McGill University, I embarked on a comparative study of Eastern Caribbean land use from which the present work was an offshoot. I express my profound gratitude to my McGill colleagues, but most especially Professor Theo Hills, for the stimulation and help they gave me at this period.

When I decided to pursue this offshoot, I received sterling advice and encouragement from Professor David Harris, then a member of the Department of Geography of University College, London. My thanks are due to him and also to other members of the University College geography department who have taken an interest in this project over the years and contributed food for thought.

Following the bibliography, I have appended a list of the many individuals – academics, government officials, and agricultural experts for the most part – with whom I had personal communication in the course of this work. To them I owe an immense debt of gratitude for the wealth of fascinating information and stimulating ideas with which they provided me. It is perhaps invidious to single out any names when all were so ready to help, but I feel I should particularly mention Professor David Edwards of the University of the West Indies' Department of Agricultural Economics at St Augustine, Trinidad, who gave me invaluable assistance in devising the questions in my 1966 survey, and Professor Guy Lasserre, Professor of Geography at the Université de Bordeaux, who, among other kindnesses, facilitated my access to many key sources of information in Paris in the spring of 1969.

It would be almost impossible to mention all the dozens of people in the islands of the Eastern Caribbean who contributed in one way or another to the progress of this study. Perhaps the best I can do is to offer my special thanks to four individuals, one in each of the four study islands, who were the catalysts who made the whole enterprise possible.

In 1966, Mr. Kenneth Monplaisir, the Managing Director of the St Lucia Banana Growers' Association, arranged for me to meet all the key participants in the island's banana industry and to visit growers in every district. And when he sped me on my way to Martinique, it was with introductions that gave me immediate access to the director of that island's banana growers' organisation. Twenty-two years later, when I reappeared out of the blue, I was welcomed as if I had been gone only a couple of months, and meetings with current leading figures in the banana industry were organised at a moment's notice.

In Martinique, it was M. Paul Emélie, poet, philosopher and *ingénieur agronome* who advised me in the 1960s and again in 1988, when he put me in touch with those currently responsible for directing the destiny of the island's banana industry.

In Dominica, the name that stands above all others is that of my dear friend, the late Miss Vanya Dupigny. She introduced me to everyone I knew in Dominica, and it was a privilege and a delight to be swept up in her dynamic orbit. Dominica will never be the same without her.

In Guadeloupe, my oldest and most faithful friend was the late M. Joseph Hazaël-Massieux, former Directeur du Service Départemental d'Agronomie. Through him I gained insight into the complexities of Guadeloupean agricultural institutions, which might otherwise have remained a closed book, and his letters were a source of pleasure and enlightenment to me for over twenty years.

To these friends, then, for themselves and as representatives of the many more who were so kind to me on their islands, my sincerest thanks.

Two other friends must receive special mention, neither of whom has lived long enough to see the completion of this work. M. Dany Victorin, of the Services Agricoles in Martinique, introduced me to wide variety of farmers in out-of-the-way districts and was an excellent and most informative companion. Mr. Stanley Iton, Vincentian by birth but a Montrealer by adoption, had an intimate knowledge of the workings of Eastern Caribbean peasant agriculture, and to accompany him in the field was a rare treat. He had a talent for establishing a rapport with farmers and drawing out of them the real reasoning behind seemingly irrational land use decisions, and I miss both his friendship and his wise insights.

The original figures for this book were primitive, manually drawn affairs. I am indebted to Kevin Hagen for the metamorphosis of the maps, and to Isabel Trigger and Rosalyn Trigger for wrestling the recalcitrant graphs into their Excel strait-jackets.

Finally, I want to acknowledge a special debt to my spouse, who contributed not only intellectual stimulus but also technical assistance on a heroic scale.

Acronyms

ACP	African, Caribbean, and Pacific (countries party to the Lomé Convention)
ASSOBAG	L'Association Bananière Guadeloupéenne
BDS	Banana Development Scheme
CAP	Common Agricultural Policy (of the European Common Market)
CARICOM	Caribbean Common Market
CARIFTA	Caribbean Free Trade Association
CATAG	Co-operative for pest and disease control (Guadeloupe)
CBEA	Caribbean Banana Exporters' Association
CDC	Commonwealth Development Corporation
CEAB	Comité Economique Agricole Bananier des Antilles Françaises (Coordinating body for ASSOBAG and SICABAM; succeeded the CNBA in 1969)
CGM	Compagnie Générale Maritime
CGT	Compagnie Générale Transatlantique
CIB	Comité Interprofessionnel Bananier
CNBA	Comité National Bananier Antillais
CNIB	Comité National Interprofessionnel Bananier
DBGA	Dominica Banana Growers' Association
DBMC	Dominica Banana Marketing Corporation
DDSA	Direction Départementale des Services Agricoles
DOM	Départements d'Outre-Mer
EC	European Community (also referred to as the ECM and EEC)

EC$	Eastern Caribbean dollar
ECM	European Common Market
EEC	European Economic Community
FEDEG	Federation of SICAS, Guadeloupe
FOB	Free On Board
FORMA	Fonds d'Organisation et de Recherche des Marchés Agricoles
GATT	General Agreement on Tariffs and Trade
GDP	Gross Domestic Product
GIEB	Groupement d'Intérêt Economique Bananier
GIPAM	Groupement d'Intérêt des Producteurs Agricoles de la Martinique
GMP	Green Market Price
GWP	Green Wholesale Price
HIR	Hurricane Inez Rehabilitation Scheme
IBD	Inland Buying Depot
ICTA	Imperial College of Tropical Agriculture
IFAC	Institut des Fruits et Agrumes Coloniaux
IRFA	Institut de Recherches sur les Fruits et Agrumes (successor to IFAC)
NRDF	National Research and Development Foundation (St Lucia)
ODEADOM	Office de Développement de l'Economie des DOM
OECS	Organisation of Eastern Caribbean States
ORSTOM	Office de la Recherche Scientifique et Technique Outre-Mer
SATEC	Société d'Aide Technique et de Crédit (after 1965, Société d'Aide Technique et de Co-opération)
SICA	Société d'Intérêt Collectif Agricole
SICABAG	SICA Bananière de la Guadeloupe
SICABAM	SICA Bananière de la Martinique
SICAPEB	SICA des Producteurs et Exportateurs de Bananes
SICAPEMO	SICA des Petits et Moyens (Guadeloupe)
SIGBA	Société d'Intérêt Guadeloupéen Bananier
SLBGA	St Lucia Banana Growers' Association
STABEX	European Development Funds for Export Stabilisation
UNIBA	Union Bananière
USAID	United States Agency for International Development
UWI–ISER	University of the West Indies - Institute for Social and Economic Research
WD	Wagon-Départ (Price of goods leaving importing port; roughly equivalent to GWP)
WINBAN	Windward Island Banana Growers' Association Ltd.
WI$	West Indian dollar

Survival by Association

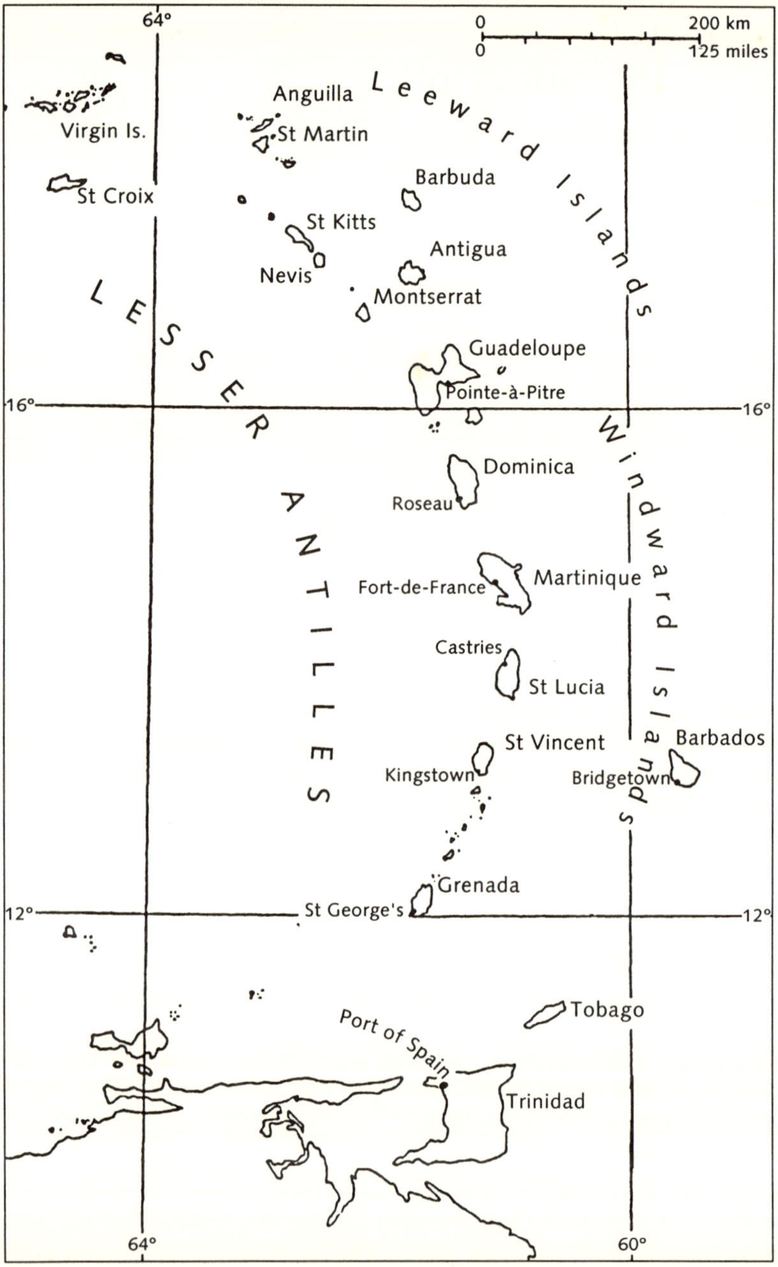

Figure 1.1
The Lesser Antilles

1 Introduction

LAND USE ANOMALIES

In a utopian world, crops would presumably be arranged so that their distribution conformed as closely as possible with the physical conditions most favourable for their growth. In the real world, optimal physical conditions are seldom a prime consideration in agricultural land use decisions; history, politics, and economics conspire to confound the determinist prescriptions of soils, relief, and climate. Paradoxically, some farmers struggle to grow crops under conditions of gruelling adversity, while elsewhere other farmers, blessed with land of far superior physical endowments, are paid to refrain from growing the same crops. Neighbouring areas with strong physical similarities often show strikingly different patterns of land use, especially when they are divided by an international boundary.

Land use differences in neighbouring jurisdictions are not necessarily limited to the choice of crops. The same crop may predominate on either side of a border but be cultivated in radically different ways. On one side, independent small farmers may grow a cash crop in combination with a variety of subsistence crops, using little or no fertiliser, seldom replanting, employing only manual labour, and being content with very low yields. On the other side, the same cash crop may be restricted to vast plantations owned by foreign companies and cultivated by labourers paid by the hour or by the task. The pressure to maintain high yields per hectare and per worker may dictate purestand cropping with heavy inputs of chemical fertiliser and pesticides, the mechanisation of labour where possible, and regular replanting or rotation of crops.

Even the spatial arrangement of the crop in relation to the physical geography may present startling contrasts on either side of a border. Where huge plantations monopolise its cultivation, it may be found only on gently sloping plains and valley bottoms, but where production is dominated by peasant smallholders, it may be restricted to the rugged highland and interfluve areas, while the lowlands are devoted to an entirely different crop.

Sometimes, the reasons for land use anomalies are obvious. Economic and political relationships often provide the key. Countries are selected as sources of imports not for their physical attributes but for their potential as mutually advantageous trading partners. Governments that have repeatedly proclaimed their commitment to free trade have often simultaneously erected, or at least maintained, an elaborate structure of tariff and nontariff barriers. In the colonial era, such barriers were often not designed specifically to protect the products of a single country so much as to encourage and channel trade between that country and its imperial possessions. In this way, patterns of agricultural land use became established that involved growing certain crops in far from ideal conditions or at rates of pay making the cost of production much higher than the price such commodities fetched on world markets.

In the period immediately following the Second World War, the Caribbean provided several examples of the establishment, revival or encouragement of crops for export to overseas markets in which it would have been impossible for them to compete without the protection of tariffs or quotas, and often both. This was so in both British and French islands: sugar and bananas were produced at prices that were generally well above those of Cuban or Central American sugar and bananas; citrus fruit was exported from the British islands to Britain; pineapples from Martinique to France; and copra and coconut oil circulated within the Commonwealth Caribbean from producing islands to processing and consuming islands, protected by common tariffs against competition from cheaper foreign vegetable oils. The purchase of tropical primary produce from relatively high-cost colonial sources, rather than low-cost dollar-area producers in Central America, was dictated by the need to conserve dollars to pay off war debts to the United States.

By the 1960s, at least so far as the British territories were concerned, the colonial era was drawing to a close. The European Economic Community had come into being with the Treaty of Rome in 1957, and there was a strong possibility that Britain would join. Such a development implied a phasing out of Commonwealth trade links on preferential terms and a realignment towards European trading partners. While strong, diversified economies might have been able to contemplate with equanimity trading realignments that would inexorably lead to the decline of some sectors, the small, fragile economies of the Caribbean territories, especially those dependent on only one or two crops, were in a far more vulnerable position. The relentless logic of economic rationalization suggested their early extinction as exporters of primary produce. Surprisingly, however, as late as 1995, among those crops that had risen to prominence as a result of the unusual conditions existing in the mid-1940s, one - the banana - was still of overwhelming importance in several Eastern Caribbean economies as well as in two major European markets. How had it survived?

In the 1990s, this has become a question of crucial importance not only for the banana growers of the Eastern Caribbean but for all farmers whose livelihoods are in jeopardy as a result of major realignments in patterns of world trade. In the Eastern Caribbean, the search for a factor common to both French and Commonwealth islands that might explain the entrenchment of land use patterns that no longer accord with present-day economic and political realities leads by a process of elimination to a single candidate: the producers' association. In the Eastern Caribbean, surviving industries are those which, when their future was threatened, had, or developed, effective institutional structures to protect and promote their interests. The prime examples of such organisations were the banana growers' associations of the Windward Islands. This book explores just how influential they have been in preserving a precarious status quo. If they had not existed or had been of a different character, would there have been any difference in the quantity of bananas grown, the areal distribution of banana cultivation, the type of farmers involved in the industry, or the methods that they used? If these associations did indeed make a difference, in what ways did they do so, and how important were the effects of their intervention? Flowing from this is the question of how the role of such institutions is determined and defined: is it primarily by the circumstances to which their creation was a response or by the ideological and philosophical traditions of those who decided to create them?

The critical role of these agencies has not hitherto been demonstrated or even investigated in depth. All these questions can be considered only in the context of the external economic relationships and the social and physical environments of the banana-exporting islands. Only when the impact of these other factors has been acknowledged and assessed can attention be turned to the real focus of this book. The analysis of growers' association operations not only sheds light on reasons for interisland variations in land use patterns, it also reveals the potential of such organisations to engineer the very survival of their industry, even against seemingly overwhelming odds.

Assessing the degree to which institutional intervention may influence the agricultural landscape requires, ideally, a comparison of two discrete areas with similar physical endowments and socioeconomic relationships, in one of which all the growers of specific crops are members of active producer associations, while in the other, all farmers function independently, with no institutional manipulation of any aspect of production or marketing. While it would be difficult to identify two areas that fulfilled all these criteria in the 1960s, neighbouring Eastern Caribbean islands of French and British affiliation did provide very favourable conditions for making such comparisons. While none of the Lesser Antillean islands provided the ideal control by being without any form of producers' association for its major crop, the extent of institutional intervention in various aspects of production, transport, and marketing varied greatly from island to island, as did the character of the institutions concerned. Moreover, it was possible to choose four islands, two with a British and two with a French colonial past, that were at least comparable in their physical potential and economic relationships and that all shared the same crop, bananas, as their foremost export. Being islands, these territories provided discrete units for study that were of limited and relatively manageable size and presented no problems of boundary definition. It is true that data on Lesser Antillean land use, while abundant, were not always in a form that facilitated interisland comparison: units of measurement differed in British and French islands, and class boundaries were rarely compatible. But this is a problem inherent in any comparative research on two areas of sufficient cultural distinctiveness to make them appropriate subjects for such a study.

GROWERS' ASSOCIATIONS: ORIGINS AND IDEOLOGY

The history of organisations that promote or protect the interests of the growers of various agricultural products extends at least to the early years of the twentieth century. Wheat farmers of the Canadian prairie provinces pioneered such organisations, forming provincial wheat pools to effect the orderly marketing of a crop that the average isolated farmer was not well-placed to market (Veeman and Veeman 1988). As early as 1910, groundnut farmers in French West Africa were forming *sociétés de prévoyance*, initially to organise the distribution of groundnut seed on credit and later to provide extension services and market their members' crop (Caswell 1985, 80,113). In 1926, the Imperial Economic Committee on Marketing advocated establishing associations for banana growers, both in Jamaica, where the trade was well-established, and in the Windwards, where it was in its infancy. Jamaican experience had shown that unorganised growers were vulnerable to exploitation, and the committee suggested two possible models for the proposed organisations: the California Fruit Growers' Exchange, based on binding contracts between grower and association, and the New Zealand system of statutory control over exported fruit. It also cited the example of the Associated Growers of British Columbia, who controlled the marketing of 83 percent of the apples grown in that province and, as of 1925, consigned them to a single agent in the United Kingdom. An enactment of the government of British Columbia had made it an offence for any person to solicit fruit from a member of a cooperative organisation (Commonwealth Economic Committee 1926, 24–5,265).

In 1937–38, cocoa producers in British West Africa, dissatisfied with a system in which large European trading companies controlled rural buying of commodities and selling of agricultural inputs, held back their cocoa from the market. Their actions provoked an investigation by a commission of enquiry that suggested establishing a state-sponsored cocoa-buying organisation of producers. The eventual outcome, after wartime experience of government control of the market, was the Gold Coast Cocoa Marketing Board, set up in 1947. Its primary purpose was to secure the most favourable arrangements for purchasing, grading, and selling Gold Coast cocoa; it was to purchase cocoa from farmers at uniform prices to be fixed seasonally. Its mandate went well beyond straightforward marketing, however. For the benefit and prosperity of the producers, it was to assist the development of the Gold Coast cocoa industry by all possible means. By 1952, the board had made grants of over twenty-five million pounds sterling towards fighting cocoa disease, expanding Takoradi harbour, and endowing the faculty of agriculture at the University College of the Gold Coast. Thereafter, the board became increasingly politicised and, eventually, fell entirely under government control. By the 1970s it was no longer primarily a marketing organisation, but a complex economic, political, and social organisation, an instrument of the government for promoting national development or national welfare (Arhin 1985, 38–40,49).

Britain and France have pursued widely divergent colonial and postcolonial policies in various parts of the world, and their differing strategies of agricultural development have drawn more attention in West Africa than in the Caribbean. In a discussion in 1954 of the purpose and effectiveness of produce marketing boards in British West Africa, it was suggested that, while their formation had resulted initially from the presence, at the end of the Second World War, of established export monopolies and from criticism of prewar marketing arrangements, these factors had been reinforced by "certain vague attitudes widely current over the last ten or fifteen years" (Bauer and Yamey 1968, 151). The "attitudes" were more specifically identified as the idea that it was both practical and desirable to stabilize producer prices using marketing boards; a belief in the irrelevance of prices; a dislike of intermediaries and traders, who were viewed as "speculators"; and a desire to socialise peasant saving and agricultural investment and direct the production and distribution of cash crops. It was asserted that the powers of the boards that had been created went far beyond those necessary for price stabilisation (151–3).

In French Senegal, by contrast, while there was postwar legislation to promote cooperative marketing, the groundnut trade was dominated by a few French companies, operated mainly through African and Lebanese intermediaries. Producers mortgaged future crops to traders for credit that would tide them over the preharvest season (Caswell 1985, 79–80).

While these West African arrangements were not precisely duplicated in the Eastern Caribbean, institutions in the Caribbean did tend to reflect similar philosphical orientations: price stabilisation and the socialisation of peasant saving and investment were priorities in the British islands, while some degree of speculation by commercial intermediaries was acceptable in the French islands. Between the 1960s and the 1980s, ideological changes in both Britain and France had repercussions in their overseas trading partners, and the situation of the partners was further complicated by their changing relations with their former colonial overlords. The French islands were progressively being integrated as *départements* into the unitary state of France, while the British islands, which were becoming independent, were forming new economic groupings and ideological orientations.

The literature on produce marketing boards is generally written from the perspective of the economist or the political scientist: it rarely studies the effect of such institutions on patterns of agricultural land use. But one would expect that redistributing produce receipts, providing guaranteed markets, and judiciously subsidising inputs and transport might be critical in determining which classes of farmers find it worthwhile to participate in a particular industry, and thus also in determining the location and intensity of cultivation. That this subject has so far failed to attract much attention from geographers seems to reflect a view that the geographer's task is to reveal the influence of spatial variables on the social process and to speculate about the future consequences of changes in current spatial arrangements (Schaefer 1953, 248–9). There is surely also a need, however, to reveal the influence of the social process on spatial variables. A geographical approach seems ideally suited for this task, which does not appear to engage any other branch of social science.

In the 1960s, when the first stage of this study was undertaken, growers' associations and produce marketing boards were widely regarded as making a positive contribution to the organisation and conduct of local, interregional, and international trade. Their role was to ensure fair returns for all the participants in their industry. By discouraging speculation and exploitation and facilitating access to markets, they were increasingly involving themselves in supply management. When overproduction threatened to undermine price levels, producer associations might cooperate to limit or control the supply of their commodity reaching the market, while if supplies were inadequate to meet demand at certain seasons, they might boost production so that rivals would not gain a foothold and destabilize their position. Thus, the gluts and shortages that were a hazard of unregulated trade could generally be avoided, and steady supplies at relatively stable prices could be maintained. If these prices were somewhat higher than prices in unregulated markets, consumers usually benefited from reciprocal trading advantages that assured them a steady and profitable market for the goods they themselves produced. They could therefore well afford to pay for the produce they had to purchase.

In the 1970s and 1980s, the virtues of supply management were called into question by aggressive proponents of free trade. To the more extreme disciples of this doctrine, any interference with the free operation of the marketplace was anathema. The laws of supply and demand should prevail, and producer marketing associations, the agents of supply management, should be dismantled and abolished. Only then might consumers obtain produce at the lowest possible price, as was their birthright. Territories, often former colonies that had long enjoyed traditional protected markets for their export crops, were confronted by the possibility that their entire economies might be sacrificed on the altar of the General Agreement on Tariffs and Trade (GATT). While their traditional trading partners scrambled to gain admission to huge new trade blocs, vulnerable producers of primary agricultural commodities contemplated desperate expedients to stave off economic annihilation.

THE ISLANDS

Understanding how institutional structures may affect land use and how ideology and pragmatism interact to determine the form of these structures is impossible without setting the four islands chosen for special examination here in their physical and historical context.

The Commonwealth Windward Islands of Dominica and St Lucia and their French neighbours, Martinique and Basse-Terre Guadeloupe, form the central portion of an arc of tropical volcanic islands that extends for over 700 kilometres, bounding the eastern margin of the Caribbean Sea. The four islands range in area from 616 to 1100 square kilometres and in population from 80,000 to 330,000. They share a long and chequered colonial past, a precarious present, and an uncertain future.

In the seventeenth and eighteenth centuries, these islands acquired an importance out of all proportion to their size and natural resources by virtue of their strategic location, which controlled the approaches to the wealthy New World colonies of Spain, and their accessibility as a source of tropical agricultural produce. They were among the earliest tropical lands to be colonised by European planters of tropical crops; the ease of exporting produce from coastal plantations far outweighing the handicap of the rugged terrain that afflicted most of these volcanic islands. In terms of land use patterns, these small islands, separated by thousands of miles of ocean from their metropolitan markets, represented the very antithesis of Von Thunen's isolated state: the isolated state turned inside out, as it were, with the most intensive cultivation around the coastal margins, while inland, agricultural activity became more and more attenuated.

In the nineteenth century, however, the locational advantages once enjoyed by the Eastern Caribbean island colonies dwindled as innovations in bulk transportation, accompanied by the freeing of trade, permitted opening up extensive inland continental areas of virgin soils and gentle relief. In the islands, all but the most favoured districts abandoned the traditional mainstay, cane, and were obliged to experiment with novel crops, mainly tree crops not as yet widely adopted in other parts of the tropical world, or to fall back on subsistence agriculture.

In other parts of the world, agricultural transformations that involved an abrupt decline in the demand for labour frequently resulted in depopulation; the Scottish Highland clearances of the nineteenth century are a case in point. In the Eastern Caribbean, the exigencies of cane cultivation and sugar manufacture had led to the importation of many thousands of African slaves, resulting in far higher populations than would have developed in territories whose agriculture was simply geared towards self-sufficiency. While the decline of the sugar industry was followed by very considerable emigration from the small islands, outlets were not unlimited, and there was pressure on the remaining population to find alternative export crops.

One commodity that rose to prominence in world trade shortly after sugar ceased to be viable in all but the most level and accessible districts of the Lesser Antilles was the banana. The development, in the late nineteenth century, of rapid, temperature-controlled cargo vessels permitted this fruit to enter world trade for the first time. Shipments quickly became substantial, but it was on large, foreign-owned plantations in Central America and the Greater Antilles that most of these bananas were produced. Martinique and Guadeloupe began to export bananas to France on a moderate scale in the 1920s, and there were attempts to begin regular banana exports from the British Windwards to Canada in the 1920s and 1930s, but in none of the islands of the volcanic arc was this crop identifiable as a potential economic saviour that would restore the fortunes of areas where sugar production (or, in the case of Dominica, lime plantations) had ceased to be viable.

Established patterns of trade were disrupted by the Second World War, and when tropical fruit exports began to increase again in the late 1940s, they developed along very different lines from the exports of the prewar period. Thus, although the Caribbean islands were relatively high-cost producers of bananas, since they were sterling-area or franc-zone producers, Britain and France gave them all the tariff and quota protection necessary to ensure that they monopolized these metropolitan markets and excluded dollar-area fruit.

From the late 1940s onwards, the banana industry in the Lesser Antilles grew at an astonishing rate, attracting both peasant and estate growers. Since supply could not initially meet demand in the protected British and French markets, prices were relatively high and permitted satisfactory profits to all sectors of the industry. By the 1960s, bananas were the leading export of every island from

St Vincent to Basse-Terre Guadeloupe, and in some islands, were almost the only crop grown for export. Referred to in the British Windwards as "green gold," they appeared to be the key to an agricultural prosperity that had eluded the islands since they had lost their preeminence as sugar producers in the early nineteenth century.

By the mid-1960s, the situation was less auspicious. Markets were saturated, prices were weakening, and the European Common Market was posing a threat to both Commonwealth and French banana growers: neither group had any assurance that it would be protected from the competition of lower-cost dollar-area bananas for much longer.

Such was the context of the banana industries in the mid-1960s in the four central islands of the volcanic arc. Despite their broadly similar colonial backgrounds and the more or less parallel development of the postwar banana industry, however, the distribution of banana cultivation varied dramatically from island to island in relation to physical conditions, the intensity of cultivation, the yields obtained, the class of farmer involved, and the amount of manpower required per unit of area and of output. For the most part, French islands and Commonwealth islands were at opposite ends of the scale.

EXPLAINING ANOMALOUS LAND USE PATTERNS: STRATEGY

Since the possible influence of seemingly minor differences in economic relationships, social factors, or environmental constraints on land use patterns cannot be overlooked, the first part of this book is devoted to an assessment of their importance. This is followed by an analysis of the nature, role, and impact of banana growers' associations in the four islands in the 1960s, the period when inter-island differences were most extreme. Considerable, some might say excessive, attention is paid to the technical aspects of banana production; experience has convinced me that without this, the general reader is unlikely to appreciate just how intractable are many of the problems confronted by Windwards farmers. Finally, an examination of the evolution of both associations and land use patterns since the 1960s adds a fourth dimension to the analysis.

It was the volcanic landforms of the Eastern Caribbean, rather than their seemingly anomalous land use patterns, that first engaged my interest in the region. In the course of fifteen months' fieldwork in 1961-62, however, I could not help wondering why it was that from one island to another, areas of very similar physical characteristics often showed quite dissimilar land use patterns, while, conversely, the same crop might be imposed on areas strikingly different in their physical geography. The chance to carry out research on the factors underlying land use decisions in the four central islands of the volcanic arc came to me in 1966-67. Armed with a lengthy questionnaire, I visited 160 farmers in Dominica, Guadeloupe, Martinique, and St Lucia.

The survey was designed to elucidate the key factors determining or influencing land use decisions in the French as compared with the Commonwealth islands, and it therefore covered as wide a range as possible of farm types and practices. Only during the course of the survey did I recognise that banana growers' associations might exert a major influence and might possibly be a key factor in inter-island differences. Thereafter I focused more closely on the role played by these organisations and farmers' attitudes toward them. Ideally, I would have revisited the earlier respondents to supplement the initially rather cursory information gathered on this subject; but in fact, it was already too late. Radical changes were made in the structure of the St Lucia Banana Growers' Association in August 1967, transforming it from a grower-controlled organisation with mass participation in decision making into a statutory body under a strong measure of government control, much more closely resembling the Dominican model.

As it turned out, 1966-7 was an ideal reference point for this study: the banana industry in all four islands had reached levels of production and areal extent that would not be substantially surpassed for a decade or more. For the first time, all four were confronted by saturated markets; and for the last time, each had a banana growers' association that was significantly different in many respects from those of any of the other three.

While it was supplemented by other material from a variety of sources, the 1966-67 survey data formed the core of this study, but determining the most fruitful method of interpreting it was in itself a major challenge. Since none of the prevailing orthodoxies seemed to provide an ideal methodology, I adopted a pragmatic approach and tackled the problem on two fronts. On the one hand, I identified all those factors whose contributions were known and more or less understood - the physical background, economic relationships, and agrarian structure, for example - and I attempted to assess their impact. Insofar as there were some generally accepted causal relationships between these factors and agricultural production (such as, at the simplest level, that bananas will not grow successfully where rainfall is less than two metres a year and the deficit cannot be made up by irrigation), this approach might be described as deductive. On the other hand, for those factors whose effects were not well understood, I used statistical analysis to try to identify correlations with observed features of land use. In this class were such diverse factors as accessibility, production costs, chemical inputs, and sources of agricultural information. When regular correlations could be discerned, I attempted to identify causal mechanisms.

In February 1988, I returned to the Eastern Caribbean to see how both organisations and land use patterns had evolved since my last visit in 1970. Major changes had taken place in the structures and activities of growers' associations, which had tended to converge. Changes in the spatial distribution and intensity of banana growing and in the character of participation were also apparent. I had to take into account sociopolitical and economic developments of various kinds, but allowing for these, I attempted to assess how far changes in the growers' associations might have been responsible for the observed changes in land use patterns.

In real life, it is generally impossible to find two areas that are identical in every way except for the one factor whose significance is to be tested. At best, one can examine three or four areas that, between them, contain most or all of the phenomena and structures considered relevant for the test. Studying an area over a period of time, however, provides an ideal opportunity for evaluating the effect of changed social mechanisms on land use within (more or less) the same environment. It might be argued that studies in historical geography perform a similar function, but in fact, the perspective is quite different. In this book, I use the present to test conclusions made in the past, whereas the historical geographer essentially uses the past (selectively) to test conclusions drawn in the present.

SOURCE MATERIAL

My source material was of three kinds: raw data (comprising information I collected from farmers, surveys of peasant agriculture in Martinique and St Lucia conducted by McGill graduate students in 1964, and computer printouts giving production information for Dominica and St Lucia in 1986–87), interviews with a wide variety of people interested in Lesser Antillean agriculture, and published and unpublished documentary material.

Raw Data

I interviewed 160 farmers in Guadeloupe, St Lucia, Martinique, and Dominica between May and October 1966 and June and August 1967, using a questionnaire developed with the assistance of Professor David Edwards of the University of the West Indies.

Sampling methods were eclectic. In Guadeloupe, there were then no comprehensive records of farm ownership or location. Since farmers were reluctant to divulge any but the most general information unless approached through a trusted intermediary, randomly accosting farmers in the villages or in the fields did not seem promising. So I asked various intermediaries to arrange meetings with as many farmers as possible. The different institutional affiliations of the intermediaries ensured that farmers representing diverse types of operation would be covered. Thus, three mayors of *communes* provided introductions (mainly to small farmers in the case of Communist mayors, and to medium-sized farmers in non-Communist *communes*); agents of the government's technical assistance organisation (SATEC) conducted me on visits to holdings on former estate land being subdivided under its aegis; the director of the Service d'Agronomie of the departmental agricultural service arranged visits to several farms; and officers of the farmers' union did likewise. In addition, I found that some casual social contacts were prepared to give more or less detailed information.

Altogether, twenty-two farmers were surveyed. I attempted to ensure that coverage was as widespread as possible geographically, by including farms of various sizes and from most districts of the island. The sample was not random in any statistically accepted sense, since it was composed of farmers expected to be cooperative, but at least it represented a broad spectrum of viewpoints by including people who were on good terms with government agents as well as those highly critical of the establishment and the status quo.

In St Lucia, a list of all banana growers, but not all *farmers*, was available from the growers' association. I was assured that since all farmers grew some bananas, the list could, in fact, be taken as a list of all farmers. This seemed a plausible assertion at the time, since the number of registered banana growers actually exceeded, by as much as 2000, the number of farmers recorded in the 1961 census. I discovered later that a few farmers in the driest parts of the southwest did not grow bananas; but wherever rainfall was adequate, virtually all farmers were banana growers.

A range of growers, from small to large, was sampled by picking names from the list for each district based on the number of stems sold the previous week. Since banana production was not closely correlated with the size of holdings, the sample did not necessarily give a complete range of sizes for each district; and since small farms were in fact far more numerous than large ones, the large farms were proportionately overrepresented. There was a limit to how many farms could be sampled, however, so it seemed preferable to ensure that all types were covered; statistical randomness, even with stratified sampling, risked leaving possibly critical gaps. Altogether forty-eight farms were surveyed; officers of the local banana growers' association located and introduced the selected interviewees.

In Martinique, as in Guadeloupe, no lists of farmers were available, but agronomists at the Direction Départementale d'Agriculture arranged for me to visit each district with extension officers who knew the local farmers and would introduce me to a "representative sample." In practice, it transpired that the representativeness of the sample was qualified by the ethnic background of the escorting officer: those who were white and *métropolitain* in origin apparently had rapport only with the white Creole owners of the large estates, while those who were Martiniquan non-white Creole in origin were acquainted with all except this group. Thus all types of farmers were interviewed, but not in all districts. I filled some gaps by visiting farmers with a spray-plane operator whose friendships with clients were not constrained by ethnic boundaries. The total sample was twenty. While it was doubtless somewhat weighted in favour of those who had good relations with the establishment, it also contained a number who were very critical of the status quo.

It is interesting to note, apropos the randomness of samples, that among both St Lucian and Martiniquan interviewees, I was able, when analysing results, to recognize certain individuals interviewed in the 1964 McGill Survey (which used a cluster sampling technique) and in a 1965 banana-costing survey carried out in St Lucia by the Barbados-based Institute for Social and Economic Research (which used a stratified sample of fewer than fifty farmers). This could have been a coincidence; but because those individuals were prominent members of the community and known to hold strong views about agriculture, one must wonder whether, even in a random sample, there are social factors making it more likely for outspoken community members to be included.

In Dominica, the agriculture department arranged for me to visit each district with the local extension officer. Again, there were no lists of farmers, but each officer took me to the houses of large-, medium-, and small-scale farmers known to him and likely to cooperate. In some districts, more extrovert officers accosted people by the roadside, but they were not, as a rule, nearly as informative as the farmers who were approached more formally.

The extension officers were all Dominican and were not constrained by the ethnic inhibitions of their Martiniquan counterparts. All the same, the sample was not entirely representative, since it generally excluded farmers who had no dealings with the extension service. To test how typical the seventy Dominican interviewees were, they were compared in as many respects as possible with means derived from the 1961 agricultural census. These comparisons suggested that while the farming standards (as reflected by yields) of the 1966 sample were well above average, the regional crop choices in the 1966 sample conformed well with the 1961 pattern. All interviewees grew bananas, except for a handful in the extreme southwest, where it was too dry.

While the statistical rigour of the 1966–67 sample was by no means unimpeachable, I felt that if appropriate allowances were made where the sample was probably not representative, it did cover the gamut of regional and socio-economic situations in each island well enough to be used in some types of statisical analysis. Some farmers responded to the questionnaire fairly directly without expressing personal opinions, but others were prepared to spend several hours discussing the issues in depth. These discussions were particularly valuable, since they revealed reasons for agricultural decisions that might never have emerged in a study based solely on pre-formulated questions.

In 1970, I returned to Dominica, revisited eight farmers, and interviewed four new ones. In 1979, after Hurricane David, I attempted to contact six farmers from the 1966–67 sample and found four still involved in agriculture: the other two had died some years earlier. When I revisited the four islands in February 1988, the St Lucia Banana Growers' Association and the Dominica Banana Marketing Corporation gave me access to their computer records on growers. For St Lucia these records included each grower's production in 1984, 1985, and 1986 and pinpointed, as "not active", growers who had not sold fruit for some time, while for Dominica they gave each grower's 1987 production and estimated acreage in bananas. For each island, these figures were grouped by district. It did not prove possible to reinterview any of the 1966–67 samples for St Lucia and Dominica; twenty-one of the St Lucia sample were traced on the list (which contained over 12,000 names), but seven of these were classed as "not active." In Dominica, 6000 growers were listed, but only six of the 1966 sample could be identified, since in many cases several growers shared the same name. In Martinique, I managed to trace and revisit one farmer from the 1966 sample.

The two hundred 1964 McGill Survey schedules, to which I had access, were used mainly for reference purposes rather than statistical analysis. They were confined to smallholdings and were concerned with crop combinations, features of holdings (their size, the number of parcels, the stoniness of the soil, and so on), the composition of farm households, and the educational level of farmers.

Interviews

During the 1960s, I visited the various campuses of the University of the West Indies and the University of Puerto Rico to consult economists, agricultural economists, and sociologists familiar with the problems of the Eastern Caribbean. In 1969 I spent a week in Paris meeting French government officials in the ministry for overseas *départements* and territories responsible for policy in the Antilles. In the islands, both in the 1960s and in 1988, I met with civil servants in various departments, especially agricultural departments; officers and technical personnel of banana growers' associations and other crop marketing organisations; soil scientists, agronomists, nematologists, and other specialists attached to research institutions in the Eastern Caribbean; the managing director of Geest West Indies, the purchaser of all Windwards bananas; and politicians responsible for agricultural policy decisions. Many of these people were glad of an opportunity to make comparisons with neighbouring islands, since liaisons between similar institutions in French and Commonwealth islands were often poorly developed.

In 1988 particularly, I was struck by what might be termed the "Rashomon Syndrome." Different individuals speaking about the state of the banana industry in their islands gave sometimes startlingly different versions of recent and current trends and developments. Only by comparing many points of view and evaluating them in the light of field visits and growers' association statistics could I draw any confident conclusions about the real situation.

Documentary Material

Within the islands, local public libraries and archives were a fruitful source of historical background material, while government departments and growers' associations provided a rich haul of reports, memoranda, and statistics, published and unpublished. In St Lucia, the National Research and Development Foundation (NRDF) now has an extremely useful documentation centre in which copies of theses, reports, and papers concerning St Lucia have been assembled for consultation. Elsewhere in the Caribbean, I consulted university libraries in Barbados, Jamaica, Trinidad, and Puerto Rico.

In Montreal, through the McGill Centre for Developing Area Studies, I had access to an extensive collection of statistical material on the Caribbean, as well as several unpublished theses, geographical and anthropological, dealing with various aspects of Lesser Antillean agriculture. The Département d'Anthropologie at the Université de Montréal, which has for a number of years had a special concern with the French Antilles and their problems, also made accessible some interesting theses germane to my study.

In London, in addition to the University of London library, those of the Royal Geographical Society, the Colonial Office, and the West India Committee (now housed in the Institute of Commonwealth Studies) proved particularly useful, while in Paris, the Bibliothèque Nationale yielded works obtainable nowhere else.

Technical Matters

I turn now to technical matters. Units of measurement posed a problem, since the French islands used metric measures, while the Commonwealth ones kept official records in imperial units. Furthermore, the farmers themselves frequently employed prerevolutionary French measures such as the *carré* (3.3 acres) and the *toise* (fathom) - not to mention bags, pots, and tins of indeterminate capacity. Because the difference between the metric tonne and the imperial long ton is only 1.6 percent (1 long ton = 1.016 metric tons), I have left the long tons unconverted: they are indicated by the spelling of "ton." However, in general, all units of length and area have been converted to metric units; but the imperial original has also been given when it makes more sense in terms of class boundaries or when the original was obviously just an approximation in the first place. To say that a piece of land was 1600 metres distant when the farmer had said it was a mile away would give an air of precision that was probably neither justified nor intended.

Currency is also a potential source of confusion. The French islands use the French franc, and in the 1960s, the Commonwealth islands used the West Indian dollar (WI$), pegged to the British pound sterling at the rate of WI$4.80 = £1. But from 1976 onwards, the WI dollar, now known as the Eastern Caribbean dollar (EC$), has been pegged to the United States dollar at EC$2.70 = US$1.00. For purposes of comparison, I have generally used the WI/EC dollars and converted other currencies to these dollars at the exchange rate appropriate for the period.

The *département* of Guadeloupe consists of the two large, contiguous islands of Grande-Terre (limestone) and Basse-Terre (volcanic), in addition to several smaller island dependencies. In this book, "Guadeloupe" (also known as Guadeloupe *proprement dite*) normally refers only to the volcanic island of Basse-Terre Guadeloupe; when there is any possibility of ambiguity, I have used the term "Basse-Terre Guadeloupe", meaning specifically the western, volcanic island.

2 The Economic Context of Eastern Caribbean Banana Industries

Ever since bananas became an exportable commodity in the latter part of the nineteenth century, the location and relative importance of different zones of production and their relationship with actual and potential markets has been in constant flux. Economic environments have mutated, creating windows of opportunity for areas formerly at a disadvantage and insurmountable obstacles for once-flourishing producers. This study spans more than two decades, and many changes took place while it was under way. In this chapter, the focus is on the economic context of the mid-1960s, when the initial surveys were carried out. The subsequent evolution of that context and, in particular, the ways in which the situation in the late 1980s differed significantly from that in the earlier period, will be analysed in chapter 9, in conjunction with a discussion of related political, social, and technological changes.

THE WORLD TRADE IN BANANAS

While world trade in bananas was estimated by 1967 to involve between 4 million and 5 million tons of fruit annually, the origins of the trade are quite recent (Arthur et al. 1968, 3). It began only a century ago and has grown to major proportions only within the past seventy years. The banana was widely cultivated throughout the tropical and subtropical world for centuries as a fruit and, in some areas, as a staple food crop, but it was too perishable to withstand lengthy voyages in slow sailing vessels. Only with the advent of steamships did it become accessible to consumers in temperate latitudes, and then only to those within a limited range. Refrigerated cargo vessels extended this range, but the fruit can withstand a voyage of two or three weeks at the most, while the high cost of using specialised vessels to transport a cargo whose value is so low in relation to its bulk makes a much shorter haul economically desirable. Consequently, while such tropical commodities as sugar, cocoa, tea, and rubber, which are all rendered less perishable and more valuable in relation to their bulk by some processing in their country of origin, were long produced for export only within a single continent or a few restricted localities having peculiarly propitious physical or human conditions, banana production for export was taken up or promoted in almost every part of the tropical world that had access to a temperate market.

Since physical and economic limitations prevent the transport of bananas halfway round the globe, it is unrealistic to speak of world markets and world trade in the crop. In fact, for trading purposes there is a series of more or less closed subsystems: the Western Pacific, Southern Africa, Southeastern South America, and the North Atlantic. The Eastern Caribbean falls squarely within the North Atlantic subsystem, since its choice of markets is effectively limited to Western Europe and Eastern North America (Arthur et al. 1968, 49; Simmonds 1959, 284,328).

THE NORTH ATLANTIC BANANA TRADE

Within the North Atlantic subsystem, every exporter has, in theory, a choice of markets, while every importer can choose between several sources of supply. Sociopolitical considerations have, however, sharply narrowed the range of both choices, but while these constraints have distorted the patterns that purely economic considerations might have produced, they have not resulted in the complete isolation of any elements of the subsystem. Even where trade is completely bilateral, with a single supplier and a single consumer, the threat of giving access to other suppliers if sociopolitical commitments become too burdensome can be used to influence price levels.

Production in the subsystem is dominated overwhelmingly by the Ecuador-Colombia-Central American zone, which produces well over half the world's export bananas and which in the mid-1960s supplied virtually the entire markets of North America, West Germany, and the Benelux countries and up to 40 percent of the Italian market. Britain, however, drew her supplies almost entirely from Jamaica and the Commonwealth Windward Islands, while France drew two-thirds of her bananas from the French Antilles and one-third from West Africa. In addition to Central America, the Caribbean, and West Africa, the Canary Islands were a significant production zone, since they were mainland Spain's main source of supply, and they also exported small quantities of fruit to the United Kingdom, France, West Germany, and Italy.

Few generalisations can be made about the production zones of the North Atlantic subsystem beyond the fact that they lie in or close to the tropics, mainly in areas of low per capita income. Bananas are grown intensively and extensively, on unfertilised virgin soils and on soils requiring heavy fertilisation, in flat areas where transport and disease control are cheap and easy and in rugged areas where they are expensive and difficult, in low-rainfall areas where irrigation is necessary, and in areas where hurricane risks are high. In some areas, production is dominated by vast plantations, while in others, peasant growers produce most of the crop.

While in parts of Central America banana workers earned as little as WI$1.00 a day in the mid-1960s, in the French Antilles the rate was WI$5.00 a day, and, in addition, the employer was liable for social security contributions of approximately WI$2.50. It is not surprising, then, that production costs varied widely, especially since some exporting areas had to contend with both physical handicaps and high labour costs. For 1964–65, assuming comparable packaging, the respective FOB values for French Antillean, Windwards, and Central American bananas would have been approximately £43, £30 and £20 per ton (calculated from figures in Persaud 1966 and *La Banane* 1967).

What was remarkable, given this wide range of FOB values, was the narrow range of retail prices in consumer countries. In Canada, the United Kingdom, France, and Germany, bananas sold for roughly WI36¢ a pound in the mid-1960s, although the on-plantation costs of the French bananas were almost double those of the Commonwealth Caribbean bananas shipped to Britain and four times those of Central American fruit sold in Canada and West Germany (*La Banane* 1967, 2:33–9). This was presumably a reflection of the fact that, while in less wealthy countries rising income levels were accompanied by rising banana consumption, once a certain level of per capita consumption was reached in the wealthier countries (between 7 and 10 kilograms per year), consumption levels ceased to be very responsive to variations in price. Switzerland, with the most expensive bananas in Western Europe, had one of the highest levels of consumption, while in North America, even substantial price-cutting failed to boost demand above a 10-kilogram-per-year ceiling. Since in those countries importing bananas from low-cost areas, the trade is usually effectively monopolised by one or two very large companies, it would seem that prices tend to be geared to what the market will bear, rather than the laws of supply and demand.

The degree of vertical integration between banana grower and wholesaler is highly significant in the economic relationships of the North Atlantic subsystem. After leaving the field, a stem of bananas must be packaged, transported to port, loaded onto a specialised ship, conveyed to the importing country under carefully controlled conditions, and then unloaded and despatched to ripening facilities in the region of retail sale. Finally, the ripened bananas, possibly repackaged, must be transported from ripening room to retail outlet.

When vertical integration is taken to its furthest extreme, a single company may own plantations, ships, and ripening facilities and carry out all the necessary processes, from planting to ripening, to put a stem of fruit on the retail market. The United Fruit Company, for long by far the most important and influential company in the North Atlantic subsystem, traditionally operated in this way, although by the 1960s the company tended to purchase bananas from other growers rather than run its own plantations, presumably because only marginal profits were accruing from plantations.

At the opposite end of the scale, the French Antillean banana trade was conducted with minimal vertical integration. At its most extreme, growers sold their bananas by the roadside to an intermediary who transported them to the port and resold them to an exporter. They were then shipped to France in the banana boats of the Compagnie Générale Transatlantique (CGT), the shipping company which had a monopoly of maritime trade between the French Antilles and the *Métropole*. The exporter's agent at the metropolitan port then endeavoured to resell the bananas to a ripener, who in turn supplied ripened fruit to retailers. By the mid-1960s, however, most growers were responsible, either individually or in groups, for exporting their own bananas. There were a small number of exporters who also owned ripening facilities in France, but in general, at least three different interests were involved between the field and the retailer.

The Commonwealth Windwards–United Kingdom trade fell somewhere between these two extremes. In each island, all growers belonged to a growers' association to which they sold their bananas. The association wrapped the bananas and, in some cases, conveyed them to the exporting port, selling the fruit of the entire island to the exporter, Geest, who also owned or leased the banana boats. Geest imported the fruit into the United Kingdom and transported it to the company's own regional ripening facilities.

While the highly integrated operations of, for instance, United Fruit in the mid-1960s did not seem to bring lower prices to the consumer, because a single company controlled banana handling facilities in both exporting and importing zones it had enormous power over its sources of supply and price levels. Control of ripening facilities virtually denied access to would-be newcomer importers, while control of exporting and shipping facilities denied alternative outlets to producers. Moreover, while a profit had to be shown on the whole trade, profits might be foregone on individual segments, permitting the vertically integrated operation to indulge in lengthy price-cutting wars to undermine rivals.

The British trade is a case in point. In the 1960s, roughly half Britain's bananas were imported from Jamaica, 77.5 percent of these by the then United Fruit subsidiary, Elders and Fyffes. Without the intervention of the British government, Elders and Fyffes could, and almost certainly would, have destroyed the Jamaican banana industry by importing lower-priced bananas from alternative sources, ultimately in Central America. Jamaican producers might have been denied access to the specialised shipping required to send their fruit to Britain, and even if they had managed to lease ships, they might have been unable to ripen and distribute their bananas in Britain. Moreover, the Windwards industry would have been unable to compete with low-cost foreign bananas and would doubtless also have been rapidly ruined (*Jamaican Weekly Gleaner*, 2 February, 1971).

On the other hand, computations made in 1966 indicated that Jamaican bananas could theoretically have been sold in Eastern Canada, a market shared for the previous twenty-five years between two great companies, Standard Fruit and United Fruit, at lower prices than those current for the Central American and Ecuadorian fruit imported by these companies. Their stranglehold on ripening facilities and distribution, however, made any attempt to initiate an independent Jamaica-Canada trade inadvisable, especially since the two companies could indulge in protracted price-cutting (Beckford and Brown 1966).

The North Atlantic banana trade, in which both French and Commonwealth islands of the Eastern Caribbean participated, was, then, a complex structure whose form was determined only partially by strictly economic considerations. The entry into and survival within this trade of such relatively high-cost producers as these Eastern Caribbean islands is explicable only within this context.

THE DEVELOPMENT OF THE EASTERN CARIBBEAN BANANA INDUSTRIES

While France and Britain were among the earliest countries to import bananas on a large scale, their Eastern Caribbean colonies were by no means hasty in assuming a major exporting role. But this was not a result of insouciance. It is true that as early as 1890, when direct steamship service was established between the Windwards and Canada, the advantages of entering the trade had been stressed (Nicholls 1890) and that by 1907 the Compagnie Générale Transatlantique had provided refrigerated holds suitable for banana shipment on its vessels to France (Kervégant 1935, 517). Nevertheless, only minimal quantities of bananas were actually exported at these early stages because of two economic realities: first, physical conditions, particularly the rugged terrain, were not conducive to the successful exploitation of a bulky and fairly delicate crop like bananas; and second, other crops providing either better or more dependable returns were being cultivated in the islands at this period, so that incentives to adopt a new alternative were small.

While little progress had been made by the 1920s in countering the problems posed by ruggedness, falling prices, disease, and hurricane damage had reduced the viability of almost every other crop and provoked tentative moves in each of the four islands to initiate export banana industries. These initiatives met with uncertain fortunes but provided valuable experience when, in the late 1920s and early 1930s, new economic policies of the metropolitan powers made bananas more attractive for Eastern Caribbean farmers. In the British islands, the initiation of regular shipping services between the Windwards and eastern Canadian ports, subsidised by the Canadian government, was a critical factor, while the French Antilles were given an entrée into the French market by means of tariff protection and quotas: in 1928, the duty on noncolonial fruit was raised, and in 1931–32, foreign bananas were subjected to an import quota, and the duty collected on them was channelled back to Antillean producers (*La Banane* 1967, 1:3, 2:10). As a result of these measures, Antillean exports mounted rapidly at the expense of those of the Canary Islands, formerly France's main source of supply.

The export of bananas from the Eastern Caribbean lapsed completely during the Second World War, but in the immediate postwar period the British and French demand for fruit from nondollar sources encouraged renewed exports under favourable circumstances. While the Canadian market had been lost irrevocably to Central American bananas, the British market was now closed to them by a quota restriction of 4,000 tons a year on banana imports from dollar-area countries. Bananas from non-Commonwealth sources were subject to an import duty of £2.10.0 a ton, raised in 1956 to £7.10.0, the equivalent, roughly, of a 20 percent preference at 1956 prices (Morgan 1962, 126). Once established behind this substantial tariff and quota barrier, Windwards banana production was further safeguarded against low market prices by price assistance and price adjustment schemes operated by the United Kingdom and Windwards governments between 1955 and 1964. In 1967, when overproduction by Caribbean producers had brought price levels precariously low, a cartel was set up, with the approval of the United Kingdom government, to share the market in agreed proportions between Jamaican and Windwards bananas. Elders and Fyffes and Geest agreed not to ship bananas from other sources for sale in the United Kingdom unless, between them, the Caribbean producers could not fulfil the requirements of the British market (*Sunday Times*, 31 January 1971).

A similar degree of protection was afforded to French Antillean producers in postwar years. Their competitive position was assured initially by a 20 percent tariff on foreign banana imports, and in 1962, when this became inadequate, the French president decided that an "organised" banana market in France was the solution. The franc-zone producers of France's former African colonies (Côte d'Ivoire, Cameroun and Madagascar) were to supply one-third of metropolitan France's requirements, while Martinique and Guadeloupe were to supply the remainder.

Without these various forms of protection, there would have been no export banana industries in the Eastern Caribbean in the 1960s. While the period after the Second World War had seen some improvement in internal communications, the islands retained, after all, most of the physical disadvantages that had made them nonstarters in the early years of the century. The terrain was rugged, the soils often poor and subject to erosion, and always requiring heavy applications of fertiliser. Disease control was expensive and difficult, and hurricane damage a constant threat. Furthermore, wages, uniformly low in prewar days, were sharply differentiated by the 1960s; and the opening up of new low-cost production areas in West Africa represented an even more serious menace than the ever-present Central American surpluses, since the West African producers could play upon French Community or British Commonwealth affiliations to justify some access to French and British markets.

Seasonal fluctuations in supply and demand were yet a further problem that afflicted both sets of islands. Except in the highest, wettest areas, there is a pronounced spring dry season in the Eastern Caribbean. This would naturally cause a trough in production in the summer months and a peak during the winter. But demand patterns in the importing countries did not accord with this rhythm. Consumption was affected by the severity of the winter climate, which might hinder distribution and prevent sales in outdoor markets, by competition from locally grown summer fruits, and by the idiosyncracies of different national tastes: some peoples, for instance, eschewed bananas in a heat wave. In the United Kingdom, consumption rose above the annual mean from April to September, to a maximum in June and July, and fell below the annual mean from October to March, to a January and February minimum. In France, consumption was above the annual mean in the period from March to June and in November, (the maximum was in May), while the periods from July to October and December to February formed two troughs, with the extreme low falling in August (*La Banane* 1967, 1:24; Persaud 1966, 54).

Competitive, low-cost producers can often avoid the worst effects of such seasonal fluctuations by arranging to supply complementary markets, but where an industry only exists by virtue of special protection and is tied to a single market, this is impossible. If summer shortfalls and winter gluts were to be avoided, production had to be carefully scheduled to peak in the less naturally favourable early summer months. Moreover, these already high-cost producers laboured under yet another handicap, since they had to maintain equipment and installations to handle peak demand, even though for much of the year these facilities were operating at only seventy-five percent of their capacity.

In spite of an array of disadvantages that became more rather than less acute with time, over a period of fifteen to twenty years, both the British Windwards and the French Antilles succeeded in developing very substantial export banana industries from almost nothing. In 1965, Guadeloupe and Martinique together exported 250,000 tons of bananas, while Dominica and St Lucia exported 130,000 tons. The precariousness of these highly protected industries cannot, however, be overemphasised. While the banana industries initially benefited France and Britain by permitting them to obtain supplies of tropical fruit without spending scarce foreign currency (notably dollars), by 1966 this was no longer a major consideration. However, since the French islands were politically an integral part of France, and the Commonwealth islands retained some degree of dependence on Britain, the two metropolitan countries were not necessarily spending more on expensive bananas than they would have been obliged to spend on salvaging the Eastern Caribbean islands from the economic ruin that would inevitably have ensued from the collapse of their banana industries.

The vulnerability of the Eastern Caribbean banana industries placed them in an uneasy relationship with the rest of the North Atlantic subsystem. Even though their trades were almost entirely bilateral and highly protected, they were by no means isolated from external influences. This was less true in the 1950s, when rapidly expanding production still fell far short of potential demand. By the mid-1960s, however, demand was virtually satisfied and seasonal gluts were liable to depress prices. Martinique tried briefly to divert surplus fruit to alternative markets. Receipts per ton for bananas shipped to North America were much lower than for bananas shipped to France. But provided that shipping and marketing costs could be covered, the sale of a few thousand tons of bananas annually on the North American market was expected to be more profitable than destroying the surplus or sending it to France at the risk of saturating the market and depressing price levels there. The North American operation was only marginal, however, and was discontinued after 1966.

The only other solution to the problem of market saturation was a very rigorous control on production and shipment. This solution implies a high degree of regulation right down to grower level, with cooperation between growers within individual islands and between exporters from different islands supplying the same market. The 1962 decree of the French government assuring the Antilles of two-thirds of the metropolitan market also provided for a division of this share in a fixed proportion between Martinique (53.73 percent) and Guadeloupe (47.27 percent). While this decree restrained the islands from shipping excessive quantities of fruit to France and driving down prices to their mutual detriment, overproduction by growers was still a problem.

In the case of the Commonwealth Windwards, satisfactory price levels in the United Kingdom market could be sustained only with Jamaican cooperation. Until 1966, when Windwards production threatened to overtake that of Jamaica, Jamaica was not anxious to come to any agreement to share the United Kingdom market in fixed proportions and limit the total Jamaican export. However, after a period of low prices in a saturated market had proved as uncomfortable for Jamaican producers as for their Windwards rivals, an accommodation was reached that accorded roughly half the market to Jamaica and half to the Windwards.

Such arrangements were satisfactory as long as conditions permitted production to be sustained at a constant level, in accord with demand. Since producers had no outlet for casual disposal of surpluses, however, production levels had to be maintained at very close to the quota limit. If drought or disease affected yields, a shortfall was therefore inevitable, leading to a loss in export earnings and giving cheap foreign fruit an entry into the metropolitan market.

Finally, if an exporting island was dependent on a metropolitan government for the tariff protection and market organisation that permitted its industry to survive, it was also at that government's mercy concerning price levels. For two decades in France there had been a government-imposed retail price ceiling on bananas of Fr2 per kilo. But by the late 1960s, it was claimed that this ceiling permitted only the narrowest of profit margins to handlers at all stages. It was their misfortune, however, that the price of bananas was included in the cost of living index (to which many wage levels were automatically geared) and that the government, in consequence, had strong economic and political reasons for holding down banana prices. It therefore countered by raising the ceiling price to Fr2.20, but, at the same time, it authorised imports of Ecuadorian bananas to ensure that prices would not in fact rise substantially above the old ceiling.

The European Common Market introduced an additional complication into the North Atlantic subsystem and its relationships with Eastern Caribbean banana producers. It was agreed under the terms of the Treaty of Rome, signed in 1957, that over the next thirteen years, the six member countries would adjust their own quota and tariff arrangements for banana imports to conform with a single Common Market standard. At that date Germany, the largest banana importer among the Six, had a free market and no import duty. France, the second largest, imposed a 20 percent duty on foreign bananas; Italy, which had a measure of state control over the industry, imposed a 36 percent duty on all but Somalian imports and the Benelux countries had a 15 percent import duty and a free market. It was agreed that by 1970, there should be a common external tariff of 20 percent for all foreign bananas imported into the market, except bananas of associated states, mainly African, which were to enjoy entry at a somewhat lower rate. Meanwhile, member countries would gradually work towards conformity; Germany, for instance, would introduce a 6 percent duty initially, rising to 12 percent in 1966. In addition, internal markets were to be freed, quotas were to disappear, and bananas were to cross the frontiers of member countries without encountering any barriers.

Since it was noted in an annexe to the treaty that bananas from the French overseas departments counted as a "European" agricultural product, producers in the French Antilles were optimistic that their rapidly expanding production, which risked saturating the French market before long, would enjoy access to a much larger market in the other member countries, and particularly Germany, once Central American bananas had to surmount a 20 percent tariff barrier.

By the mid-1960s, however, it was evident that far from benefiting its Antillean banana producers, France's membership in the Common Market was liable to spell their ruin. In the first place, franc-zone West African producers were providing such strong competition in the French market by 1962 that only the establishment of an organised market, with quotas, permitted the Antillean industry to survive; but the aim of the Common Market was the elimination of such quota arrangements. In the second place, while a 20 percent tariff had seemed adequate in 1957 to ensure that Antillean bananas would be able to compete with Central American fruit, by 1966, because of rising production costs in the Antilles, the removal of internal tariff barriers would have permitted Central American bananas to undercut those of Martinique and Guadeloupe, even in their traditional French market, unless a common external tariff far higher than twenty percent was imposed. Finally, it was becoming clear that the Germans had no intention of permitting French Antillean bananas to encroach on their market at the expense of low-cost Central American fruit. Despite the treaty provision for the gradual introduction of tariff barriers, West Germany annually applied for, and obtained, permission to import a duty-free quota at least equal to its expected annual consumption. Germany argued that this was essential to safeguard traditional commercial ties with the Latin American banana-producing countries that provided a market for German manufactures. In 1966, Germany was still importing its entire banana supply duty-free (*La Banane* 1967, 2:14).

Nor could Antillean producers sit back and wait for full implementation of the treaty in 1970, complacent in the knowledge that if the 20 percent tariff proved inadequate, they would be protected and compensated by the Common Market's Common Agricultural Policy (CAP). The CAP provided that for products insufficiently protected by the common external tariff, a minimum reference price was to be determined, taking into account production and marketing costs. If, as a result of overproduction or the import of cheap foreign produce, the market price fell below the reference price, the market agency would intervene and buy produce grown within the Common Market at the reference price. This operation was to be financed from the Common Agricultural Fund, which, in turn, was to be financed by a compensatory levy on the cheaper imported produce. By 1964, seven different fruits produced within the Six, mainly in France and Italy, were protected in this way; but calls for Antillean bananas to be similarly safeguarded met with resistance, mainly from the Germans.

Their opposition centred on two points: it was claimed, first, that Antillean bananas were not of the quality demanded by their market and, second, that they were not actually a "European" fruit (*La Banane* 1967, 2:5). The fact that the shipment of Martiniquan bananas to Hamburg, attempted in 1964, was a failure, even at "world market" prices (*La Banane* 1967, 1:13), supported the first objection: German importers declared that the fruit was unacceptable to consumers. But Antillean exporters suspected that since their fruit had proved quite acceptable on the discriminating American market, the German objection was simply a ploy to ensure that Germany could not subsequently be obliged to accept Antillean fruit under the terms of the Treaty of Rome. Officials in Paris suggested that no matter how far Antillean growers went to satisfy the tastes of the German market, further unreasonable requirements would always be set up to exclude their product. ("They would say they had to be red, or 35 centimetres long.")

The second objection, that Antillean bananas were not "European," remained in dispute. In the Antilles, the somewhat cynical view was expressed that, while in the complex commodity negotiations in Brussels, French negotiators would certainly press for the support and protection of their Antillean bananas, in the final analysis, Antillean claims would be sacrificed as a pawn in return for German concessions on some matter more vital to metropolitan French interests.

EXPORT BANANAS AS AN ELEMENT IN EASTERN CARIBBEAN ECONOMIES

In all four islands under study, export banana industries expanded from virtually nothing in 1945 to multimillion-dollar enterprises by 1965. While banana industries had been established in all the islands by 1952, in none of them were bananas the most valuable export. But by the mid-1960s, bananas were far more valuable than any other exports in three of the islands, and, although Guadeloupean statistics do not differentiate the products of volcanic Basse-

Table 2.1
Value of main agricultural exports, 1952 and 1962

	Dominica		*St. Lucia*		*Martinique*		*Guadeloupe*[a]	
	1952	*1962*	*1952*	*1962*	*1952*	*1962*	*1952*	*1962*
TOTAL DOMESTIC EXPORTS								
WI$ (thousands)	4,451	7,571	2,542	7,566		60,000		45,000
Ancien francs (billions)					7	17	7	13
MAIN CROPS (PERCENTAGES)								
Bananas	24	64	2	78	33	44	38	45
Sugar	-	-	49	5	28	30	43	44
Rum	-	-	-	-	27	13	?	5
Citrus and citrus products (limes, oranges, grapefruit)	43	26	-	-	-	-	-	-
Copra, coconut oil	6	6	25	13	-	-	-	-
Pineapples	-	-	-	-	10	8	-	-
Cocoa	4	2	15	1	-	-	8	-
Bay oil	1	2	-	-	-	-	-	-
Coffee	-	-	-	-	-	-	4	-
Total	78	100	87	97	98	95	86	94

Sources: Dominica, Colony of (1955, 4); Persaud (1966, 32,34); Martinique (1964, 38,44,74); ORSTOM (1965, 4); Lasserre (1961, 530,681,735,740,961).
[a]Basse-Terre only, estimated.

Terre Guadeloupe from those of Grande-Terre and Marie Galante, it is certain that if this distinction were made, bananas would have been well ahead of any other crop in Basse-Terre. Table 2.1 illustrates the position of banana exports in relation to exports of other leading crops in two sample years, 1952 and 1962.

The figures for Basse-Terre Guadeloupe (listed here simply as "Guadeloupe") are estimates, based on the presumption, which Lasserre's data (1961) justify, that virtually all the *département*'s bananas and approximately half its cane were grown on Basse-Terre in the sample years. In all the islands, exports consisted almost wholly of a small range of agricultural products: nonagricultural goods occupied a trivial position in export lists. By 1965, bananas comprised between 60 and 85 percent of island exports by value and had risen to this preeminence within a remarkably short time. Thanks largely to this one crop, island exports had increased by 70 to 200 percent in ten years. This is a remarkable achievement, given that the island economies had always been strongly orientated towards external trade. So great was their traditional concentration on tropical export crops that they had long been obliged to import not only manufactured goods, but even many essential foodstuffs.

In 1962, the per capita gross domestic products (GDPs) of St Lucia and Dominica were WI$314 and WI$331 respectively; 22 percent of St Lucia's GDP and 18 percent of Dominica's were contributed by export agriculture (Persaud 1966, 37). The per capita GDPs of Martinique and Guadeloupe were WI$740 and WI$700 respectively; 27 percent of Martinique's GDP and 32 percent of Guadaloupe's were contributed by agriculture (Andic 1965, 74–5). These percentages include produce destined for the local market, but the percentage contributions of *export* agriculture in the French islands probably closely resembled the contributions in the Commonwealth ones. The difference in the per capita value of agricultural production in the French and Commonwealth islands is partly a result of higher productivity in the French islands, and partly a result of higher commodity prices.

In all four islands, then, export agriculture accounted for approximately one-fifth of the total GDP. While export bananas contributed between 12 and 17 percent of total GDPs directly, a much higher proportion of the islands' GDPs depended on the income generated by banana exports, particularly in the import and retail trades and services. In the French islands, government-financed enterprises (administration, education, public works, and the like) would presumably have been unaffected by vicissitudes in the banana industry, since expenditure was financed directly by the French treasury, but in the Commonwealth islands, revenues from the industry were a significant proportion of government income, and without them, reductions in government spending, with further repercussions on the GDP, would probably have been inevitable.

An industry that employed only a few workers and generated income and profits that were mainly spent abroad might through its decline or disappearance substantially reduce the GDP without materially affecting the living standards of the mass of the population. This was far from the case for banana growing in the Commonwealth Windwards, where income from the industry was spread over a remarkably high proportion of the population. Even in the French islands, where the number of proprietors of banana-growing holdings was much smaller and the industry was concentrated in relatively few hands, a large number of workers were employed since the possibilities for mechanising banana cultivation were limited.

It was difficult to obtain accurate employment statistics for the industry, since much of the labour was part-time, family labour was often employed, and in the Commonwealth islands, many growers farmed only part-time on very small holdings. It was estimated (SICABAM 1965) that one worker was required for each hectare of bananas in Martinique and Guadeloupe, which would suggest 8,000 and 6,000 banana workers respectively in these islands. In St Lucia and Dominica, enquiry suggested a similar labour requirement per hectare, but cultivation was much more extensive, so figures of 13,000 and 10,000 respectively might be a reasonable estimate. If these figures are multiplied by a factor of four or five to take account of each worker's dependents, some idea is gained of the proportions of island populations deriving some or all of their income from banana cultivation: 10 or 15 percent in the French islands, and possibly as high as 70 percent in St Lucia and Dominica.

That the banana industry was a mainstay, in the Commonwealth islands *the* mainstay, of the island economies and that involvement in the industry was widespread throughout their populations is indisputable. It might, however, be argued that since the industry developed so swiftly and suddenly from a small base, its collapse would at worst have meant a return to the status quo, and might more optimistically have been expected to induce the rise of substitutes. A closer investigation reveals fallacies in such arguments.

In the first place, the population of all the islands had increased substantially since 1945: by 1965, it had grown by between 30 and 35 percent (Martinique 1964, 15; Welch 1968, 227,229); but at the same time, the terms of trade had moved against tropical primary produce, rendering imported manufactured goods more expensive, while traditional Caribbean exports such as sugar and cocoa fetched lower prices than formerly.

By the mid-1960s, the situation was further aggravated by the seemingly irreversible decline of the sugar industry, once the mainstay of three of the four island economies. Reasons for the decline were both economic and social. Except on some of the larger operations in northern Guadeloupe, processing equipment and methods of transporting cane to central factories had been inefficient and out of date, and while, theoretically, sugar production might still have been viable in some districts of St Lucia, Martinique, and Guadeloupe where it had recently been abandoned, substantial investment would have been needed to revive it. In contrast, the change to bananas in marginal sugar areas had required relatively little capital investment. Moreover, while sugar production might have been viable for companies or large estates owning both canelands and factories, by the mid-1960s, the small, independent cane farmers who had traditionally supplied up to one-third of the factories' cane found returns too marginal to be worthwhile.

The revival of sugar was a dubious proposition economically; socially, it was even less conceivable. Even in these islands of perennially high unemployment, it was impossible by 1965 to recruit an adequate and efficient labour force for the sugar industry: workers preferred almost anything, or even nothing, to work in the cane fields. Even if there had been an adequate labour force in the early part of the crop season, by midseason numbers would have dwindled so that cane-cutting extended far beyond the period of optimum yield; often, large parts of the crop remained unharvested.

Workers disliked sugar for various reasons: cane is an unpleasant crop to work with; manual harvesting requires sustained hard labour in hot sun. In contrast, banana or tree-crop cultivation provides a more varied routine under less gruelling conditions. Moreover, bananas provided round-the-year employment, while cane-cutting was highly seasonal. Furthermore, the history of sugar as a slave crop made it repugnant to a rising generation that was increasingly socially and politically aware, and the estate- and factory-owners in post-slavery times had done little to mitigate the suspicion and distaste with which the industry was regarded. The gulf between the living standards of employers and employees had always been so vast that assertions by the former that they could not afford higher wages must always have had a hollow ring.

When, in the 1960s, the employers confronted genuine financial difficulties, they could hardly have expected much sympathy or cooperation from their workers, especially since their difficulties were caused in some measure by their own failure to modernise when times were better. Since the 1930s at least, labour relations in sugar had been abysmal, with repeated strikes in most of the islands. In St Lucia strikes prompted the closure of Dennery Factory, the island's third largest, in 1957, and of Roseau Factory, its last, in 1963. In Martinique, after a violent strike in 1959, one of the largest estates sold its best cane land to the government for subdivision in the land reform of 1961, the *réforme foncière*. Even in Guadeloupe, where overt labour problems had been less crippling than elsewhere, absenteeism was a problem. The most ominous portent for the sugar industry, there as elsewhere, was its failure to recruit young workers from the rising generation: every year, the average age of the labour force increased by one year.

Undoubtedly, the banana industries, which offered more attractive prospects to both workers and landowners, helped to undermine sugar and accelerate its decline in many areas where bananas were a feasible alternative. On the other hand, even in islands such as St Kitts, with virtually no alternative employment, there were labour troubles, a shortage of workers, and a tendency to retreat from the more marginal cane lands.

In Dominica, limes rather than sugar had been the mainstay of the economy before the rise of bananas, but while the lime industry did not suffer from the social stigma of sugar, its restoration to preeminence would hardly have been more gratifying. By the mid-1960s, restrictions on importing lime products into Britain (the chief market) from dollar-area sources had been lifted, giving access to Mexican lime oil and lowering prices substantially. Although Dominica's production capacity probably did not fall much below that of 1952, because income from limes was considerably reduced, 1950 living standards would have been impossible to maintain with the lime industry of 1965, even with an equivalent output.

Since turning back the clock was clearly out of the question, the only yardstick for determining how crucial were bananas to the island economies is the facility with which substitutes might have replaced them. It was not as if the banana industry itself had developed in response to the decline of any other industry. The rise of bananas preceded the decline of sugar, which achieved its highest-ever production in St Lucia in 1956 and in Martinique in 1963, years after bananas had become well established. In Guadeloupe, sugar production was still expanding annually in 1966. Limes were still reasonably profitable in the early 1950s when Dominicans began large-scale banana production. Indeed, since optimum physical conditions for bananas differ considerably from those for sugar or limes, bananas tended at first to be established where traditional mainstays were quite unimportant because of rugged terrain or high rainfall.

In the early days, bananas were largely grown by farmers who had previously concentrated on subsistence food crops, possibly obtaining a small cash income from minor tree crops. It is true that once bananas were well established, there was a widespread transfer of both land and labour from sugar to bananas, especially in St Lucia and Martinique; but this was in response to the greater profits per hectare and more attractive working conditions offered by bananas, rather than to any intrinsic failure of the sugar industry. Thus, the recent history of sugar and limes provides no evidence that the collapse of bananas would induce the development of an equally volatile substitute.

In any case, it is difficult to conceive of any substitute which could have compensated for the failure of the banana industry. It was able to take root and flourish only because of the peculiarly favourable conditions after the Second World War, when quotas and tariffs provided an unusual degree of protection for colonial produce on metropolitan European markets. By the 1960s, metropolitan governments were reluctant to support such measures, since restricting dollar-area imports was no longer necessary. Without protection, virtually no tropical crop could be grown more economically in the Eastern Caribbean than elsewhere.

Inevitably in these rugged islands, soil conservation and transport costs were high, while wages were far higher than in Africa, Asia, or much of tropical Central America. For example, excellent grapefruit were grown in Dominica, but production costs exceeded the price on the United Kingdom market, except for a brief period in early autumn when prices were unusually high because the South African season was over and Mediterranean fruit not yet available. While Dominican grapefruit growers did their best to exploit this marginal advantage, if excessive quantities of Dominican fruit had been shipped, prices would doubtless have fallen to unremunerative levels. Moreover, even this trade rested on the exclusion of dollar-area supplies. If Martinique and Guadeloupe had taken up the production of grapefruit, they should in theory have enjoyed a privileged position as the sole Common Market producers of this fruit. In all probability, however, other member countries would have been even more reluctant to accept Antillean grapefruit than Antillean bananas as a European fruit.

There were several minor crops, such as nutmegs and bay, that were grown profitably in one or another of the Eastern Caribbean islands simply because these islands had happened to have adopted them early on and therefore had specialised knowledge of agricultural and processing methods, which gave them an advantage over potential rivals. To expand any of these crops would, however, have been counter-productive, since world demand was limited and increased production would merely have lowered prices.

It would be unrealistic, then, to imagine that the failure of any of the Eastern Caribbean banana industries would have been merely a temporary setback. A failure would have brought a massive dislocation of island economies, leaving a large proportion of their populations with no independent cash income and little alternative but to depend on subsistence food crop production to a far greater extent than they had had to before the establishment of bananas fifteen or twenty years previously.

COMMONWEALTH AND FRENCH BANANA INDUSTRIES: ECONOMIC PARALLELS AND DIFFERENCES

To place the banana industries of the four islands in the proper economic perspective requires evaluation of the relative importance of the economic factors that encouraged dissimilar patterns in the industry and factors that favoured conformity.

The differences can be summarised fairly briefly. In the French islands, banana production was somewhat less dominant in the GDP and export totals than in the Commonwealth islands, and bananas employed a much smaller proportion of the total population. The survival of a major alternative crop, cane, provided a somewhat wider, if not much less precarious, base for the French islands' agricultural economies. Since political and economic integration of the French Antilles with France-in-Europe permitted unrestricted emigration, marginal participants might have felt less urgency to remain in the banana industry. Moreover, there was less pressure to maximise production in the French islands, because a favourable balance of trade was not essential for the *départments* as a whole, nor was it even a particularly useful goal. In the Commonwealth islands, however, the failure to balance imports and exports jeopardised their pursuit of political independence, or semi-independence, since economic viability was felt to be a precondition for self-government. These differing circumstances probably accounted for some restraint in the French islands in the drive to expand banana production wherever and whenever possible, a restraint that was quite lacking in the St Lucian and Dominican industries, especially in the early 1960s.

The higher wages in the French islands obliged growers to use labour as intensively as possible and further restricted the production of bananas under marginal conditions. French growers were to some extent compensated for their higher labour costs by substantially higher FOB prices: WI$250 a ton, compared to WI$135–$150 a ton for Windwards bananas. Such price levels were possible because France's major banana suppliers cooperated under the auspices of the Comité National Interprofessionnel Bananier (CNIB); but the Windwards producers never managed to cooperate in this way with their Jamaican rivals. These higher price levels, however, turned banana-growing into a game played for much higher stakes in the French than in the Commonwealth islands and significantly restricted participation, since failure incurred a risk of heavy losses.

On the other hand, there were many compelling parallels between the banana industries in the two sets of islands, both historically and in the mid-1960s. In the context of world banana trade as a whole, export banana cultivation in all four islands had developed only recently; in all four, bananas had expanded rapidly in the 1950s and early 1960s until by the mid-1960s supply had begun to exceed demand in the respective markets, even though considerable capacity for increased production still existed. While large-scale plantation operations had initiated export banana cultivation in most other major production areas, throughout the Eastern Caribbean bananas had originally been adopted most enthusiastically by small farmers. Estate owners had, for the most part, entered the industry more cautiously. Although, especially in the French islands, estate production did play an important role, the units of production were still generally very small compared with units in Central America or West Africa. Moreover, complete vertical integration of banana industries, with a single company growing, exporting, shipping, importing, ripening, and wholesaling the crop, was never characteristic of either set of islands, although, again, vertical integration was common elsewhere in the North Atlantic subsystem.

The geographical relationship of the two sets of islands to their markets was very similar. Each shipped almost its entire production to a single importing country with whom it had close political ties. The two markets had much in common: both were old-established markets with banana consumption seemingly close to saturation point. Both were open to Eastern Caribbean exports only by virtue of special protection from tariffs, quotas, and "organised" markets that not only favoured Eastern Caribbean exports but also partially or completely excluded exports from elsewhere. In both cases protection depended on goodwill and frequent renegotiation, rather than on any long-term guarantees. The fluid economic situation of the mid-1960s and an emphasis on reducing tariffs and developing new economic groupings, such as the European Common Market, made the future of the industry in all of the islands even more uncertain.

3 The Character of Land Occupancy

Variations in rural population density, land tenure, or farm size may account for significant variations both in the choice of crops and in techniques of cultivation observed in neighbouring areas with similar physical potential and constraints. From a global perspective, the four Eastern Caribbean islands exhibit a rather narrow range of interisland variation in land occupancy. Whether or not this variation has had a significant impact on land use and, more specifically, patterns of export banana cultivation can be assessed only by an island-by-island analysis. The issue is more complex than it might at first appear, since, in addition to examining interisland variations and their effect on land use, one must realize that land use may, in turn, affect agrarian structure, rendering it a dynamic rather than a merely static element in island land use systems.

Finally, there is also the question of whether banana growers are typical of their island's farmers: are the size of their farms and the forms of land tenure typical, or is it possible that only some conditions of tenure or some sizes of holdings permit profitable participation in export banana production? Again, did preexisting conditions of tenure constrain entry into the industry, or did the exigencies of the industry lead to modifications in agrarian structures in islands where it became a major economic force? While it is not possible to provide definitive answers to all these questions, some light can be shed by examining other characteristics of banana growers, such as their age, the length of time they have worked their holdings and the means by which they acquired them, and their educational and ethnic backgrounds, and by discussing how closely these farmers conform with the general profile for their island.

DENSITY OF RURAL SETTLEMENT

Table 3.1 is compiled from data for 1960–61. To estimate rural populations, the populations of the leading urban centres have been subtracted from the island totals. The term "area in holdings" in the census reports for the Commonwealth islands has been taken to correspond with the *territoire agricole* of the French islands. Each term represents the area in private ownership or to which private owners laid claim. The remainder belonged to the Crown or State and was mainly forested highland, much of which was unsuited to cultivation.

In crude terms, Martinique was three times as densely populated as Dominica: a difference explained, to some extent, by the fact that when the islands were settled in the seventeenth and eighteenth centuries it was primarily to exploit their sugar-producing potential, and in this respect, Dominica quickly proved disappointing. Variations in density are, however, much less extreme when the rural population is related only to the area in holdings (Table 3.1). Moreover, variations between districts within a single island are far greater than those between islands as a whole. Thus, within Basse-Terre Guadeloupe, the commune of Trois Rivières had 3.36 persons per hectare in holdings, while Goyave had only 0.66, and in Dominica, the parish of St Patrick had 2.4, while St Luke had only 0.35 (Lasserre 1961, 2:472; *WI Census of Agriculture* 1968). This suggests that density of settlement was at least to some degree a function of land quality and hardly to be regarded as in any way an independent variable.

While the two French islands were more densely populated than the two Commonwealth ones, there was no sharp dichotomy between the two sets. Possibly a more sensitive indicator is the relative availability of agriculturally workable land. It is, however, difficult to define "agriculturally workable" in this context, for the concept is a subjective one and affected by economic conditions as well as by government policy concerning, for instance, conservation. Certainly, in Martinique, there were no plans to alienate any of the land within the *forêt domaniale* (state-owned forest lands), and indeed, there was a feeling that in the past, too much land had been cleared for agriculture in areas whose relief and soils made forest cover desirable. In Guadeloupe, however, it was primarily economic

Table 3.1
Rural settlement density, 1960–61

	Martinique	*Guadeloupe*[a]	*Dominica*	*St Lucia*
Area of island (km^2)	1,100	848	767	616
Area in holdings (km^2)	800	480	300	330
Area in holdings (%)	73	56	38	54
Area in crops (km^2)	320	250	135	181
Island area in crops (%)	29	29	17	29
Holdings area in crops (%)	40	52	45	52
Area in pasture (km^2)	200	c.50	17	21
Island area in pasture (%)	18	6	2	3
Holdings area in crops and pasture (%)	65	63	51	57
Total rural population	196,000	104,000	45,000	61,000
Persons per hectare	1.78	1.23	0.59	1.00
Persons per hectare-in-holdings	2.45	2.17	1.50	1.84
Persons per hectare-in-crops	6.1	4.2	3.3	3.0

Sources: WI Census of Agriculture, 1961 (1968) (Commonwealth Islands); Lasserre (1961) (Guadeloupe); Martinique (1964). (Préfecture de la Martinique).
[a]Basse-Terre only.

considerations rather than conservation that discouraged the alienation of any more *forêt domaniale.* There were probably several thousand hectares of moderately sloping land between 300 and 500 metres above sea level in windward Guadeloupe that, had they been in Dominica, would have been considered quite acceptable for agricultural settlement. In Guadeloupe, however, they were regarded as too inaccessible and too deficient in insolation for profitable cultivation. It was suggested that where new roads crossed the central mountains, some of the lands immediately adjacent might be sold as market-garden plots, although doubts were expressed that the soils were really suitable.

In St Lucia there were still a few small blocks of Crown land in 1967, mainly around the margins of the forest reserve areas, that were considered suitable for sale for agriculture purposes, and, in addition, there were scattered holdings that had reverted to the Crown and were available for resale. In Dominica in 1966, there were 4,000 hectares of Crown land destined for agricultural settlement, most of which had been allocated by the late 1960s, if not legally alienated. While in Dominica and, to a lesser extent, St Lucia, the settlement of supposedly virgin Crown lands was still put forward in the 1960s as a panacea for the problem of pressure on the land, in the French islands, redistribution of the existing *territoire agricole* was seen as the only real solution.

LAND TENURE

To understand the complex network of land tenure arrangements in the Eastern Caribbean in the 1960s, it is necessary to know something of the history of land apportionment in the area. At the end of the eighteenth century, practically all of the land then alienated was held freehold in large estates on which slaves produced sugar and coffee for the profit of their European owners. In the sugar areas, estates might vary in size from forty to several hundred hectares, while in coffee-growing districts they were usually somewhat smaller: upwards of sixteen hectares. There were few independent smallholders, except for small settlements of poor whites squeezed into marginal areas and a few escaped slaves in the mountains.

With the abolition of slavery in the 1830s and 1840s, however, a strong demand for land arose among the thousands of former slaves who wished to leave the estates and become independent cultivators. They could not usually afford initially to buy more than a hectare or so, and since most of the best and most accessible land was already tied up in large estates, they were frequently obliged to acquire land on the periphery of the area then in holdings, often on interfluves or some distance inland. This problem was mitigated to some extent in the mid-nineteenth century when repeated economic crises afflicted the planter class, arising from emancipation, changes in the technology of sugar production, and the freeing of trade. Estates that did not find ready purchasers during the ensuing spate of bankruptcies might be broken up and sold as peasant holdings. Divided estates and the sale of government lands, however, provided only a few thousand holdings in each island. Not only were many ex-slaves unable to purchase land, but there was often resistance by the plantocracy to the development of peasant freeholding, since they felt this would jeopardize their labour supply. Consequently, in Dominica, for instance, the planter-dominated legislature attempted to prevent the sale of crown land in blocks of less than 40 acres.

Thus, while individual freehold tenure was the ideal of large and small farmers alike, those who were unable to attain the ideal were forced into a multiplicity of compromises: shared freehold tenure, sharecropping on leased holdings, cash rental of land, various forms of shared occupancy between owner and tenant, and squatting. The peasants were forced to compromise because of their poverty or the planters' obstruction; the planters were obliged to compromise, sometimes because they lacked the capital to develop their land and farm it directly and sometimes because they could not recruit enough labour and therefore had to provide incentives or use indirect methods to keep their land in cultivation.

One of the most widespread tenure problems in the four islands in the 1960s had arisen from the practice of sharing freeholds in undivided tenure. This system was not unusual in areas where both land and money were limited, so that when a parent died leaving many children, there was no possibility of all except one leaving to farm elsewhere or of one being able to buy out the inheritances of the remainder. Thus, three or four generations after the original purchase, a five-acre plot of land might be held in undivided ownership by dozens of descendants. In Dominica, where the vested interests had legislated against the sale of small blocks of land, a further complication was introduced by the nineteenth-century practice of forming groups, or "companies," to buy large blocks. As a result, in the 1960s the co-owners, sometimes numbering hundreds, were often not related at all. All the co-owners of a plot of "family land" or "company land," as it was known, had right of usufruct on any part of it, regardless of whether they had planted or cultivated any crops, so that unless an amicable agreement could be reached between all of them, those who ventured to sow and cultivate ran the risk of having someone else reap. In the French islands, anyone who wished might compel a legal division of their family land, although this was often hardly worthwhile, for it might bring the individual only a few acres or less. In the Commonwealth islands, however, division could not be made without the agreement of all the co-heirs, and frequently many had emigrated and were untraceable. The extent of undivided freehold tenure was hard to assess, but it has been estimated that in St Lucia, it involved 64 percent of all cultivable land (SLBGA 1966a, 1).

The landowner who had difficulty obtaining a reliable labour supply or had areas of marginal land whose direct cultivation by wage labour would seldom be profitable resorted to sharecropping. The metropolitan sugar companies, which amassed huge estates in Guadeloupe in the wake of bankruptcies of Creole planters in the mid-nineteenth century, found a solution to their labour problem in the system known as *colonage*. On their more marginal lands, they leased small plots, seldom more than a few hectares, to landless peasants who agreed to grow cane on a specified proportion of the plot and to deliver the crop to the company factory for crushing.

A proportion of the cane, often a third, was to go to the landowner as rent; the *colon* was required to work as a wage labourer only on the company's estates and not elsewhere.

Over the years, the requirements of *colonage* became less rigorous, but the system was still widespread in Guadeloupe in 1966. In the late 1950s, it was estimated that in Basse-Terre Guadeloupe, *colons* contributed 8 percent of all the cane crushed by the sugar companies (Lasserre 1961, 2:654). A similar system existed in the sugar valleys of St Lucia, and while it was customary mainly in cane-growing areas, no doubt owing to the relative ease of controlling the sale of this crop, it was also recorded among banana growers in Dominica. In Martinique, however, it was never very important, even in cane areas; the Creole plantocracy had been more successful there than elsewhere in ensuring that a very high proportion of the cultivable land remained in their hands, so that until quite recently, labour supplies were assured without the inducement of *colonage*.

Cash rental of land was another possibility for agricultural workers with no land or not enough to render them independent of wage labouring. In the French islands, however, it is doubtful whether many landowners were prepared to rent land to small farmers, so cash rental does not seem to have been very important: it might have involved a few hundred holdings, at most. Since development capital could be borrowed relatively easily, an estate could prosper more readily with direct cultivation. On the other hand, in St Lucia and Dominica the owners of much of the estate land had no capital to finance development directly; and in addition, many small and medium-sized holdings belonged to emigrants to Britain who may have had vague intentions of returning sometime but, meanwhile, were glad to rent to relatives and neighbours. Migration from the French islands was, proportionately, on a somewhat smaller scale (Welch 1968, 230).

The establishment of permanent tree crops on a large scale is an expensive undertaking, involving heavy outlay on clearance and preparation of land and purchase of young plants followed by a lengthy period, often five years or more, during which the young trees must be tended and there is no return on this investment. Estate owners unable to finance tree crop establishment directly sometimes arranged for small farmers to tend their young trees, in return permitting the farmers to cultivate subsistence crops and bananas in the spaces between the trees. The tenants might also be required to clear land and plant the tree crops for the owner in the first instance. In the mid-1960s, this form of tenancy was encountered

Table 3.2
Land tenure on the four islands

	Total number of farms	*Owned*[a]	*Colonage*	*Rental*	*Mixed tenure*	*Rent-free*[c]
Guadeloupe[b] (1957)	12,000	6,000	4,000	500	1,500	?
Dominica (1961)	8,667	6,614	?	1,390	580	83
Martinique (1935)	6,541	4,775	1,500	226	?	?
St Lucia (1961)	12,699	8,358	(2,264	)	1,260	804

Source: WI Census of Agriculture, 1961 (1968); Doeuff (1968,4); France (1966, 273).
[a]or in owner-like possession.
[b]Basse-Terre only; approximate numbers.
[c]Or nominal rent.

only in the Commonwealth islands, and especially Dominica. In the French islands, estate cultivation of tree crops was unimportant, so there was no reason for shared occupancy.

Squatting was also more prevalent in the Commonwealth than in the French islands, although it was said to occur quite extensively within the limits of the *forêt domaniale* in leeward Guadeloupe until the 1950s. Statistics on squatters are hard to come by; indeed, because there were no cadastral surveys and many landowners had no title deeds, it was often difficult to determine who really was a squatter. It was estimated in 1967 that outside the central forest reserves, 60 percent of St Lucia's Crown lands were occupied by squatters, and there were even a few within the forest reserves themselves. While some squatters in both Commonwealth islands probably still practised shifting cultivation, using slash-and-burn-methods on Crown land that they had little intention of purchasing, many had farmed the same piece of land for years, in some cases since the Second World War, when squatting was, in fact, sanctioned to increase home food production. In areas where it was government policy to alienate land for agriculture, settled squatters were given first claim to the land. Those who been prevented from purchasing their land only by the lengthy bureaucratic procedures involved in survey and alienation were probably already looked upon as "in ownerlike possession" (Table 3.2).

SIZE DISTRIBUTION OF LAND HOLDINGS

Figure 3.1 compares holding-size distributions in the four islands in the early 1960s. Because the data from censuses taken at different

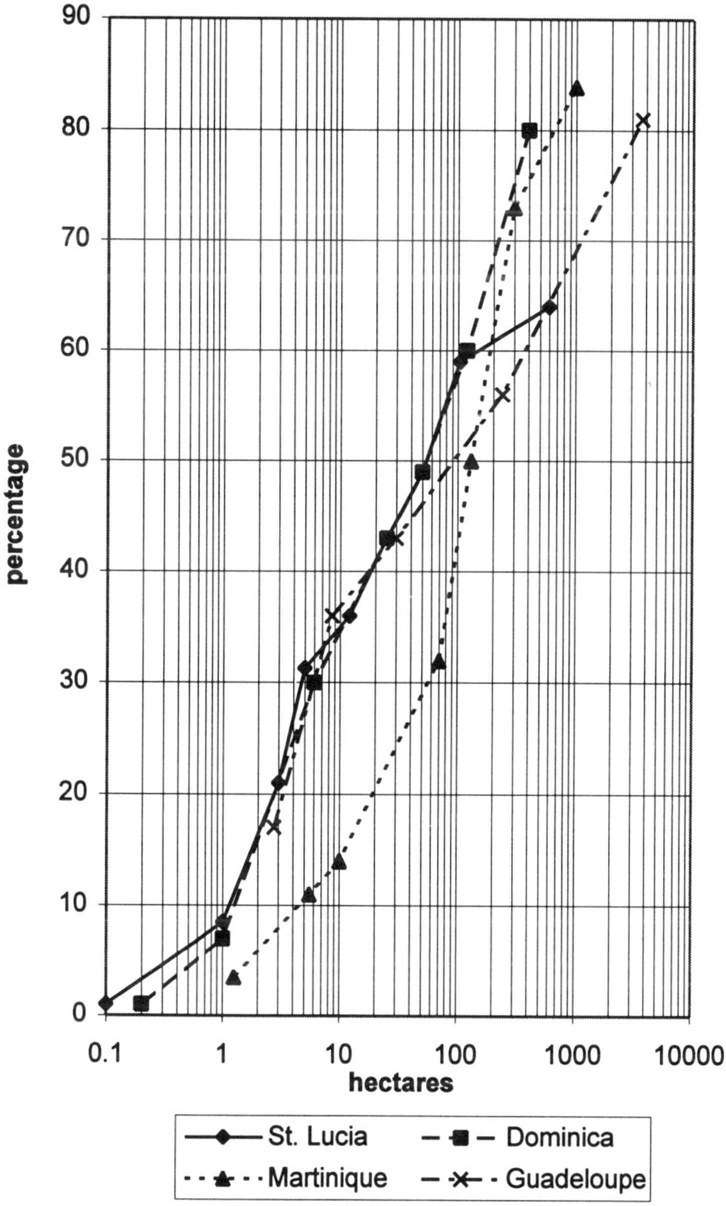

Figure 3.1
Agrarian structure of Martinique, Basse-Terre Guadeloupe, Dominica, and St Lucia. Cumulative percentages of land in holdings smaller than a given area
Source: West Indies Census of Agriculture, 1961 (1968); Lasserre (1961); Doeuff (1968).

dates with incompatible size-group boundaries and different criteria for what constitutes a "farm" were difficult to reconcile, this cumulative graph seemed the most reasonable way to represent the disparate data on a common basis. For each island, the mean holding size within each size group is plotted against the percentage of the total area of land-in-holdings in farms or properties of that size or smaller. The plotted points for each island are joined by straight lines to show the overall pattern for individual islands, since there are insufficient data to sketch in the curves which in reality link these points.

Size distributions in the two Commonwealth islands are remarkably similar for holdings of less than 100 hectares, and the pattern for Guadeloupe, especially Basse-Terre, conforms very closely with the Commonwealth islands if only properties are considered. However, the large area farmed by sharecroppers would modify the Basse-Terre Guadeloupe graph considerably if leasehold farms were included. For Martinique, the lack of census data for the 1950s and 1960s makes comparison problematical. Doeuff (1968), uses 1935 figures and suggests that until the 1960s, the pattern had not altered significantly. Burac's study, however, shows, at least for the Centre-Nord region on which it is based, a very different distribution of property (1975, 5). While he points out that the *réforme foncière* instituted in 1961 was responsible for some redistribution, it seems unlikely that the dramatic evolution from the 1935 situation to that recorded by the cadastral survey of the early 1970s took place wholly in the 1960s. More probably, in Martinique as in the other islands, there was a substantial expansion of the smallholder class during the 1950s, so that by 1960 it too may well have had nearly 30 percent of its land in holdings of less than five hectares.

A further 25 to 30 percent of the area in holdings in each island was in holdings of between 5 and 100 hectares; but whereas in Dominica, St Lucia, and Martinique, most of the remaining 45 to 50 percent was in holdings of 100 to 1,000 hectares, this size group accounted for only 18 percent in Guadeloupe, where 32 percent was in holdings of over 1,000 hectares. In Basse-Terre, a single company owned 8,585 hectares, 17 percent of the total (Lasserre 1961, 2:647).

It is worth noting that these four islands resembled each other in agrarian structure far more closely than the nearby islands of St Vincent or Barbados: St Vincent had a significantly higher proportion of its land in smallholdings, Barbados a much lower proportion: Barbados had 15 percent in holdings under 4 hectares and a further 1 percent in holdings under 10 hectares; St Vincent had

40 percent in holdings under 4 hectares and a further 12 percent in holdings under 10 hectares (*West Indies Census of Agriculture* 1968).

Like the land tenure forms, the agrarian structures of the 1960s were a legacy of more than two centuries of chequered economic history. The significance of the similarities and differences in the size distribution of landholdings in Dominica and St Lucia revealed by Table 3.3 can be appreciated only in the context of long-term trends, since size distribution is constantly evolving in response to political, economic, and social pressures.

By the end of the nineteenth century, the original division of the islands into large estates for the production of sugar and coffee had changed considerably. The impact of successive crises in the sugar industry varied greatly from island to island. In Dominica, where sugar had always been marginal, the white Creole plantocracy had almost disappeared, while in St Lucia and Guadeloupe it was much weakened, and Guadeloupe's best sugar lands had passed into the hands of metropolitan sugar companies. In Martinique, whose plantocracy had been shielded from the rigours of the French Revolution by an interlude of British rule, the greater resources and solidarity of the long-established white Creoles ensured that bankrupt estates were kept in local hands rather than sold to metropolitan interests. Moreover, despite the varying fortunes of the original white Creole landowning families, in all four islands many of the large estates that had been created in the eighteenth century still existed in the latter half of the twentieth century. Some, indeed, had been consolidated into much larger properties, notably in Guadeloupe.

Despite the post-Emancipation efforts of the plantocracy to inhibit the development of a class of peasant smallholders, either by legislating against the sale of government land in small lots (Dominica) or by cooperating to buy up bankrupt estates so that they were not fragmented or sold to former slaves (in Martinique), many small farms had been created in all four islands by the end of the nineteenth century. They were located mainly in the hillier and less accessible districts, in areas where estates marginal for sugar production had gone bankrupt, or in the interior, in areas not previously considered worth settling.

It is difficult to obtain figures showing the evolution of holding-size distribution in the first half of the twentieth century. In Dominica and St Lucia, agricultural censuses were held in 1946 and 1961. Unfortunately, the 1946 census does not record holdings of less than one acre. Table 3.3 shows that while the number of large estates remained relatively stable, there was a great, in St Lucia a

Table 3.3
Size distribution of holdings over one acre in Dominica and St Lucia, 1946 and 1961

	Holding-size groups (acres)							
	1–	*5–*	*10–*	*25–*	*50–*	*100–*	*200–*	*500+*
Dominica, 1946 (total 4,895)	2,760	979	776	199	89	44	34	31
Dominica, 1961 (total 5,309)	3,273	1,244	493	127	77	35	36	24
Change, (total +414)	+513	+265	–283	–72	–12	–9	–2	–7
Percentage change (+8.5 overall)	(+21	)	(–36	)	(	–13		)
St Lucia, 1946 (total 2,980)	857	827	917	242	62	38	26	17
St Lucia, 1961 (total 6,175)	4,337	1,068	463	154	63	38	33	19
Change, (total +3,195)	+3,484	+241	–454	–88	+1	0	+7	+2
Percentage change (+107 overall)	(+221	)	(–47	)	(	+6.5		)

Sources: West Indian Census, 1946 (1950); West Indies Census of Agriculture, 1961 (1968).

spectacular, increase in the number of small holdings and a substantial decline in the number of medium-sized holdings. The division of land on inheritance may have been responsible for much of the shift, since there had been a substantial increase in population over the period.

For Guadeloupe, estimates of property distribution in 1952 and 1960 can be derived from figures given by Lasserre (1961, 1:419,427). These figures (Table 3.4) suggest a dramatic restructuring similar to the restructuring in Dominica and St Lucia. It should be noted, however, that class boundaries in Table 3.4 are different from those in Table 3.3. While in Guadeloupe, the class of *petites propriétés* includes all holdings of less than ten hectares, it is likely that, as in the Commonwealth islands, the dramatic rise in the number of holdings came mainly in the 0–4 hectare class, especially as the average holding size in this class is under 2 hectares.

In Martinique, there was an agricultural land census in 1935–6. Despite the introduction of land reform legislation in 1961, however, a brochure published by the prefecture in 1964 reproduced the 1936 data on agrarian structure almost unchanged (see Table 3.5), although it included a note on the *réforme foncière* implying that the data referred to the situation in 1958 and that the *réforme* had effected some modest changes since then. Doeuff, summarising the achievements of the *réforme foncière* up to 1968, still had no more up-to-date data at his disposal. A cadastral survey carried out in the early 1970s suggested a considerable change since 1936, however. Figures were available only for the Centre-Nord region (Table 3.5) and may not be typical of Martinique as a whole, but the Centre-Nord region alone had far more holdings under three hectares than the entire island had in 1935–6.

Evidently, then, in French as well as in Commonwealth islands, the 1950s saw a big expansion in the overall number of holdings: but the expansion was almost wholly in the smallholder category, while the percentage of land in medium-sized holdings showed a substantial decline.

In the 1960s, the number of smallholdings continued to grow in all four islands. By 1965, the number of *banana growers* in St Lucia (12,479) and Dominica (10,602 in 1964) exceeded the total number of land holdings in 1961 (Persaud 1966, 12). In Dominica, the sale of Crown land in lots of about five acres, often to farmers who had been working it unofficially for some years, permitted the continued expansion of the smallholder class. In St Lucia the growth of smallholdings was mainly at the expense of medium-sized and large properties. Some owners of medium-sized holdings were pre-

Table 3.4
Estimates of holding distribution in Guadeloupe, 1952 and c.1960

	Holding-size groups (ha)			
	<10	*10–50*	*50–500*	*>500*
1952 (total, 7,666)	4,700	2,600	355	11
c.1960 (total, c.16,653)	16,000	600	40	13
Change (total, +8,987)	+11,300	-2,000	-315	nil
Percentage change (total, +117)	(+240)	(-77)	(-89)	(different definition)

Note: These are estimates for the whole *département*. The 1952 figures, in particular, may represent only a rather rough approximation (derived from Lasserre 1961,419,427).

pared to sell part of their land to raise capital for road-building, while some owners of large estates sold marginal land on their periphery hoping that this would assure them of a pool of local labour. However, this strategy sometimes proved counterproductive if the smallholders who bought the land could produce enough that they did not need to work for wages on the estates.

In the French islands, there was little unalienated land suitable for agriculture left by 1960, and to counter political unrest, land reform measures were introduced to bring about extensive changes in the holding-size structure of the islands. Limits were set on the maximum area that could be farmed directly by an individual or company owner (from 100 to 300 hectares, depending on the quality of the land, and whether it was owned by companies or individuals). Property in excess of the limits was to be sold, rented, or leased to sharecroppers. This reform was to be effected in stages over the succeeding five years.

While the pace of reform was not nearly as rapid as the planners had envisaged, by 1967, 2,028 additional smallholdings had been created in Guadeloupe and 616 in Martinique (Doeuff 1968, 44–5, 52–3). In the deteriorating economic climate of the later 1960s, however, momentum was lost, partly as a result of diminishing government financial assistance but chiefly because land redistribution had no real economic rationale. Peasants acquiring holdings had to pay such high prices for the redistributed land that for the next ten or fifteen years, while repaying their government loans, they could expect to be worse off as independent farmers than as wage labourers. The ideal of reform was to create holdings of three to

Table 3.5
Size distribution of holdings in Martinique, 1935–36 and the early 1970s

	Holding-size groups (ha)						
	0–	*3–*	*10–*	*40–*	*100–*	*200–*	*500–*
1935–36, number (total 6,536)	4,696	1,019	456	157	126	71	11
1935–36, area (total 80,354 ha)	5,876	5,924	8,993	10,669	17,381	21,099	10,412
Percentage of total area	7.3	7.4	11.2	13.3	21.6	26.3	12.9

	Holding-size groups (ha)					
	0–	*3–*	*5–*	*20–*	*50–*	*100–*
Early 1970s number (total, 6,825)	6,494	142	106	30	25	28
Early 1970s, area (total, 15,851 ha)	3,767	547	904	996	1,888	7,689
Percentage of total area	23.7	3.5	6.1	6.3	11.9	48.5

Sources: Doeuff (1968,4); Burac (1975,5).
Note: The data for the 1970s refer only to the Centre-Nord region, which has about 20 percent of Martinique's land-in-holdings.

five hectares that farmers and their families could operate without employing extra labour; but the crops that could be grown on holdings of this size were not likely to generate an acceptable residual income. So in fact, few of the landless were able to afford the luxury of becoming peasant proprietors.

POTENTIAL IMPACT OF LAND OCCUPANCY ON LAND USE

When placed in a continental or even a regional context, the population densities, tenure forms and holding-size distribution of these four islands fell within a fairly narrow range of variation. On a local scale, however, each island exhibited some distinctive characteristics; the question is, can these help to explain variations in the extent, distribution, and methods of banana cultivation?

Variations in rural population density might be expected, other things being equal, to result in corresponding variations in the availability of land and, consequently, land prices. But comparisons between all four islands are difficult, since many things, such as the availability of credit and crop prices, were not equal between Commonwealth and French islands. Nevertheless, the economic

Table 3.6
Land prices, 1966–67 (WI$ per acre)

	Martinique	*Guadeloupe*	*St Lucia*	*Dominica*
Uncleared government or Crown land	–	900	720	36–72
Cleared, with banana potential	2,880+	1,200–3,600	600–1,440	480–1,200
Land established in bananas	5,520+	2,400–7,200	2,400–6,000	1,200–2,400

Source: Personal communications, 1966–67.

structures of Dominica and St Lucia were comparable, so their land price differentials may be significant (Table 3.6).

Such variations are important because cheap land encourages extensive methods of cultivation, since it may cost less to invest in land than in fertiliser. Furthermore, cheap land that is available to almost anyone will have a marked impact on the labour market. Usually, only the landless will work regularly as wage labourers on estates. Thus, where land is cheap, labour is likely to be scarce and unreliable, and even estate owners with no shortage of capital may be obliged to adopt crops that require relatively little labour, even if returns per acre are low. If they do grow bananas, they may have to use unsophisticated techniques with low yields, rather than cultivating intensively and risking disaster because their work force is not prepared to operate according to a critical time schedule and standard.

Each form of land tenure tends to encourage or favour some crops or methods of cultivation at the expense of others. Thus, while freehold tenure is generally regarded as the ideal, since it provides complete freedom of choice over land use, it disposes the prudent freeholder to look to the long-term enhancement of the capital value of the holding, rather than to maximise short-term profits. There was a feeling in the Commonwealth islands that permanent tree crops, well-established, added more to the value of a holding than did a banana plantation. Thus, unless a holding was so small that its owner could not hope to make a living from tree crops, bananas might be established only on a temporary basis, between young citrus and/or coconuts, to tide the owner over the expensive establishment phase. Within a few years, the permanent crops would crowd out the bananas, and even if the tree crops brought low returns for several years, farmers were very reluctant to cut them out and substitute a more lucrative short-term crop.

On the other hand, where land was vested in the family or group, short-term crops were usually favoured, while permanent tree crops were avoided. While it was usually possible to agree on the allocation of plots for subsistence provision crops, the uncertainties and potential for conflict inherent in this form of tenure made the planting of citrus, cacao, or coconuts, with their high establishment costs, a dubious proposition. Coheirs would have as much legal right to harvest the crops as the planter, and constant surveillance throughout the harvest period would be impracticable. Bananas, on the other hand, occupied an intermediate position: since a stem is harvestable for only a brief period, vigilant planters had a reasonable chance of harvesting their own; and the high value of a single stem discouraged its casual removal by coheirs, unless they were prepared for trouble. However, how family land was used or, indeed, whether it was used at all depended on ancillary factors: whether there was pressure for land in the area, whether the holding was large enough for all the co-owners to farm their portions without impinging on neighbours, and, if not, whether the co-owners could purchase other holdings, whether there was some concord among the co-owners, and whether they would refrain from reaping what they had not sown. In Dominica, family land was frequently left uncultivated, since co-owners preferred to buy and operate their own holdings; but in St Lucia, although conflicts often arose, family land was generally cultivated, usually in bananas, because family land was all that most farmers had. In the French islands, whether or not land was held in undivided tenure does not seem to have been critical in terms of crop choice, presumably because tree crops were not very important, and relatively few peasant farmers were involved in the banana industry.

Sharecroppers normally had to devote a substantial portion of their land to a crop specified by their landlord. In Guadeloupe, where sharecropping was most widespread, the crop was always cane. While there were areas in which bananas would have flourished had not *colons* been obliged to plant cane, on the whole it would probably be fair to say that in Guadeloupe, land use in this case determined tenure form rather than vice-versa. Because the sugar companies were resolved to produce cane on their lands, they promoted a tenure form that facilitated cane production. In the French islands, from 1961 on, sharecropping was carefully regulated, giving tenants some security of tenure and ensuring that a proportion of tenants' holdings might be set aside for provision crops. In the Commonwealth islands, however, sharecropping was an ad hoc arrangement between landlord and tenant, and the landlord usually received one-third of the crop. Because sharecroppers' tenure was insecure, tree crops were not cultivated, and while bananas often were, it was not worth the sharecropper's while to cultivate too intensively, since increased fertiliser input, for instance, would produce diminishing marginal returns.

Cash rental also normally precluded tree crops because of long-term insecurity of tenure, and it was anyway normally the resort of farmers who could not afford heavy establishment costs. The choice of crops and intensity of cultivation were influenced by whether it was a lessors' or a lessees' market. In St Lucia, the strong demand for land during the peak years of the banana boom led to a lessors' market with relatively high rentals, and tenants grew purestand bananas as intensively as they could; while in Dominica, where many lessees were working the land to oblige friends and neighbours who had gone to England, a mixture of bananas and subsistence crops was more usual. In parts of the island where communications were poor, tenants practised shifting cultivation on large, virtually abandoned estates, securing a new plot from the owner every two or three years. Some bananas were grown, but provisions were the usual product of such tenancies.

Shared occupancy of the land inevitably involved mixed cropping, with coconuts or citrus belonging to the landlord and bananas or provisions to the tenant. Landlords operating this system found it in their interest to have tenants grow bananas between the tree crops, since the fertiliser applied to the bananas benefited the landlord's coconuts or citrus.

Squatting used to be associated with the shifting cultivation of provision crops, but by the 1960s, squatters in the Commonwealth islands were major participants in the banana industry. Remote forest holdings were usually cultivated by primitive, extensive techniques and were the first to be abandoned when prices declined. On the other hand, squatters who expected to purchase the land they occupied often farmed intensively and did not hesitate to plant permanent tree crops, even to an extent that would eventually exclude bananas.

The size distribution of land holdings seems to have had a bearing both on the percentage of the area in holdings that was cultivated and on the choice of crops. It is demonstrable in the Commonwealth islands that the larger the holding-size group, the smaller was the percentage of that group's area in cultivation (Table 3.7). The indications are that a similar pattern existed in the French islands, although there is no way of deriving detailed statistics from the available French data.

In Guadeloupe, 55 percent of the entire *territoire agricole* was cultivated; but of the area controlled by 24,000 medium-sized and

Table 3.7
Percentage of area-in-holdings in crops, Dominica and St Lucia, 1961, by size group

	Holding-size group (acres)									
	0–	*1–*	*5–*	*10–*	*25–*	*50–*	*100–*	*200–*	*500+*	*total*
Dominica (%)	97	82	57	48	42	38	37	35	29	44
St Lucia (%)	94	86	68	63	41	43	45	56	27	52

Source: WI Census of Agriculture, 1961 (1968).

small holders and *colons* (which together had an average holding size of 2.4 hectares), 64 percent was cultivated, while of the area controlled by 51 large estates (averaging 757 hectares), only 44 percent was cultivated (Lasserre 1961,1:429). In Martinique, the high percentage of land in large holdings and the relatively high percentage of uncultivated land in holdings point to a similar pattern. There are a number of possible explanations. Large landowners may have held idle land for speculation, or as fallow land, while the smallholders needed every available square metre to fulfil their families' needs. Large landowners may have been unable to obtain the labour necessary to exploit their holdings to the full, while smallholders could rely on family assistance. Smallholders, with unpaid family labour, may have found it worthwhile to cultivate marginal areas on which it would have been uneconomic to deploy a paid labour force. Large landowners may have deliberately kept a proportion of land out of production to create a shortage of jobs and keep the local labour force amenable. Whatever the cause, the effect was clear: whether or not bananas were in fact grown on a plot of land capable of growing bananas might be determined by the total size of the holding of which the plot formed a part.

Holding size did not simply affect whether or not a piece of land was cultivated; it also helped to determine what crops were grown. Some crops can be grown economically only on a large scale, particularly when elaborate processing with expensive equipment is necessary before they can be exported. Where this is so, the owners of large estates may collaborate to exclude small growers and reserve the production of such crops for their own land. Other crops involve laborious agricultural or marketing procedures for which paid labour would be uneconomic, so that such crops are often confined to smallholdings operated by family labour. Yet other crops bring in high returns on total investment but low returns per hectare, and these are consequently restricted to farmers with plenty of land to spare.

Table 3.8
Distributions of major crops in Dominica and St Lucia, 1961, by holding-size group

	Holding-size group (acres)									
	0–	*1–*	*5–*	*10–*	*25–*	*50–*	*100–*	*200–*	*500+*	*total*
DOMINICA (PERCENTAGES)										
Land controlled	1.1	12	11	10	5.6	6.6	6.4	14.9	32.3	100
Land in crops	2.5	22.5	14	11	5	6	5	12	21	100
Banana stools	4.7	23.6	23	10.8	4.5	4.7	(	28.7	)	100
Coconut trees	1	16	8	14	6	4	3	14	33	100
Provisions	7	69	11	5.5	2	2.5	1.5	1	0.5	100
Grapefruit trees	0.1	4	4	9	7	6	22	24	24	100
Lime trees	0.8	14	6	11	3	6	6	20	30	100
ST LUCIA (PERCENTAGES)										
Land controlled	2	16	10	9	7	5	5	12	34	100
Land in crops	3	27.5	14	11	5.5	4	5	13	16	100
Banana stools	2.9	29.5	16.9	14.6	5.9	3.1	(	30	)	100
Coconut trees	1.3	14	9.4	10.4	5.6	4.9	9.1	18	26	100
Provisions	13	43	27	9	2	1	3	1	1	100

Source: WI Census of Agriculture, 1961 (1968).

For each size group, Table 3.8 shows the relationships in the Commonwealth islands between the percentage of land area controlled, the percentage of land area cultivated, and the percentage of various major crops grown. It emerges from this table that provisions were overwhelmingly a smallholder crop in both islands, while grapefruit were entirely an estate crop in Dominica. Bananas were grown by all groups, but were disproportionately numerous on holdings of less than ten acres, while coconuts were also a universal crop, but disproportionately numerous on the largest holdings. Limes followed a very similar pattern in Dominica, but limes and grapefruit were of negligible commercial importance in St Lucia.

It is not possible to produce detailed statistics for the French islands, but such information as is available bears out the idea that there also, certain size groups concentrated much more strongly on certain crops than did other groups. Provisions would seem to have been the province of the small farmer, as in the Commonwealth islands; but banana cultivation showed quite a different pattern, being largely the preserve of the medium-sized and medium-large farmer.

While evidence of interrelationship is strong, there is some question whether it is holding-size structure that influences crop choice or crop possibilities that influence holding-size structure. In St Lucia, for instance, the postwar rise of the banana industry was accompanied by a great expansion in the number of holdings in the one- to ten-acre range. It might be argued that the profitability of smallholder banana growing led to the proliferation of smallholdings, rather than that the large number of smallholdings permitted the spread of banana growing. Similarly, the decline of medium-sized holdings noted on several islands might be attributed to the decline of cacao, a crop well-suited to holdings of 10 to 50 acres so long as it fetched satisfactory prices.

Undoubtedly, in the sugar islands in the eighteenth and nineteenth centuries, it was the requirements of sugar manufacturing that controlled the size of holdings: advances in technology made consolidation necessary. In the twentieth century, however, while there is still evidence of some flexibility, a large mass of smallholders strongly attached to their land has introduced an element of stability, or possibly inertia, into the system. In any case, it is doubtful whether a single crop has remained overwhelmingly dominant in this century for long enough to impose its optimum holding-size requirements, as sugar did in the first two centuries of colonisation. Finally, it is worth noting that while the immense company-owned estates of Guadeloupe permitted the economic operation of many of Guadeloupe's sugar factories to continue beyond the 1960s, in Martinique, failure to consolidate led to the progressive abandonment of cane in many areas. However, banana and pineapple cultivation were profitable alternatives for the Martinique estate owners, crops which the Guadeloupe sugar companies did not, on the whole, find worthwhile, even under ideal physical conditions.

BANANA GROWERS: TYPICAL EASTERN CARIBBEAN FARMERS?

If it is difficult to determine the exact nature of the associations between forms of land occupancy and types of land use by looking at either in a general way, an alternative strategy is to focus on the farmers involved in the export banana industry and compare them with the islands' farmers as a whole. Were the size of banana growers' holdings or the manner in which they held them in any way atypical? If so, was there anything anomalous about the farmers themselves, such as their age, farming experience, or educational or ethnic background? These personal characteristics might provide a clue to whether participation in the banana industry was strongly influenced by the preexisting agrarian structures or whether it was the industry that had induced changes in these structures, either by attracting farmers who possessed certain attributes or by squeezing out those who lacked them.

HOLDING-SIZE PROFILE OF BANANA GROWERS

In the mid-1960s, all four islands had banana growers in each category of holding size, from less than one hectare to over 200 hectares. However, the percentage in each category varied from island to island: the differences between French and Commonwealth islands were particularly marked.

Tables 3.9, 3.10 and 3.11 demonstrate once again the difficulty of reducing data from the four islands to common denominators. Apart from the fact that Commonwealth data are usually in acres and French data in hectares, size-class boundaries are often at such irregular intervals that it is difficult to extrapolate or interpolate consistently. A further problem is that whereas Commonwealth data are classified according to holding-size, French data on banana holdings are classified according to the area in bananas rather than the overall area of the farm on which they are grown. Menauge suggests that the average Guadeloupean banana grower had 45 percent of

Table 3.9
Distribution of export banana growers in St Lucia and Dominica, by holding-size group

		Holding-size group (acres)						
	Total	*0–*	*1–*	*5–*	*10–*	*25–*	*50–*	*100+*
ST LUCIA (1961)								
Holdings (no.)	12,686	4,284	6,130	1,365	571	183	63	90
Holdings with bananas (no.)	9,458	2,393	5,015	1,205	532	177	56	82
Holdings with bananas (%)	75	56	82	88	93	97	89	91
DOMINICA (1961)								
Holdings (no.)	8,667	2,115	4,290	1,410	546	131	78	97
Holdings with bananas (no.)	7,292	1,704	3,571	1,285	455	118	67	92
Holdings with bananas (%)	84	81	83	91	83	90	86	95

Source: West Indies Census of Agriculture, 1961 (1968, 87,102,181,196).

Table 3.10
Distribution of export banana growers in Martinique (Centre-Nord), by holding-size group

		Holding-size group (ha)				
	Total	*0–*	*5–*	*20–*	*50–*	*100+*
Holdings, 1971 (no.)	6,825	6,636	106	30	25	28
Banana holdings, 1972 (no.)	146	101	19	14	12	-
Estimated holdings with bananas (no.)[a]	146	81	25	14	12	12
Holdings with bananas (%)	2	1	24	47	48	43

Source: Burac (1975, 5,115).
Note: Banana holdings are classified according to banana acreage rather than holding acreage. The Centre-Nord has about 10 percent of Martinique's banana growers and 18 percent of its banana acreage.
[a]"Estimated holdings with bananas" is a rough approximation, based on the assumption that bananas occupy about 45 percent of the total holding (Menauge 1974,53).

his or her land in bananas (1974, 53), but he does not indicate whether this pattern was consistent throughout all size groups. In the Commonwealth islands, the pattern was by no means consistent (see Table 3.8). In 1961, the average St Lucian farmer had 27 percent of his holding in bananas, the average Dominican farmer, 13 percent; but the percentage of a holding devoted to bananas varied inversely with its size, so that in St Lucia, 61 percent of the area of holdings less than 0.4 hectares carried bananas, declining steadily to 11 percent for holdings over 40 hectares. For Dominica, the range was from 48 percent of the smallest holdings to a mere 6 percent of the largest (Persaud 1966, 9; *WI Census of Agriculture* 1968, 181).

While these points should be borne in mind, it is nevertheless clear that while in St Lucia and Dominica bananas were grown on most holdings in all size groups, even those of less than an acre, in the French islands bananas were predominantly a crop of the medium-to-large landowner and were generally absent from holdings of less than five hectares (12.5 acres) (Table 3.12). So far as it was possible to judge, this dichotomy became, if anything, even more pronounced between the early and mid-1960s. In the Commonwealth islands, there were substantially more banana growers in 1966 than there had been in 1961; the number of holdings had risen, and participation in the banana industry was almost universal, except where limited by inadequate rainfall or extreme inaccessibility. None of the Dominican farmers interviewed in 1966 had given up banana cultivation. Low prices had induced one or two to stop

Table 3.11
Distribution of export banana growers in Guadeloupe, by holding-size group

		Holding-size group (ha)				
	Total	*0–*	*6–*	*10–*	*20–*	*50+*
Holdings, 1960 (no.)	16,653	(16,000	)	(600	)	53
Banana holdings, 1970	2,298	2,090	(142	)	(66	)
Estimated holdings with bananas[a]	2,298	(2,090	)	(142	)	66
Holdings with bananas (%)	14	(13	)	(24	)	?100

Source: Lasserre (1961); Menauge (1974, 54).
Note: Parentheses indicate range of hectare class size.
[a]See note *a*, Table 3.10. Banana holdings are classified according to banana acreage.

harvesting fruit from their more remote parcels, but others planned to start growing export bananas as soon as the roads then under construction gave them access to the port of Roseau.

In Guadeloupe, however, while Lasserre had counted a total of approximately 4,100 growers in 1960, Menauge recorded only 2,298 in 1970, and he suggested that numbers had declined by 30 percent between 1960 and 1966 and a further 19 percent between 1966 and 1970. Growers with the smallest holdings had suffered the greatest decline: almost a third of growers with less than a hectare of bananas gave up the crop between 1966 and 1970 (Lasserre 1961, 2:659,684,742; Menauge 1974, 53,61). The pattern was similar in Martinique, with an estimated 3,077 growers in 1963 declining to 1497 in 1972, although the number of farmers with over 20 hectares of bananas increased slightly from 101 to 120 over the same period (*La Banane* 1967, 1:14; Burac 1975, 115). By the mid-1960s, most farmers in the French islands with less than five hectares available for banana cultivation considered this crop too risky, so that peasant participation in the industry, a significant factor in the 1950s, was dwindling, and bananas were becoming increasingly the preserve of the medium-sized and large grower.

The clear contrast between the scale of operations of typical banana growers in French and Commonwealth islands is also revealed by comparing the banana acreages of holdings producing bananas for export. In 1961, 40 percent of St Lucia's export banana acreage and over 60 percent of Dominica's were on holdings with less than one hectare of bananas. But in Martinique, the 1959 figure was only 17 percent, declining to a mere 7 percent in 1963, while in Guadeloupe in 1964, only 10.5 percent of the island's export banana acreage was on holdings with less than 2 hectares in bananas (*La Banane*

Table 3.12

Distribution of banana growers, by holding-size group, 1966–67 Survey

	Interviewees with bananas (%)	*Total number of interviewees*	*Holding-size group (ha)*					
			0–	*1–*	*5–*	*10–*	*50–*	*100+*
St Lucia	100	45	3	16	7	8	3	8
Dominica	97	68(70)	5	34	19	8(9)	1	1(2)
Martinique	34	7/8(22)	-	1?(4)	0(1)	5(10)	0(1)	2(6)
Guadeloupe	65	11(17)	0(1)	3[a](6)	4[a]	3(4)	0(1)	1

Note: Numbers in parentheses indicate total number of holdings surveyed in size-group.

[a]Not necessarily growers of export bananas; may grow bananas for provisions.

1967, 1:14,16). While total areas in bananas for export remained relatively stable in the French islands throughout the 1960s, so that the decline in the acreage share of growers with less than a hectare in bananas indicated a significant shift toward larger-scale units of cultivation, there was no evidence of a similar shift in the Commonwealth islands at this period. Regardless of the size of their operations, St Lucian farmers interviewed in 1966 all said that they were maintaining or expanding their banana acreages. Farmers in Dominica, where discouragingly low prices in the winter of 1965–66 had not been mitigated by price support, spoke of retrenchment, but such talk was not restricted to any particular size group.

FORMS OF TENURE ASSOCIATED WITH BANANA CULTIVATION

Banana growers in the French islands generally had freehold ownership of the land they cultivated, although there were individuals who rented additional land from other family members. Sharecropping was not practised by banana growers; farmers who were obliged to have recourse to sharecropping probably lacked the resources to risk entering the banana industry.

In the Commonwealth islands, the majority of banana growers interviewed in 1966 owned the land they cultivated, but various other forms of tenure were encountered. Several respondents grew bananas on family land. In theory, this practice was risky, since growers had no legal recourse if their crop was harvested and sold by other family members. St Lucian farmers cultivating family land frequently complained of difficulties with co-owners but continued using such land, *faute de mieux*. In Dominica, while farmers who had other options usually avoided planting bananas on land in co-ownership, farmers who had only family land did not hesitate to grow bananas on it and did not appear to find this practice a source of conflict, probably because the much lower pressure on land resources in most districts of Dominica would have made conflict harder to justify.

In St Lucia, four growers rented some or all of their land, but no sharecroppers were encountered. Although sharecropping, or *métayage*, had been commonplace in the sugar areas only a few years earlier, it was not regarded as a satisfactory form of tenure by banana growers. In Dominica, the large areas of unalienated Crown land complicated the situation. Five growers were squatting on Crown land, although four of these had applied to purchase their holdings and were waiting for them to be surveyed. Undoubtedly, many farmers in Dominica were, in effect, practising shifting cultivation on Crown land, and others were doing likewise on estate land considered too marginal for direct cultivation by its owners. Several growers practised sharecropping in some form. Some grew only bananas, giving about a third of the crop to the landowner in lieu of rent. Some had more complicated agreements: for instance, landowners permitted other people to grow bananas and provisions on the land rent-free; in return, tenants were expected to tend interplanted tree crops, and in some cases to plant and establish the young trees. Some farmers interviewed were cultivating, rent-free, land belonging to friends or relatives who were overseas.

STATIC AND DYNAMIC TENDENCIES IN AGRARIAN STRUCTURES

In the 1960s, it was evident that some forms of tenure and sizes of holdings were more propitious for banana cultivation than others. My interviews in 1966–67 revealed that while perhaps half the growers of export bananas had acquired their land and vocation involuntarily, through inheritance, the remainder had taken some initiative to acquire a holding and had actually chosen to become full- or part-time farmers. I obtained information from some farmers about their approximate ages and other personal characteristics, and the length of time they had farmed their holdings, and tried to determine whether these factors shed any light on the relationship between the development of the banana industry and the evolution of agrarian structures, and certain patterns could be discerned. Tables 3.13 and 3.14 show the approximate ages of farmers interviewed and the length of time since they had acquired their holdings.

The average age of farmers in all four islands at this period was in the mid-fifties and was believed to be increasing by about a year annually. The farmers interviewed were thus probably a fairly representative sample. A few were young, a few were in their seventies or eighties, but most appeared to be between 40 and 70. The younger ones were not, in most cases, owners of freehold holdings. One or two rented or sharecropped land, while others worked on family land or on holdings belonging to parents or grandparents. Evidently, land was generally acquired, either by inheritance or purchase, by the middle-aged. Even bearing this in mind, however, it is clear that in Dominica and, especially, St Lucia, there had been a strong upsurge in the acquisition of property between six and ten years before the time of the survey. This upsurge coincided with a period of rapid expansion in the banana industry in both islands, spec-

Table 3.13
Age distribution of farmers surveyed, 1966–67

	Young (under 35)	*Middle-aged (35–60)*	*Elderly (60+)*	*Total sample*
	Number (%)	*Number (%)*	*Number (%)*	*Number*
Martinique	2(10)	12(57)	7(33)	21
Guadeloupe	1(7)	10(67)	4(27)	15
St Lucia	7(16)	28(64)	9(20)	44
Dominica	13(20)	45(68)	8(12)	66

tacularly rapid in St Lucia. Since there was no dramatic change in the pattern of land availability in the Commonwealth islands in the 1950s and 1960s, nor were there any special government incentives to buy land, it seems likely that it was anxiety to participate in what they perceived as a profitable industry with a bright future that drove many middle-aged people to acquire land holdings at that period.

This conclusion is reinforced by Tables 3.15 and 3.16 which reveal the personal characteristics of farmers in the mid-1960s. While in each island, there was a nucleus of farmers who had farmed all their lives and had never had any other occupation (except, on the French islands, compulsory military service), there were also substantial numbers on every size of holding who had formerly pursued other careers and, in many cases, pursued them still, part-time. In all the islands there were businessmen, doctors, and lawyers, often with no background in agriculture, who had purchased large estates. There were returned emigrants, especially in St Lucia and Dominica, who had bought medium or small holdings with savings accumulated abroad; and there were former policemen, clerks, teachers, and carpenters, tailors, and other artisans who had managed to save enough capital to buy small plots of land.

It should also be noted that the fact, or expectation, of inheriting land did not necessarily predispose the heir to a lifelong career in agriculture. While in St Lucia, two-thirds and in Martinique, four-fifths of those who had inherited land had been full-time farmers all their lives, in Guadeloupe the small sample was evenly divided, and in Dominica, more than half of those with inherited land had pursued or were pursuing other means of gaining a livelihood.

It was difficult to relate an early or lifelong commitment to agriculture to agricultural training. In the French islands, no respondents admitted to having received formal instruction in agriculture

Table 3.14
Duration of tenure of land holdings

	Length of tenure, in years (date of acquisition)								
	0–5 (1961–6)	*6–10 (1956–60)*	*11–15 (1951–5)*	*16–20 (1946–50)*	*21–25 (1941–6)*	*26–30 (1936–40)*	*30+ (1936–)*	*Total responding*	*Average (in years)*
	Number (%)	*Number (%)*	*Number (%)*	*Number (%)*	*Number (%)*	*Number (%)*	*Number (%)*	*Number*	*Number*
Martinique	0	3(25)	1(8)	3(25)	2(17)	1(8)	2(17)	12/24	22
Guadeloupe	3(43)	0	1(14)	1(14)	0	1(14)	1(14)	7/22	15
St Lucia	1(4)	10(38)	6(23)	2(8)	1(4)	3(12)	3(12)	26/48	18
Dominica	5(12)	11(26)	9(21)	8(19)	6(14)	1(2)	2(5)	42/70	15

Table 3.15
Working history of farmers surveyed on the four islands, 1966–67

	Martinique	*Guadeloupe*	*St Lucia*	*Dominica*
Lifelong farmers	11(6)	6(2)	21	31
Farmers with experience in other jobs	8(1)	5(3)	14	34
History unknown	4(1)	6(4)	13	5

Notes: For Martinique and Guadeloupe, the figures in parentheses represent banana growers. In St Lucia and Dominica, all respondents were banana growers.

at school or college, and only about 14 percent in the Commonwealth islands said they had formal training. Most respondents claimed to have learned about farming from parents and friends, neighbouring estates where they had once worked, or by "trial and error."

Although many women owned land in their own right, most respondents in the 1966–67 survey were male. Where men were present in a household, they automatically assumed that their cooperation was being sought. Consequently, the only women respondents were widows, spinsters living alone, and women whose spouses were overseas. There was little evidence of gender bias toward or away from banana cultivation: one Dominican respondent said that she was awaiting her son's return from England to enter the export banana industry, but this was evidently because her holding had hitherto been too remote from the motorable road for the feasible extraction of export bananas, and her son's return was expected to coincide with the arrival of the road in that district.

While the ethnic background of those who actually cultivated the bananas in each of the islands was very similar, the backgrounds of the owners of the banana lands were somewhat more varied. In both Martinique and Guadeloupe, a high proportion of the larger holdings were owned by local white Creoles (known as *békés*, particularly in Martinique). The metropolitan sugar companies that still owned large tracts of land in Guadeloupe had little interest in growing bananas, although they had grown them extensively in the 1950s, when it had been thought that cane might benefit from being grown in rotation with bananas. Many white Creole growers were also engaged in exporting bananas, their own and, in some cases, other people's as well. Some Martiniquan banana growers also owned ripening facilities in metropolitan France, although this was said not to be true of Guadeloupeans.

Table 3.16
Full-time and part-time farmers on the four islands, 1966–67

	Martinique	*Guadeloupe*	*St Lucia*	*Dominica*
Full-time farmers	17	19	42	52
Part-time farmers	5	2	5	17

In the Commonwealth islands, ownership of banana lands was not concentrated in the hands of any particular ethnic group. In Dominica, the white Creole landowning class had long since practically ceased to exist. Two large estates were owned by the Commonwealth Development Corporation, there were one or two British expatriate landowners, and Geest, the shipper and importer of all Windward bananas, owned two large estates in the north of the island. While these were all major producers, they did not dominate the industry. In St Lucia, several larger estates were still in the hands of local white Creole families, one or two very large estates were owned by expatriate British whites, and Geest had holdings of about 1,200 hectares in the former sugar valleys of Cul-de-Sac and Roseau. Nevertheless, these growers did not occupy a dominant position in the St Lucia Banana Growers' Association (SLBGA), since it had been constituted before most of them had become involved in the industry.

Since in the Commonwealth islands, all export bananas had to be sold to the island growers' associations, which alone had the right to sell them to the shipper-importer, there was no opportunity for any ethnic group to control the industry by engineering some form of vertical integration. Thus, even Geest had to sell the bananas from his estate to the SLBGA and buy them back to ship to the United Kingdom.

While the actual cultivation of bananas was carried out by people with very similar ethnic and socioeconomic characteristics in all four islands, there were, then, certain interisland differences in the control or ownership of the land on which the bananas were grown. Peasant smallholders participated on a very limited scale in the French islands, while owners of medium and large estates controlled the industry. In Martinique as a whole, and in the banana-growing districts of Guadeloupe, these estate owners were very often white Creoles.

CONCLUSION

It cannot be denied that there were interisland variations in the character of land occupancy and that some of these may have had some influence on the way in which export banana production was carried on. The variations that have been discussed, however, were not generally closely aligned with the striking variations in the character and location of banana cultivation that will be described in the following chapter. While the holding-size structure of farms exporting bananas was quite different in French and Commonwealth islands, the overall patterns of holding-size distribution were fairly similar for all four islands. The range of tenure forms was also similar, but while export banana growers in Dominica and St Lucia ran the gamut from freeholders to squatters, most banana growers in Martinique and Guadeloupe were freehold landowners.

All four islands saw changes in agrarian structures in the 1950s and 1960s; while high birthrates and laws of inheritance that give all acknowledged offspring a share of their parents' land may permit smallholdings to proliferate, the number of small farms is actually likely to increase only if there is a marketable crop that makes farming such properties economically attractive. It seems likely that in the Commonwealth islands, the existence of a banana industry in which both large- and small-scale growers could participate encouraged the adoption of agriculture by many people who might otherwise not have bothered to cultivate or take much interest in land they had happened to inherit.

The export banana industry was dominated by a particular ethnic group in the French but not the Commonwealth islands; while this may have influenced the development of different types of institutional structures in the two sets of islands, there is no evidence that it had any inherent responsibility for interisland land use differences: within individual islands, banana growers of European and African descent followed the farming practices of their fellow islanders, rather than any ethnic stereotype.

4 The Environmental Context of Banana Production in the Eastern Caribbean

Evidently, the strikingly different relationships between export banana cultivation and the island environments in neighbouring French and Commonwealth territories in the Eastern Caribbean in the 1960s cannot be adequately explained either by the economic associations of the territories or by their agrarian structures. While these topics could be considered on an island-wide basis, the third potential source of interisland variation, the physical environment, cannot be treated on such a broad canvas. The environment must be investigated not only island by island, but in some cases, district by district, before its influence on the character and distribution of banana cultivation can be assessed.

This chapter sets out the basic physical geography of the islands, their landforms, climate, and soils, and then proceeds to describe the distribution of banana cultivation in the 1960s, drawing attention to the often quite dramatic interisland differences in the relationship between the crop and the physical environment. Having demonstrated the lack of congruence between patterns of banana cultivation and the primary features of physical geography, the chapter then turns to secondary features of the environment that are often influenced by the natural landscape but not absolutely determined by it: infrastructure, preexisting land use patterns, and labour resources. While such factors are more subject to human manipulation than, say, relief or climate, they may nevertheless stimulate dynamic change, or conversely, lead to stagnation and inertia.

PRIMARY PHYSICAL FACTORS

If the suitability of physical conditions had been a prime consideration in decisions about agricultural land use, it is doubtful whether Eastern Caribbean farmers in the 1960s would have grown any major export crops, since all could have been produced under better physical conditions elsewhere. In fact, however, it is very often limiting factors rather than favourable conditions that are relevant in land use choices: whether land is too precipitous to be cultivated at all rather than whether it is flat enough to be worked easily and whether rainfall in the driest months of an average year is inadequate for a crop to survive, rather than whether rainfall in the driest months of a dry year is abundant enough for the crop to flourish.

While the four islands are composed of roughly similar landscape elements, they vary somewhat in ruggedness and mean altitude. Each is aligned along the Lesser Antillean volcanic arc (Figure 1.1) and consists of an assemblage of Tertiary and Quaternary volcanic centres, some long extinct and reduced by denudation to low hills, others active within the past 50,000 years and, in the case of Montagne Pelée in Martinique and La Soufrière in Guadeloupe, as recently as this century. Each island is composed of a mixture of flow lava, domes, and pyroclastics, the last being by far the predominant element, although solid lavas often form conspicuous features in the landscape. While there are domes of acid composition and some basic flow lava, most of the material ejected from Central Lesser Antillean volcanoes is andesitic. Since each of the four islands is situated toward the western side of the Lesser Antillean submarine ridge, they all tend to be asymmetrical, with steep leeward (western) slopes and gentler, more extensive windward slopes (Welch 1966, 331–2). St Lucia's highest peak is just under 1,000 metres; the other three islands have volcanoes rising to just under 1,500 metres. Thus, in composition, general configuration, and height, the four islands are fairly similar.

In detail, however, there are differences that must be taken into account when assessing land use potential, since they might have a bearing on accessibility, possibilities for mechanisation, scale of operations, and temperature and insolation. Figure 4.1 shows height range within 4-square-kilometre squares for each of the islands, and Table 4.1 gives the percentages of their land surface areas that fall within each relief-range class. Dominica is considerably more rugged than the other three, with far less gently sloping land at low

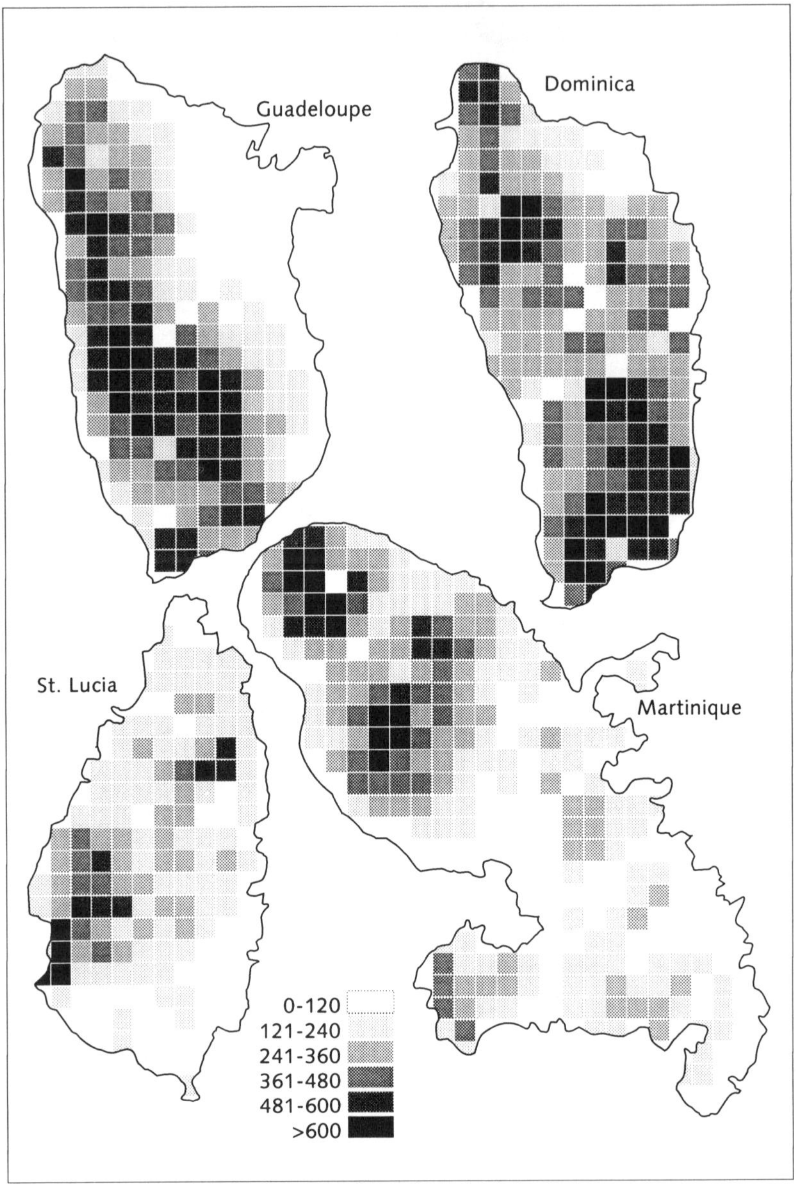

Figure 4.1
Relief amplitude: Height range in metres within 2 × 2 km squares

Table 4.1
Island areas in each relief range class (Fig. 4.1)

Relief range within 4-km² squares (in m)	*Guadeloupe*	*Dominica*	*Martinique*	*St Lucia*
		(percentages)		
0–120	27.5	5.6	26.8	24.5
121–240	18.4	10.1	32.1	44.4
241–360	17.9	34.1	25.0	19.2
361–480	14.3	23.4	8.2	4.6
481–600	15.9	17.9	2.9	3.9
601–720	5.8	7.8	2.6	3.3
721–840	0	0.6	1.8	0
>841	0	0.6	0.4	0
Total	100	100	100	100

altitudes. Dominica and St Lucia lack *planèze* slopes (little-dissected aprons of volcanic ash) such as exist on the eastern flanks of Montagne Pelée in Martinique and the Soufrière volcano in Guadeloupe. Southern Martinique and northern St Lucia, but not Dominica or Basse-Terre Guadeloupe, have areas of low, rugged, heavily eroded hilly country of pre-Pliocene age. St Lucia has considerable areas of level land, but it is largely restricted to the floors of three major valleys, penetrating deep into the interior but effectively isolated from each other by rugged mountainous interfluves.

While such physical differences might have been highly significant for sugar cane, whose economic viability depends on central processing facilities that are accessible to an extensive surrounding area, they were not critical for banana production. Some of the islands have a higher proportion than others of gently sloping land with easy access to exporting ports, but all have well above the minimum area of accessible land on which bananas could be grown necessary to justify the establishment of regular shipping facilities. By comparison, Montserrat, an island north of Guadeloupe and composed of very similar landscape elements, simply did not have a large enough area with banana-growing potential to justify scheduling calls by a banana boat (Table 4.2).

In the four islands, bananas were in fact being grown successfully on a variety of relief types: flat valley floors, steep valley sides, and the *planèze* slopes of recent volcanoes. While the islands did differ in physical detail, then, their differences did not critically restrict their banana-growing potential.

Table 4.2
Areas and dimensions of the four islands and Montserrat

	Area (square km)	*Maximum length (km)*	*Maximum width (km)*
St Lucia	616	40	22
Martinique	1,100	61	26
Dominica	767	43	23
Guadeloupe (Basse-Terre)	848	43	24
Montserrat	85	16	9

A similar assessment can be made of the climatic differences. The climates of the Central Lesser Antilles are determined by regional controls - the elevation of the sun and the pressure and circulation patterns over a large area of the Caribbean, North Atlantic, and neighbouring parts of North America - and local factors - insularity, altitude, and relief.

Regional controls tend to produce similar conditions throughout the four islands, even though northern Guadeloupe is 320 kilometres from southern St Lucia. The configuration of the Caribbean Basin and the confluence near the Central Lesser Antilles of the warm waters of the North and South Equatorial Currents have combined to cause a northward extension of warm, humid equatorial characteristics (Lasserre 1961, 1:181). Cloud cover, whose variability is largely dependent on local factors, is of far greater significance than latitude in its effects upon insolation. The mean annual temperature in all four islands is close to 26°C at sea level, and there is a range of only 2°C between the monthly means of the warmest and coolest months. Normal diurnal ranges are 8–10°C. At least at sea level, therefore, temperatures are never low enough to inhibit the cultivation of any crop requiring tropical or equatorial temperatures.

The four islands, which lie between the high pressure cells of the North Atlantic and the low pressures of the Intertropical Convergence Zone, are wholly within the zone of the Easterly Trades and very rarely experience winds from any other quarter. It is variations within the easterlies that account for the different types of weather that affect these islands from day to day and from season to season: the passage of disturbances which may result in ascending air currents and rainfall. The potential frequency of such rainfall depends not on the latitude of individual islands, but on the relative strengths and positions of the pressure systems that affect the area as a whole. Between January and March, northeasterly winds prevail, and the humid, unstable air of the Trades may be overlain at a relatively low level by a less humid inversion layer, inhibiting the development of strong ascending air currents that might lead to precipitation. At times, however, easterlies originating farther east intrude into the region bringing a thicker layer of moist, unstable air with a much greater potential for heavy rainfall should disturbances trigger it off.

In late April or early May, there is a major change in the configuration of North Atlantic and North American pressure systems, so that throughout the northern summer, the humid layer of the Easterly Trades attains greater thickness in the Caribbean area. Conditions are ideal for the development of troughs of low pressure bringing heavy rain and squally conditions. Since it is not until December that winter pressure and circulation systems are reestablished in the North Atlantic, the rainy season persists in the Central Lesser Antilles for several months after the southern retreat of the overhead sun (Lasserre 1961, 1:189,195).

In the Central Lesser Antilles, then, there is a single drier season between December and May and a wet season from May to December, with about two-thirds of the annual rainfall falling in the wetter half of the year. Depending on the time and intensity of changes in regional pressure and circulation, the length and intensity of the dry season may vary considerably from year to year, and it may be more or less continuous or intermittent. In a single season the rainfall at two similarly located stations may vary substantially according to the paths of rain-producing disturbances within the Easterly Trades, but in any particular year, conditions will tend to be either drier or wetter than average throughout most of the region. Thus, in some years, especially in low rainfall zones, there may be two or three months of more or less continuous drought, while in other years the "dry" season may be almost as wet as the rainy season.

While conditions over a broad region determine the potential of airmasses for instability and the release of precipitation, the amount of rain that actually falls is largely determined by local conditions, particularly relief. Annual rainfall totals vary from as little as a metre in some low-lying coastal areas to over ten metres on the summits of the highest mountains. As rainfall increases, relative variability decreases; at low rainfall stations, the driest years may record only a third as much rain as the wettest, while in moderately well-watered areas, the driest years record half as much rainfall as the wettest (Lasserre 1961, 1:174).

Local peculiarities of relief may affect rainfall in various ways: for instance, owing to a foehn effect, rainfall at a given altitude is generally lower on leeward (west coast) than on windward (east coast) slopes. This effect is less pronounced in Martinique and St Lucia than in Guadeloupe and Dominica, presumably because the first two islands have a greater proportion of lowland and a different disposition of low east-west cols. Despite some interisland variation in the precise relationship between rainfall and relief, however, rainfall maps of the four islands (Figure 4.2) show that the pattern is broadly similar in all four. Dominica has very little low-lying land and the proportion of its area that receives less than 2 metres of rain a year is smaller than the other three islands. The fact is, however, that all four have sufficient land with relief that does not entirely inhibit agriculture and rainfall that is at least adequate for a wide range of tropical and equatorial crops, so that relief and rainfall cannot be the key factors in interisland land use variations.

Windstorms, which may occur at any season, and hurricanes, which are generally restricted to the rainy season between July and October, are of great concern to farmers considering the cultivation of vulnerable tree crops. Several hurricanes or tropical storms pass through the Eastern Caribbean every year, but their paths vary. In the Central Lesser Antilles, hurricanes may devastate one island three or four times in a decade or even twice in a single season, while another island may remain relatively unscathed for thirty years or more. Over the one and a half to three centuries for which records exist, there is no conclusive evidence that any one of the four islands has been more prone to hurricanes than the other three.

At the time of my 1966–67 survey, Dominica had not been seriously afflicted since 1930, but Guadeloupe had borne the full brunt of Betsy (1956), Cleo and Helena (1963), and Inez (1966). Several Guadeloupeans suggested that the frequency of hurricanes in their island explained the dearth of permanent tree crops there compared with Dominica, where they were abundant. However, when I asked about the impact of hurricanes David and Frederick, which hit Dominica with extreme ferocity in 1979, I was told that they had been followed by an increase in the planting of permanent tree crops, especially citrus, since it had been observed that while all bananas had been lost throughout the island, citrus losses had been only partial, except close to the path of the eye of Hurricane David.

Thus, while hurricanes and windstorms undoubtedly have a major economic impact, their effect on land use is conditioned by the economic context as a whole, and they do not appear to have been

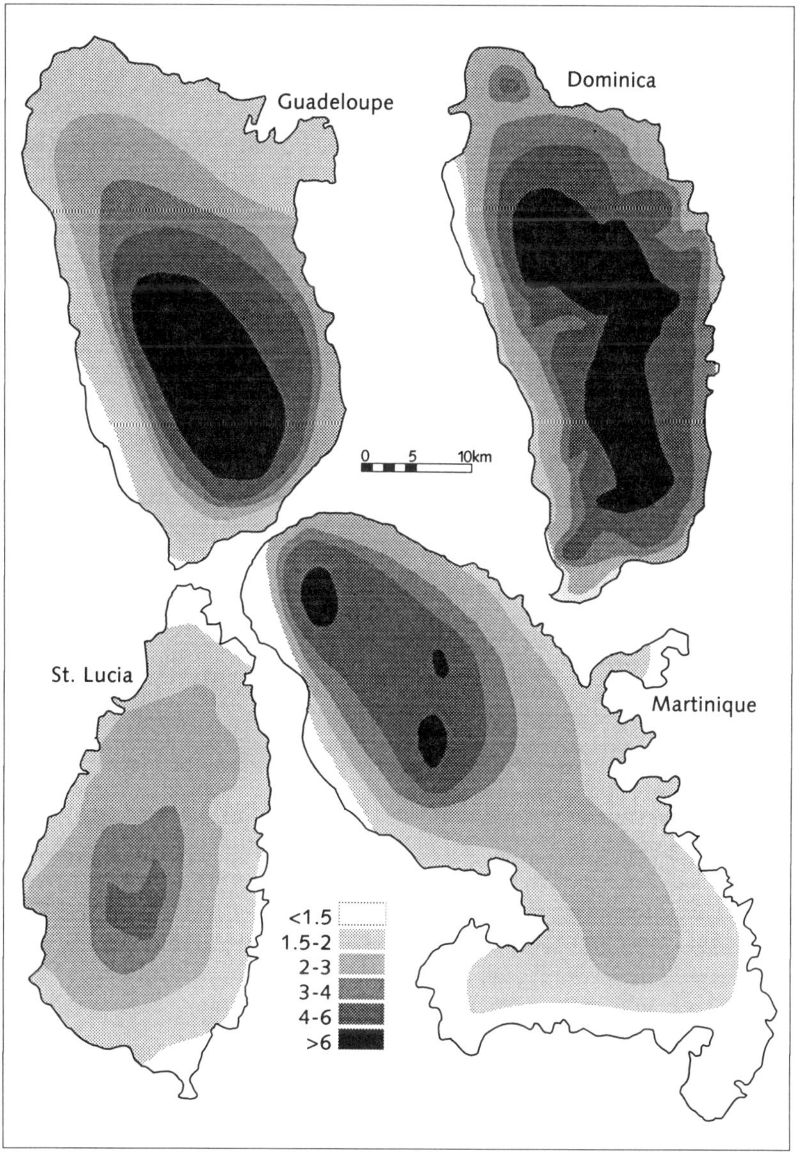

Figure 4.2
Guadeloupe, Dominica, Martinique and St Lucia: Mean annual rainfall in metres
Sources: Lasserre (1961); Lang (1967); Marieu (1966); Stark et al. (1966).

an absolute limiting factor for any form of land use. There were complaints in some islands that certain windward (east coast) valleys were particularly subject to wind damage, but nowhere had this deterred farmers from planting bananas, the most vulnerable of crops. At most, it had been a contributing factor in the discouragement of intensive cultivation.

The soil types of the four islands are a third element of possible significance for land use. Figures 4.3 to 4.6 show the island-by-island distribution of the various classes of soils in the Central Lesser Antilles, according to a synthetic classification that permits interisland comparison on the same basis (Welch 1987, 1–11). Since parent materials and climate are major factors in soil formation and these cover a similar range in all four islands, it is not surprising that most soil classes found in one island also occur in the other three.

The relative proportions of each class vary somewhat (Table 4.3) owing to the different disposition of relief elements of different ages, and it seemed possible that this might be significant for assessing comparative land use potential. For instance, during the 1960s it was suggested in the French islands that the protosols on the eastern slopes of Montagne Pelée and the young kandoid soils in the south-eastern part of Guadeloupe provided a superior medium for banana-growing, while the older kandoid soils of northern Guadeloupe were not satisfactory for this purpose. In fact, however, experience has shown that while better yields can certainly be obtained on some soils than on others, most Lesser Antillean soils, provided they are well-watered and appropriately fertilised, can be made to grow bananas. Thus, while the soil maps provide an interesting summary of comparative distributions of certain combinations of climate and parent material, they do not indicate in any precise way the relative potential of each island for growing specific crops. Except where soil erosion has rendered cultivation physically impossible, it is hard to think of any major agricultural options that have been ruled out in the four islands by unsuitable soils.

Thus, while relief, climate and soil conditions are not identical on the four islands, they have enough in common that they cannot be responsible for the major differences in the character and location of banana cultivation. Undoubtedly, there were physical differences in the islands' agricultural potential; but since none of the four was being exploited to its physical limits in the 1960s, these differences cannot in themselves be regarded as critical in determining the character of contemporary land use.

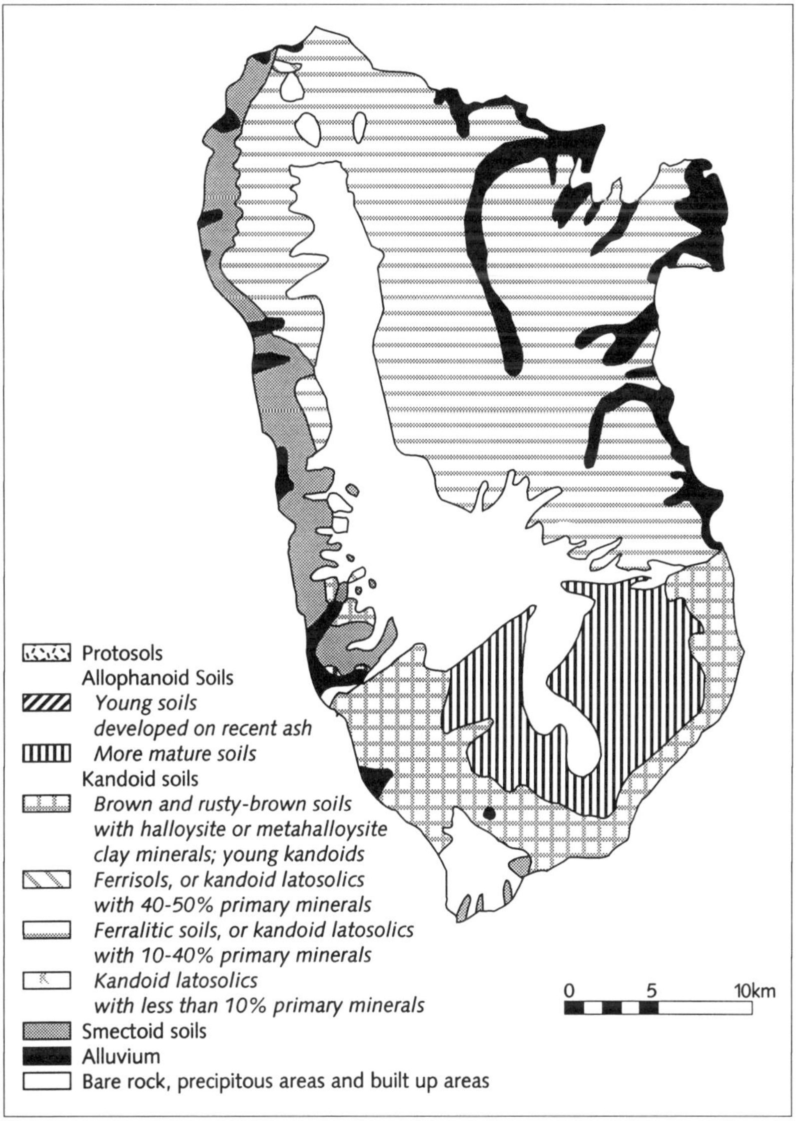

Figure 4.3
Guadeloupe: Soil types
Sources: Welch, derived from Carte des Sols des Antilles à 1/20 000e: Guadeloupe (1970); Colmet-Daage and Lagache (1965); Colmet-Daage and Gautheyrou (1974).

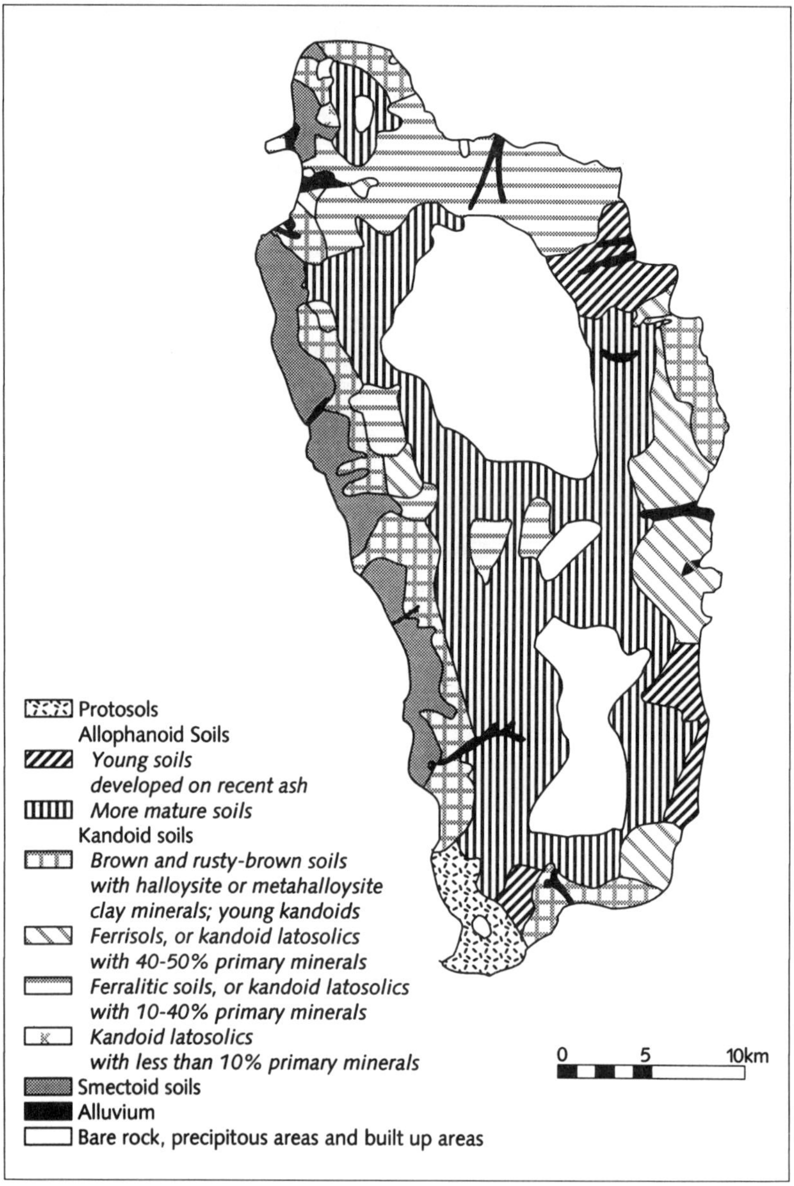

Figure 4.4
Dominica: Soil types
Sources: Welch (1987), derived from Lang (1967).

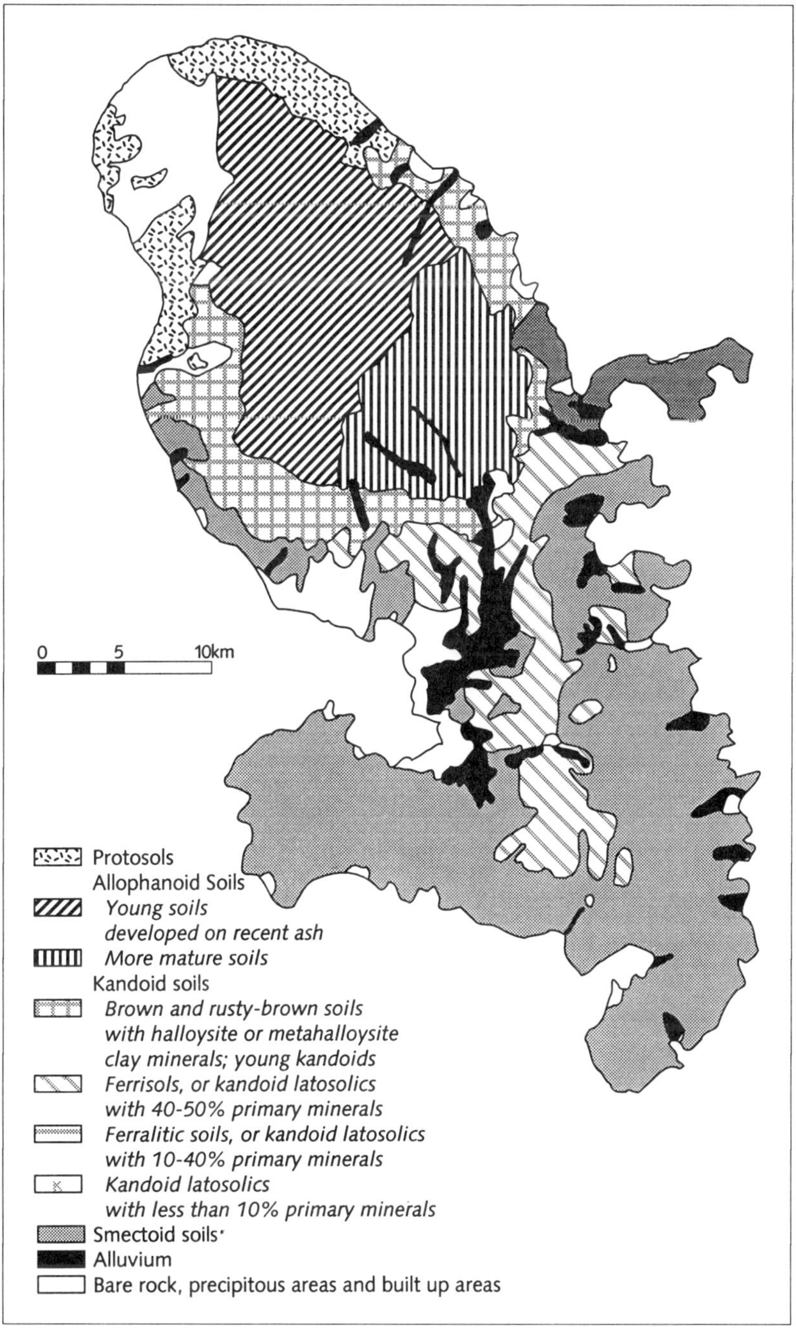

Figure 4.5
Martinique: Soil types
Sources: Welch (1987), derived from Carte des Sols de la Martinique à 1/100 000e, n.d.; Colmet-Daage and Lagache (1965); Colmet-Daage and Gautheyrou (1974).

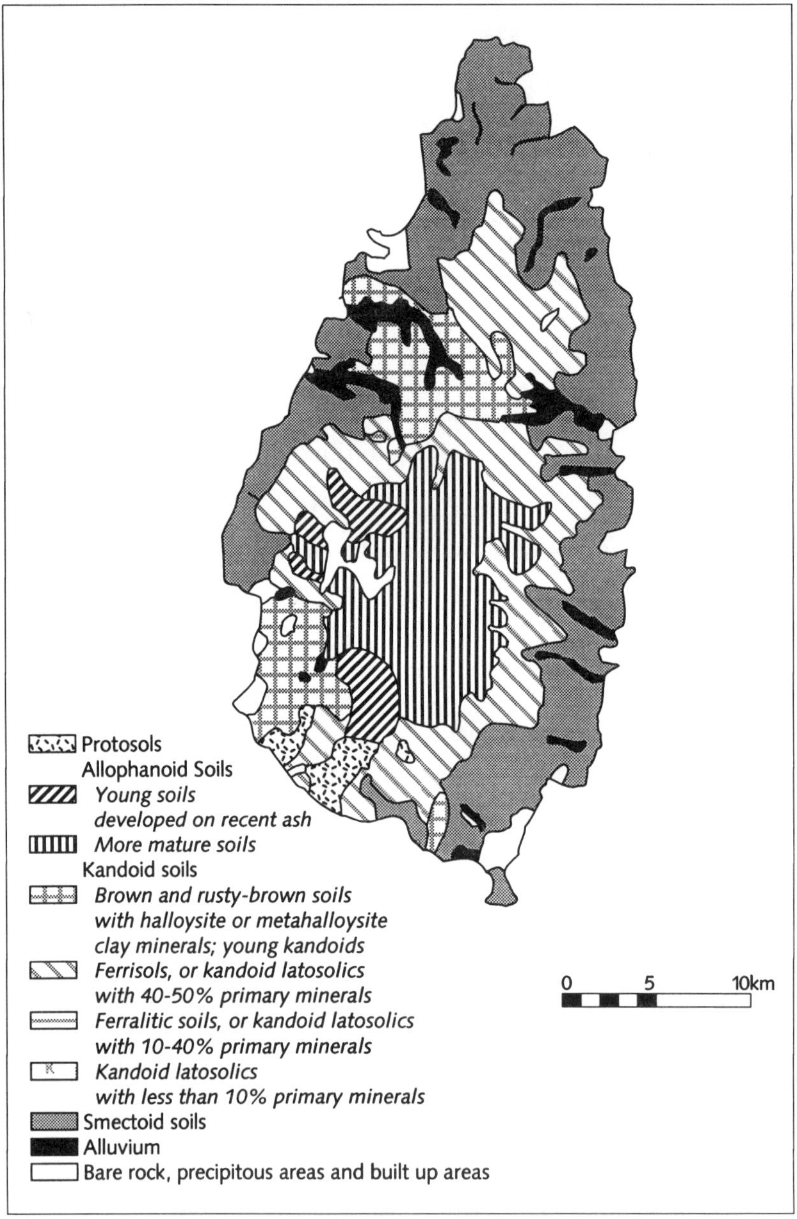

Figure 4.6
St Lucia: Soil types
Source: Welch (1987)), derived from Stark, Lajoie, and Green (1966).

Table 4.3
Land surface in the four islands occupied by each soil class

Soil Classes	*Guadeloupe*	*Dominica*	*Martinique*	*St Lucia*
1. Protosols	-	2.43	4.20	1.47
2. Allophanoid soils:				
A. Young soils developed on recent ash	0.03	4.71	16.83	3.49
B.and C. More mature soils	11.53	32.26	8.34	13.59
3. Kandoid soils:				
A. Young Kandoid	13.60	10.61	7.73	9.39
B. Kandoid latosolics with 40–50% primary minerals	0.14	6.75	8.60	21.20
C. Kandoid latosolics with 10–40% primary minerals	38.67	11.58	-	-
D. Kandoid latosols with less than 10% primary minerals	-	0.23	-	-
4. Smectoid soils	6.11	8.49	42.46	43.29
5. Alluvium	8.14	1.54	5.44	4.43
6. Bare rock, precipitous and built-up area	21.78	22.54	6.39	3.13
Total	100	100	100	100

Source: Figures 4.3, 4.4, 4.5, 4.6.

LOCATION OF BANANA CULTIVATION

Maps of the distribution of banana cultivation in the early to mid-1960s reveal remarkably different patterns on different islands, as do tables of export banana production on a parish-by-parish or commune-by-commune basis (Figures 4.7 to 4.10; Tables 4.7, 9.14, below). In both St Lucia and Dominica, there were areas of banana cultivation in almost all districts; the crop was absent from high forest reserve areas, and from some of the more arid coastal regions, but otherwise it would have been meaningless, in these islands, to speak of banana-growing or non-banana-growing areas, although certainly there were some districts where production was more intensive.

In the French islands, the situation was quite different. Again, bananas were absent from the highest and most heavily forested parts of the interior and from arid coastal areas, except where conditions were suitable for irrigation. Beyond this, however, most export

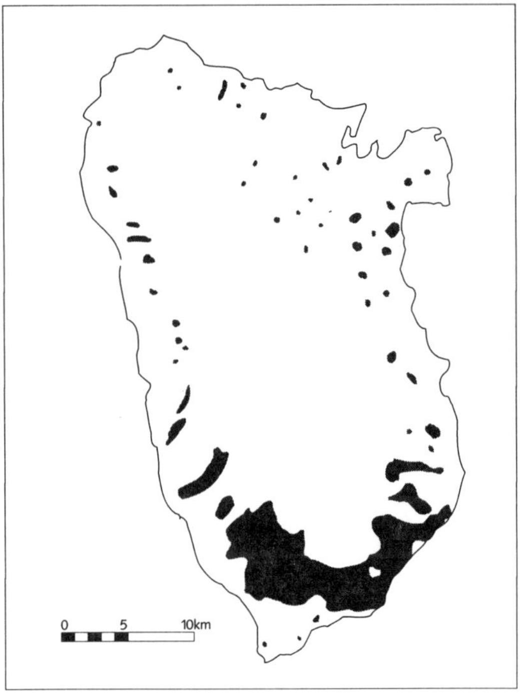

Figure 4.7
Guadeloupe: Distribution of banana cultivation, c. 1960
Source: Lasserre (1961).

banana production in Guadeloupe was concentrated in the southern half of the island, with five of sixteen communes, all contiguous, accounting for 78 percent of the island's acreage in 1964 (*La Banane* 1967, 1:17). In Martinique, the regional concentration was less obvious. Banana cultivation was quite widely distributed in the central and northeastern parts of the island; but it was still far more aggregated than in St Lucia or Dominica and was almost entirely absent from most of the west. The more concentrated nature of banana cultivation in the French islands was reflected by the statistics. Combined purestand and mixed stand plantations totalled approximately 10,000 hectares in Martinique, 8,000 hectares in Guadeloupe, 15,700 hectares in Dominica and 13,500 hectares in St Lucia (*La Banane* 1967, 1:12,17; Momsen 1969, 41): this at a time when the combined production of the two French islands was about two and a half times that of the two Commonwealth islands.

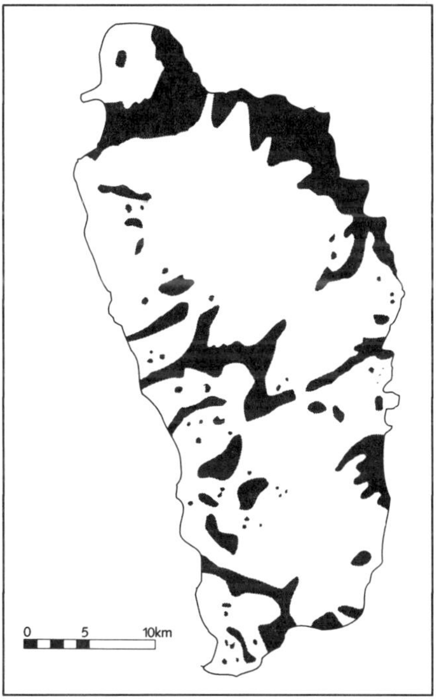

Figure 4.8
Dominica: Distribution of banana cultivation, 1966
Source: Momsen (1969).

RELATIONSHIP WITH PHYSICAL GEOGRAPHY

The absolute physical limitations for banana production in these islands are inadequate rainfall, compounded by a lack of access to irrigation water, and excessively steep slopes, where erosion has removed or would remove surface soil under cultivation. Reduced insolation at high altitudes and podsolisation with mineral pans causing impeded drainage are inhibiting factors, but have not proved a complete deterrent to banana growers in some instances.

In Martinique, most bananas were grown below 300 metres, although around Morne-Rouge (Figure 4.13) bananas extended to about 400 metres above sea level. Cultivation was restricted to the less rugged areas: on the four square kilometre grid of Figure 4.1, only squares with an elevation range of less than 360 metres contained areas of banana cultivation. The main banana areas received

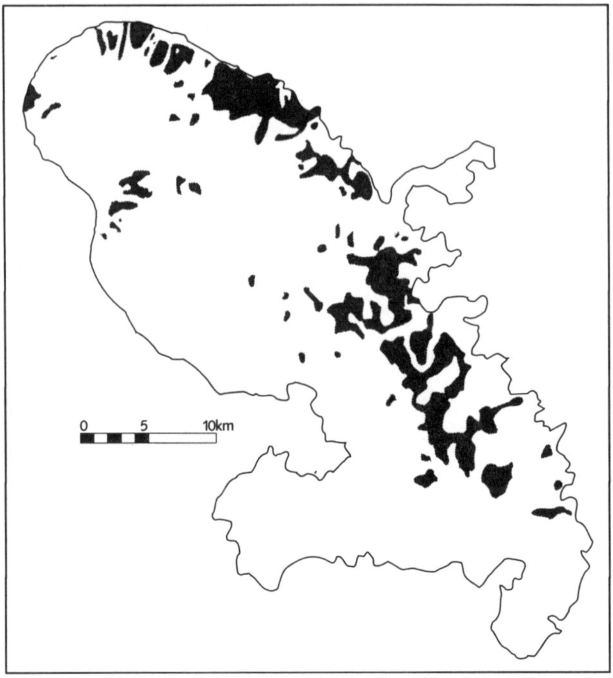

Figure 4.9
Martinique: Distribution of banana cultivation, c. 1965
Source: Carte des cultures et d'occupation des terres de la Martinique (n.d. [pre-1967]).

between 2 and 4 metres of rain annually, although bananas were grown in the Morne-Rouge–Fonds-St Denis district, with up to 5 metres, and at Vauclin, with only 1.5 metres (but with some irrigation).

In Guadeloupe, the relationship of banana cultivation to the physical conditions was substantially different. Bananas were cultivated from sea level (in Trois-Rivières and elsewhere) to an altitude of 600 metres around Matouba (St Claude) and the Plateau du Palmiste (Gourbeyre). The most important growing areas were over 300 metres in elevation. Bananas were also grown in areas with elevation ranges (within 4-square-kilometre squares) of 240 to 480 metres, extending, in Trois-Rivières, into areas with ranges up to 600 metres, and, in the valleys and heights of the leeward coast, 720 metres. There was no banana cultivation on the extensive areas of moderate

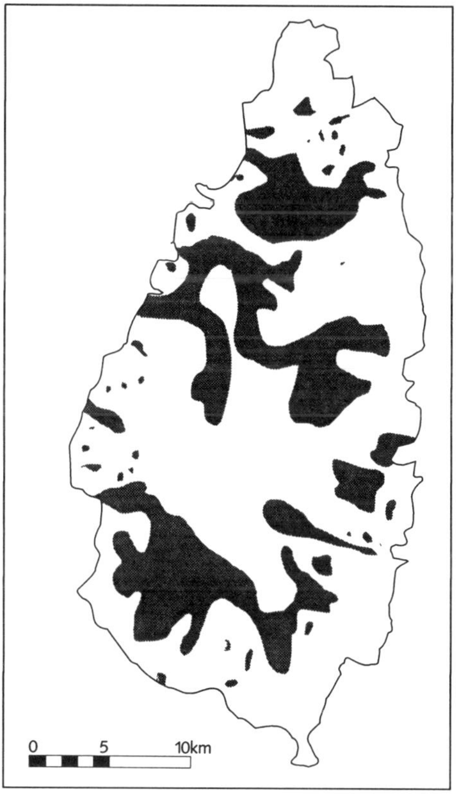

Figure 4.10
St Lucia: Distribution of banana cultivation, 1965
Source: Momsen (1969).

relief on the eastern slopes of the northern mountains. Rainfall in the main banana-growing areas was from two to six metres.

In St Lucia, most banana cultivation was carried on between sea level and 300 metres, with a more pronounced concentration within river valleys than in any other island. Inland of Soufrière (Figure 4.14), bananas extended to about 600 metres. Areas with a relief range (within 4-square-kilometre squares) up to 480 metres were used fairly indiscriminately, while areas with a range of 480 to 600 metres were not impinged upon very much, since they were mainly within forest reserves. There were small encroachments on the reserves, however, and even the squares with a relief range over 600 metres all had

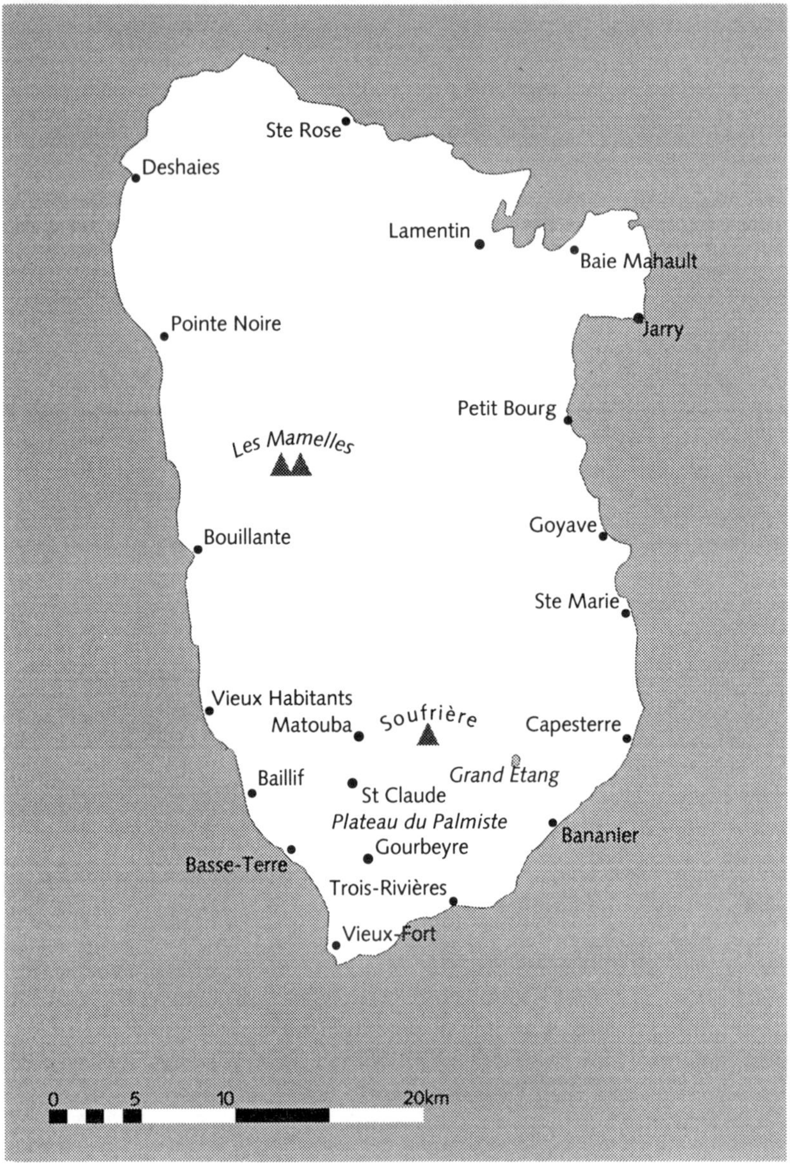

Figure 4.11
Guadeloupe: Location of names mentioned in text

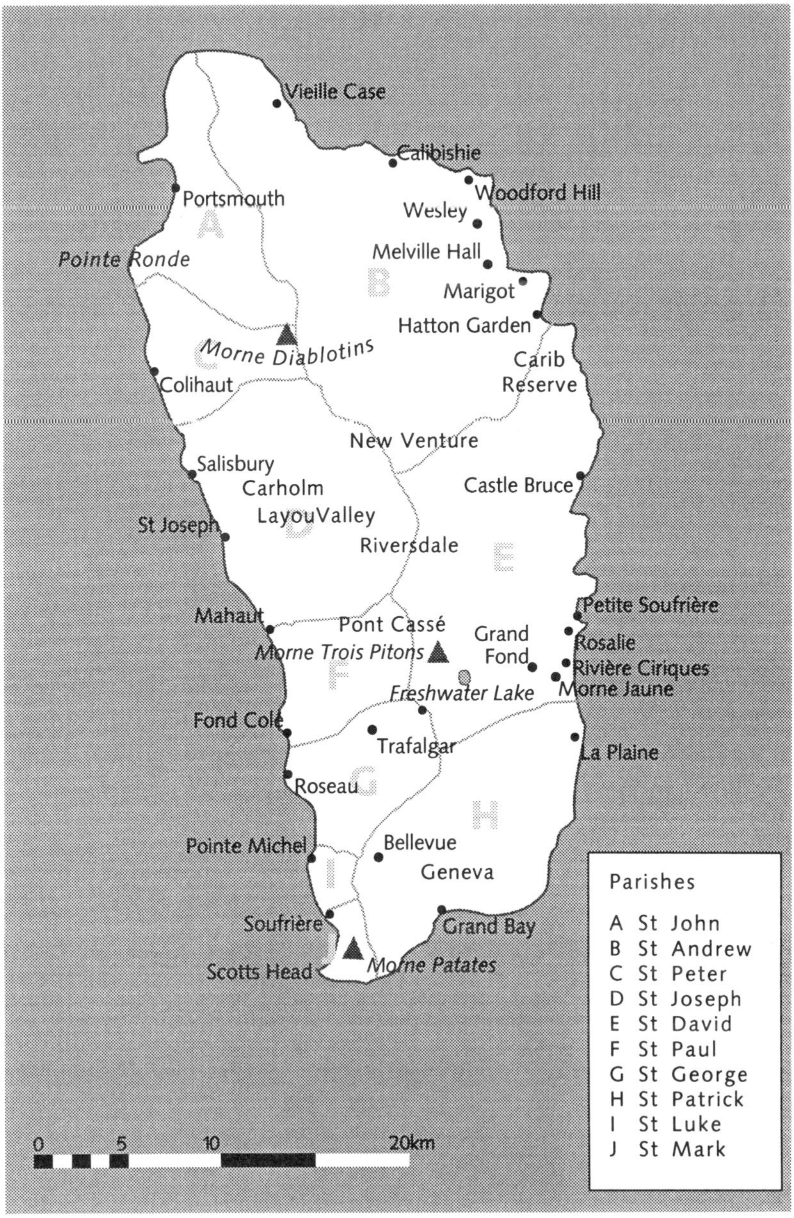

Figure 4.12
Dominica: Location of names mentioned in text

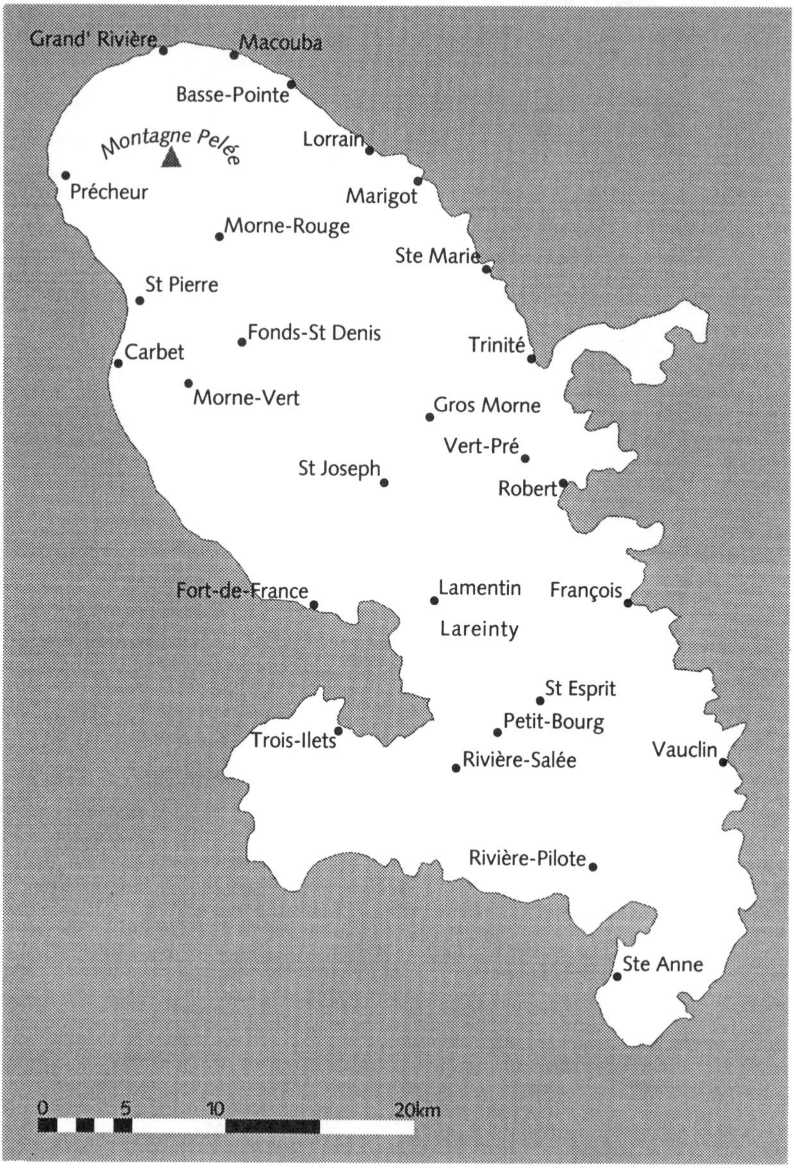

Figure 4.13
Martinique: Location of names mentioned in text

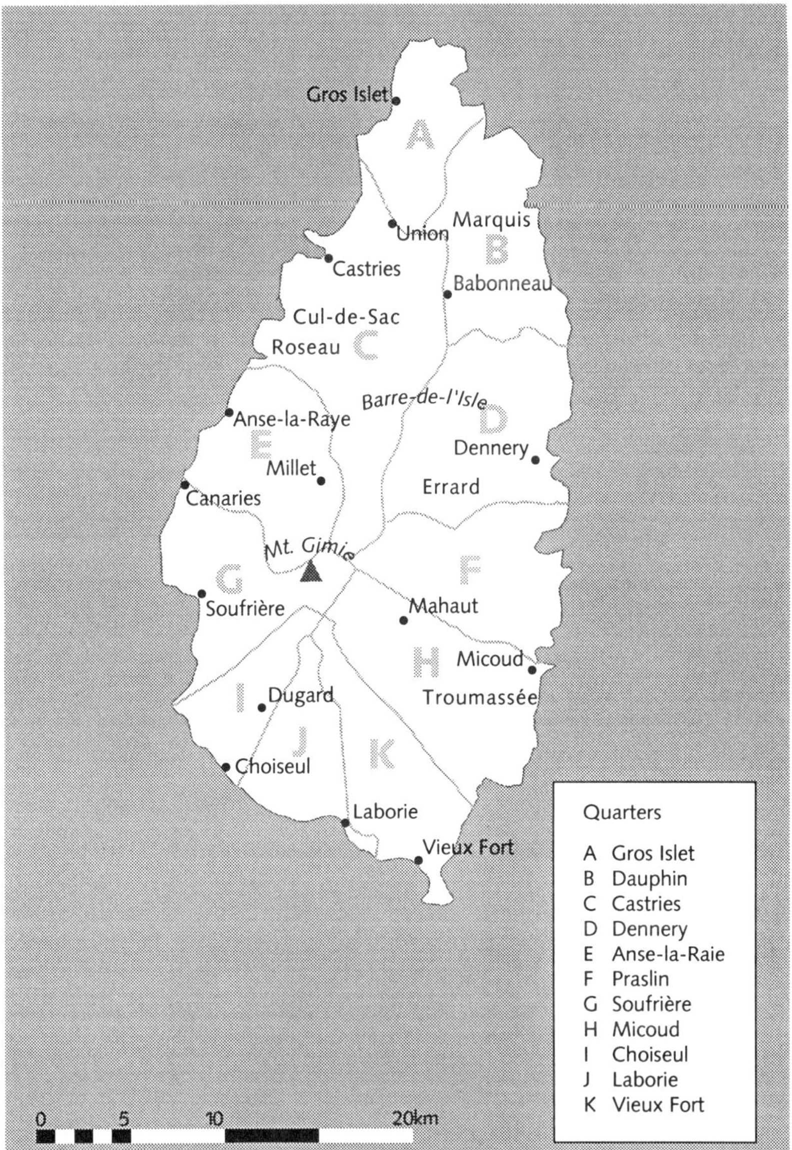

Figure 4.14
St Lucia: Location of names mentioned in text

patches of banana cultivation. Bananas were grown in areas where rainfall averaged 1.75 to 3 metres, but they were also found where rainfall was as low as 1.5 metres and as high as 4 metres.

In Dominica (Figure 4.12), banana cultivation extended from sea level to over 800 metres in inland areas of relatively gentle slopes. In the northeast (St Andrew), where a third of Dominica's bananas were grown, they were found mainly below 300 metres; but on the leeward side of the island, in the central plateau area and in the southeast inland of Morne Jaune, they were frequently cultivated up to 600 metres above sea level. While there was a concentration of bananas in areas with a relief range of less than 360 metres, banana cultivation frequently extended into squares with a range up to 600 metres along the leeward coast, and even over 840 metres in the southwest and in the northern peninsula. Most bananas were grown in areas with 2 to 4 metres of rain annually, but there were some in zones with as much as 8 metres.

Tables 4.4, 4.5, and 4.6 summarise relationships between banana-growing areas and relief and rainfall. It is apparent that banana cultivation within any island was not narrowly restricted by exacting requirements of rainfall, altitude, or relief. Irrigation is usually essential, however, where annual rainfall falls below two metres. All four islands had some potentially irrigable land, but in the 1960s this was being exploited only very locally. Very high rainfall presented no real problems once leafspot disease could be controlled by spraying.

In the 1950s the pattern had been rather different. The spread of leafspot disease in high rainfall areas had caused a decline in production, and the problem was so serious in Guadeloupe that growers were starting to abandon banana cultivation at higher altitudes and to concentrate production in coastal areas, despite the risk of drought. By the 1960s, however, leafspot disease could be controlled by spraying, and even in Guadeloupe, where both high and low land was available, bananas had been reestablished in the higher areas and phased out at lower levels (Lasserre 1961, 2:657–9).

Besides having higher rainfall, high altitudes have lower temperatures and reduced insolation. In the Eastern Caribbean these variables seldom reach critically low levels for banana production, but they do reduce the rate of growth. Consequently, while at sea level, an exportable stem of bananas can be harvested nine months after planting, at 600 metres up to eighteen months is required. Between October and February, vegetative growth is very slow and few bunches start to develop. Growth resurges in March, bunches are

Table 4.4
Elevation of banana-growing areas of the four islands

	Martinique	*Guadeloupe*	*St Lucia*	*Dominica*
Elevation at which banana cultivation was most widespread	sl.–300m	300m–400m	sl.–300m	sl.–300m
Highest elevation at which banana cultivation occurred	400m	600m	600m	800m
Lowest elevation at which banana cultivation occurred	sl.	sl.	sl.	sl.

Note: sl. = sea level.

Table 4.5
Relief range of banana-growing areas

	Range within 4-km² squares, in metres			
	Martinique	*Guadeloupe*	*St Lucia*	*Dominica*
Range at which banana cultivation was most widespread		<480	<480	<360
Maximum range at which banana-growing took place	360	720	>600	>840

Source: Figures 4.1, 4.7–4.10.

"shot" (begin to develop) in May, and the harvest period is concentrated in the winter months (*La Bananeraie Guadeloupéenne* 1984, 7). On the other hand, bananas that have matured slowly are said to be of better quality: that is to say, they are more resilient and bruise less readily. With modern packing techniques, resilience is not of great significance, but in the 1960s it did confer the worthwhile advantage of lower rejection rates.

It might be expected that soil variations would have influenced banana distribution, but a comparison of soil maps (Figures 4.3 to 4.6) with maps of banana distribution in the four islands (Figures 4.7 to 4.10) makes it clear that there are no soil types in the islands on which banana cultivation is impossible. In Martinique, Dominica and St Lucia, bananas were cultivated on all soil types, with no detectable concentration on any particular type. There was little

Table 4.6
Average annual rainfall in banana-growing areas, in metres

	Martinique	*Guadeloupe*	*St Lucia*	*Dominica*
Rainfall range in main banana-growing areas	2–3	2–6	1.75–3	2–4
Maximum rainfall for banana growing	5	6	4	8
Minimum rainfall for banana growing	1.5	1.75	1.5	2

Source: Figures 4.2, 4.7–4.10.

banana cultivation in areas of smectoid soils, although enough to suggest that with an adequate water supply, bananas would grow satisfactorily on such soils. Banana cultivation was also very localised on mature allophanoid soils; but large areas of these soils fell within forest reserves where high rainfall and rugged terrain made any disturbance of the natural vegetation a threat to the stability of the soil cover. In Dominica in particular, hardpan formation and resultant drainage problems also limited the suitability of extensive tracts of allophanoid soils. Even so, bananas were sometimes planted where such land adjoined the main transinsular road. In Martinique, there were no ferrallitic soils with less than 40 percent of primary minerals, but in St Lucia and Dominica such soils were widely used for banana cultivation.

In Guadeloupe, the case was different. Although bananas were grown on all soil types, the bulk of the export crop was concentrated in areas of younger soils in the southern third of the island. Only small, scattered patches of bananas were cultivated on ferrisols and ferrallitic soils. A reason often suggested for this concentration was the presence in the south of heavy clay soils of high fertility, in which bananas rooted more firmly than in lighter soils. This made them more resistant to wind damage. Moreover, it was also claimed that nematodes did not flourish in these heavy soils, and this was why nematode infestation posed a far less severe problem in Guadeloupe than in the other three islands. In fact, however, bananas in southern Guadeloupe were by no means restricted to this one soil type. They were also grown intensively on allophanoid soils, both young and not so young. It seems unlikely, then, that soil types alone provide an adequate explanation for the concentration of Guadeloupe's export banana industry within a relatively restricted sector of the island.

Certainly, some soils are more suitable for banana cultivation than others. Individual farmers frequently said that between one part of their holding and another or, particularly, between one parcel of land and another, there were marked differences in the bunch weights that could be achieved, the susceptibility of banana mats to wind damage, the response to different types of fertiliser, and the number of years of ratooning that were practicable. (Ratooning is the practice of harvesting several successive stems from the same mat or rootstock, without uprooting and replanting it.)

In most cases, however, accessibility overrode soil fertility in determining where a banana grower's main efforts should be concentrated. Furthermore, since soil depletion, erosion, and nematode infestation were the results of intensive cultivation combined with inadequate levels of husbandry, the differences in fertility between one parcel of a holding and another might result directly from the relative inaccessibility of one parcel, rather than any intrinsic variations in soil type.

SECONDARY ENVIRONMENTAL FACTORS

Infrastructure

So far as the export banana industries of the Lesser Antilles are concerned, in the 1960s 'infrastructure' meant, essentially, ports and roads. Any irrigation was on a small scale, and generally the initiative of private individuals. Electricity was not necessary, nor was piped water - although a water supply was required at boxing facilities if shipment in boxes, a development whose merits were still being debated at this period, was to replace the traditional method of shipment on the stem.

The question of ports is straightforward. When banana industries were established or reestablished on the islands in the late 1940s and early 1950s, it appears to have been of very little significance whether an island had deep-water harbour facilities with alongside docking or whether banana boats were obliged to anchor hundreds of metres offshore and be loaded by lighter. Martinique and St Lucia had good deep-water harbours, but Dominica and Basse-Terre Guadeloupe did not, and while the deep-water port of Pointe-à-Pitre was readily accessible to the northern part of Basse-Terre Guadeloupe, the bulk of the bananas were from the start exported through the southern port of Basse-Terre, which had an open roadstead.

It is true that during the 1960s, as the volume of banana exports increased, deep-water port facilities in Dominica (Roseau) and

Guadeloupe (Basse-Terre) came to be regarded as a virtual necessity, since it was anticipated that loading would be cheaper, with deep-water facilities, and less liable to damage the fruit than when it had to be transported to vessels offshore by lighter. However, enthusiasts for deep-water ports may have over-estimated their benefits. In St Vincent, the change from loading by lighter to loading alongside brought no reduction in costs either to the shipper or to the banana growers' association (Iton 1970, personal communication). Moreover, no one has ever demonstrated that bananas loaded alongside arrived in the United Kingdom or France in better condition than those loaded by lighter. Thus, there would appear to be no evidence that the superior port facilities gave any special impetus to the banana industry in the islands or districts where they existed.

Since transporting a bulky and delicate crop over rough roads contributed significantly to the costs of production, proximity to an island exporting port might have been expected to confer an advantage on some growers, remoteness, a disadvantage on others. In Guadeloupe, there was indeed a great concentration of banana cultivation in the communes closest to Basse-Terre. However, it would have been perfectly feasible to export bananas from Pointe-à-Pitre, and this was in fact done when the volume of bananas produced in the northeast became large enough.

The 1961 census figures, tabulated parish by parish in Dominica and quarter by quarter in St Lucia, reveal no concentration of banana cultivation in the neighbourhood of exporting ports (Table 4.7). In Dominica, the parishes of St Joseph and St Andrew, with less than 35 percent of the island's land-in-holdings, together accounted for almost 56 percent of the stems harvested. Neither of these parishes is close to a port. On the other hand, St John, in which the port of Portsmouth is located, together with St George and St Paul, the parishes containing and closest to Roseau, produced only 23 percent of Dominica's bananas even though they contained 30 percent of the island's land-in-holdings. In St Lucia, the quarter of Dennery, the most distant from either exporting port, had 19 percent of the island's land-in-holdings and accounted for 41 percent of stems cut.

It was not possible to obtain figures for Martinique on banana production in different communes. Land use maps constructed from aerial photographs taken in the late 1950s suggest, however, that proximity to the exporting port of Fort-de-France was not of overriding concern, since export bananas were grown on the northern slopes of Montagne Pelée, in the area of Grand' Rivière, 45 kilometres from Fort-de-France. In the mid-1960s it was suggested that

Table 4.7
Banana stems cut, by parish (Dominica) or quarter (St Lucia), 1961

	Land-in-holdings (%)	*Stems cut (%)*	*Number of stems cut per acre-in-holdings*	*Number of stems cut per cultivated acre*
Dominica	100.00	100.00	29.21[a]	66.05[a]
St John	8.44	5.62	19.45	44.67
St Peter	6.64	2.82	12.42	67.72
St Joseph	12.57	21.72	50.46	126.91
St Paul	11.06	9.12	24.10	56.47
St George	10.88	8.36	22.46	49.67
St Luke	1.59	0.53	9.76	17.27
St Mark	3.39	1.47	12.70	18.37
St Patrick	11.56	9.53	24.08	43.79
St David	11.82	7.03	17.36	59.07
St Andrew	22.06	33.79	44.75	81.92
St Lucia	100.00	100.00	70.22[a]	136.75[a]
Castries (urban)	1.22	0.48	27.56	40.75
Castries (rural)	9.37	14.11	115.72	157.82
Soufriere	9.49	5.95	43.87	90.75
Vieux Fort	12.44	2.64	14.90	58.58
Anse-la-Raye	13.11	13.44	71.75	136.96
Choiseul	3.24	0.49	10.51	13.77
Dennery	19.49	41.10	148.06	284.01
Gros Islet	14.44	10.96	53.20	121.09
Laborie	5.18	1.16	15.68	25.91
Micoud	12.02	9.73	56.83	86.89

Source: Derived from WI Census of Agriculture, 1961 (1968, 85,94,179,186).
[a]Island average.

the small east coast port of Trinité might be developed as a banana-exporting port, since it was more central than Fort-de-France to the main banana-growing districts of the island, but, as in the case of Basse-Terre and Roseau, the question was one of building facilities to accommodate a preexisting industry, rather than locating an industry near preexisting facilities.

McQuillan (1968) investigated the relationship between estate-to-port transport costs and agricultural production in Dominica in 1967. He compared the relative costs of transport to port for different crops grown on the same estates to determine whether lower transport costs might explain why a particular crop was predominant in a particular region. McQuillan could find no strong relationship between transport costs and variations in production, although he did not appear to take into account the possibility that if transport costs had been a critical factor, crops whose transport costs were uneconomically high would probably not have been grown at all.

The question of roads is more complicated. Figures 4.15 to 4.18 show road networks in the late 1950s or early 1960s (depending on the publication date of the maps on which these figures are based). A comparison with Figures 4.7 to 4.10, showing the distribution of banana cultivation very shortly after this, reveals quite different relationships in French and Commonwealth islands. In Martinique and Guadeloupe, export bananas were concentrated entirely in areas close to roads. In Martinique, no block of banana plantations was more than one kilometre from a "departmental" or "national" road, and the most distant margins of plantations were, at most, three kilometres from these roads. Most blocks were in fact traversed or skirted by roads, and all banana growers who were interviewed in the survey of 1966–67 had holdings by roads. In Guadeloupe, the distribution was similar. One kilometre was the maximum distance of the *margins* of banana-growing areas from departmental roads. Many of the larger estates also had a network of feeder roads, so that no bananas had to be carried more than a few hundred metres. Many of these roads had not been built or were not all-weather roads when the industry first began to develop after the Second World War. Many feeder roads were built specifically for the extraction of bananas, and expansion of the road network and of banana cultivation often went hand in hand, particularly in southern Guadeloupe.

On the other hand, in both the French islands there were physically suitable areas well served by road systems in which little or no banana cultivation took place. Northeastern Guadeloupe and several well-watered inland districts of Martinique are examples. When major new roads were built, such as the Deux Mamelles road, completed in 1961 across northern Basse-Terre Guadeloupe, their primary purpose was to improve communications between the major towns and isolated rural communities, rather than to open up new agricultural land.

In St Lucia and Dominica, while there was a concentration of banana growing in areas less than one kilometre from the roads, it was by no means restricted to such zones. In leeward St Lucia, there were small pockets of cultivation up to three kilometres, as the crow flies, from the nearest road, and several growers that I interviewed in 1966–67 had holdings between one and two kilometres

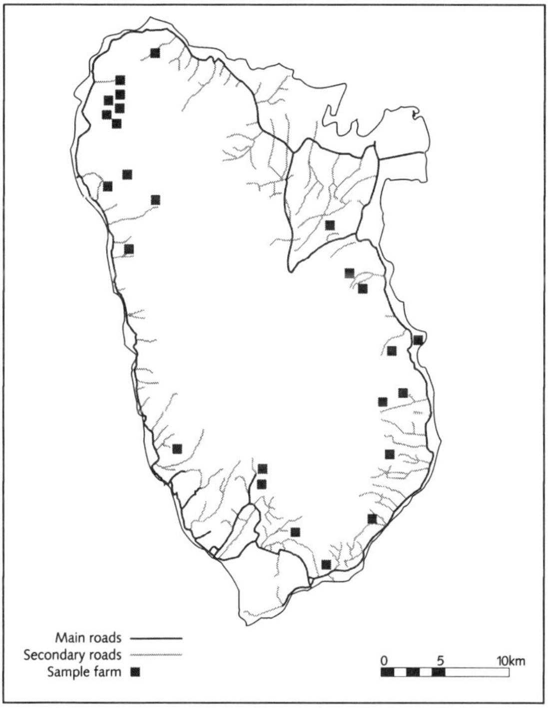

Figure 4.15
Guadeloupe: Location of surveyed farms, and road network, 1958

from a public road as the crow flies, often a much greater distance on the ground; 4.5 kilometres was the maximum cited. In Dominica, several growers that I interviewed in 1966–67 had holdings at least three kilometres as the crow flies from any road, and in the Colihaut district on the leeward coast, one farmer claimed to have a holding ten kilometres' walk from the nearest accessible road. Several others in this area had holdings almost as remote from which banana crops were sometimes extracted.

The average distance from the road (on the ground) of 48 holdings surveyed in St Lucia in 1966–67 (Figure 4.18) was 0.5 kilometre, with three respondents claiming distances of 4 kilometres or more; but in Dominica (Figure 4.16), the average distance was 1 kilometre, and 11 holdings out of 70 were more than 4 kilometres from the road. Several respondents remarked, however, that they only occasionally harvested bananas on their remoter holdings, when prices were unusually favourable; and some farmers had holdings which, although otherwise suitable, could not be used for banana produc-

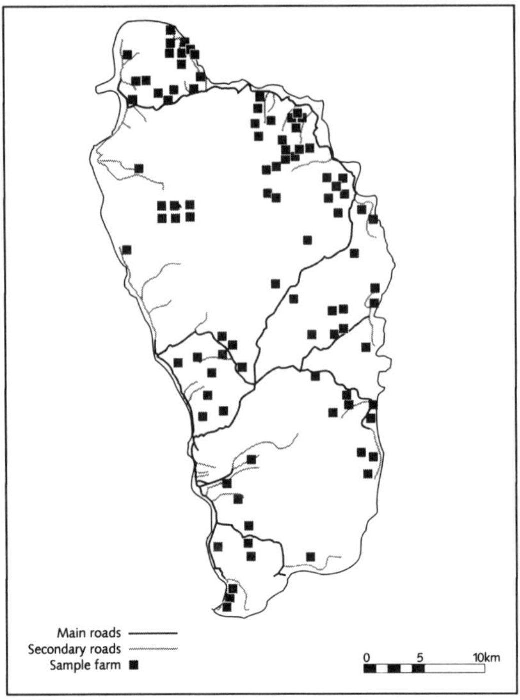

Figure 4.16
Dominica: Location of surveyed farms, and road network, 1963

tion because of their distance from any road. One such area was inland of Marigot, on the northeastern coast.

A lack of roads certainly limited early large-scale participation in the export banana industry in areas such as the Carib Reserve, but when prices were attractive or when no alternative source of cash income was available, Dominican and St Lucian farmers were prepared to transport their fruit for remarkable distances on foot. In the 1950s, bananas were headed from the Grand Fond-Rivière Ciriques area on the east coast of Dominica to the Roseau Valley via the Freshwater Lake, a distance of 12 kilometres. Naturally, however, the volume of fruit that could be extracted such distances in this way was limited. In the 1961 Census, the Dominican parishes of St Peter and St David, with exceptionally poor road systems, had among the lowest numbers of stems cut per acre-in-holdings.

Between the late 1940s and the mid-1960s, there was a substantial expansion of the road system in both St Lucia and, particularly, Dominica. Until 1958 it had been impossible to drive from the west to the east coast of Dominica, except in the narrow northern part

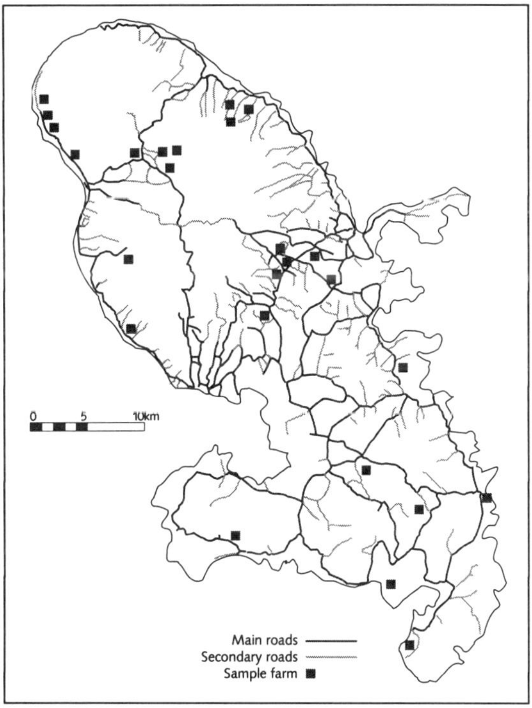

Figure 4.17
Martinique: Location of surveyed farms, and road network, 1958

of the island. The road system in the north had been quite separate from the system radiating from Roseau, the capital, in the south. From Roseau roads extended only northward to the Layou River, inland to Riverdale and Trafalgar, and southwards to Pointe Michel and Grand Bay. While much of this road construction was a social priority, linking isolated communities and bringing them access to Roseau, a corollary was ribbon cultivation of bananas alongside the transinsular roads, a feature which shows clearly on Momsen's map of 1966 (1969). Thus, while nearness to roads was not essential for banana production, it was certainly desirable. Bananas were grown, for instance, at Pont Cassé, in an area where hardpan formation caused major drainage problems, and reduced insolation doubled the time taken to produce a harvestable stem of bananas. Moreover, in many areas in both Dominica and St Lucia, private individuals or groups of farmers had used their own resources to extend roads and cut feeder roads to provide better access to their land for trucks

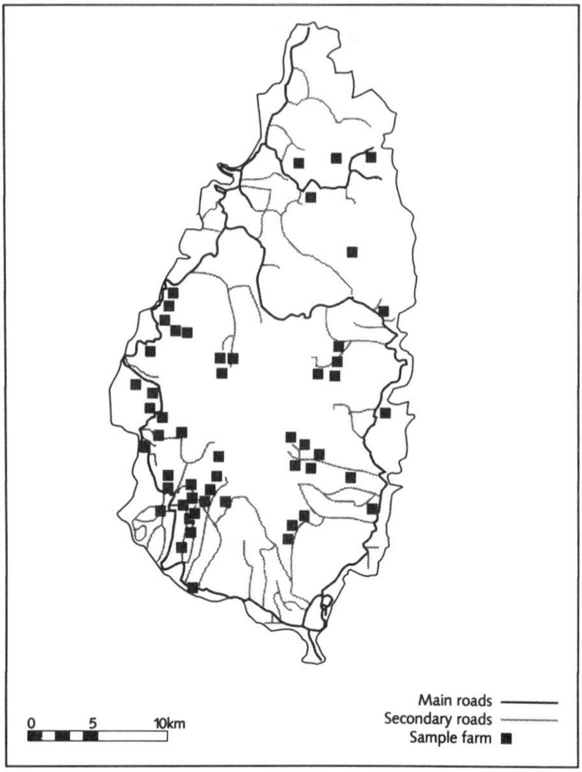

Figure 4.18
St Lucia: Location of surveyed farms, and road network, 1974

and jeeps. One St Lucian farmer, with a holding of 40 hectares, had spent WI$31,000 to construct two kilometres of road from the main Barre de l'Isle road near Dennery, northward to his holding. Farmers in the valleys of northeastern Dominica had also built feeder roads themselves. Virtually the only areas in St Lucia and Dominica with roads but without banana cultivation were areas with inadequate rainfall or in Forest Reserve zones.

The intensive banana cultivation practised in the French islands required a heavy input of fertiliser (three tons per hectare per crop), a sustained input of labour, and facilities for easy extraction of the crop. This intensive cultivation could not be carried on more than a few hundred metres from a motorable road. In the Commonwealth islands, remoteness did not become an absolute barrier to banana cultivation until fairly extreme limits were reached, limits determined by a delicate balance of market prices, the cost of inputs and the level of inputs required. By employing extensive methods and little or no fertiliser and by using family labour that was not costed by the day or task, farmers might cultivate bananas, on an attenuated scale, far beyond the limits a conventional economic appraisal would dictate.

Pre-Existing Crop Distribution

So far, the discussion has been conducted as if bananas were the only feasible crop or, at least, the one farmers would choose first, unless adverse conditions ruled them out. How far was this really the case?

In fact, it is physically possible to grow an enormous variety of crops on the islands, and before bananas assumed the dominant position in island economies that they held in the mid-1960s, much of the land they then occupied was planted in other crops, some grown primarily for subsistence, others for export. By far the most important, in three of the four islands, was sugar cane.

By the mid-1960s sugar, which until ten years earlier had been the mainspring of the island economy in Martinique, Guadeloupe, and St Lucia, had sunk to a secondary role in the first two islands and had disappeared entirely from the third.

In St Lucia by 1965, all the land which had previously been in sugar cane was planted in bananas. The three "sugar valleys" of Roseau, Cul-de-Sac, and Dennery, which in 1956 had produced the highest tonnage of sugar for export in the island's history, had abandoned cane, one by one, and switched to bananas. It is by no means certain that St Lucia's sugar industry could have survived long, even in the absence of bananas with their rival claims on land and labour. The yield of sugar per ton of cane crushed was low compared with those on the major sugar-producing islands (Harrison 1965, 12), and while the central factories were very small by modern standards, the ruggedness of the terrain separating the three valleys made consolidation unfeasible. The industry suffered from recurrent labour problems. Nevertheless, the Roseau and Cul-de-Sac operations might have continued to be viable for some years had there been no more attractive alternative. As it was, the more vulnerable section of the sugar industry, at Dennery, began to experience difficulties as early as 1957. Less than 75 percent of the Dennery factory's supplies of cane normally came from company lands, and the small farmers who had hitherto contributed the balance were already turning to bananas, to which their generally hilly, well-watered holdings were for the most part better suited. Bananas also brought them higher returns varying less with the seasons. The Dennery factory ceased to operate in 1958; thereafter, company lands were planted entirely in bananas.

Sugar Manufacturers Limited, the company operating the Roseau and Cul-de-Sac factories, began a limited programme of banana cultivation on their own lands in 1957, and by 1959 planned to increase banana production in the Cul-de-Sac Valley and concentrate sugar production at Roseau (Harrison 1965, 35). In 1964, however, all sugar production ceased. Evidently, the company had concluded that bananas were simply more profitable. The fact that sugar production did continue at Roseau for nearly four years after Geest Industries acquired a majority of shares in Sugar Manufacturers Limited suggests that the economic advantage of one crop over the other was probably marginal from the company's point of view; but social factors finally swung the balance in favour of bananas (Harrison 1965, 24–5).

In the early years of banana establishment, the existence of a major and initially viable sugar industry in St Lucia had an important influence on where bananas were grown. At first, they were excluded from much of the more level, easily worked land, which belonged to sugar companies. This meant, however, that when sugar production was abandoned, large tracts of land became available that could easily be converted to purestand banana cultivation. The dilemma of whether long-term tree crops should be conserved did not exist.

In Martinique, it is more difficult to trace a clear relationship between the rise of the postwar banana industry and the sharp decline of sugar in the mid-1960s. Although a number of smaller and less efficient factories had closed in the 1940s and 1950s, the area in cane actually reached a maximum in 1963: 14,000 hectares, with ten factories producing 93,000 tonnes of sugar. Between 1963 and 1966, however, four factories ceased operations, production fell to 62,000 tonnes, and the area in cane declined to 9,500 hectares. This rapid decline was the result of a 40 percent increase in wages over four years, during which the price of sugar had remained the same. The hilly terrain limited the possibilities for mechanisation, and the lack of vertical integration meant that unprofitable field operations could not be compensated for by profitable factory operations. Unlike Guadeloupe's sugar factories which derived the bulk of their supplies from their own company lands, Martinique factories were generally supplied by independent landowners with holdings of 50 to 200 hectares. The industry had been caught in a vicious circle: marginal proprietors went out of cane production, supplies to some factories fell below economic levels, and these factories then closed, and leaving cane farmers in the immediate neighbourhood too far from a factory to continue in cane production.

Unlike St Lucia's cane lands, the abandoned cane lands in Martinique did not automatically go into banana production. Some of the land was owned by proprietors of holdings too small to gain access to the export banana industry, and some was in areas too dry or otherwise unsuitable for bananas. Nevertheless, Marieu's (1966) map showing factories closed between 1939 and 1966 reveals that most were located in areas producing large quantities of bananas in the mid-1960s (89).

Additional impetus to the decline of cane cultivation was given by the land reform policy which came into effect in Martinique and Guadeloupe in 1961. The policy put limits on the area of land that an individual could own and forced the break-up of a number of large properties. Even though some of the new holdings would have been well suited to mechanised cane cultivation, their new owners, with large loans to repay, were obliged to seek crops giving them higher returns per hectare than cane. It was difficult for isolated, independent small farmers to enter the banana industry, but smallholders who were settled on subdivided estates, with the assistance and encouragement of government agencies to set up co-operative marketing organisations, seem to have had little hesitation in doing so. In 1968, for instance, 26 of the first 336 smallholders established on the former Lareinty estate lands in Lamentin were growing bananas, although most did not devote their entire holdings to this crop (Graham 1970, 31).

Although economically viable sugar factories required a large, accessible catchment area of good cane land, cane was also cultivated in many districts of Martinique solely for the manufacture of rum, for which the island had an excellent reputation. Since rum distilleries could operate on quite a small scale and remain economically viable, relatively small areas of land suitable for cane but too remote to supply a central sugar factory could be used to grow cane for distilleries: land in leeward coastal areas, for instance, and in the south. Many of these scattered, isolated cane lands were probably too dry for successful banana cultivation; but even if their land was not too dry, distillery owners with quotas for rum production often found this sufficiently profitable that they would not lightly change to another crop. Moreover, while the change from cane to bananas would have been a relatively simple matter, to reverse the procedure if economic changes made this desirable would have been much more difficult. Quite apart from the problem of reactivating disused industrial plant and recruiting skilled workers to operate it, there would have been the problem of reacquiring rum quotas that had lapsed or been sold.

Although some land that was formerly planted in cane was certainly used for banana cultivation in the 1960s, the expansion of the banana industry in Martinique was not for the most part directly at the expense of cane. For one thing, by 1962 Martinique was already producing more bananas than the market could absorb, and yet sugar factories closed down in the four following years at an accelerating rate.

Furthermore, even in the major cane-growing districts, substantial areas were normally left fallow or used as pasture, and it was consequently possible in the 1950s for landowners to plant bananas without initially cutting back on cane acreages.

Thus, the precise effect of cane cultivation on the pattern of banana growing in Martinique is difficult to characterise. Cane must certainly be taken into acount when examining land use patterns in detail, but on a broader scale, it is hard to see how bananas were either helped or hindered by preexisting cane.

In Guadeloupe, the situation was different again. Until the mid-1960s, a very high proportion of the cane land was held by the metropolitan-owned sugar companies, who also owned the sugar factories. These factories were backed by far greater resources than the locally owned factories of Martinique, and because their long-term interests lay in sugar production, they were unlikely to switch to banana cultivation for short-term gain. All the same, it was not in the interest of the factory companies to plant their entire acreages in cane, since Guadeloupe's sugar production exceeded the quota that it could sell at a guaranteed price in France. (Martinique, on the other hand, was by the 1960s increasingly failing to fill its quota). In the late 1950s and early 1960s, therefore, several companies devoted substantial parts of their holdings to banana cultivation. In fact, until a satisfactory method of controlling leafspot was developed, there was a tendency to plant increasing quantities of bananas on the gentle lower slopes of eastern Basse-Terre Guadeloupe and even, in one case, in limestone Grande-Terre, even though rainfall was low for bananas in these areas, and some irrigation was necessary. It was supposed that if bananas were grown in rotation with cane on such lands, the heavy applications of fertiliser for bananas might increase the yields of the cane that succeeded them. By the mid-1960s, however, it had been demonstrated that while fields previously cultivated in bananas did indeed produce higher tonnages of cane, the sucrose content was lower and actual yields of sugar per hectare were not significantly higher. Consequently, there was a return to growing bananas on hillier, more inland sites, and they disappeared completely from Grande-Terre and most of northern Basse-Terre.

Thus, the cane industry in Guadeloupe did affect the location of banana growing, but in different ways from those described for St Lucia and Martinique. In St Lucia, cane initially formed a barrier to banana growing in certain areas, but as the banana industry gathered momentum and the sugar industry faltered, cane was overwhelmed and abandoned, providing large blocks of land for pure-stand bananas. In Martinique, the possibility of adopting banana cultivation may have prompted the closure of sugar factories and rum distilleries in some districts, but in many others, cane was able to hold its own, or if it did cease to be viable, it was replaced by pineapples, pasture, or even fallow. In Guadeloupe, however, companies that had huge resources, holdings extending across areas of widely varying relief and climate, and abundant "spare" land for experimentation were able to adopt banana cultivation on a large scale. They could move it from the lowlands to the hills or, in some cases, simply abandon it, creating a very volatile land use situation. Cane could scarcely be regarded as a barrier to banana cultivation in Guadeloupe and may, in some cases and at certain periods, have facilitated its spread.

In the islands where sugar had dominated the economy until the 1960s and in those areas of the islands where the climate and terrain permitted the cultivation of either crop, the relationship between cane and bananas was by far the most significant in its influence on land use options perceived and adopted. Other options existed: in the French islands, for large landowners, cattle-rearing, either for beef or dairying, was often a possibility, and in Martinique, pineapples were also a viable crop in some areas. These options served limited markets, however, so that their viability was assured only if they were carried out on a modest scale, and their importance as an alternative to bananas was thus only locally significant.

Much more widespread was the cultivation of vegetables and ground provisions. In most cases, these crops were grown primarily for consumption by the cultivator's family; any surpluses were sold either locally or in the larger towns. Since provisions and vegetables were rarely exported and local markets were limited, there was little temptation for farmers to transfer large acreages to such crops. Even if satisfactory returns per hectare were possible in theory, any sudden expansion would lead to gluts and falling prices. In Martinique and Guadeloupe, some farmers concentrated almost entirely on vegetables and ground provisions, but this was generally for socio-economic reasons not directly related to theoretical calculations of the profitability of these crops relative to bananas. In none of the islands was there evidence that bananas and ground provisions were in direct competition for land. In the Commonwealth islands particularly, where mixed farming was the rule, the spread of export banana cultivation inadvertently brought about an increase in the quantity of ground provisions (such as dasheen) harvested. In the first place, ground provisions were often planted as a pioneer crop between the stumps in newly cleared forest land, until roots and stumps had rotted sufficiently to permit the planting of bananas. Once bananas were established, the ground provisions planted between benefitted so much from the fertiliser applied to the bananas that yields were substantially increased. In St Lucia, it was reported that the price of a bag of dasheen had actually declined as a result: what had some years previously sold for WI$12 to WI$15 would fetch only WI$9 in 1966 (Williams 1966, personal communication).

As for the "vegetables," - such crops as carrots, cabbage, tomatoes, and cucumbers, normally grown in temperate lands - they had always been cultivated on a very modest scale, except in a few districts where suitable soils and climate had encouraged a local tradition of specialisation in such crops. Where such traditions were established, there was little temptation for farmers to abandon them in favour of banana growing, since, even though these vegetables were more vulnerable than most tropical crops to pests, diseases, and adverse weather conditions, they provided, potentially, much higher returns per hectare than did bananas.

In any case, neither pineapples, livestock, vegetables, nor provision crops represented a real barrier to establishing bananas. Any farmer periodically reevaluating crop choices could adopt or reject these options individually, year by year. This was not the case with cane, whose abandonment by a few farmers could undermine the viability of a factory, force it to close and free hundreds, sometimes thousands, of hectares of land for alternative uses. Nor was it the case with tree crops such as coconuts, coffee, cacao, or citrus fruits, which might take five years or more after planting to bear, and several more years after that to reach their full productive potential.

Scattered trees providing fruit for local consumption were a common element in the landscape in Martinique and Guadeloupe, but although one or two large landowners did speak speculatively in 1966 of their intention to establish plantations of lime trees or avocado pears, there were hardly any primarily commercial plantations of fruit trees in either island. In fact, both Martinique and Gaudeloupe imported limes and grapefruit from Dominica. The suggestion that hurricanes were to blame for the scarcity of fruit trees is difficult to prove or disprove, but, in any case, there was clearly no incentive to plant citrus fruit for export to metropolitan France because its former North African possessions had traditionally supplied all its requirements.

The production of vegetable oil from locally grown coconuts was not an economic proposition in the French West Indies: without a protective regional tariff barrier, the oil could not have competed against lower-cost imports. Thus, coconut plantations were not an element in their landscapes.

In fact, the only remaining tree crops of any significance in the French islands were coffee and cacao. The reputation for high quality enjoyed by Guadeloupean coffee, for many decades an important crop in the valleys of leeward Basse-Terre, enabled the local product to command premium prices. Nevertheless, only a handful of estates still grew coffee commercially in the mid-1960s; of farmers interviewed who had grown coffee, most reported that they now neglected it or were eliminating it, since the labour costs of harvesting it were too high. In fact, bananas had been expanding at the expense of coffee ever since 1928, when a high proportion of the trees were destroyed or damaged by a particularly devastating hurricane (Lasserre 1961, 1:669).

A common practice, however, had been to interplant bananas and coffee. Both agronomically and economically, this had been regarded as a mutually advantageous combination. Since coffee was more deeply rooted, it took soil nutrients from a greater depth than did shallow-rooted bananas, and it benefited from the fertiliser applied to the bananas to such an extent that coffee yields per hectare were as great in mixed coffee-banana plantations as in purestand coffee plantations. The bananas benefited, in turn, from the reduction in weed growth resulting from the shade cast by the coffee trees. Bananas brought in year-round income, but banana prices often fluctuated dramatically. Coffee, on the other hand, was seasonal, but returns were dependable. Thus, in the late 1950s there were 3,000 hectares of mixed coffee and bananas in the southern banana-growing district of Guadeloupe (Lasserre 1961, 2:691–2).

By the mid-1960s, however, returns from coffee were said to be negligible, and with one exception, no fresh plantings were reported. Along the Grand Etang road in Trois Rivières, while at lower levels bananas and coffee were still a common combination, new banana plantations on freshly cleared land were entirely purestand, and even in the former coffee-growing strongholds of the leeward coast valleys, banana growers were reported to be cutting out coffee. On the other hand, smallholders who had little hope of entering the export banana industry often maintained their coffee, at least sufficiently to provide for home consumption. One medium-sized estate owner (with approximately 20 hectares) was actually eliminating bananas and planting purestand coffee, claiming that coffee could still be profitable if processed by the grower and that in the mixed banana-coffee combination the coffee flowers were often damaged when the bananas were sprayed to control leafspot.

In Martinique, coffee had never, in modern times, been as important a crop as in southern and leeward Guadeloupe. Conditions were less suitable for the prized Arabica variety, which could command premium prices in overseas markets. Only one farmer interviewed reported to me that he still harvested coffee, and his plantations had been seriously damaged by Hurricane Edith in 1963. Another farmer, in the Morne Rouge area south of Montagne Pelée, mentioned that his father had had several hectares of coffee, but it had been largely destroyed by Edith and was not worth harvesting from the trees that were left.

In general, then, coffee could not be said to have obstructed the spread of bananas in the French islands. Indeed, the coffee-banana combination, which was mutually advantageous for many years, might be said to have fostered the spread of bananas in the former coffee areas of southern Basse-Terre Guadeloupe.

For cacao, the situation was more straightforward. In Guadeloupe, certainly, the hurricane of 1928 provided an impetus for replacing cacao with bananas, since a cacao-banana combination was not regarded as complementary. By 1961, however, even in the former cacao-growing areas of southern Guadeloupe, farmers did not hesitate to tear out cacao trees in full bearing, so much more profitable was banana cultivation (Lasserre 1961, 2:692). In the late 1950s, cacao was still moderately important in some of the leeward coast valleys of Basse-Terre Guadeloupe; its relatively low labour costs were credited with its survival, often in out-of-the-way areas from which the extraction of bananas would have been difficult and costly (Lasserre 1961, 2:737). By the mid-1960s, however, it was generally regarded as not worth harvesting, since harvesting costs were said to exceed returns by about 300 percent.

In Martinique, a farmer in the heights of Lorrain mentioned that there had once been a good deal of cacao on his property, but it had long since been replaced by bananas. One other farmer had several hectares of cacao, mixed with coffee, but this cacao too had been severely damaged in 1963, and he did not feel that current prospects for the crop justified replacing it.

Since St Lucia and Dominica moved in a different economic orbit from the French islands, the relationship between the profitability of bananas and that of other tree crops was substantially different. Although banana prices were still above those received by Central American producers, they were little more than half the prices received by Martiniquan and Guadeloupean growers. Wages were also very much lower in St Lucia and Dominica, particularly when the social security contributions that employers in the French West Indies were required to pay were taken into account. This meant that for crops such as cacao, which received no special protection in either set of islands and was exported at world prices, the difference in profitability relative to bananas was far less in the Commonwealth islands and the point at which cacao ceased to be profitable at all was reached much later.

On the other hand, coconuts, which were protected by a regional oils and fats agreement, were guaranteed a market at renumerative prices in the Commonwealth islands, while they had apparently never been considered a worthwhile crop in the French ones (Barbados 1964). Citrus fruit production had also been encouraged at various times in the Commonwealth islands, either by tariff or quota preferences in the United Kingdom, and under favourable circumstances, citrus could be grown profitably. Although St Lucia and Dominica were on the same footing so far as cartels and tariffs were concerned, the manner and degree to which they had taken advantage of them differed.

In St Lucia, the sugar industry continued to provide a source of cash income in several districts until the 1960s, and apart from this, alternative opportunities for wage earning had been available in Castries since before the turn of the century and, on the United States air base in Vieux Fort, since the 1940s. Consequently, before the rise of the export banana industry, the emphasis, at least among smallholders, was upon subsistence food crops: a variety of scattered fruit trees and coffee were grown primarily for home consumption. The substitution of bananas for some of the provision crops was a simple choice with no long-term implications.

Coconuts were already a well-established crop in St Lucia by the 1950s; since they had low labour costs but provided relatively low returns per acre, they were favoured by larger estates, but most holdings recorded at least a few trees (West Indies Census of Agriculture 1968, 200; 1966–67 Survey). There is, however, no evidence that coconuts provided a real barrier to planting bananas; in fact, in some cases coconuts actually fostered the spread of bananas. On a parish-by-parish basis, the 1961 census figures show no obvious relationship, and certainly no clear negative correlation, between banana and coconut densities. However, census data relating to districts extending from watershed to coast are not, in this instance, a very effective tool for making such distinctions.

There was undoubtedly some differentiation between bananas and coconuts based on climate. Although there is a broad zone in which conditions are favourable for both crops, coconuts take longer to mature and start bearing at higher altitudes. On the other hand, coconuts can thrive in drier conditions than bananas will tolerate without irrigation. Thus, a pattern of high coconut densities allied with low banana densities was more likely to reflect inadequate rainfall for banana cultivation than the exclusion of bananas by an established tree crop. Moreover, if owners of large holdings extending across both low- and high-rainfall zones, or owners of two or more parcels of land located in different rainfall zones, show low overall densities for each crop, this should not be interpreted as the result of competition for space. Statistics might obscure the fact that each crop was planted at high density in the zone optimal for its cultivation.

Agronomically, bananas and coconuts were in fact regarded as a highly satisfactory crop combination. It is true that banana densities had to be reduced when the coconuts were young, but this was only a temporary phase; and the output, in nuts per tree, of the coconuts, was increased by up to 300 percent as they benefited from fertiliser applied to the bananas, although it would have been uneconomic to apply fertiliser to the coconuts by themselves. In areas where rainfall was marginal for banana growing without irrigation, farmers reported that although purestand banana plantations were not viable, they had planted bananas beneath their coconuts. The bananas barely repaid the cost of their cultivation, but the improved coconut yields made the operation well worthwhile. Among 48 banana growers that I interviewed in all parts of St Lucia in 1966, all of whom had at least a few coconut trees, not one reported having eliminated any coconuts in favour of bananas or having any intention of doing so.

Cacao was almost as widely grown as coconuts in St Lucia; more than three-quarters of the 1966 survey respondents had some trees. As a companion crop for bananas, however, cacao was far less satisfactory than coconuts. In the first place, while coconuts had different, though substantially overlapping, climatic requirements from bananas, the area in which cacao could be grown fell entirely within the zone most suitable for banana growing. Since the cacao remains a low, bushy tree, it can be interplanted with bananas only if the density of both crops, measured as trees or plants per hectare, is permanently reduced. Agronomically, there seems to be no particular advantage in intermingling the two crops; economically, as soon as one crop becomes markedly more profitable than the other, the farmer must consider eliminating the less profitable crop. The greater value-to-weight ratio of cacao and the more flexible time of harvesting must encourage its retention in more inaccessible areas, even when returns from cacao are somewhat low compared with returns from similar acreages of bananas. Moreover, because cacao takes four or five years to bear and will go on bearing for fifty years, while bananas produce harvestable fruit in nine months and may require replanting every two to five years, farmers are discouraged from converting too hastily from cacao to bananas. This explains why, even after several years of very low cacao prices, most St Lucian farmers still retained some cacao trees in the mid-1960s.

None of the farmers surveyed was planting or had any immediate intention of planting new cacao. Several said that they had neglected their cacao, or had harvested only a small proportion of the potential crop. It had proved almost impossible to find a market for the 1964 and 1965 crops (Raveneau 1967, personal communication). Several farmers said that they were cutting out their old cacao, although in most cases, this was old seedling cacao, up to fifty years old and more, and not recently planted, high-yielding clonal cacao. In general, there was little evidence that cacao provided a serious barrier to the expansion of banana cultivation. The greatest acreages in cacao were on medium-sized and large estates, which usually had sufficient unexploited land at the beginning of the period of banana expansion to take up the new crop without, initially, encroaching on the old.

The only district in which there was evidence of real competition between bananas and older-established tree crops was in the quarter of Soufrière. Table 4.7 (above), which is based on 1961 census figures, shows that in terms of stems of bananas cut per cultivated acre, Soufrière was well below average: 90 stems were cut in Soufrière, compared with an island average of 136.75 and a figure of 284 stems in the quarter of Dennery, with the highest number of stems per cultivated acre. Unlike the other quarters with below-average figures, Soufrière does not contain large areas with insufficient rainfall for banana cultivation. Consequently, while most of the other quarters with low banana densities also had low cacao and citrus densities, the cacao density in Soufrière was three times the island average and the citrus density almost double the island average. Indeed, almost two-thirds of the cultivated land-in-holdings in Soufrière must have been occupied by cacao and citrus: 60 percent by cacao alone. Thus, although by 1966 farmers interviewed in Soufrière, as elsewhere, said that they were cutting out cacao and replacing it with bananas, this switch was being carried on gradually: in one case, only part of the cacao was being removed so that bananas could be interplanted with the remainder.

If there were only a few localities in St Lucia in which established tree crops significantly reduced the amount of cultivable land-in-holdings available for banana cultivation, in Dominica the situation was much more complex. The rugged terrain had precluded the construction of even a single central sugar factory in the island, so that cane cultivation had been of little importance for more than 50 years before the development of the banana industry. What cane was grown, mainly in the drier districts, supplied a handful of distilleries producing rum for local consumption. The mainstay of Dominica's economy, at least for the first three decades of the twentieth century, had been limes. After lime cultivation had received setbacks from disease, hurricanes, and the collapse of the lime market in the 1920s, there had been some diversification into oranges, grapefruit, and coconuts. Cacao had been of moderate, but fairly widespread significance from the late nineteenth century onwards.

The distribution of various tree crops in Dominica before the post-war growth of the export banana industry had been strongly influenced by the state of communications. Until the late 1950s, only a small surrounding area was linked by motorable roads to Roseau, the capital and chief port. In the north, a road linked Portsmouth, the second port, with the coastal settlements of St Andrew's parish as far south as Hatton Garden. Everywhere else, produce had to be headed or carried on pack animals, or transported in canoes and lighters, which was easy along the sheltered leeward coast, but much more difficult from the windward coast settlements, exposed to the full force of the Atlantic rollers.

While it could not be claimed that the shortcomings of Dominica's communications infrastructure determined what was grown in various parts of the island, they certainly eliminated a number of options in those districts that were least well served. Thus grapefruit, for instance, a crop that seemed to have considerable potential in the 1930s and 1940s (especially after the Second World War when U.S. production was excluded from the United Kingdom market), was concentrated heavily in the parishes close to Roseau, the site of the island's only packing plant and consequently the sole exporting port. A few estate owners had planted grapefruit in the hinterland of Portsmouth, presumably hoping that increased production there would justify a second packing plant. By 1966, however the plant had not been built, and most of the northern production went to waste. By this time there were road links, albeit circuitous, with Roseau, but the telephone system between Roseau and the north had virtually broken down. This made it extremely difficult for northern growers to coordinate harvesting (which could take place only when the fruit was dry) and hire of lorries in Roseau to transport the fruit.

Oranges, on the other hand, being destined largely for local Caribbean markets, were shipped in barrels without special waxing or grading, and could therefore be exported from either Roseau or Portsmouth. They were widely grown in all leeward parishes, but were unimportant in the windward areas.

In districts more remote from exporting ports, only crops with a relatively high value-to-weight ratio and crops that could be carried undamaged over rugged terrain were worth considering. Thus, cacao, which underwent its initial processing locally, was grown in most areas with a suitable climate. Coconuts, which were processed to copra on the estates and, until 1966, exported from Portsmouth and Roseau in that form, were also widespread, but were particularly important in the northern windward areas. Bay was a major crop in the southern windward areas: its leaves could be distilled locally, and the resulting oil shipped in drums by canoe to Roseau.

A pattern of regional differentiation of established tree crops in Dominica was obvious in the late 1950s (Fentem 1960, 8). It was borne out by the information collected in the 1961 agricultural census, by my survey in 1966–7, and by a survey restricted to estate production carried out by McQuillan in 1967 (1968, 39–48). For such conspicuous variation in tree crop densities between different districts of Dominica to be apparent even when the regional division used was the parish gives strong support to the contention that accessibility largely determined the original establishment of the pattern. Parishes, after all, extend from coast to watershed and encompass a wide range of physiographic and climatic conditions. If my 1966–67 survey data for relative densities of bananas, citrus, and coconuts is tabulated on a parish-by-parish basis, it is quite consistent with the 1961 census pattern (Welch 1989, 201).

The effect of this pattern on the spread of export banana cultivation was twofold. Where there were mature coconuts, oranges, or grapefruit, it was usually possible to interplant bananas; sometimes this was actually beneficial to the established tree crops. Many farmers were anxious to take advantage of a crop that provided a dependable income all year round. On the other hand, since citrus and coconuts were seen as a long-term investment enhancing the value of a holding, there was rarely any question of removing them in favour of bananas, so that banana densities were limited, particularly in the main citrus areas, and opportunities for purestand plantings were restricted.

Among the 70 farmers that I interviewed in the 1966–7 survey in Dominica, 43 grew both bananas and citrus, and the relative densities of these crops suggest that the two were indeed negatively correlated. Farmers with a high density of one crop tended to have a low density of the other. It was evident from responses to the 1966–7 survey questionnaire (reproduced in the appendix) that farmers with established citrus had limited space available for banana planting. Several farmers had recently reduced banana densities as grapefruit and orange trees planted a few years earlier had matured. Others were still planting more citrus trees and intended to reduce or eliminate banana production as the citrus reached maturity. None of those interviewed, however, intended to expand banana plantings or increase their density at the expense of established lime, orange, or grapefruit trees.

Preexisting crop patterns, then, exerted some influence in all four islands on the rate at which banana-growing spread, its intensity in the mid-1960s, and its location within each of the islands. Nevertheless, while St Lucia's recent land use history had much more in common with Martinique's than with that of Dominica, the character and location of banana growing in St Lucia bore a much closer resemblance to that of its Commonwealth sister than that of its French neighbour.

Human Resources

Who actually cultivated the bananas - the owners themselves, the owners' unpaid relatives, or paid employees - was another potential source of interisland variation. The 1966–7 survey encompassed the full spectrum, from owners of smallholdings who did all the cultivation and harvesting themselves, with no assistance, paid or unpaid, to owners of large estates, resident in town or even overseas, whose land was both managed and cultivated by paid employees without any direct intervention by the owners.

In general, labour arrangements varied according to the size of the holding more than any other factor. In all four islands, owners of really small holdings performed all or most of the labour unaided, no matter what crop was grown. On slightly larger holdings, especially in the Commonwealth islands, unpaid family labour was often pressed into carrying harvested bananas to buying points, and paid labour was used occasionally, particularly for clearing land. In all four islands, there were respondents - but very few - who used exchange-labour groups (known in all four islands as *coup de main*). This practice had evidently been very widespread when most small farmers grew mainly subsistence crops and had hardly any cash income, but it seemed to have largely gone out of favour as the banana industry had drawn small farmers into the cash economy (Romalis 1968, 172).

Most of the farmers with medium-sized holdings (over 4 hectares) employed paid labour, although often very erratically, according to need and availability. Since they were often unable to afford to maintain a stable labour force, they were liable to have to pay well above minimum wage rates to the workers they did employ. Payment by the task rather than by the day was also quite common on medium-sized holdings.

On larger estates over 20 hectares, paid labour, generally paid by the day, was the norm. Some estates kept an extremely stable labour force and managed to organise their workload so that they had no need for extra workers to carry bananas to the roadside, even though bananas could be harvested in the Commonwealth islands only on the day before the weekly call of the banana boat. (In the French islands, banana boats called more frequently, so that periods of harvesting were less restricted.) A stable labour force was easier to maintain if a second major crop, less exacting than bananas - coconuts, for instance - was also grown. On all four islands, however, even on estates of 20 hectares or more, the size of the labour force often varied over time by 100 percent or more, although there was usually a nucleus of full-time workers.

Only four of the estates I visited in 1966-67, two in St Lucia and two in Guadeloupe, were run by managers rather than by owners.

Holding size was undoubtedly of greater significance than any purely local factors in determining the nature of the labour force. The question remains to be answered, however, whether this general pattern was modified to any degree by the kind of crops that were grown. It was asserted in all the islands, for instance, that *colonage*, or sharecropping, was rarely encountered in the banana industry, although it had been common in the cultivation of cane, and indeed, none of the banana growers I interviewed in 1966 had a conventional sharecropping agreement with a landlord/landowner. Straightforward cash rental was the normal rule. On the other hand, in the Commonwealth islands but not in the French ones, I encountered a variety of ad hoc arrangements in which labour was traded for a share of the produce: in most cases, bananas. In Dominica, farmers with exceedingly remote holdings sometimes offered a share - as much as two-fifths - to anyone who would assist in carrying out stems of bananas to distant buying points. Estate owners who had insufficient capital to cultivate their land directly sometimes permitted farmers with insufficient land to grow bananas on estate land between permanent tree crops such as coconuts and citrus. Sometimes these farmers were expected to plant the tree crops themselves, at an agreed spacing; sometimes their obligation extended only to keeping the land between the tree crops free of weeds. The landowner benefited chiefly from the fertiliser applied to the bananas, which was liable also to benefit the deeper-rooted tree crops belonging to him.

There was considerable interisland variation in the number of labourers employed per hectare, particularly on larger estates (Tables 4.8 and 4.9). This may simply have reflected intensity of cultivation, on the one hand (for instance, planting densities were generally higher in St Lucia than in Dominica), and the degree to which cultivation had been mechanised (by the use of weedicides, mechanical ploughing and motor transport), on the other. The labour force was, after all, drawn from persons of very similar ethnic and socioeconomic background in all four islands. Indeed, it was alleged that many of the workers in Guadeloupe's banana industry were illegal immigrants from Dominica.

One factor that was not common to all four islands, however, was the incidence of bilharzia, which was absent in Martinique and Dominica, was said to occur in some areas of Guadeloupe, and was believed to be widespread in St Lucia (Monplaisir 1966, personal communication). The incidence of bilharzia was particularly high in the former sugar valleys, whose nearly level floors were crisscrossed by slow-flowing drainage ditches: Richefond, near the old Dennery factory, recorded an infection rate of 50 percent in 1968, and in 1970, 91 percent of its inhabitants in the 15 to 19 age group tested positive for the disease (Jordan 1985, 38, 53, 82). Because bilharzia was so debilitating, it may have had a significant impact on the productivity of affected St Lucians and may thus have been a factor in the higher number of workers employed per hectare in St Lucia.

A number of farmers in each of the islands cited difficulty in obtaining an adequate labour supply as an impediment to the optimal exploitation of their holdings. The problem varied considerably from island to island, however, and even within individual islands, the availability of labour evidently varied markedly from district to district.

In Guadeloupe, a labour shortage was cited as a problem in only a few isolated cases. In Deshaies, in northern leeward Basse-Terre Guadeloupe, some respondents claimed that the difficulty of obtaining labour restricted the area of cultivation. Young people, it

Table 4.8
Average labour force, by holding-size group, 1966–67 Survey

	Holding-size group (ha)				
	0–	*1–*	*4–*	*20–*	*40+*
Martinique	–	npl	4	12	65
Guadeloupe	npl	npl	7	10	–
St Lucia	npl	1	5	17	75
Dominica	npl	<1	3	6	34

Note: npl = no paid labour.

was said, did not like to work on the land. Elsewhere, however, a shortage of labour was not even mentioned as a problem, except by one farmer in the heights of Capesterre who claimed in a general way that while the owners of large holdings experienced no difficulty, smallholders sometimes had trouble finding labour, and usually paid people a little extra. They did not, however, make social security payments on their employees' behalf. Even in a situation in which there was a large labour surplus, it would be understandable that the offer of only occasional employment with no social security benefits might not prove attractive to someone with other means of subsistence.

Indeed, most of the evidence seemed to suggest that there was an abundant supply of labour in most of Guadeloupe. It was reported that unions for agricultural labourers had made very little headway, since employers had implied that they would not hire union members. Many banana growers simply refused to pay the social security contributions that they were required to make on behalf of their workers; some were said to owe millions of francs. Such a situation could not have persisted had there been any difficulty in obtaining labour. The employers' position was said to be further strengthened, moreover, by the presence of a large pool of Dominican immigrants, most of them illegal and in no position to insist that social security payments should be made on their behalf. I was informed that there were as many as 15,000 Dominicans working in the banana plantations, although there was no way of verifying this statement, which was probably an exaggeration. The fact that it was possible to increase sugar output from 117,000 tonnes in 1958 to 168,000 tonnes in 1965 indicates the relatively abundant labour supply in Guadeloupe at this period. Many Dominicans were said to come specially for the cane harvest, and the failure of

Table 4.9
Average paid labour force by holding-size group, 1961 Census

	Holding-size group, in acres (hectares)								
	0–	*1–*	*5–*	*10 (4–)*	*25–*	*50– (20–)*	*100– (40+)*	*200–*	*500+*
St Lucia	0.054	0.454	1.462	2.774	4.142	6.762	11.605	47.0	186.789
	(	0.426	)	(3.106	)	(6.762)	(	61.567	)
Dominica	0.086	0.351	0.558	1.758	4.893	6.154	11.222	25.621	72.958
	(	0.330	)	(2.364	)	(6.154)	(	31.989	)

Source: West Indies Census of Agriculture, 1961 (1968).

Guadeloupean workers to organise left them powerless to prevent this incursion.

In only one instance was it suggested that labour problems had had some negative effect on the expansion of the banana industry. Sugar companies were said to have abandoned bananas and reverted to growing only cane on factory land in northeastern Basse-Terre Guadeloupe, partly because when both crops were grown, it was hard to get workers to work in the cane fields, since cane cutting was much more unpleasant than tending bananas. Moreover, since bananas required 250 work-days per hectare per annum, as against only 140 days for cane, the conversion of large acreages from cane to bananas might have created local labour shortages.

In Martinique in 1966 and 1967 there was a much greater preoccupation with the labour supply than in Guadeloupe. Shortages were regarded as particularly critical in the cane industry; officers of the *services agricoles* told me that after the cane harvest had been in progress for a couple of months, absenteeism became an increasingly serious problem extending the harvest far beyond the period of highest sucrose content. The unions, however, would not permit this labour deficit to be made up by imported labour, and the unions, in Martinique, were extremely powerful. They were political rather than trade unions, and encompassed not only agricultural labourers but workers in all types of occupations, rural and urban. The unions strongly resisted attempts to alleviate the labour shortage by introducing new methods of cultivation and some degree of mechanisation, because they felt, understandably, that these innovations might reduce the demand for labour and weaken their members' bargaining position. The agricultural labour shortage was of quite recent origin. In 1963, which was the peak year for sugar production, the labour supply had been adequate to produce 90,000 tonnes of sugar. In 1966, it had been barely adequate to produce 64,000 tonnes. Part of the scarcity was believed to have been brought about by the conversion of a substantial area, estimated at 1,500 hectares, of cane land to banana plantations, which required much more labour per hectare (*La Banane* 1967, 1:14). It was also suggested that there was an accelerating rural exodus; young people in particular were selling any land they had in order to buy taxis and move to town (Emélie 1967, personal communication). Whatever the cause, the future of the cane industry was said to be in jeopardy, since shortages had driven up wages much more rapidly than the price received by the sugar producers had increased, and several of Martinique's less profitable sugar factories were expected to close.

Despite the labour crisis in the sugar industry, farmers in the 1966–67 survey revealed considerable regional variations in the labour market. The greatest concern over labour shortages was expressed by farmers in the central part of the island, in St Joseph and Gros Morne. Here it was claimed that there were "just a few old people" left prepared to do agricultural work, and one farmer in Gros Morne told me he had to pay a man twenty-five francs (WI$12) for a four-hour working day, and had had to recruit him from as far away as Ste Marie. Several farmers, responding to a perceived labour shortage, said they were concentrating on livestock production, since livestock required far less labour than either cane or banana production. For example, two smallholders in Morne Rouge (in central-northern Martinique) remarked that because they had had difficulty finding workers and would have had to depend on hired labour at well over the minimum wage, they had decided to concentrate on livestock and not to take up banana production, even though it was potentially profitable. Near St Esprit in central-southern Martinique, the owner of a medium-sized holding with 10 hectares of bananas and 17 hectares of pasture said that because of labour problems, he intended to give up bananas and move entirely to livestock production. He had ten employees working full time on his banana cultivation and a further ten employed occasionally for cutting, heading, and packing. He reckoned that with the whole property in pasture, a labour force of three or four would be adequate, with occasional help for fencing, for instance.

Although in some areas labour was felt to be so scarce that employers had to pay premium rates or adopt less labour-intensive forms of land use, in other areas labour was not regarded as a problem. Despite great seasonal fluctuations in labour requirements near Le Prêcheur, for instance, on the western slopes of Montagne Pelée, small farmers reported no difficulty in obtaining workers for fifteen francs (WI$7) a day, little more than the minimum wage. Social security contributions, which would have amounted to an extra 45 percent, were generally ignored. In Lorrain and Morne-Vert, both northern communities fairly remote from Fort-de-France, labour shortages were never mentioned as a problem.

It is hard to generalise about the effect of inadequate or poorly distributed labour supplies on agricultural land use in general, and the banana industry in particular, in Martinique in the mid-1960s. To some extent, a vicious circle had been created: the conversion of cane lands to banana cultivation had absorbed all surplus labour, so that agricultural workers could eschew unpleasant seasonal work in the cane fields and demand higher wages, which the banana industry was profitable enough to pay. The sugar industry could not support higher wages, so landowners were obliged to close sugar factories and convert more land to bananas, thereby aggravating the labour shortage. Even in areas where, for climatic reasons, banana cultivation was impossible, the high wage levels commanded by banana workers elsewhere had tended to drive up wages, creating difficulties for both the cane and livestock industries. On the other hand, for a certain class of farmers, the shortage and high cost of labour in the banana-growing regions were actually instrumental in keeping or driving them out of banana production. The low labour requirements of livestock rearing and dairy farming, for instance, made them an attractive option even in areas in which substantially higher profits per hectare could theoretically have been obtained from banana production.

The problem of labour scarcity was most acute in areas readily accessible to Fort-de-France and was most strongly felt by medium and small-scale farmers. They told me that the owners of large estates had no real problem recruiting labour, for a variety of reasons, from the fact that, in the banana industry at least, large-scale growers could offer steady employment and assured social security contributions, to the fact that growers traditionally dispensed paternalistic favours that made their workers beholden to them. Scarcity of labour was attributed to such causes as the movement of young workers, especially, to Fort-de-France and the possibility, for parents of large families, of drawing a reasonable income from family allowances after putting in the requisite minimum period of employment each year. Interestingly, no one cited emigration to metropolitan France as a cause, although it was relatively easy to migrate at this period.

In St Lucia, as in Martinique, the difficulty of finding an adequate labour supply was often cited as a problem, but its seriousness varied from one district to another. Especially along the leeward coast, from Soufrière northwards, the labour shortage was said to be acute. In some cases it actually limited the area that owners of medium-sized holdings were able to cultivate. One Canaries estate owner said that he needed fifteen workers but could only get four or five. It was claimed that emigration to the United Kingdom had decimated the labour supply and that when it became difficult to emigrate to Britain, workers migrated seasonally to the U.S. Virgin Island of St. Croix. In Anse-la-Raye, it was said that while female labour was available, most of the male labour force preferred fishing to agricultural work.

Elsewhere, in several of the windward valleys, such as Errard and Mahaut, and at Millet in the centre of the island, labour was in such short supply that workers had to be recruited from other districts and boarded by the week by their employers. The chief source of this migrant labour was the Choiseul-Laborie area of southwestern St Lucia, where much of the agricultural land was badly eroded and the rainfall was inadequate for successful banana cultivation. In other districts, such as the Troumassée-Mahaut area in the east, farmers remarked that it was precisely because there were so many banana growers in the district that it was difficult to obtain labour.

As in Martinique, owners of small and medium-sized holdings claimed that it was easier for owners of large estates to maintain an adequate work force, perhaps because large estates often provided transport to and from the workplace. However, one estate owner pointed out that in addition to providing easier working conditions, he made sure that he provided steady employment: peasant farmers, who required only occasional assistance, had to pay substantially higher rates.

The fact that labour could in most cases be obtained if premium rates were paid suggests that there was a large body of agricultural workers who preferred to subsist on their smallholdings unless offered a worthwhile financial inducement to work elsewhere. Thus, when farmers claimed that they were unable to extend their cultivation or exploit their land to its full capacity, it is possible that this was only because the land in question was too marginal to exploit profitably with labour paid above the minimum rate. On the other hand, if greater financial inducements had been offered, workers might have been drawn off their own tiny holdings, bringing a decline in banana production by this sector. Thus, the pattern of production might have been changed, but without much change in the overall volume.

In Dominica, as in the other islands, labour was in short supply in some areas, while other areas evidently had a surplus. Overall, however, the shortage appeared to be more acute and more widespread in Dominica than in the other islands. This shortage was hardly surprising, since, even though Dominica was by far the least densely populated of the four, a substantial portion of the work force had emigrated to the United Kingdom: people who were young to middle-aged in the mid-1960s. Younger Dominicans were emigrating to the Virgin Islands. Most young people, it was said, preferred almost any occupation to agriculture. Trades such as building and motor mechanics were favoured, and government jobs were sought after because they provided paid holidays, sickness benefits, and pensions. Locally, fishing was more attractive than farm work, especially along the leeward coast. Moreover, because most of the rural population had some land of their own, they were not forced to work for other people to survive.

The labour shortage in Dominica was further aggravated by the inadequate motorable roads: stems of harvested bananas often had to be headed several miles from smallholders' properties. Since harvesting could only take place within the forty-eight hours before the loading of the banana boats, all fruit had to be headed out on one or two days a week, and carriers could command premium rates on those days, earning enough that it was hardly worth their while to work for lower rates on other days.

Only one area of Dominica actually had a labour surplus in the mid-1960s: the district of Grand Bay, a large, spread-out village on the south coast, where there was some pressure on the land, and workers were prepared to work on estates as far away as Portsmouth. Labour for the Castle Bruce–Rosalie area in eastern Dominica was also recruited from Grand Bay. Elsewhere, the only place in which the labour supply was felt to be even satisfactory was in the north coast village of Calibishie. In every other area, one or two respondents said labour was a problem, albeit one of varying severity.

In the southwest, owners of large estates could maintain an adequate labour force provided that they offered steady employment; otherwise, they might be obliged to send lorries to pick up workers from considerable distances. Smallholders, who could offer neither steady employment nor free transportation to and from work, had to offer well above the minimum rates to induce anyone to work for them.

In the northwest and in the east from La Plaine northwards to Woodford Hill, the labour problem was considered acute. In the village of Colihaut, for instance, it was said that bananas often wasted in the fields because there were not enough carriers, and the owner of a Point Ronde estate said that while he needed ten workers, he had been unable to find more than four. In Marigot, Wesley, and Woodford Hill, in the northeast, small farmers complained that they could not always get their fruit to the buying point, and they claimed that even when they offered premium rates, people preferred to work at Woodford Hill and Melville Hall, large estates belonging to Geest and the Commonwealth Development Corporation (CDC). They surmised that this was because the large estates were more accessible, and the workers there were less closely supervised. It was acknowledged, too, that the large estates did offer steadier and more reliable employment. Even so, the large estates complained that a serious shortage of workers was inhibiting them from cultivating the estates as efficiently as they would have liked. At the

CDC's Melville Hall, there were fields of coconuts that could have been interplanted with bananas, had sufficient labour been available, while Geest's Woodford Hill was cultivated rather extensively, in patches, to spread the risks of wind damage, since not enough workers could be recruited to cultivate the estate intensively.

In three of the four islands, then, the pattern and, in some cases, the intensity of banana cultivation had been modified by shortages of labour, both local and island-wide. To some extent, the high labour demands of banana cultivation had created this labour deficit. It was less acute, often nonexistent, in areas unsuited to banana cultivation. As in the case of preexisting land use patterns, however, islands with similar labour market characteristics did not necessarily share similar patterns of banana cultivation.

CONCLUSION

A careful examination of the distribution of export banana cultivation in these four Eastern Caribbean islands in the mid-1960s fails to reveal any consistent relationships either with primary physical factors such as relief, climate, or soils, or with elements of the island landscapes that might have been strongly influenced by physical factors: infrastructure, preexisting land use, and the distribution of the potential work force. While there were interisland variations in many of these factors, there was no sharp dichotomy between French and Commonwealth islands. Nevertheless the most striking difference in the distribution of banana cultivation was between concentrated, aggregated cultivation in the two French islands and extensive, widely dispersed cultivation in the two Commonwealth islands. In the following chapter, the analysis of the ways in which Eastern Caribbean bananas were cultivated and brought to market only serves to emphasise the division.

5 Methods of Production and Disposal

One of the most remarkable features of banana production in the Eastern Caribbean in the 1960s was that in different islands, the same fruit, destined for comparable metropolitan markets, was produced not only in dissimilar locations and by different types of growers but using widely varying methods of cultivation and disposal. Even within a single island, variations might be substantial. Between the most sophisticated farming operations in the French islands and the most rudimentary ones in the Commonwealth islands, the gulf was immense. In this chapter, I shall describe banana cultivation in its least and most intensive forms and begin to consider why such widely divergent farming systems found favour among different sectors of the community. I shall also trace, in broad outline, the radically different paths by which harvested fruit was transferred from field to market in different islands.

It was by drawing upon case studies of individual farmers in a variety of circumstances that I was able to build a composite picture of the way in which the banana industry operated (Welch 1989, appendix B). The case studies were of farmers who were particularly forthcoming and informative when I interviewed them in the course of the 1966–67 survey. They shed much light on the reasons for land use decisions that to a supervicial observer seemed eccentric, and they often provided a rationale for actions patently at variance with the received opinions of the "experts."

CULTIVATION

Under favourable conditions bananas may be cultivated with some success with a minimal input of cash or sophisticated capital equipment. In Dominica in the 1960s, it was not unusual for farmers squatting on Crown lands to grow bananas, practising a form of shifting agriculture. Frequently, cultivation was on extremely steep slopes, partly *faute de mieux,* but also it was said that some farmers actually preferred such terrain because for a few years nutrients were continually washed down from higher levels, so that soil exhaustion was less rapid. Also, it was not necessary to stoop and bend when cultivating and weeding such land.

Clearance, whether of virgin or secondary forest, was by hand and normally consisted of felling large trees and leaving them to rot in situ, while other cleared vegetation might be burnt. The farmer usually planted whatever variety of exportable banana was most readily available. Lacatan was the most common variety. Often, different types of suckers would be mixed with "bullheads" (the corm of a plant that had already fruited) in the same field. Other crops, generally ground provisions, might be planted between the bananas.

Once the bananas were established, the farmer would take whatever steps were necessary to prevent them from being overwhelmed by weeds, provided the price of bananas made this worthwhile. Suckers springing from the plant mat would be allowed to proliferate unchecked and the crop would probably be sprayed regularly to control leafspot only if the new plantings were in an area already containing an appreciable number of bananas.

Under such conditions, many plants would fail to produce bunches, and others would give unmarketable fruit, either because of scarring or because the stem was below the acceptable weight. Harvested bunches would be headed out along steep and muddy footpaths, often for several miles, to the nearest buying point, where they might still be rejected. Some farmers with distant holdings cut stems more than 24 hours before the buying period opened and then recut them to try to make them appear fresher than they were.

Needless to say, marketable yields under these conditions were extremely low, often less than two tons per hectare. Fields were not systematically replanted at regular intervals; plants that blew down might be replaced, but after a few years, when the soil was exhausted, such plantations were abandoned and the farmer might move on to establish new banana fields elsewhere. Such shifting cultivation was not restricted to Crown lands. Farmers often rented small plots on uncultivated estate land and subjected them to a similar cycle of depletion and abandonment.

While such methods produced very meagre results and may have inflicted serious long-term damage on the land, they required very little cash outlay by the farmers who, unless they attributed a cash value to their own labour, might consider any receipts from banana sales as pure profit. There was virtually no risk of incurring any financial loss.

At the opposite extreme, some farmers felt it worthwhile to invest whatever capital and labour were necessary to ensure the maximum possible annual yield per hectare on their land. Very often, these farmers occupied lowlands and valleys that had long been cleared and cultivated, but where necessary, clearance was carried out with power saws and heavy machinery for tearing out old roots. In Dominica, land clearance was reported to cost about WI$100 per hectare for labour alone; in Guadeloupe, a figure equivalent to WI$1,200 was cited. Drains were dug across cleared land, where necessary, and steeper slopes were contoured or terraced. Where pan formations impeded soil drainage, the subsoil might be ploughed to break up the hardpan.

Particularly, but not exclusively, in the French islands, farmers interested in maximizing cash profits per unit of land planted purestand bananas at the maximum recommended density, which varied according to altitude. Below 250 metres above sea level, 2,500 mats per hectare was the favoured maximum. Preferred varieties of planting material were Robusta (Poyo) and Giant Cavendish (Grande Naine), the latter mainly in Martinique. Since it was desirable that all the plants in a field should be of the same size and develop at the same rate, uniform planting material was used; bullheads were preferred. They were planted in deep holes, and fertiliser was applied at planting and at regular, specified intervals thereafter. The type of fertiliser used depended on local soil conditions, but ideally, at least three tons per hectare per year were applied. Windbreaks were planted where necessary at appropriate intervals, and where nematodes and borers were a problem, appropriate chemical controls were used. Planting time was chosen, where possible, to ensure that the fruit could be harvested during the period of peak demand and highest prices, the length of time required to produce harvestable bunches varying from about nine months at near sea level to eighteen months or more at an altitude of 600 metres.

Once the plantation was established, weeds were controlled either chemically or by hoeing and cutlassing, and most suckers were removed from the mat shortly after they appeared, although one "follower" was left to develop five months or so after the initial planting, to provide a second harvest about six months after the first. Leafspot control was carried out at regular intervals, sometimes as frequently as once every eleven days in high-rainfall areas, often by aerial sprayplane. Where there was a risk of lengthy dry periods, plantations were irrigated. Maturing bunches were propped where necessary to reduce losses through falling and covered in blue polythene "sleeves" to prevent scarring. At time of harvesting, bunches were carried not more than 200 to 300 metres to feeder roads or narrow gauge railways and transported by truck or rail to packing stations. After three to six harvests, or as soon as yields started to decline, fields were uprooted and replanted, or if nematode infestation was a problem, left fallow for some months before being replanted.

Employing such techniques, some farmers achieved annual yields of over 40 tonnes per hectare. On the other hand, some farmers claimed to adhere to all, or nearly all, of these practices, but obtained much lower yields, while others obtained quite high yields with a much less rigorous application of prescribed practices.

If by conscientiously following prescribed practices, it was possible to obtain yields ten or even twenty times greater than those achieved by farmers who did not make the requisite investments of labour and capital, why, in St Lucia and Dominica especially (where average yields in 1966 were only 6 and 3 tons per hectare respectively, compared with 25 and 20 tonnes in Martinique and Guadeloupe), did not more farmers take the steps necessary to increase their yields per hectare?

One possibility is that they were simply unaware of the techniques that might be employed to produce better results. While this may have been so in a few cases, it seems unlikely to have been a widespread phenomenon. Bananas had been grown commercially in both islands for over fifteen years, and both government agricultural extension workers and growers' associations had carried on campaigns more or less continuously to apprise farmers of improved techniques of cultivation. In particular, the importance of fertiliser was emphasized through various schemes involving credit, subsidy, or even, in the wake of hurricanes, free distribution of nitrogen-phosphorus-potassium (NPK) fertilisers. It is therefore hardly conceivable that any farmers were unaware of the value agricultural experts placed on fertiliser as a means of sustaining or increasing yields. And yet, except perhaps when it was free, many failed to use it, or used only insignificant amounts. I encountered farmers who could recite the entire range of techniques advocated by extension officers and the precise quantities of fertiliser recommended, but who admitted to yields of only one ton per hectare. They followed none of the prescribed procedures, claiming that they could not afford to do so.

It was true that sources of credit were limited, particularly for farmers who did not own the land they farmed and thus had no collateral. Nevertheless, many of the farmers interviewed could have obtained loans for agricultural inputs, had they so desired. The fact was that for a variety of reasons, they did not consider the risk of indebtedness worth taking.

In the first place, many small farmers in St Lucia and Dominica had holdings a mile or more from the nearest motorable road. Several already had considerable difficulty recruiting enough labour to carry their crop to the road within the narrowly restricted cutting period, and an increase in yields would have presented insurmountable problems. Even if labour could have been found, the wage demanded for carrying out the augmented crop might well have been so high that the additional receipts would have been less than the extra fertiliser and labour costs.

While some of the lowest yields were recorded on some of the remotest holdings, there were other instances where remoteness could not explain low yields. Despite the repeated assertions of agricultural experts that bananas were best grown as a purestand crop and that the drawbacks of mixed cultivation more than countered its advantages, most small farmers in St Lucia and Dominica, and indeed many medium- and large-scale farmers, still grew bananas mainly in combination with other crops, primarily provisions in the case of smallholders and tree crops in the case of larger landowners.

So far as the mixed cultivation of bananas and provision crops was concerned, because there are no comparative-cost surveys, it is hard to say whether net returns per hectare would have been greater if provisions had been grown on a separate part of the holding, rather than in combination with bananas. Agricultural experts felt that it was wasteful to permit fertiliser intended for bananas to be shared by the interspersed provisions, but farmers often claimed that the increased yields from provisions justified growing the two crops together, even if banana yields were reduced. (Evidently nobody thought it worthwhile to buy chemical fertiliser for provision crops alone.) As I mentioned in the previous chapter, however, some St Lucian farmers did remark in 1966 that as a result of growing provisions in fertilised banana fields, production of, for instance, dasheen had risen to a point where its market price had been significantly depressed. The officers of the banana growers' associations certainly did not favour mixed cropping, in part because they felt it diverted fertiliser (in some cases supplied at subsidised rates) from the specific crops it was intended to benefit, but mainly because it greatly increased the area that had to be sprayed for leafspot. Spraying was carried out by the associations and financed by a cess, or levy, collected from growers on the poundage of bananas they produced rather than on the area they had that required spraying.

While the mixed cultivation of bananas and tree crops also increased the cost of leafspot control, it was viewed in a somewhat less negative light by agricultural experts. By the mid-1960s, however, because of low coffee prices, there was very little mixed cropping by export banana growers in either of the French islands, which certainly accounts for some of the discrepancy in yields per hectare between the Commonwealth islands and their French neighbours.

While it was conventional wisdom that approved agricultural practices would significantly improve yields of marketable bananas, it was almost an article of faith among those most influential in the industry, the officers of the agricultural departments and banana growers' associations, that chemical fertilisers were the main key to increased production. I was told that the distribution of subsidised fertiliser in Dominica in 1964 (after extensive damage to bananas as a result of Hurricane Edith which passed directly across neighbouring Martinique in September 1963) was responsible for an increase in average stem weights in the following year and an increase in production generally. Conversely the decline in fertiliser use once it was no longer subsidised was held responsible for the drop in production in both Commonwealth islands in 1966. A careful investigation of the facts, however, suggests that the relationship between yields and fertiliser use was not entirely simple and straightforward.

To begin with, positive island-wide correlations between fertiliser use and mean stem weight are hard to establish. Mean stem weights were not recorded in the French islands, where bananas were boxed for export. There are annual records for the Commonwealth islands for mean stem weights of exported bananas, but when supplies were short the minimum acceptable stem weight was sometimes reduced from the usual 18 pounds to as low as 16 pounds. Consequently, it is impossible to determine the actual relationship between fertiliser use and variations in mean stem weight.

On the other hand, when annual yields per hectare of exported bananas in Dominica between 1961 and 1968 are compared year by year with half the sum of fertiliser used per hectare for the export year and the preceding year, the two factors show an extremely strong positive correlation ($r = 0.9103336$, with less than a 1 percent chance that this result was accidental). Even this correlation should be treated with some caution, however, since it assumes that the acreage figures for the years in question are accurate, or at least bear a constant relationship to the real figures. (The 1966 acreage given in the Dominica Banana Growers' Association annual report for 1968 (DBGA 1969) is less than half the more carefully researched figure recorded by Momsen (1969) for the same year.)

I assessed the relationship between yields and fertiliser use per hectare reported by farmers interviewed in 1966 for Dominica and St Lucia individually and for Martinique and Guadeloupe together, since the samples were rather small in these last two islands. In the case of Dominica, the correlation coefficient r was 0.45618, significant at the 1 percent level; for St Lucia $r = 0.5809532$, significant at the 0.1 percent level; and for Martinique and Guadeloupe $r = 0.7289659$, significant at the 4 percent level.

I made the same calculation for 16 farms surveyed in St Lucia in 1965 for the UWI-ISER Banana Costing Survey (Persaud 1965). In this case, I plotted total purchased inputs rather than fertiliser alone against yields and found that $r = 0.54861$, significant at the 4 percent level. However, if one example in which both inputs and yields were exceptionally high is removed from the sample, then for the remaining fifteen farms, r equals only 0.3444672, which is not significant even at the 10 percent level.

Regression lines plotting fertiliser use per hectare (x) against yields (y) are very similar for Dominica and St Lucia and show a clear positive correlation in each case (Figure 5.1), although not nearly as strong as that for the French islands (Figure 5.2). For the Commonwealth islands, at 1966 figures, every WI$100 invested in fertiliser should have produced, on average, an additional 2.2 to 2.3 tons of bananas per hectare. For the French islands, however, every WI$100 invested in fertiliser should have yielded an additional 4 tons of fruit per hectare.

Such a discrepancy requires explanation. Perhaps fertiliser was more effective in Martinique and Guadeloupe because farmers followed recommended agricultural practices more conscientiously. Perhaps, too, the fact that banana growing in the French islands was largely restricted to the better agricultural land accounted for

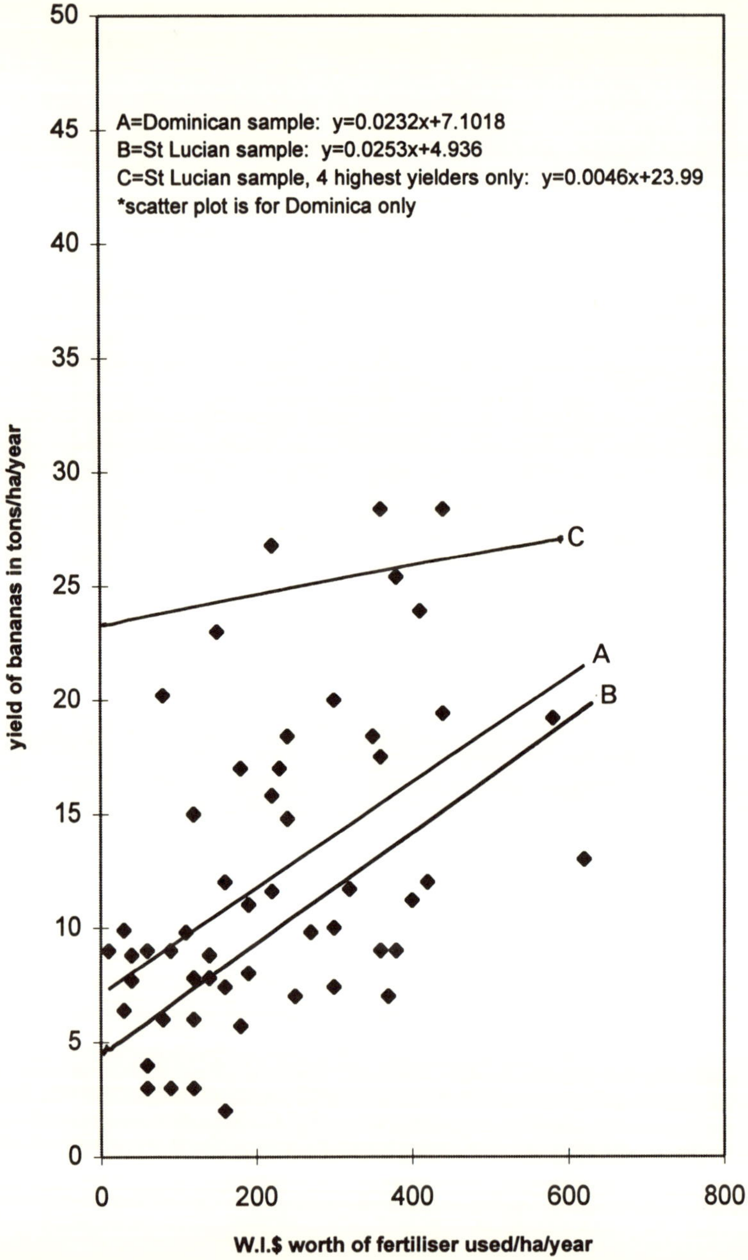

Figure 5.1
Dominica and St Lucia, 1966–67 Survey data: Regression lines for banana yields in relation to fertiliser use per hectare

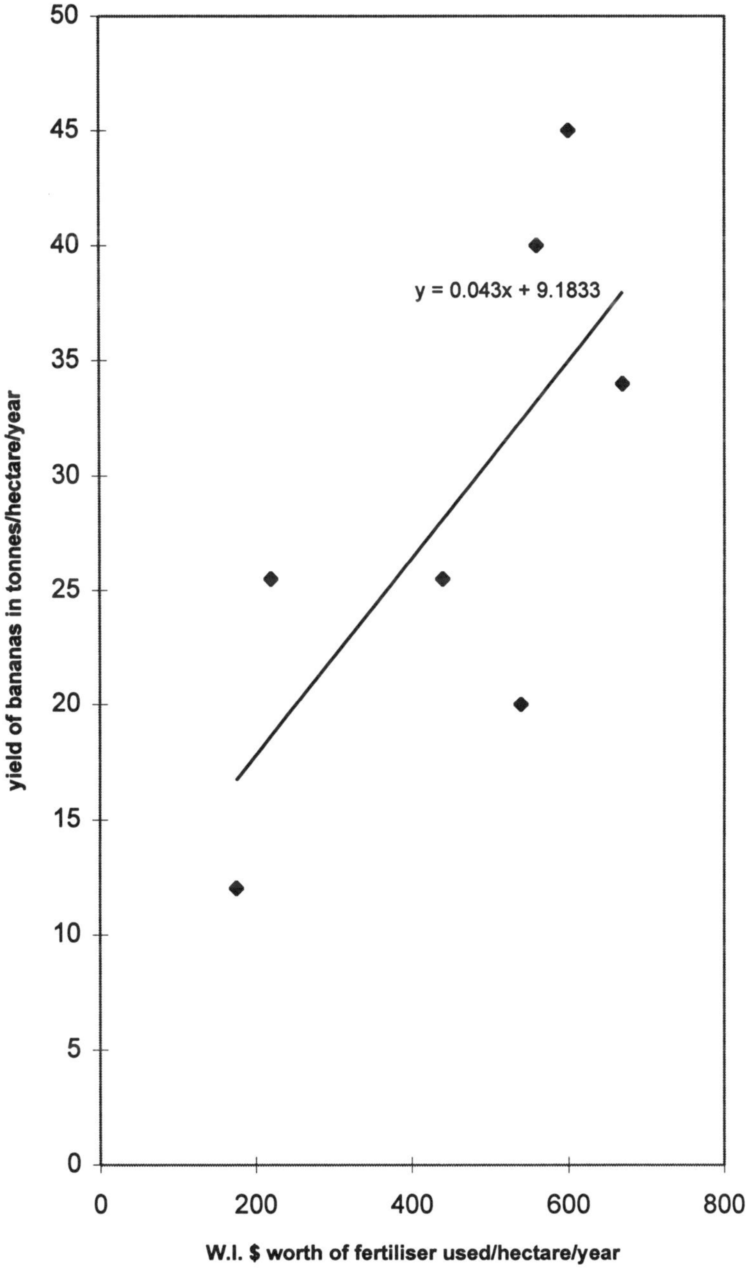

Figure 5.2
Guadeloupe and Martinique, 1966–67 Survey data: Regression line for banana yields in relation to fertiliser use per hectare

the stronger response to the fertiliser applied. The most likely explanation, however, lies in the prevalence of mixed cropping in Dominica and St Lucia. The actual density of bananas on most of the holdings surveyed in the Commonwealth islands may have been half that on the French islands, and much of the effect of the fertiliser may have been diverted to improving yields of interplanted provisions, coconuts, or citrus.

Whatever the cause, the difference was likely to be self-perpetuating, especially when the market was saturated and there was little prospect of selling much more fruit. Even if a St Lucian or Dominican farmer was convinced by statistical evidence that an extra WI$100 worth of fertiliser per hectare would be likely to yield an additional 2.25 tons of fruit, worth approximately WI$200, he or she might well conclude that this increase was inadequate to cover the addditional expense of harvesting the increased yield.

If expanding total production was not desirable in 1966, would it not have paid farmers to try to grow the same quantity of fruit on a smaller area, with more intensive fertiliser use producing greater yields per hectare, a smaller area to be weeded, and more land left available for alternative crops? This might have been an attractive proposition if the relationship between fertiliser use and yields had been obvious and constant, but in the Commonwealth islands, and especially Dominica, it was by no means obvious. Statistically, a positive relationship can be discerned, but the scatter of points on the graph is so great that any individual farmer might have easily assumed that fertiliser application had an almost random effect on yields. In Martinique and Guadeloupe, all farmers spending WI$500 or more per hectare on fertiliser achieved yields of 20 tons or more; but in both Dominica and St Lucia there were farmers who claimed to spend WI$500 per hectare on fertiliser, and yet they achieved yields far lower than 20 tons, in some cases only 10 tons per hectare. On the other hand, there were several farmers in Dominica who claimed to be achieving yields of over 20 tons per hectare with a fertiliser input of less than WI$200.

To sum up, while there is little doubt that greater use of fertiliser would, overall, have produced higher yields in the Commonwealth islands, yields would not necessarily have reached the levels achieved in the French Islands. In any case, there were neither markets nor labour to deal with much larger harvests. Moreover, while every additional WI$100 expended on fertiliser in the Commonwealth islands yielded an average of 2.25 tons of bananas, with a value to the grower of approximately WI$200, in the French islands, where fertiliser was almost the same price per ton but banana receipts were on an average much higher (7 to 8 cents per pound, compared with 4 cents in the Commonwealth islands), every WI$100 worth of fertiliser yielded an additional 4 tons of bananas with a value of approximately WI$670. (The annual production figures for the four islands are given in Table 5.1.)

DISPOSAL

Although cultivation practices differed in the Commonwealth and French islands, there was a substantial degree of overlap, but the ways the harvested crop was brought to market were radically different.

In St Lucia and Dominica, all export bananas were bought from the farmers by the island's banana growers' associations, which maintained buying points throughout the islands and buying stations in the exporting ports. Within certain periods specified in advance, growers brought their bananas on the stem to these points, where the fruit was weighed and inspected, and, provided it met the minimum standards specified by the association, accepted for shipment. The grower received immediate payment at a price that was basically the same for all growers and was determined in relation to the "Green Market Price", the price at which non-Windwards bananas were sold to the green ripeners in the United Kingdom (SLBGA 1964, 4).

Accepted stems were wrapped and then transported to the ports, two in each island, in lorries hired by the associations. At the port of export, the bananas were sold to Geest Industries, which bought all exported Windward Island bananas and leased or owned the boats in which they were carried to the United Kingdom. There was an agreement that Geest would buy all stems of a certain quality from the four Commonwealth island growers' associations (in Dominica, St Lucia, St Vincent, and Grenada), and the associations were obliged to keep Geest informed of anticipated production levels to ensure the appropriate provision of cargo space.

In Martinique and Guadeloupe, the different history of the banana industry and, in particular, the fact that it had traditionally been dominated by estate rather than peasant producers resulted in a completely different set of structures and institutions for getting the crop from the grower to the market in metropolitan France. Estate growers assembled their harvested bananas at their own estate packing sheds, where they were cut off the stem, washed and dipped in fungicide, and packed in cardboard boxes stamped with the grower's mark. The boxes were then transferred to the exporting port, where

Table 5.1
Banana production of the four islands in tons

Year	Dominica	St Lucia	Guadeloupe	Martinique
1925	175	-	904	-
1926	125	578	1,431	-
1927	113	-	1,342	-
1928	42	-	1,246	-
1929	-	-	527	-
1930	30	-	2,278	-
1931	-	-	4,290	-
1932	-	-	11,718	4,547+
1933	275	278	16,439	9,396+
1934	475	275	16,734	-
1935	900	755	26,246	-
1936	-	1,358	35,194	42,000
1937	1,435	1,387	47,712	-
1938	879	1,259	50,281	37,000
1939	529	931	45,904	28,000+
1940	-	-	22,887	-
1941	875	725	7,382	1,801
1942	225	28	2,274	109
1943	50	1	3,119	66
1944	50	0.5	2,540	-
1945	50	1	10,470	-
1946	45	1	19,009	3,263
1947	91	19	31,844	10,961
1948	184	25	48,731	28,307
1949	1,508	1	48,766	41,788
1950	4,643	26	58,599	52,027
1951	6,501	233	68,938	72,348
1952	9,808	625	72,155	62,448
1953	13,571	1663	69,389	59,701
1954	16,233	3,540	76,914	60,954
1955	15,034	5,170	66,415	60,826
1956	22,357	10,440	57,045	88,238
1957	17,325	12,092	79,427	96,579
1958	20,315	13,070	94,097	94,400
1959	27,880	30,503	116,481	131,426
1960	28,415	28,461	115,223	126,207
1961	28,756	40,433	122,362	137,760
1962	28,239	49,469	118,058	151,250
1963	30,738	53,311	108,567	116,984
1964	42,232	60,926	54,806	85,991
1965	49,756	80,533	75,690	117,717
1966	42,919	83,744	91,800	232,700
1967	46,796	69,107	85,000	214,500
1968	54,909	71,467	111,500	221,900

Sources: McFarlane (1964, 89); *La Banane* (1967, 1:12,15); Persaud (1966, 27); Hoy (1962, 263); see also Table 9.5.

exporters arranged to load them onto the banana boats of the Compagnie Générale Transatlantique, which had a monopoly of the shipment of goods and produce between metropolitan France and the Antillean *départments*. Sometimes exporters would handle the produce of several estates; often the exporters were themselves owners of large estates.

The bananas remained the property of the grower until they were unloaded at the metropolitan port and sold to wholesale ripeners there. Indeed, in the case of Martinique, where family links between estate owners tended to be stronger, groups of growers often owned ripening facilities in France so that their produce did not pass out of their ownership until it was sold to wholesale distributors. Only on the sale of their produce in the *métropole* did growers receive any payment for it. If the fruit of a particular grower could not be sold by the exporter's agent, because of its poor condition on arrival in France or simply because of a glut on the market, the grower would receive nothing for it, but would still have to pay the costs of shipment. These costs could result in a substantial debit note.

Small growers, who could not afford to operate their own packing sheds and were unlikely to have family or business ties with an exporter, were clearly at a disadvantage in this system. In the 1950s, small farmers had been dependent upon *ramasseurs*, agents of exporters who came around in vans and bought the fruit of peasant growers on the stem for cash. This system might be satisfactory when demand was strong and prices high, but when demand was weak, farmers were often obliged to accept very low prices or were left with their produce unsold. By the 1960s, there were various grower groups set up to combat this problem, and in particular, there had been an effort to organise small growers into Sociétés d'Intérêt Collectif Agricole, or SICAS, to operate their own packing facilities and make their own contracts for shipping space with the CGT. These groups worked with varying degrees of success. Their drawback was that members received no payment until their fruit was sold in the *métropole*, and if by mischance it could not be sold or fetched a very low price, they might receive nothing but a debit note for shipping costs.

None of the factors, physical or human, that have been considered so far can adequately account for observed interisland differences in the character and location of banana production, and particularly the major French-Commonwealth dichotomy. It is time to turn to a factor that does at least have the potential for creating a division along this axis: the producers' associations.

6 Institutional Structures: The Origins, History, and Character of Eastern Caribbean Banana Growers' Associations

In a world of untrammelled laissez-faire capitalism, there would be no place for producer associations. Either vertically integrated companies would compete to bring produce from the field to the consumer at the lowest prices consistent with profitable operation, or the produce would be bought and sold by a chain of middlemen, which might include processers, shippers, and wholesalers. Each change of ownership would be freely negotiated according to the laws of supply and demand. In theory, this system should provide the consumer with produce at the lowest possible prices. In practice, it does not necessarily do so since it permits major producers or wholesalers to eliminate competition by artificially depressing price levels until competitors are forced to withdraw from the market.

At the time of the postwar development or revival of Eastern Caribbean banana industries, the market situation was, in any case, by no means one of untrammelled laissez-faire capitalism. For social, political, and economic reasons, Britain and France were anxious to foster banana production in the Eastern Caribbean islands, and while prices obviously could not be allowed to rise above levels acceptable to the consumer, the metropolitan authorities were more concerned that supply should expand to satisfy demand than that the forces of the marketplace should operate freely within the tariff and quota constraints they had imposed. Thus, it was not in the interests of governments to discourage the formation of producers' associations, even if their activities were liable to distort market forces that would otherwise have led to the survival of only the fittest, that is to say, the physically well-endowed and most efficient.

Nevertheless, while island-wide producer organisations of one kind or another existed almost from the start in Dominica and St Lucia, they were much slower to become established in the French islands. To understand why, it is first of all necessary to examine the reasons for the creation of such organisations. It is only in the light of these raisons d'être that the role of individual banana growers' associations in the mid-1960s can be appreciated. By this period, each of the four islands had a single banana producers' association that purported to represent all of the island's growers and promote the interests of the export banana industry as a whole.

THE RATIONALE FOR PRODUCERS' ASSOCIATIONS

Almost every form of produce destined for shipment overseas requires some form of preparation and packing, if not more elaborate processing, before it can be exported. While large-scale producers may be able to maintain and staff their own facilities for carrying out the necessary operations, medium-sized and small farmers usually lack the resources to set them up or the volume of production to exploit them economically. The Gros Michel variety of bananas grown before the Second World War was extremely resilient and could be shipped on the stem with a minimum of packaging; but the Panama-disease resistant varieties that replaced them in the 1940s and 1950s were far more fragile and required careful handling and packaging, initially on the stem and later in boxes. Thus, unless smaller growers were to be dependent on the good graces of larger growers in their neighbourhood, should there be any, to wash and wrap their fruit, it was essential that cooperative facilities of some sort be set up. The same considerations applied to the transport of fruit from the growing areas to the exporting ports. Large-scale growers owned or could rent trucks; small growers could only do so through cooperative arrangements.

The ravages of leafspot disease afflicted large and small growers indiscriminately, particularly in higher rainfall areas. While an arrangement that left individual growers responsible for spraying their own bananas might have been the least costly for large growers, especially those with purestand plantations, there were drawbacks in leaving disease control to the individual. The fields of growers who sprayed inadequately or too infrequently could become pools of disease that could easily spread and afflict the plantations of more conscientious and affluent neighbours. Thus, disease control was another area in which the common interest suggested some degree of coordination.

Provided that soil conditions are reasonably propitious, the subsistence crops traditional in the Eastern Caribbean, and even commercial and semicommercial tree crops such as coconuts, citrus, and cacao, can be grown with very little capital outlay for such items as chemical fertilisers. Bananas, on the other hand, are a demanding crop requiring substantial applications of expensive imported fertiliser if they are to be grown intensively on the same piece of land for any length of time. If small growers are to benefit from bulk-buying, they need an organisation to handle purchases of supplies and then make them available on terms that small farmers can afford.

Even large growers are unlikely, individually, to be able to fund research into disease control and the development of better plant varieties and better agricultural practices - unless, that is, they are in a league with the United Fruit Company (now Chiquita). Research may be undertaken or funded by government agencies, but these agencies may not share the priorities or the commitment to a specific crop of farmers already involved in its production. Consequently farmers may find it worthwhile to divert a portion of their own profits to a research agency under their control.

The islands of the Eastern Caribbean are from time to time traversed by hurricanes and windstorms that may wreak havoc in banana plantations. In the worst instances, an entire island's production may be reduced to almost nothing for nine months. Provided several such storms do not come in quick succession, large producers may be able to finance replanting from their own resources or to obtain the necessary credit. On the other hand, if smaller producers who may have already bought fertiliser on credit lose a high proportion of their crop, they may be unable to afford the necessary investments to resume production. Unless there is an effective state-funded system of disaster relief, crop insurance of some kind may provide the only safeguard against a substantial body of farmers dropping out of banana production entirely in the wake of a really destructive storm. It is, however, the most vulnerable farmers who are least likely to be able to negotiate individually with insurance companies; they will probably be able to obtain protection only through contracts negotiated collectively by their associations.

When producers' organisations provide various facilities to all growers, the more efficient (often, though not always, the larger) producers may, to some extent, subsidise the less efficient. If these facilities are not provided, however, the overall level of production may decline to a point where it is no longer worthwhile for shippers to call at a port. If the production of a region falls below a critical level, shippers could justify using alternative sources of supply. Once such sources gain a foothold in the market, they may expand production to supply the entire requirement, and render the limited production of an island's few really efficient growers superfluous.

Not only production but also marketing of a somewhat fragile and perishable export crop may be risky and fraught with pitfalls for an individual small-scale producer with limited means, few contacts, and no direct access to markets. An organisation responsible to growers, acting as intermediary between producers and wholesalers, and having access to market information is in a much stronger position to negotiate price levels and shipping contracts. Since demand and price fluctuate seasonally and not necessarily in accord with the normal peaks and troughs in production brought about by in the Eastern Caribbean climate, both buyers and sellers may benefit from some sort of intermediate organisation that can inform growers about how to schedule their production to make the most profit, and provide inducements for growers in areas where climatic conditions give them the option of choosing their harvesting season to concentrate their production in the periods of peak demand.

If supply exceeds demand at certain periods, competition among growers to sell their produce may reduce prices to a level where production costs exceed receipts and the more marginal are driven out of production entirely. Only by withholding surplus fruit from a saturated market and either destroying it or diverting it to other, less profitable markets may price levels be maintained at satisfactory levels. Individual growers cannot take such action, however; only an organisation in a position to compensate those whose produce has to be withheld can undertake such manipulations.

Conversely, if much of an island's crop were destroyed by windstorms or hurricanes and several months' production lost, there would be little that individual growers could do to ensure that fruit from alternative sources of supply obtained temporary - and only temporary - access to their market. United in an association, they would be in a much better position to see that whatever short-term arrangements were made did not jeopardize their long-term interests and might even be turned to their profit.

Finally, there are many small farmers whose financial resources are so slender that they could not afford the cash inputs required for fertiliser, for instance, or to pay labourers for carrying harvested bunches, unless they saw immediate returns for their harvested crop. While various mechanisms may be employed to pay growers for their produce at the moment it leaves their hands, unless payment is made through an agency with no interest in profiting from the small growers' weak bargaining position, the growers may have to trade a substantial percentage of their profit for the convenience of instant cash.

There were thus many reasons why the formation of producers' associations would have been in the interest of many, if not all, Eastern Caribbean banana growers. Such associations may be formed either through the direct action of governments, which may create more or less independent statutory bodies to control and regulate the industry in the best interests of the majority of the growers, or they may be formed by the voluntary association of growers in a cooperative body, with or without government encouragement and regulation. An association may embrace all the growers on an island or just certain groups or individuals who feel they have a common interest in associating.

It is interesting, before examining the activities and impact of banana growers' associations in St Lucia and Dominica, Martinique and Guadeloupe, to look at their origins and histories, as well as the character of their membership and the structure of their decision-making bodies. Such an investigation sheds considerable light on the reasons why associations in different islands have come to such diverse conclusions about what policies their members' best interests demand. How successful these policies and activitities have been in promoting members' interests and how significant they have been in influencing the distribution and character of banana cultivation on the ground are at the heart of this assessment.

ORIGINS AND HISTORIES OF ISLAND BANANA GROWERS' ASSOCIATIONS

By 1966, each of the four leading banana-producing islands had a single, island-wide banana producers' association. These associations were significantly different and had developed by distinctly different paths. The oldest could trace their origins, in some form or other, to the early 1930s, while the youngest was, effectively, less than a year old.

Proposals to form growers' associations were first made by an Imperial economic committee as early as 1926. The committee was anxious to see export banana cultivation, which was then in its infancy in St Lucia and Grenada, develop as a complementary source of supply to the hurricane-prone Jamaican trade. It felt that development was impeded by the lack of responsible authorities representing the growers and advocated the establishment of associations of growers and exporters in the banana-growing colonies, in Jamaica, St Lucia, and Grenada, and in Dominica when it too joined the trade. The associations were to be under government auspices to ensure they were thoroughly representative. Their purpose was to negotiate with shipping lines, guarantee regularity of supplies, and promote improved agricultural methods (Commonwealth Economic Committee 1926, 45, 264–5).

An association was indeed established in Jamaica in 1929: the Jamaica Banana Producers' Association Limited, formed "for the purpose of reserving a greater share of the value of the banana trade to the growers" (McFarlane 1964, 40). At that time, the United Fruit Company dominated Jamaica's banana trade with both the United States and the United Kingdom, and growers had become dissatisfied with their share of the final selling price. The new association soon acquired its own refrigerated ships and challenged United Fruit for the United Kingdom trade. United Fruit was obliged to compete with the association for supplies, and growers, mainly smallholders, could sell to whichever body offered higher prices (McFarlane 1964, 40).

St Lucia and Dominica were making rather uncertain beginnings at export banana production and took somewhat longer to establish associations. Shipments of bananas from the Windward Islands were first made in the 1920s, but the industry faltered with the onset of Panama disease. In the 1930s, however, exports were resumed with the provision of regular shipping facilities to Canada. In 1934, the Dominica Banana Association was founded "to market bananas and regulate and control their export" (McFarlane 1964, 43), and in St. Lucia in the same year a similar organisation, the St. Lucia Banana Association, was established by government legislation "to create a body corporate to market bananas and to regulate and control the export thereof." Under this ordinance, which remained in force, with only minor amendments, until its repeal in 1953, the association had the sole right of export of bananas from St Lucia, but the government retained some control over the association: its board could be dissolved and replaced by appointees of the Governor if it was judged to be performing its duties inadequately (Biggs, Bennett, et al. 1964, 34).

The St Lucia Banana Association did not on the whole deal directly with growers, but rather with dealers who bought bananas from farmers, mainly peasants. The dealers' profit was restricted, however, which gave some protection to the peasants, as did the fact that dealers' buyers competed for their fruit.

After the Second World War, the failure of St Lucian farmers to respond to renewed market opportunities for export bananas provoked a visit by a team of experts in 1951; the team concluded that the association in its statutory form was not the most appropriate type of controlling authority. It recommended that the St Lucia Banana Association should be replaced by the St Lucia Banana Growers' Association, to be modelled on the All-Island Banana Growers' Association of Jamaica. This association, which was governed by an elected board of directors, had been formed in 1946 as a company limited by shares in which only growers were eligible for membership (Biggs, Bennett, et al. 1964, 36). The Jamaica Banana Producers' Association had become purely a shipping agency (Simmonds 1959, 304–5, 326).

In 1953, the St Lucia ordinance of 1934 was repealed, and the St Lucia Banana Growers' Association Limited (SLBGA) was incorporated as a company limited by shares and vested by law with the sole right to export of bananas from St Lucia. Until the mid-1960s, its constitutional position as *the* authority responsible for the well-being of the island's banana industry remained unmodified, despite the fact that in 1953 its Jamaican prototype was limited to the administration of technical aspects of the industry, such as leafspot control and the programme of subsidised fertilisers, while a statutory body, the Banana Board of Jamaica, was established to select and purchase fruit, pack and transport it to the docks, and conduct high level negotiations with shipping companies (Simmonds 1959, 304).

The complete range of activities that the SLBGA was authorised to undertake is set out in its *Memorandum and Articles of Association* (1953). Essentially its objectives were to promote and protect the interests of the banana growers of St Lucia; to foster research into all aspects of the industry and take steps to improve agricultural methods and disease control; to act as agent for growers in purchasing, collecting, marketing, and shipping fruit; to enter into contracts with buyers or dealers; to enter into profit-sharing agreements that might benefit the association; to purchase or charter shipping or aircraft; to deal in merchandise such as fertilisers and agricultural equipment; to invest funds and lend or borrow money; and to acquire lands or buildings, wharves, and machinery (SLBGA 1953, 1–4).

The Articles of Association set out the organisation and structure of the SLBGA in great detail. Every owner or occupier of land on which there were at least thirty banana mats or who had produced and sold for export at least fifteen stems of bananas during the previous calendar year was entitled to be enrolled as a registered grower and become a member of a district branch of the association. District branches might be formed when there were at least fifteen potential members and might elect delegates (up to a maximum of 291 for the whole island) to vote at general meetings. The business of the association was to be conducted by a board of directors numbering from five to fourteen persons, two of whom might be co-opted. It might appoint five of the directors to form an executive committee. The chairman of the board was to be elected annually (SLBGA 1953, 7–16).

Until 1958, the directors were exclusively large growers and businessmen, but thereafter small growers gradually replaced large growers on the board of directors. Because some of the new directors were aligned with a rival political party, the then Labour Government was concerned that an organisation embracing so many thousands of grower-members and controlling what was by then by far the most important sector of the island's economy might be manipulated for party-political ends. It sought to persuade the board to amend the association's articles to insulate the banana industry as far as possible from political interference (Biggs, Bennett, et al. 1964, 36). However, the board would not agree, and consequently, in December 1962 the government passed an amendment to the ordinance of 1953 to prevent elected members of the legislature and persons serving on the executives of political parties from serving as directors of the association.

As a result of this legislation, one director resigned from the board and three others, in order to remain, resigned from the executive of a political party, but the government's apprehension (or possibly that of the larger planters) about the politicisation of the board was not allayed, particularly when small growers gained control of it in 1963. That year, the government appointed a Commission of Enquiry into the industry. Reporting to the Commission, larger planters professed that while they were in favour of the industry being run by the growers, they felt that circumstances might arise, if they had not already arisen, in which government intervention might become necessary. The commissioners suspected that the larger planters simply desired to take control of the industry and replace the old association with one conducted solely on commercial lines (Biggs, Bennett, et al. 1964, 35).

Although the Commission found little fault with the way the association had run the industry so far and although it admitted that a form of canvassing for election to the board had been taking place for some time, "principally along the lines of workers being influenced to vote for their employers," the commissioners expressed concern that "the organised group approach to election of directors might result in control of the industry being exercised by a board which, due to incompetence, mismanagement, neglect, or other reasons, might adversely affect the industry and therefore the general economy of St Lucia."

The commission therefore recommended that the "Government should take powers which would enable it to dissolve the Board of Directors of the Banana Growers' Association" if it considered the board was performing its duties inadequately, abusing its powers, or indulging in political activity (Biggs, Bennett, et al. 1964, 41,43). As an alternative, should such an amendment not meet acceptance, it recommended that draft legislation be prepared to establish a statutory banana growers' association. It recommended further that the statutory board should consist of fourteen voting members (six large growers, six small growers, and two official members, one of whom should be the Financial Secretary) and that intermediate between the district branches and the parent body, there should be area councils, which might provide a more effective channel of communication for representations from small growers. Recommendations were also made regarding, for instance, the minimum size of district branches, and the undesirability of delegates and especially directors being paid employees of the association (Biggs, Bennett, et al. 1964, 46–9).

Delegates held an extraordinary general meeting in February, 1964 and rejected the idea of a statutory board. In March, nevertheless, the government presented a bill to make the association a statutory body on the lines recommended by the commission, but two dissenting ministers left the ruling Labour Party as a result, and in April the government fell. In the subsequent election campaign, the future of the association was the major issue. The United Workers' Party (UPW), a new party formed by the erstwhile opposition and dissident ex-Labour members, promised that, above all, the SLBGA would remain a producers' association. In June, the UWP formed the new government (Romalis 1968, 242–5).

Over the next three years, the association was at the centre of intense political manoeuvring, and the entire board was voted out and replaced in 1967. In August 1967, the UWP government, which had won power on a platform of opposition to government intervention in the banana industry, passed a bill (almost identical with the bill its members had so strenuously opposed in 1964) making SLBGA a statutory body. It gave the government power to change the number of board members and dissolve the board, and the Premier, who was also the Minister of Finance, had ultimate control over the association's right to assume any loans (Romalis 1968, 264).

The history of the Dominican association over the same three decades was less turbulent. The Dominica Banana Association, set up as a statutory body in 1934, was the agency with which the buying company, Antilles Products, contracted in 1949 to buy all Lacatan bananas grown in the island for the next fifteen years (Dominica, Department of Agriculture 1949).

In 1959, the government of Dominica felt obliged, for reasons which were obscure by the time of my visit in 1966, to intervene in the affairs of the banana industry. (Biggs, Bennett, et al. (1964) imply that the intervention was necessary: without it, the industry might have been seriously retarded.) As a consequence, under the Banana Ordinance Act of 1959, the Dominica Banana Growers' Association (DBGA) superseded the Dominica Banana Association. The DBGA was nevertheless still a statutory body. Membership was open to growers with a minimum of thirty mats, and the association was run by a board consisting of ten members, six elected and four appointed by the government. Two of the government appointees were generally the Chief Agricultural Officer and the Financial Secretary (*WINBAN News*, April–June 1967, 6). Even though it was a statutory body, the DBGA in the early 1960s differed very little, for all practical purposes, from the SLBGA. A provision for the dissolution of the board by the government in certain circumstances was, however, incorporated in its ordinance (Biggs, Bennett, et al. 1964, 45).

In 1966–67, large growers were still well represented on the board of the DBGA, and the chairman was a large grower. While it was asserted in some quarters that the large growers were manipulating board policy to their advantage, that view had evidently not acquired a wide enough currency to provoke demands for a major change in the board's composition.

The individual associations in the four Commonwealth Windward Islands each had the sole right to export bananas from their island, and each had signed separate agreements with the buyer, Geest. However, an umbrella organisation, the Windward Islands Banana Growers' Association (WINBAN), looked after their common interests. WINBAN originated in 1956, when representatives of the governments and the banana associations of Dominica, St Vincent, and Grenada were invited to a meeting in St Lucia to discuss common problems affecting the banana trade and to consider joint action for their solution. As a result of this meeting, WINBAN was formed in 1958 as a consultative and advisory body; it was a company limited by guarantee and not having share capital. Its headquarters were in St Lucia. The subscribers to the Memorandum and Articles of Association were the four corporate or statutory associations or bodies in Dominica, St Lucia, St Vincent, and Grenada. In practice, each island association was represented on WINBAN by one director and one representative (Biggs, Bennett, et al. 1964, 37).

WINBAN was administered by a general manager and a secretary and was mandated to undertake a wide range of activities. It was responsible for periodic negotiation with the purchasing company to maximise returns to growers and with governments to obtain subsidies for price stabilisation schemes. It negotiated with Jamaican counterparts and the United Kingdom government to secure an agreed proportion of the market for Windwards banana production. It undertook the bulk purchase of fertiliser and other materials required by the banana industries (Biggs, Bennett, et al. 1964, 37). In 1959 it introduced a hurricane insurance scheme, and in 1963 it opened a banana research centre in St Lucia (Romalis 1968, 84–5).

In the Commonwealth Caribbean, monolithic producer associations came into existence almost as a matter of course as soon as a crop began to assume a significant role in an island's economy, but in the French islands, producer associations were created at a much later stage and without the aura of inevitability. On the other hand, at a national level the French were quicker than the British to introduce organisational structures to encourage and protect their colonial Caribbean banana industries. In 1931, France imposed quotas and tariff barriers to protect its Antillean banana production, and in 1932, the Comité Interprofessionnel Bananier (CIB) was created (Menauge 1974, 17). Based in Paris and composed of representatives of colonial planters, wholesale importers, and shippers, the CIB was intended to ensure that suitable port facilities existed, that banana cargoes arrived in France at a rate and rhythm adjusted to market demand, and that the industry received favourable publicity. In short, its purpose was to reinforce the French government's policy of support for colonial bananas (Dardet 1939, 163).

Evidently the first CIB lapsed or was disbanded, for in 1951 the French government instituted a new CIB composed of thirty-five members representing producers from the franc-zone, shippers, importers, ripeners, and government representatives. Their mandate was, again, to study the requirements of the market and regulate shipments to meet them, and to represent the industry in negotiations with the government (*La Banane* 1967, 2:10). They held monthly meetings to monitor supply and demand and to coordinate the timing and destination of banana shipments (France 1966, 162). The CIB continued in this form until 1968, when its failure to respond adequately to falling prices, declining exports, and an erratic French market led the government to set up a sixteen-member

Comité Restreint Interprofessionnel Bananier, which left the original CIB with a more limited role (Menauge 1974, 171–2).

Considering the early date at which the banana industry developed institutions at a national level, the slowness of Martiniquan and Guadeloupean growers in developing all-embracing local organisations seems all the more surprising. Indeed, under the aegis of the colonial government, an association was formed in Guadeloupe as early as 1933 to select fruit, oversee transport, and organise sales. Two similar groups were formed in Martinique at the same time (Dardet 1939, 164). Members of the Guadeloupean association, L'Association à Forme Coopérative des Producteurs de la Guadeloupe, were expected to ship their produce in the vessels of the Compagnie Générale Transatlantique, and might receive a bonus if local regulations regarding the preparation of fruit for export were respected. The principal function of the association was to negotiate a shipping contract for producers with the Compagnie Générale Transatlantique (Menauge 1974, 164).

The fate of the Guadeloupean association is not related by Menauge, but, presumably, it failed to attract or hold a substantial membership, since in 1939, on the outbreak of the Second World War, the French government announced that it would assure the export of French West Indian fruit, no matter what the cost, if the participants in the industry joined together in a single organisation under government control. Such a group was formed in May 1940 (Menauge 1974, 164), but what became of it when the Allied blockade effectively terminated banana exports is not clear. As Menauge remarks, the government was anxious more or less from the earliest days of the industry that its participants should all group themselves in a single, unified organisation; but only in periods of crisis for the banana industry did it take action to promote this goal (104).

The first recorded instance of any island-wide cooperative movement in the postwar period was CATAG, a Guadeloupean cooperative for pest and disease control. CATAG was established in 1955, and its articles of association were approved in 1958. A board of directors was elected by members, and the board appointed a manager to run the cooperative. The aims of CATAG were to provide special equipment and trained staff to apply pesticides and disease control agents either aerially or by knapsack sprayer; to supply the required products (fungicides, insecticides, nematicides); and to set up workshops and other buildings to service, repair, and store equipment (Guadeloupe 1964).

How successful CATAG was in prosecuting these aims is hard to determine. Since the French government's Fourth National Plan

(Quatrième Plan), covering the period 1962–65, called for the general application and enforcement of plant protection measures and suggested that leafspot control should be effected by assisting plant protection cooperatives such as CATAG (Durand 1964, 4), it would appear that when this plan was drawn up in 1961, the objectives of CATAG were not being fully implemented.

It was external forces that finally convinced French West Indian banana producers of the need for joint action on a broader front. By 1958, supplies reaching the French market had begun to exceed demand, and the Ivory Coast, where production was rapidly expanding, had set up a powerful marketing organisation. In 1960, some participants in the banana industries of Martinique and Guadeloupe suggested establishing a professional organisation, that would be directed towards

1 achieving uniformity in the standard of production by assisting small producers to improve the quality of their fruit;
2 bringing the control of exports and transportation under a single management;
3 relating production strictly to sales, unifying the selling process, and controlling it up to delivery to dealers and, to a certain extent, up to the stage of retailing (Durand 1964, 9)

There were at this time three groups or associations in Martinique and five in Guadeloupe with which some but not all growers were affiliated. These groups took joint action mainly to secure and distribute shipping space, but they did not present a coordinated front. They could not, for instance, collaborate to divert surplus production to alternative markets, or even to dump it in the sea, when saturation of the French market led to depressed prices there.

On 29 January 1961, the Société d'Intérêt Collectif Agricole Bananier de la Martinique (SICABAM) was formed, and initially, 80 percent of the island's producers joined as members (La Banane, I, 1967, 3). Although encouraged by the government (Durand 1964, 9), SICABAM was a private organisation, a Société d'Intérêt Collectif Agricole (SICA) of the type defined by law in the French civil and penal codes. Its mandate was "to carry out or to facilitate all arrangements relating to the organisation of production, packaging, preparation for packing, handling, shipping, transportation, and dispatch to French and foreign markets of bananas produced by its members and clients" (SICABAM 1964, 1). It was also to promote technical and scientific research on production, handling, and transportation and to seek assistance from appropriate persons or specialised agencies;

to study and implement all measures for plant pest control; to define and apply approved standards of quality; and to promote sales of bananas produced or collected by its members (Durand 1964, 9–10).

SICABAM's immediate objectives, in 1961, were to unify the industry, that is, to bring all producers into SICABAM; to secure the restriction of imports of foreign bananas into France with quotas giving priority to fruit from Martinique and Guadeloupe; to negotiate a single freight contract with the shipper (CGT); and to establish an equalisation fund to compensate producers whose bananas were diverted to foreign markets at periods of suplus production (Durand 1964, 2).

These four immediate objectives were achieved within three years. By June 1962, all Martiniquan planters belonged to SICABAM (*La Banane* 1967, 1:3). The association's swift success in attracting the twenty percent who had initially remained outside may have owed something to the fact that under French law, such associations could oblige even nonmembers to abide by their rules (Arneaud 1969, personal communication).

On 4 January 1962, after arbitration by the French President, two-thirds of the French banana market was allocated to the overseas *départements* of Martinique and Guadeloupe, while the remaining third was allocated to franc-zone African states. Two months later, the Comité National Bananier Antillais (CNBA) was created, with delegates from SICABAM and its Guadeloupean counterparts, to coordinate exports from the two islands (SICABAM 1964, 3; *La Banane* 1967, 1:3).

In June 1962, an equalisation fund, the Caisse de Péréquation, was set up in Martinique. This fund was financed by a cess levied on bananas shipped to metropolitan ports and was used to compensate producers whose fruit had to be sold in foreign markets at prices that did not cover production costs. In November, SICABAM signed a single freight contract with the Compagnie Générale Transatlantique (*La Banane* 1967, 1:3), which replaced about seventy contracts between exporters and the shipping company (SICABAM 1964, 2).

Once it had put in place the mechanisms necessary to ensure the continuing viability of Martinique's banana industry, SICABAM clearly had a long-term role to play in effecting the smooth operation of these mechanisms. In 1965, it was transformed from a SICA into a producers' group, eligible for government subsidies. This was a recognition that it controlled the banana industry and could regulate levels of production (Emélie 1967, personal communication). It was administered by a council composed of twelve to eighteen members named by the general assembly, which was composed of all shareholders. Its initial capital was fixed at Fr113,500, divided into 227 shares of Fr500 each, and the shares were allocated to members according to the tonnage they had shipped in the previous twelve months: one share for every 600 tons shipped. Would-be subscribers could band together to acquire a share, provided they formed a legally constituted group, a SICA, for example. At least 80 percent of the shareholders had to be growers; the remainder might be exporters who were not growers, provided their activities would further the objectives of SICABAM. Each shareholder had at least one vote and an additional vote for every 600 tons shipped, up to a maximum of five votes. The presence of one-sixth of the shareholders was usually required for a quorum, but more were required in some cases, such as the approval of changes in the statutes.

Council members were required to hold at least two shares during their term of tenure, ostensibly as security for any actions they might take. The council of administration of SICABAM appointed the director general, who might be a shareholder, but not a member of the council (SICABAM Dossier, 1966).

By 1965, the total number of shares had risen to 320 (SICABAM Dossier, 1966), but by 1967, overproduction had made established shareholders reluctant to expand membership further. They disagreed about whether newly formed SICAs should be able to acquire shares in SICABAM directly or should have to apply to the Union des SICA for a portion of the shares already held by the SICA sector. It was anticipated that this problem would have to be resolved by the arbitration of the departmental prefect (Emélie 1967, personal communication).

While the question of access to membership may have provoked some controversy in the latter part of the 1960s, the general management of SICABAM proceeded very smoothly, with a steady expansion of the functions for which it was responsible. In 1966, accounting operations were computerised; a cool storage shed was built to permit daily cutting; and plans were made to improve port handling facilities (SICABAM Dossier, 1966; Léobon 1967, personal communication).

In Guadeloupe in 1960, efforts to unite the various producer groups into a single organisation representing all growers met with less immediate success, since the preexisting groups were deeply divided on matters of policy and outlook. The largest group, accounting for about 60 percent of the island's exports, was the Société d'Intérêt Collectif Agricole des Producteurs et Exportateurs de Bananes (SICAPEB). Its members were mainly older planters and proponents of a scheme to build a banana port on the Rivière-Sens, in the commune of Gourbeyre (Menauge 1974, 164). As with SICABAM, operating capital was obtained from shares sold to member-growers, who were entitled to one share for every 120 tons of bananas loaded during the preceding twelve months. In 1964 there were 125 members, and the Société was run by a board of 18 officers elected from the membership at annual general meetings (Guadeloupe 1964). SICAPEB was concerned primarily with negotiating shipping contracts with the Compagnie Générale Transatlantique and distributing shipping space among members according to applications received.

The second largest group in the early 1960s was the Société d'Intérêt Collectif Agricole Bananière Guadeloupéenne (SICABAG). SICABAG was run by a younger group of planters and accounted for 20 to 25 percent of the island's exports. It resembled SICAPEB, except that it was administered by a smaller (twelve-member) board, and it performed essentially the same functions, namely, negotiating shipping contracts with the Compagnie Générale Transatlantique and allocating shipping space to members. Its members favoured the creation of a banana port in the town of Basse-Terre (Menauge 1974, 164).

The third group, known either as the Société d'Intérêt Collectif Agricole des Petits et Moyens (SICAPEMO) or FEDEG, the Guadeloupean Federation of SICAs, was of negligible influence in the industry, accounting for only 3 to 5 percent of exports, about 2,000 tons a year. Its membership consisted of 9 banana-growing SICAs (St Claude, Gourbeyre, Baillif, l'Habituée, Goyave, Bananier, Capesterre, Trois-Rivières (Regrettée) and Trois Rivières (Schoelcher) with a total membership of about 250 (Arthur, Houck, and Beckford 1968, 61). FEDEG was run by a board of directors composed of seven members. While Durand (1964, 10) suggested that its objectives were similar to those of SICABAM, SICAPEB, and SICABAG, a description of its mandate in 'Banana Growers' and Marketing Co-operatives and Associations in Guadeloupe' (Guadeloupe 1964) does not mention the negotiation of contracts with the Compagnie Générale Transatlantique, but speaks rather of its role in furnishing members with agricultural supplies and equipment, improving the marketing of members' crops, and seeking economic prices for them.

A number of large growers, accounting for as much as 10 to 12 percent of exports, remained outside any of these organisations throughout the early 1960s (Menauge 1974, 163). The government's Fifth National Plan (Ve Plan) speaks of the indispensability of creating the Société Interprofessionnelle Guadeloupéenne Bananière (SIGBA), which was to facilitate the export of the island's fruit to foreign countries, especially those within the European Common Market. Contemporary newspapers mention several acronyms for the organisation that the government hoped to see formed, and at the Banana Demonstration Tour in Guadeloupe in February 1964, UNIBA, a union of banana associations, was described as if it actually existed, although it is mentioned nowhere else. Its purported aims were very similar to those of SICAPEMO.

It was only in 1964, however, after a series of hurricanes had inflicted crippling damage on the Guadeloupean banana industry, that the various rival groups finally became convinced of the necessity of presenting a united front. After Hurricane Cléo crossed the island in August 1964, an organisation (SIRAP) was formed to buy bananas in Martinique or elsewhere and resell them in the French market under Guadeloupe's quota. This was the first real step towards unity, and the local administration hoped it would be the foundation of a more comprehensive professional association uniting planters and exporters, to be called L'Union des Producteurs et Exportateurs de Bananes de la Guadeloupe (UNIPEBAG). This scheme was rejected by the planters, but the administration made the granting of hurricane relief subsidies dependent upon an agreement among the different parties to negotiate unity. Thus at the end of 1964, a committee was formed to study the problem, and out of this study, in March 1965, emerged SICA-ASSOBAG (Menauge 1974, 165).

L'Association Bananière Guadeloupéenne (ASSOBAG) superseded all the earlier organisations and claimed to embrace all the island's banana growers. It negotiated a single freight contract with the Compagnie Générale Transatlantique and represented the planters in negotiations with the government (*La Banane* 1967, 1:7). It was constituted in a fairly similar manner to its Martiniquan sister organisation, SICABAM. Nongrowers could make up no more than 10 percent of the membership, and shares were allocated to members according to the tonnage they had shipped: one share for every 120 tonnes of fruit exported in the previous twelve months - or, in the event of hurricane damage, one share for every 6 hectares in bananas, well-maintained.

The number of votes allocated to each shareholder was a function of the number of shares held. In 1967, there were 135 shareholders with 835 shares, but one very large planter held 73 shares (8.7 percent), while the president of the Federation of SICAS, representing 318 small growers, had only 5 shares (Menauge 1974, 166). Essentially, ASSOBAG was a big planters' club. The entire membership of 135 shareholders constituted the general assembly of the association, which elected an administrative council of 15 members for a 3-year term. The council, in turn, elected a president (who could be reelected for an unlimited number of terms) and other officers, and it nominated a director who worked under its control and supervision (Menauge 1974, 166).

ASSOBAG sought official recognition as a producers' group in July 1967. Its objectives, set out in its application for recognition, were similar to the general mandate of SICABAM. It was to effect or facilitate all operations concerned with organising the production and marketing of bananas grown or *collected* by its members. To this end, it might make any necessary investments in facilities for packing, handling and transport, disease control, and technical and scientific research on all aspects of production and handling. It might also establish mechanisms of quality control, rationalise internal transport, and facilitate the disposal of the island's banana production by researching both overseas marketing possibilities and the industrial transformation of surpluses (Menauge 1974, 166).

The cooperative groups, or SICAS, within SICABAM and ASSOBAG were regional organisations of medium-sized and small growers (many with less than one hectare in bananas) set up after 1958 to share leafspot spraying and packing-shed facilities and to arrange marketing of members' fruit in France. In the mid-1960s, there were about nine banana-growing SICAS in Guadeloupe and about fifteen in Martinique, some with over 200 members. In some cases they had been organised by the government agency Société d'Aide Technique et de Crédit (SATEC), which had been set up to provide farmers with credit and technical assistance and which was active in both French islands throughout the 1960s.

While the chief purpose of the SICAS was to ensure fair access to the metropolitan market and fair prices to the small grower, the rules and regulations of the SICAS were hard to enforce, since they were voluntary associations, and if growers saw a temporary advantage in selling their fruit independently of their SICA, there was little that could be done to stop them. Even grouped together (as FEDEG in Guadeloupe and L'Union des SICA (UNISICA) in Martinique), their influence within their island associations was very limited, since they accounted for only 3 to 5 percent of banana exports from Guadeloupe and under 12 percent from Martinique (Burac 1975, 127). In their aims and operations, the SICAS had much in common with the growers' associations of the Commonwealth islands, but because membership was not mandatory and universal and their regulations not government-enforced their potential effectiveness was greatly limited.

CONCLUSION

To some extent, the banana growers' associations may have been influenced by differing national philosophies or government policies. It seems only reasonable to suppose, however, that the composition of an association's membership and, in particular, of its controlling body would have been most significant in determining the character of its involvement in the industry. The interests of the farmer with half a hectare in mixed cultivation on a steep hillside three or four kilometres from the nearest motorable road are unlikely to have been the same as the interests of a planter with 500 hectares of purestand bananas on a gently sloping valley floor, criss-crossed by access roads or light railways. Although the political and economic situation might restrain the vigour and openness with which the controlling group pursued policies favouring its own class, it would be most surprising if the controlling group did not try to promote, or at least preserve, its own class interests wherever possible.

By examining the activities of the four Eastern Caribbean banana growers' associations and their influence in the 1960s on cultivation, transport, and marketing, their potential to determine or modify the character of land use can be assessed. To reveal the ways in which the character of those who controlled the associations influenced their policies and actions, it is necessary to compare the associations both with one another and with themselves at different stages of their evolution.

7 Banana Cultivation: Aims, Activities and Impact of Island Growers' Associations

From establishing banana plantations to harvesting the still-green fruit, growers' associations have been involved to very varying degrees in the four islands. Their activities have been concentrated in four main areas: research and extension, fertiliser credit schemes, leafspot and other pest control, and hurricane insurance and rehabilitation.

RESEARCH AND EXTENSION

The Commonwealth Islands

To understand the somewhat limited direct role of the growers' associations in banana research and extension, it is necessary to appreciate the role of various other institutions and organisations, many of them with overlapping mandates. Before 1960, most agricultural research in the Commonwealth Caribbean was done in the larger or more populous islands of Jamaica, Barbados, and Trinidad. The research was conducted mainly by scientists associated with the Imperial College of Tropical Agriculture (now the Trinidad branch of the University of the West Indies), and it was generally fundamental research: studies of soil genesis and clay minerals, for instance, and experiments in plant breeding. At the Regional Research Centre in Trinidad there was a banana breeding section whose object was to develop new varieties with all the advantages of Gros Michel and Lacatan (the two varieties of most commercial importance in the Commonwealth Caribbean before the 1960s) but none of their disadvantages, particularly, the extreme susceptibility of Gros Michel to Panama disease and of Lacatan to leafspot (*Cercospora*).

There had been very few studies, however, of the agronomy of the banana crop in the Commonwealth West Indies (Spector 1964), and, in contrast with the cane industry, in which yields on British islands compared favourably with yields of their French neighbours, banana yields on most British islands exporting the crop were abysmally low, only a fraction of yields recorded in Martinique and Guadeloupe. Thus, there was an urgent need for studies of fertiliser requirements and nutrient uptake, spacing and planting densities, crop timing, and agricultural practices generally (Spector 1964). Consequently, the Windward Islands Banana Research Scheme was initiated in 1961, with funds supplied by the United Kingdom government and WINBAN and administered by the University of the West Indies in Trinidad. Subsequently, in 1963, WINBAN assumed responsibility for the scheme, which was then financed by WINBAN, the United Kingdom government, and Geest Industries, the sole purchaser of Windwards bananas. Headquarters were established in St Lucia, and a laboratory was built there, although the new research unit continued to have access to the facilities of the Regional Research Centre in Trinidad. It also maintained close links with Rothamsted Experimental Station in England (Twyford 1964).

Priority was given to research on the fertiliser requirements of bananas, since Windward Islands soils were so diverse, and there was little information on nutrient deficiencies. Field trials were laid down on the major soil types of each of the islands, and soil and leaf samples were analysed to determine relationships between nutrient status and fertiliser response (Spector 1964).

In 1963, experiments were begun to examine the effects on yields, cropping time, nutrient and water uptake, growth habit, weed and leafspot incidence, and wind losses of square-planted bananas at densities varying from 1,700 to 5,300 per hectare. Another trial examined the effect of array (square, rectangular, or double-row planting) on bananas planted at a density of 3,000 per hectare (Twyford 1964). Researchers also tried to determine whether mixed cropping was agronomically justifiable and if so, what crop combinations were mutually beneficial, or at least compatible.

Experiments with a variety of herbicides attempted to determine which ones gave the most satisfactory weed control and under what conditions (Spector 1964). The effects of mulching bananas with black polythene sheeting were observed. Researchers also tried to determine the effectiveness of different substances in controlling leafspot. They compared the performance of Robusta and Lacatan clones under field conditions in Grenada and tried to correlate various features of the early growth of the plants with final yields (Twyford 1964). Because nematode infestation was becoming a serious problem in many districts of St Lucia and Dominica by the mid-1960s, WINBAN also hired a nematologist to search for effective remedies.

Several unresolved problems involved in improving fruit quality and reducing the costs of production were identified and were either currently under study or were to be the subject of future research. Much of WINBAN's research addressed problems that concerned banana growers in general and that were also under investigation in the neighbouring French islands and elsewhere. Mixed cropping was, however, no longer an issue in Martinique and Guadeloupe, and nematode build-up there could be dealt with by fallowing, which was impractical in much of Dominica and St Lucia. Furthermore in the Commonwealth Windwards bananas were grown on soil types not considered suitable for this purpose in the French islands. It would probably be fair to say that while WINBAN had recorded no major breakthroughs by the time I did the fieldwork for this study in 1966–67, there had been steady progress in some areas and new information of potential interest to many growers was available.

It was relatively easy for big planters to obtain information directly from WINBAN, but the dissemination of this information to a wider audience was another matter. Even though WINBAN sponsored research that was relevant to all classes of banana growers, it had only limited means for disseminating results. It did publish the *Banana Growers' Manual* (WINBAN 1986), a comprehensive guide to recommended agricultural practices issued by the banana extension committees of the four Commonwealth Windward Islands, and it also published a quarterly journal, *WINBAN News*, containing articles about the industry, research developments, hints to growers, and news of island growers' associations. The subscription rate was low, but it is not known what percentage of growers the journal reached. The centre's research scientists sometimes addressed gatherings of farmers in all four islands during organised Banana Weeks and Field Demonstration Days, but in principle extension work was the responsibility of island agricultural departments and banana growers' associations.

In Dominica, the DBGA maintained two demonstration banana plots, one in the north and one in the south. Field days organised by the agricultural department's banana field officer and the DBGA were held there periodically. Hundreds of farmers attended to hear talks by leading farmers and officers of the DGBA and the agricultural department. The field days provided an opportunity for practical demonstrations of techniques and discussions of farmers' problems (Guye 1966, 8). Nevertheless, they reached only a few hundred of Dominica's eight thousand or so farmers, and neither the DBGA nor the agricultural department felt that such efforts alone would be sufficient to bring about the improvement in yields that they regarded as essential for the future health of the industry. They were particularly concerned that many banana fields were by this time at least eight years old and in poor condition: simply increasing fertiliser applications no longer produced much response. The solution was a major rehabilitation, involving uprooting and replanting entire fields; but this was expensive either in terms of wages or labour, and entailed not only several months' loss of production, but also complications in the event of hurricane losses that will be explained in more detail below.

An opportunity for the DBGA to conduct a more aggressive extension campaign was provided by Hurricane Inez, which flattened 60 percent of the bananas in the Northern district and 25 percent in the South and East on 27 September 1966. Following this disaster, the DBGA and the agricultural department jointly launched the Hurricane Inez Rehabilitation Scheme (HIR) to induce growers who had had substantial losses to adopt recommended techniques of spacing, planting, and fertiliser application when they rehabilitated their plantations. Under HIR, farmers were to receive subsidised fertiliser on favourable terms, but only if certain conditions were met. Fields were to be replanted rather than "supplied" after the usual pattern ("supplying" meaning replacing only uprooted or damaged mats). Bananas were to be planted in purestands only (but a banana-coconut combination might be approved if the coconut canopy was not too close); planting was to be at specified densities: 3,000 plants per hectare at sea level, down to 1,500 per hectare at elevations of 600 metres or more; and four or five applications of fertiliser amounting to approximately 2.5 tons per hectare per year were to be made at specified intervals.

The personnel for HIR were either agricultural-department officers or leafspot officers from the DBGA. The leafspot officers were not fully occupied by leafspot control after the hurricane and were quickly retrained to carry out the rehabilitation scheme. Each officer was assisted by one or two specially hired labourer-assistants. Planting was to be closely supervised by the DBGA's leafspot officers and was to be accompanied by borer control treatment.

Growers found HIR attractive because they obtained fertiliser without an initial downpayment (a condition of Dominica's regular fertiliser credit scheme), and they did not have to start paying for it until they began to harvest the replanted crop. The scheme had in fact been conceived before the hurricane, but the destruction caused by Inez provided favourable circumstances for implementing it. To fund rehabilitation, the buyer, Geest, gave one-eighth of a cent for each pound of bananas the company purchased in the autumn of 1966. (This money was given to all four islands, not just Dominica (Higgins 1967, personal communication).)

In St Lucia, as in Dominica, primary responsibility for extension services was in the hands of the department of agriculture, which had twenty-two trained instructors in 1963. Their main concern, however, was controlling soil erosion on the steep slopes that were increasingly used for banana cultivation. It was felt that there were not enough instructors and that they tended to take a greater interest in the farmers who followed their advice and, consequently, to neglect those who needed it most (Biggs, Bennett, et al. 1964, 14).

The SLBGA had about thirty field officers. Their main responsibility was supervising leafspot spray gangs, but they were also required to advise growers about fertiliser requirements and borer control measures. They were not, in general, trained in agriculture, and until the mid-1960s, there was little or no official liaison between the extension staff of the agricultural department and the field officers of SLBGA.

In 1966, the managing director of the SLBGA blamed the lack of effective extension work for continuing low yields (Monplaisir 1966, personal communication). Nevertheless, some steps were being taken to address this problem. In October 1966, a Banana Week was organised by the St Lucia Banana Extension Committee, a coalition of the agricultural department's extension agents and the field staff of the SLBGA. The programme consisted of slide shows on banana production shown at five regional centres, and eighty-three demonstrations on private holdings in all parts of the island. The demonstrations, which were attended by over 2,300 adults, covered all aspects of land preparation, planting, cultivation, harvesting, and handling. Demonstrators identified bad practices, accepted suggestions from participants, and noted difficulties they had experienced when trying to improve standards of cultivation. (*WINBAN News*, April–June 1967, 8–11).

The French Islands

In the French islands, research and extension work were conducted by various organisations that shared features with analogous Commonwealth institutions but were seldom their precise counterparts. All banana research was in the hands of the Institut Français de Recherches Fruitières d'Outre-Mer, formerly the Institut des Fruits et Agrumes Coloniaux (IFAC), whose headquarters for the Western hemisphere had been located in Guadeloupe since 1950. Although IFAC served not only Guadeloupe and Martinique but also Guyane and even, to some extent, non-French countries such as Colombia and Ecuador, and while it was responsible for research on a range of tropical fruits, including pineapples, avocadoes, and citrus, nevertheless, its location in the banana-growing region of Basse-Terre Guadeloupe made it almost inevitable that banana problems would be its chief concern. This focus was further reinforced by the fact that a portion of IFAC's funding came directly from a tax levied by the French government on bananas "exported" from Martinique and Guadeloupe. A drawback of this arrangement was that funds might be severely reduced if hurricanes disrupted production, but in times of crisis, the French government might subsidise IFAC from other sources (Menauge 1974, 153).

The research interests of IFAC were similar to those of the WINBAN centre: agronomy, disease control, improving fruit quality, and lowering production costs. The most notable achievement of IFAC in the mid-1950s was the development of an effective method of controlling leafspot disease (*Cercospora musae*, Sigatoka). This disease was becoming an increasingly serious problem in all the Windwards, especially in high rainfall areas. In Guadeloupe, it threatened the very existence of the export banana industry in the high rainfall areas of southern and southeastern Basse-Terre that had traditionally been the main centres of banana production (Morue 1967, personal communication).

In the late 1950s and early 1960s, research efforts at IFAC were concentrated on maximising yields per hectare; there were trials to determine optimum planting density and pattern (Champion 1964). By the mid-1960s, IFAC's main interest was in developing banana varieties more resistant to wind damage and in improving banana quality and packing methods (Morue 1967, personal communication).

Although IFAC's sources of funding, namely, the metropolitan government and local banana growers, were similar to those of the WINBAN research centre, IFAC did not owe its existence to island growers' associations in the way that the WINBAN centre did, and its preoccupation with bananas may have resulted more from its geographical location than from the interests of those who controlled it. Nevertheless, the research interests of the two centres were very similar. If there were differences in orientation, they lay more in the way research results were communicated and in the clientele for whom they were destined. One of the scientists working at IFAC said it functioned very much like a private institution, working directly for the island's big planters by, for example, analysing soil samples for them in its laboratories (Morue 1967, personal communication; Menauge 1974, 154). On the other hand, like WINBAN, IFAC published pamphlets giving technical advice, and it produced a weekly newssheet, *Fruits Guadeloupéens,* giving agricultural and market information.

The real responsibility for extension work was, however, in other hands, and in the mid-1960s the growers' associations, SICABAM and ASSOBAG, had a very small role in it. In the French islands, as in the Commonwealth ones, extension was originally the responsibility of the island agricultural departments. In theory, the Martinique and Guadeloupe departments had always provided extension services, but it was suggested to me that, in fact, they had been organised on an effective basis in Martinique only since the mid-1950s. One or two agents of the Service d'Agronomie were stationed in each commune, a total of about twenty on the island (Emélie 1967, personal communication). In addition, each island had two or three *foyers de progrès agricole,* demonstration centres where farmers could come for advice about agricultural matters. These services were supposed to be available to all farmers, large and small.

Whether because the agricultural departments were felt to be doing an inadequate job, or simply because its mandate had not been defined carefully enough to avoid overlapping constituencies, the Société d'Aide Technique et de Crédit (SATEC) in fact covered much of the same ground as the agricultural department's extension services. SATEC, which was active in the banana industry from about 1960 to 1970, was a *société d'état,* an organisation formed and funded by the government. Initially, its agents concentrated on assisting small farmers, especially banana growers, to set up SICAS, on subdividing estates sold to the government under the *Réforme Foncière* and on settling small farmers on them.

In 1965, the SATEC changed its name to Société d'Aide Technique et de Co-opération, which signalled a withdrawal from its financial role and a shift of emphasis to technical assistance. In 1967, SATEC launched *L'Opération Banane,* designed to revitalise the industry by promoting techniques to improve both yields and quality (Menauge 1974, 159; Burac 1975, 60). This effort was to be directed particularly at small and medium-sized farmers. The Guadeloupe branch of SATEC was staffed by four officers with specialist agricultural qualifications and five monitors, or agricultural technicians, but they were involved with several facets of agriculture in the island, not the banana industry alone. They provided advice through visits to individual farms, through the publication and distribution of a manual on production techniques for banana growers, and through radio broadcasts, in Creole, on such topics as desuckering and borer control (Menauge 1974, 158–9).

Evidently even the extension work of the agricultural departments and SATEC together did not satisfy the perceived needs of the banana industry. In 1966, members of the agricultural department in Martinique told me that the SICABAM had its own technical assistance section (Jacquemart and Lamure 1966, personal communication), although this section must have been on a modest scale, since it was not mentioned by anybody else. In Guadeloupe, the board of ASSOBAG decided, in April 1968, to create the Service Agro-technique de la SICA–ASSOBAG. It was set up under the technical authority of IFAC, and run by an agronomist with solid experience in banana problems, aided by four technical assistants and eight monitors. It was concerned with improving yields and quality and made direct contact with planters. In fact, it took over the part played by SATEC in banana industry extension work, so that by 1970 SATEC had more or less withdrawn from extension work and was able to concentrate its efforts elsewhere. The Service Agro-technique de la SICA–ASSOBAG was funded by the government and the growers (Menauge 1974, 159–61).

The island growers' associations became involved in research and extension apparently in an attempt to compensate for the perceived deficiencies in the services provided by the other agencies. It might seem that if services were available, it was of no great significance who provided them. Analysis of the impact of the associations' activities suggests, however, that who provides a service often has a bearing on who receives it, and on how it is received. I concluded from conversations with small farmers in all four islands that the most likely reaction to the recommendations of "experts" was scepticism, often well-founded, and unless farmers were provided with strong inducements to adopt improved agricultural techniques, the most well-intentioned advice was likely to fall on stony ground.

In the French islands, IFAC was, in effect, the servant of the big planters, and SATEC provided guidance and close supervision and, initially, credit to farmers on smallholdings that had been carved out of large estates under the land reform programme. For small farmers outside the orbit of these organisations, however, there was no body with an obligation to assist in improving banana cultivation, and certainly, it was not a high priority with SICABAM or ASSOBAG.

Even in the Commonwealth Windwards, where growers' associations had a clear obligation to serve all classes of growers and had for some time acknowledged the need to promote agronomically desirable practices, it was often hard to detect what results the associations might have achieved. To be sure, WINBAN's experimental work had only been in progress for three or four years at the time of my 1966–67 survey, so it would have been unrealistic to expect all growers to be familiar with its latest findings. The fact is, however, that in the three subjects of particular interest to Windwards farmers, namely, the choice of appropriate fertilisers, mixed cropping, and nematode control, knowledge of advances made by WINBAN scientists seemed very limited indeed. Of 117 farmers interviewed, only 5, 3 of them large estate owners, were using fertilisers of a different composition from that supplied throughout each island by the growers' association under its credit scheme. No farmer reported having taken account of WINBAN's research when determining crop combinations or spacing of mixed crops; and despite widespread concern that banana plants were blowing down more easily, relatively few farmers (10.6 percent in St Lucia and 15.7 percent in Dominica) said they thought that nematode infestation was a problem. No one interviewed in St Lucia reported using chemical products to combat nematodes, although 20 percent did so in Dominica (in most cases employing a product not intended for the purpose). A further 3 percent were aware that there were chemicals to control nematodes but said that they were too expensive to use.

I asked the farmers I surveyed in 1966–67 about their sources of information on agricultural techniques. In St Lucia, only six of forty-eight farmers mentioned contacts with the SLBGA that might have given them access to up-to-date information on techniques of cultivation. One of the six, a manager of a large estate, had experimental plots on his land. Three were part-time SLBGA employees: a paymaster, a reception officer, and a leafspot officer. In five out of six cases, the yields obtained by these farmers were below the average of 10.4 tons per hectare for the sample as a whole! The leafspot officer, for instance, whose duties also extended to checking borer control measures and fertiliser requirements and assessing the need for drains on holdings in his district, recorded a yield on his own holding of only 9 tons per hectare. Three farmers mentioned that after Hurricane Abby in 1960, the association brought in Jamaican experts to demonstrate planting and rehabilitation techniques and advise on fertiliser application. One, but only one, spoke of acquiring information at one or two "mass gatherings" organised by the SLBGA.

In Dominica, the success of the DBGA in disseminating agricultural information to growers seems to have been even more limited. Only three of seventy farmers interviewed mentioned any contact with the DBGA that might have provided information on agricultural techniques. Two of the three were employees, and the third noted that, while he was aware of recommendations the association had made, experience had taught him that his own methods gave more satisfactory results.

Table 7.1 shows the sources of farming information of the St Lucian and Dominican farmers that I interviewed and records the number and percentage of farmers citing each source.

Both the SLBGA and the DBGA had taken some steps to improve standards of cultivation, but whether, if they had played a more aggressive role, their impact at that period would have been any greater is open to question. In both St Lucia and Dominica, over 50 percent of the farmers I interviewed had obtained some information or advice from agricultural departments or their extension officers. The average yield obtained by these farmers did exceed the yield of farmers who had relied on "trial and error," "experience," or "family training." In St Lucia, farmers who had received information or advice obtained 12.29 tons per hectare, while those who had not averaged 6.67 tons per hectare. In Dominica, the corresponding averages were 10.2 and 8.9 tons per hectare. When the data are subjected to a t-test, however, it emerges that, while for St Lucia, the difference between the two groups of farmers is significant at a 2 percent level, for Dominica the difference is not significant even at a 20 percent level. Since professional advice and expertise were held in such low regard anyway, it seems doubtful, therefore, whether it would have been especially productive, in Dominica at least, for growers' associations to put much money or effort into straightforward agricultural extension. Indeed, a number of the farmers I interviewed said that they were aware of the recommendations of agricultural officers but did not follow them because they could not afford to, or because they felt them to be inappropriate for their own circumstances.

Although WINBAN and island growers' associations had little direct impact on the agricultural techniques of the average grower, they

Table 7.1
Sources of farming information, St Lucia and Dominica, 1966–67

	Family	*School*	*ADE*[a]	*BGA*[b]	*Estates*	*T&E*[c]	*Other*[d]
ST LUCIA (48 INTERVIEWS)							
Number	10	7	22	2	–	16	2
Percentage	25.6	17.9	56.4	5.1	0	41.0	5.1
DOMINICA (70 INTERVIEWS)							
Number	20	7	28	1	10	10	6
Percentage	37.0	13.0	51.8	1.9	18.5	18.5	11.1

Note: In St Lucia, 9 of the 48 farmers did not respond; in Dominica, 16 of the 70 did not respond and are not included in the percentage calculations. Some farmers cited more than one source so that the percentages add up to more than 100.

[a] Agriculture department extension service.

[b] Banana growers' association.

[c] Trial and error.

[d] The category "Other" includes overseas agricultural institutions attended or consulted and reference to written material.

apparently had a greater impact on some of the largest growers. Several of the largest growers that I interviewed, especially in St Lucia where the WINBAN research station was located, were quite familiar with the most recent developments and some growers had had frequent personal contact with WINBAN research personnel. A very few of them managed to achieve yields equal to or even slightly above the average yields recorded on the French islands, but others admitted to yields of only 10 or 15 tons per hectare, even though their estates occupied what appeared to be some of the most suitable land in the islands for banana cultivation. In their view, the advantages of purestand planting and regular uprooting and replanting were outweighed by their own greater commitment to longer-term tree crops and their desire to minimise windstorm damage by using limited labour resources to cultivate a larger area extensively, rather than a smaller area more intensively. Inadequate capital undoubtedly discouraged several well-informed large growers from investing as much in chemical inputs as would have been necessary to bring their yields up to the levels generally attained in Martinique and Guadeloupe.

It might have been expected that where a large estate was obtaining high yields by following recommended practices, some neighbouring farmers would have adopted these practices as well (Hägerstrand 1967, 159). Evidence of this form of diffusion of information was very limited. According to several estate owners, neighbouring small farmers claimed that they could not afford new methods, which usually involved increased expenditure on inputs. Several small farmers agreed. On the other hand, one successful St Lucian estate owner reported that neighbouring small farmers had asked him about weedicides, and in Dominica, four small farmers in the Woodford Hill area said they had learnt about banana cultivation from the manager of an estate on which they had all worked. All four reported yields well above average, averaging 21 tons per hectare for the four.

A small farmer in the Layou Valley, who had at one time been an agricultural department extension officer, did say that progressive estates were generally surrounded by a progressive peasantry and that the converse was also true. He considered the Layou Valley a relatively progressive area, for this reason. The yields of the six Layou Valley farmers that I interviewed averaged 16.5 tons per hectare, well above the island sample average of 11 tons per hectare. These isolated instances suggest that while the recommended agricultural techniques did not always spread from successful, well-informed growers to their neighbours, diffusion might occur if the personality of the well-informed grower inspired confidence in the advice he might pass on.

While simply *informing* farmers either directly or indirectly through the example set by "model" farmers seems to have had limited success, there were ways of inducing or even compelling them to adopt recommended practices that proved more effective. For instance, if the right to receive certain benefits, or even to remain a participant in the industry, was made contingent on the adoption of specified practices, most growers were prepared to comply. The DBGA's Hurricane Inez Rehabilitation Scheme provided a clear demonstration of this. Initially, farmers were slow to join the scheme, but then there was a rush of would-be participants, followed by a period of waning interest, and then another rush when it was announced that the scheme would end twelve months after the passage of the hurricane. Altogether about 400 hectares were rehabilitated during the nine months of the scheme, and there were plans to restart it the following April (1968), in an attempt to ensure an increase in production in the summer months.

It is hard to gauge the impact of the scheme on standards of cultivation and, more to the point, on yields per hectare. There was a steady, if modest, increase in production in Dominica in each of the last three years of the 1960s, whereas in St Lucia, production levels fluctuated. It is thus at least possible that the scheme had a significant positive effect. On the other hand, none of the seven small or medium-sized banana growers I visited in April 1970 appeared to have been influenced by it in any way. Cools-Lartigue claims that once the rigorous supervision associated with the scheme ended, improved yields were not sustained. Average bunch weights, which had risen to 40 pounds, fell to 25 pounds as farmers reverted to old methods of cultivation (Cools-Lartigue 1969, 23,29).

FERTILISER CREDIT AND SUBSIDISED INPUTS

Although the relationship between fertiliser applications and yields was not always consistent (see Figure 5.1, above), it was generally agreed that high banana yields could not be obtained without substantial quantities of fertiliser. Agronomists recommended about 1.5 kg per mat per year, which at the recommended density of 2,000 to 2,500 mats per hectare amounted to about three tons per hectare, at a price, in 1966, of about WI$180 per ton. For large-scale growers, cultivating bananas under physical conditions that, barring natural disasters, yielded 25 tons or more per hectare, this would have been a fairly modest investment. For small growers cultivating bananas on remote holdings under physical conditions that might make response to fertiliser application unpredictable, such an investment might have been out of the question, especially if the investment had to be made months before the banana crop sales began to yield financial returns.

In St Lucia and Dominica, agricultural credit was scarce and hard to obtain, especially for small farmers with little security. In the late 1950s, therefore, growers' associations in these islands initiated fertiliser credit schemes. Approved applicants drew supplies of fertiliser purchased by their association and paid for it over the succeeding months by debiting one cent a pound from their receipts for fruit delivered to the association. In some cases, a deposit of a few dollars a bag was required. There were expenses associated with the administration of such schemes, since applicants' fields had to be inspected by field officers of the association and the clerical staff also had to be paid. Consequently, fertiliser costs were slightly higher for credit customers. Initially, government loans helped to finance the schemes, but in St Lucia, for instance, the scheme was financed by the SLBGA's own resources beginning in 1958 (Biggs, Bennett, et al. 1964, 15).

Although the SLBGA staff in St Lucia complained about some irregularities, they felt that the scheme was functioning satisfactorily for the growers. The main difficulty was that when a series of windstorms reduced production for a few months, the repayment rate dwindled, putting a strain on the association's finances (SLBGA 1966, 4). By 1966, the SLBGA owed WI$350,000 to the commercial banks, largely, it was claimed, as a result of outstanding fertiliser debts (Romalis 1968, 247).

While the DBGA's scheme resembled that of the SLBGA in many respects, it seemed in the mid-1960s to be regarded with less satisfaction. It was said that repayment imposed too much strain on growers and that many sought to evade or postpone repayment by selling their fruit in other growers' names (Cools-Lartigue 1969, 21). These complaints may well have been valid, since prices to Dominica growers fell below the four-cents-a-pound minimum maintained through price support in St Lucia during the winter of 1964–65: in December 1965 Dominica growers were receiving only two and a half cents a pound *before* deductions for repayment of fertiliser credit (DBGA 1965). Furthermore, credit repayment may have been much harder to control in Dominica because DBGA buying operations were handled by dealers. The SLBGA had more direct control through its island-wide network of buying points. A third factor was that in 1963 and 1964, substantial quantities of fertiliser were distributed free to Dominican growers when the United Kingdom provided funds to help rehabilitate plantations severely damaged by hurricanes. St Lucian farmers, who were less severely afflicted, received less free fertiliser and so were perhaps less disconcerted by the price they had to pay for unsubsidised fertiliser in 1966–67.

Whatever the reason for the relatively unfavourable perception of Dominica's scheme, the DBGA had decided by 1966 that it should be supplemented by another scheme, one that was more discriminating but that offered more favourable terms to farmers who would rehabilitate run-down plantations. Before this scheme could be implemented, however, Hurricane Inez struck the island, providing an excellent pretext for launching the project in the guise of the Hurricane Inez Rehabilitation Scheme (HIR), described earlier in this chapter.

Although the DBGA employees were satisfied with the results of the HIR campaign, board members continued to be concerned that less than one-third of the fertiliser recommended by WINBAN was used on the island's banana acreage. Some members of the board proposed that Dominica should leave the WINBAN insurance scheme (described below) and use the money saved to subsidise fertiliser sales (DBGA 1967).

In July 1968, the association did indeed withdraw from the WINBAN insurance scheme, and a cess of 0.25¢ per pound was used to subsidise fertiliser. The fertiliser was made available to growers in quarterly allocations at half the regular price; prepayment was required (Cools-Lartigue 1969, 22). By 1969, the DBGA was involved in several different schemes to induce farmers to use more fertiliser. To encouraging replanting, the HIR programme was revived as the Banana Development Scheme (BDS) and accompanied by provision of some free nematicides. Fertiliser was issued on credit, with no service charge or downpayment; delivery was free; and repayment began at the time of harvesting. If banana prices fell below 3¢ a pound, however, there was no repayment deduction; and if they were 3¢ to 4¢ a pound, only 0.5¢ a pound was deducted. At prices of 4¢ to 6¢ a pound, the deduction rate was 1¢ cent a pound; and for prices over 6¢, the rate was 1.5¢.

The old Fertiliser Credit Scheme had lapsed; it had run up a debt once downpayments were no longer required, since many recipients of credit had avoided repayment by selling their fruit in other growers' names. The scheme was resuscitated, however, in 1969, since the quarterly allocations of subsidised fertiliser were not enough, and the BDS fertiliser was not available for ratoon crops. To prevent the recurrence of abuses, more rigorous conditions were laid down than under the original scheme. A ten percent deposit was required and growers had to have sufficient production to permit repayment of their debt within three months of the issue of any allocation, at the same rates as those of the BDS. The credit limit was set at WI$125 a quarter (DBGA 1970, personal communication).

The evidence suggests that the banana growers' associations were indeed instrumental in ensuring that most farmers in St Lucia and Dominica fertilised their plantations to some extent. In the early 1960s, SLBGA and DBGA distributed well over half the fertiliser being imported into these two islands.

In 1962, the last year for which statistics are not distorted by post-hurricane distribution of free or subsidised fertiliser, St Lucia exported 49,000 tons of bananas. If all growers had participated in the credit scheme, at the then current price of WI$136 a ton, 8,136 tons of fertiliser would have been distributed. In fact, St Lucia imported 7,165 tons of fertiliser in 1962, of which SLBGA distributed 3,900 tons (54 percent). This is consistent with the fact that the larger estates in particular, but also a few well-informed and economically independent smaller growers, often preferred to buy specially formulated or cheaper fertiliser from the Agriculturalists' Association or a commercial importer. If estates over 40 hectares, producing a quarter of St Lucia's bananas, are abstracted, a very high proportion of the remaining growers must have obtained their fertiliser through SLBGA.

The situation was similar in Dominica. Given the DBGA's selling price of WI$126 a ton, the export of 28,000 tons of bananas would theoretically have entailed the distribution of 4,977 tons of fertiliser if all growers had been in the scheme. Actual fertiliser imports totalled 3,005 tons, of which the DBGA distributed 2,351 tons (78 percent). Estates of over 40 hectares produced 36 percent of the island's bananas in 1961.

Nearly all the banana growers I interviewed in Dominica and St Lucia in 1966 claimed to be using some fertiliser, although some acknowledged that the amount was very small and quite inadequate. In St Lucia, out of 48 farmers interviewed, 17 said they obtained fertiliser on the credit scheme, 10 said they bought fertiliser for cash, generally from sources other than SLBGA, and the remaining 21 did not specify. In Dominica, 14 of 70 interviewees said they obtained fertiliser through the DBGA credit scheme; 7 said they seldom or never bought fertiliser; 5 said they paid in cash, in most cases to obtain a different formulation from that supplied by the DBGA, and the remainder did not specify. It is probable, however, that in both islands most farmers did obtain fertiliser through their association's credit scheme. One well-informed St Lucian farmer said that most of the growers in his area, the remote interior district of Millet, belonged to the scheme, while another, in the southeast, remarked that it was responsible for "bringing up" the growers in his area. The scheme had enabled him to develop his banana cultivation to the point where he was no longer dependent on credit and was able to pay cash for the fertiliser he required.

The fertiliser credit schemes did have their detractors. Some farmers complained that while bananas were grown on a variety of soils, their association supplied only one type of fertiliser for the entire island and on some soils it gave no response at all. In Dominica particularly, there were complaints that there were delays in the delivery of credit-scheme fertiliser and that inadequate amounts were supplied under the scheme. Nevertheless, four of the five complainers still relied on the scheme for their fertiliser.

Two Dominican growers said that even on credit, fertiliser was beyond their means; one said that he could not afford the initial deposit. These criticisms serve to emphasize just how dependent most farmers were on credit-scheme fertiliser: the only alternative, evidently, was to do without. A farmer in leeward Dominica said that when he could not afford the ten percent downpayment required by DBGA, a year might pass without his buying any further fertiliser. Without it, the stems of bananas soon failed to achieve the minimum weight acceptable to the association, and a high proportion were rejected at the buying point.

It was widely recognized in all the islands that increasing inputs of fertiliser were required to sustain satisfactory yields and produce stems of acceptable weight. Several growers told me they had obtained good crops with little or no fertiliser when cultivating virgin soils, but in succeeding years yields had become less and less satisfactory unless they had started using it. Growers who in 1966 admitted to using no fertiliser, or only negligible amounts, had average yields of only 4.3 tons per hectare (3 tons if one questionable claim is discounted), less than half the averages of the St Lucia and Dominica sample.

Since the SLBGA and the DBGA fertiliser credit schemes were used by a high proportion of growers, despite their acknowledged drawbacks, and since growers not using the schemes often said they could not afford even the modest downpayment, it is evident that without the credit schemes many more farmers would have been unable to afford the fertiliser that was necessary to prevent production from dwindling to less than half the levels of the mid-1960s. In theory, it should have been possible, even advantageous, for farmers to buy fertiliser for cash out of their savings. In fact, however, many farmers could not accumulate the necessary cash before selling their bananas - whose growth depended on the application of the fertiliser. These people often had no access to any other source of credit.

Following extensive hurricane losses in 1963 and 1964, large quantities of free and subsidised fertiliser were distributed by the DBGA and the SLBGA. Allocations were based on acreage. There were allegations of fraudulent inflation of qualifying acreages, so anxious were farmers to take advantage of the handouts. Nevertheless, while some farmers said that the free fertiliser had boosted their production by increasing the percentage of export-weight bunches, they had felt unable to afford inputs at such a level, and bunch weights had soon started to decline again.

The deduction of one cent per pound of bananas sold under the original fertiliser credit schemes should have resulted in farmers receiving about 1.5 kg of fertiliser per plant per year, supposing that every plant bore a saleable bunch annually. (In fact, less than half did, so applications per plant were well below the recommended level.) In fact, in 1962 the associations in both islands sold growers, on credit and for cash, an average of roughly 1 kg of fertiliser per stem of bananas exported.

In the French islands at this period, neither SICABAM nor ASSOBAG was involved in the bulk buying of fertiliser, nor did they arrange to distribute it at subsidised rates or on terms of easy credit. It was suggested to me that since many of their board members were also importers of fertiliser, as well as other agricultural supplies, it was unlikely that the associations would become involved in selling anything at reduced rates (Léobon 1966, personal communication). Even local SICAs were reported to be buying fertiliser for their members through local merchants, rather than ordering it in bulk from France (Hazaël-Massieux 1967, personal communication). Presumably such small-scale enterprises did not have the necessary contacts or facilities to bypass the intermediaries. Consequently, in Martinique and Guadeloupe, bananas were grown only by those who could afford to pay cash for fertiliser or who could obtain loans from commercial banks or credit from fertiliser importers.

In Dominica and St Lucia thousands of farmers, probably a substantial majority, obtained fertiliser for their bananas through their island association's fertiliser credit scheme. Without such schemes, many, perhaps most, of these farmers would have been able to afford only very small amounts of chemical fertiliser for their bananas, or none at all. As soil fertility was depleted and virgin land became increasingly scarce, production would inevitably have declined. In

Table 7.2
Fertiliser imported into Dominica, per stem of bananas exported

Year	*Quantity of fertiliser (pounds per stem)*
1951	1.69
1952	1.36
1953	1.65
1954	1.98
1955	2.74
1962	3.03
1963	4.81
1967	3.85

Source: Colony of Dominica (1952–55); Dominica, Treasury Department (1963–64); State of Dominica (1968).
Note: This includes all fertiliser, not only that imported by the DBGA and not only that destined for use on bananas. It is doubtful, however, whether more than very moderate amounts were applied to crops other than bananas.

fact, in both islands there was a sharp increase in production in the late 1950s, at about the time the credit schemes were introduced (Persaud 1966, 28). As Table 7.2 shows, by the mid-1960s a far higher quantity of fertiliser was consumed for each stem of bananas exported than in the early 1950s.

Fertiliser credit schemes thus permitted sustained participation in the export banana industry by thousands of small farmers who would otherwise have been obliged to drop out when their soils became exhausted. The schemes also permitted far higher production levels than would have been attained without small-grower participation. Their areal impact is a matter for conjecture. Without them, banana production would probably have been restricted to medium- and large-scale holdings, most of which were located in valleys and relatively gently sloping areas. The practitioners of shifting cultivation on Crown lands and derelict estates might have been able to continue producing bananas without fertiliser, but it is unlikely that these small producers could have exerted enough influence on the industry to prevent its institutions from being modified in ways that would have made their continued participation even more precarious.

A well-informed and influential St Lucian grower, with a medium-sized holding (30 hectares, of which 8 were in bananas) remarked, in the course of the 1966 survey, that large-scale growers were trying to oust small growers from the board of the SLBGA, since the large growers felt that under the current arrangements, they were subsidising small growers. Frequent windstorm damage had resulted in slow or interrupted repayments of fertiliser credit, leaving the associations with heavy burdens of debt. Large growers, who did not use the scheme, resented the fact that SLBGA's resources had been diverted to services that gave them no advantage. The fact that large growers were at this period so anxious to gain more control over the industry suggests that given the chance, they would have effected a redistribution of resources more favourable to their interests as they saw them. An advantage, from their perspective, of making fertiliser less accessible to small growers and thereby driving them out of production would have been a much more abundant labour supply for their own estates.

Apart from exerting a major influence on who grew bananas, where they were grown, and in what quantities, the SLBGA's and the DBGA's fertiliser credit schemes had a considerable effect on other aspects of land use. Since most small farmers (as well as many medium-sized and large ones) grew bananas in mixed cultivation, fertiliser intended for banana plants inevitably benefited interplanted coconuts, citrus, and provision crops as well. Consequently, many farmers who would not have devoted time and space to long-term tree crops with the yields these gave when unfertilised, found them well worth growing in association with fertilised bananas.

Many commentators who are concerned about living standards in the small islands of the Eastern Caribbean have criticised the emphasis on crops destined for export rather than local consumption, on the grounds that export crops divert land, labour, and capital from satisfying the nutritional requirements of the local population. In the mid-1960s, however, it was claimed in St Lucia that the fertiliser applied to export bananas had also increased the yields of interplanted provision crops. While it was true that small farmers in the French islands who lacked the resources to grow export bananas often specialised in food crops for the local market, there was no evidence that Commonwealth farmers who had taken up banana growing were thereby depriving themselves or their fellow-citizens of locally grown provisions. Indeed, fertiliser credit schemes probably reinforced the practice of mixed cropping on the Commonwealth islands.

DISEASE AND PEST CONTROL

When banana industries were revived in the Eastern Caribbean after the Second World War, the favoured varieties were Lacatan and Robusta, which, unlike the formerly popular Gros Michel, were immune to the ravages of Panama disease. They were, however, highly susceptible to leafspot, which was first recognised in Dominica in 1937 and had affected most of the island by 1947 (Cools-Lartigue 1969, 19). By the mid-1950s, the disease was so serious in all the islands that yields were starting to decline. In Guadeloupe the disease had provoked a significant shift of production from the traditional high-altitude, high-rainfall banana lands of southern Basse-Terre to the drier coastal lowlands of the northeast. Spraying with water-based fungicides proved inadequate to control the disease, but an effective means of keeping it in check with an oil spray was developed at IFAC and quickly adopted throughout the region. Initially, the spray was delivered from knapsack sprays, but by the mid-1960s, substantial acreages were sprayed by aeroplane, a much more economical and satisfactory procedure where the terrain was not too steep and dissected and where the bananas were planted in purestands.

In Dominica, a leafspot control board was established as a statutory body, subject to government control, as early as 1951. Farmers were taught how to spray their banana plantations by the board's field officers, but it was the farmers' responsibility to carry out the spraying. The results of this arrangement were not satisfactory. In 1958, the leafspot control board became a subsidiary of the DBGA; spraying, now carried out by the association's own employees, became compulsory; and a cess of 0.4¢ for every pound of bananas sold was levied to finance the spraying programme. By 1968, over 800 hectares (comprising six large estates and some particularly inaccessible areas of small farms) were sprayed by plane by a Martinique-based company under contract to the DBGA. The company was paid WI$1.30 per acre, while ground sprayers were paid 60¢ an acre, or in very difficult places, 69¢. Spraying was carried out at intervals of 14 to 21 days. (Cools-Lartigue 1969, 19–20). The actual cost of leafspot spraying operations in 1965 was 0.5¢ for every pound of bananas exported (Persaud 1966, 14).

Leafspot control was also compulsory in St Lucia, where it was administered by the SLBGA and financed out of the cess of 1.125¢ a pound that the SLBGA levied to cover insurance, administration, disease control, and other expenses. The average cost of leafspot control for each pound of bananas exported was similar to the Dominica figure, although it showed greater year-to-year fluctuation. In 1963, a Martiniquan company was engaged to carry out aerial spraying in areas where this was practicable, but by 1966, the high cost of hiring spray planes had prompted the SLBGA to buy two of its own.

In the French islands, neither SICABAM nor ASSOBAG was directly involved in leafspot control in the mid-1960s. It was the responsibility of individual growers to ensure that their crops were sprayed, and one small grower told me that nearly all banana growers did spray their crop, since the fruit tended to have a poor appearance and be unmarketable if they did not (Zébus 1967, personal communication). In Guadeloupe, some smaller growers cooperated among themselves to arrange more economical leafspot spraying (Mauréaux 1967, personal communication).

The average cost of aerial spraying per pound of fruit exported was WI$0.48 (SICABAM 1965). The cost per pound was comparable with the cost in the Commonwealth islands; but spraying was very much more expensive per unit of area in the French islands. Moreover, the wettest areas might require spraying almost twice as frequently as the drier areas, creating a substantial cost differential.

While banana cultivation without leafspot control measures was virtually out of the question in the Eastern Caribbean, there were other pests and diseases which greatly reduced productivity when left untreated, although they did not place the whole future of the industry in jeopardy, as first Panama disease and then leafspot had threatened to do. The banana borer was a problem in all four islands. In St Lucia in 1966, aldrin and white lime to control borer infestation were supplied by the SLBGA out of the cess at no extra cost to growers (Monplaisir 1966, personal communication). In Dominica, free borer control was provided under the HIR. In Martinique and Guadeloupe, individual farmers undertook and paid for borer control.

Nematodes were a relatively new but growing problem in the mid-1960s. In Guadeloupe, I was told that the heavy clay soils on which much of the island's banana cultivation took place were not seriously afflicted, and no special control measures were necessary. In the other three islands, infestation was most severe where the land had been in bananas continuously, for a long period. Progressive farmers injected the soil periodically with nematicides, an expensive procedure, or left land fallow before replanting to reduce the level of infestation. Less progressive farmers did nothing, and when an unacceptably high proportion of their plants fell, they transferred their effort, where possible, to another parcel of land. None of the growers' associations subsidised nematode control directly.

The different policies of the growers' associations in the Commonwealth and French islands with regard to disease control and, particularly, leafspot spraying had clear repercussions on several aspects of banana cultivation and helped to determine where ba-

Table 7.3
Cost of leafspot control in Martinique, in wet and dry areas at different yields per hectare

Yield per hectare	*Spray cycles per year*	*Cost of Spraying*	
		Fr/kg[a]	*WI¢/lb.*
25	30	0.027	0.67
25	20	0.018	0.45
40	20	0.0113	0.28
12	30	0.056	1.35

Source: Aerial spraying costs from SICABAM (1965).
[a]Estimated total production costs, planting to packing shed ("nu hangar"): 0.40 Fr/kg; actual farm gate or packing shed prices to small growers in southeastern Guadeloupe, 1966 and 1967: 0.10 to 0.40 Fr/kg. But note that Bordaz cited a spraying cost per hectare that was *half* that given by SICABAM, 11.25 Fr/ha, not 22.50 (Bordaz 1966).

nanas could be cultivated profitably. In the French islands, where leafspot spraying was the responsibility of the individual, growers with high-density, purestand cultivations in areas level enough for aerial spraying and dry enough that only twenty spray-cycles a year were necessary could expect to keep leafspot in check far more cheaply than those in rugged, high-rainfall areas with mixed cultivation (Table 7.3). I was told that the cost of leafspot control helped to accelerate the phasing out of banana and tree-crop combinations, which until the 1950s had been traditional in parts of southern Guadeloupe and the valleys of the leeward coast. Since smallholders tended to be concentrated in the higher, more rugged areas, high leafspot control costs would have been an additional handicap to them had they ventured into export banana production. Moreover, Guadeloupean farmers claimed that aerial spraying could be carried out only on plantations of 10 hectares or more (although in a less rugged banana area of Martinique, a respondent's 8-hectare plantation was sprayed by plane). Consequently, the small grower, who had to resort to more costly ground spraying, was at an even greater disadvantage.

Since individual farmers bore the whole cost of leafspot control directly, control was not always adequately carried out in particularly vulnerable areas. In principle, spraying was obligatory. The manager of SICABAM claimed that all growers did in fact spray their bananas, but officers in the department of agriculture told me that in practice this was not the case (Jacquemart and Lamure 1967, personal communication). A farmer in St Joseph, in central Martinique, reported that although leafspot was bad in the district, many local farmers did not use adequate controls (Bordaz 1966, personal communication). The comment of a farmer in the heights of Capesterre, in southeastern Guadeloupe, that spray was *very widely* used, because otherwise the fruit had a poor appearance, implies that its use was not universal. A Trois-Rivières farmer reported that in the extremely wet area around Grand Etang, in southeastern Guadeloupe, leafspot control was poor. Farmers had started growing bananas in this area only because the construction of a road for tourism had made it easily accessible; areas physically similar but lacking such tourist attractions as the impressive Chutes du Carbet would not have been considered worth opening up for agricultural development alone.

On the other hand, the very low cost of leafspot control in relatively dry areas, such as south-central Martinique, favoured banana cultivation there. The need for irrigation and the threat of periodic losses through drought would otherwise have made banana cultivation very marginal in those areas.

If the policies of ASSOBAG and SICABAM were to the disadvantage of small holders, farmers with low yields and farmers in excessively humid or rugged districts, the assumption by the SLBGA and the DBGA of full responsibility for leafspot control and its financing might be expected to have had diametrically opposite effects. My fieldwork in 1966 and Momsen's maps (1969) of banana acreages in St Lucia and Dominica in 1965-66 generally confirm this expectation. Banana cultivation on both islands was carried on indiscriminately in areas of great ruggedness and with rainfall as high as 5 metres a year. There was no limit on the smallness of units of production: some growers I interviewed sold no more than two or three stems a fortnight. Especially in Dominica, mixed cultivation was the rule rather than the exception.

It is almost certainly true that in Dominica and St Lucia, large growers, as a whole, subsidised the disease control of small growers, since all growers contributed a constant amount for each pound of bananas produced, even though a larger area was required, on average, to produce a given weight of fruit on small than on large holdings. (Momsen (1969) gives mean yields per hectare for 1965 of 3.2 tons for Dominica and 6 tons for St Lucia, but 1961 census data suggest mean yields on estates over 40 hectares of 10.5 tons and 13.7 tons respectively.)

However, there is little reason to suppose that the elimination of small growers or the transfer of responsibility for leafspot control to the individual grower would have resulted in lower costs for the large producer. On the French islands, even with only twenty-five spray cycles a year, the cost of control for a yield of 12 tons per hectare was the equivalent of WI$1.25 per pound. The higher cost of leafspot control in the French islands was not the result of higher labour costs since most spraying was by plane in the French islands and individuals there employed the same private (French) companies as the DBGA employed. Thus, presumably because growers in the Commonwealth islands were able to negotiate a single contract and because the company was able to conduct spraying operations without reference to property boundaries, the costs per hectare were significantly lower: Fr 7 per hectare compared with Fr 22.50 in Martinique, according to SICABAM (1965). However, SICABAM's figure may be unduly inflated: a figure of Fr 11.25 was cited by Bordaz in 1966 (personal communication)!

Furthermore, the companies had more assurance of being paid by the island associations than by individual growers. The owner of an aerial spraying company in Martinique said some large growers had run up very substantial debts and ultimately had to be taken to court to extract payment (Daudin 1967, personal communication). Finally, by 1966 the SLBGA had purchased and was operating its own spray planes so that, theoretically at least, spraying could be carried out at cost, with no need to generate a profit for private aerial spraying companies. While a handful of really efficient growers might have been better off under the French system, it seems probable that even the average large grower would not.

It might be argued that if farmers in the Commonwealth islands had had to pay for leafspot control according to the area under cultivation rather than the weight of bananas produced, they would have taken steps to intensify production and increase yields, eliminating mixed cultivation in many cases. It is impossible to make any quantitative estimate of the impact of this alternative. Certainly, many small farmers with extremely low banana yields would have been forced out of export banana growing, since they could not have afforded to do without their subsistence food crops and would have been reluctant to destroy established, permanent tree crops. On the other hand, many large growers with established coconuts and citrus interplanted with bananas would also have been adversely affected; in some drier areas of St Lucia, bananas could only be grown successfully beneath coconut palms.

In fact, while the 1961 census figures suggest a well-above-average intensity of production on estates over 40 hectares, the 1966 survey provides no confirmation of such a trend (see Tables 7.4 and 7.5).

Table 7.4
Average yields according to holding size, St Lucia and Dominica, 1966–67

	Holding-size group (ha)						
	0–	*1–*	*5–*	*10–*	*20–*	*>50*	*Island average*
ST LUCIA							
Average yield (tons/ha)	3.3	9.8	12.8	–	17.5	7.8	10.4
Number (total = 38)	2	15	9	0	4	8	
DOMINICA							
Average yield (tons/ha)	8.4	10.5	10.5	12.7	6.2	18.3	11.9
Number (total = 56)	3	28	14	8	1	2	

Source: Author's Survey, 1966–67.

Table 7.5
Average yields according to area in bananas, St Lucia and Dominica, 1966

	Area in bananas (ha)						
	0–	*1–*	*5–*	*10–*	*20–*	*>50*	*Island average*
ST LUCIA							
Average yield (tons/ha)	4.5	10.0	14.7	9.6	15.3	7.9	10.4
Number (total = 38)	4	15	9	5	1	4	
DOMINICA							
Average yield (tons/ha)	11.9	10.1	11.2	11.7	16.6	–	11.9
Number (total = 56)	4	38	10	3	1	0	

Source: Author's Survey, 1966–67.

When correlation coefficients are calculated for yields in relation to holding sizes for 40 St Lucian and 53 Dominican banana growers, figures of $r = -0.0467$ and $r = 0.11102$ respectively are obtained, figures not significant even at a 20 percent level. This suggests that even if in a sufficiently large sample, cultivation on large estates was on average more intensive than on small ones, the range of variation was in practice very great, and by no means all large growers were net subsidisers under the DBGA-SLBGA system of financing leafspot control.

In summary, the delegation of leafspot control to the associations and the financing of the control on the basis of poundage rather than acreage favoured mixed cropping by all classes of growers. The system meant that growers in rugged, wet locations - typically, though not uniquely, smallholders - were not deterred by the high cost of disease control from growing export bananas.

How effective was the leafspot control carried out by the Commonwealth associations compared with the French system of control by individual growers? In principle, spraying was carried out wherever bananas were growing and with a frequency adjusted to the needs of each area, varying from nineteen cycles a year in less humid districts to thirty-six cycles in the wettest zones (Monplaisir 1966, personal communication). In practice, it is doubtful whether coverage was as complete or as consistent as my informants claimed. Between November 1966 and January 1967, no aerial spraying was carried out in St Lucia, since, it was alleged, the SLBGA had insufficient funds for spray oil (Atkinson 1967, personal communication). In Dominica too, it seems unlikely that leafspot control was entirely adequate. Bananas were grown on almost 16,000 hectares, often miles from any road, and Momsen suggests that the funds allocated by the DGBA for leafspot control were insufficient to provide comprehensive coverage. Moreover, in some of the more inaccessible areas she surveyed, growers assured her that she was the first person apart from themselves ever to pass that way (Momsen 1969, 8,20). This would seem to preclude regular visits by leafspot spraymen.

Nevertheless, only a small percentage of the farmers I surveyed in either island in 1966 said they were dissatisfied with leafspot control measures (14.6 percent in St Lucia and 8.6 percent in Dominica). A considerably higher proportion said they were satisfied (27.0 percent and 12.9 percent respectively). The great majority expressed no opinion, however, but evidently did not find the disease a problem. While the dissatisfied growers in St Lucia recorded an average yield of only 8.8 tons per hectare, slightly below the 10.4-ton average of all those surveyed, the dissatisfied growers in Dominica actually had a mean yield of 13.8 tons per hectare, somewhat above their island's average of 11.9.

My informants gave various reasons for their dissatisfaction. In St Lucia, there were claims of laxness by local spraymen, especially in areas notorious for infestation by *fer-de-lance* snakes. In both islands, some farmers had picked quarrels with their association's spraymen that had led to the withdrawal or banishment of the spraymen. In some cases, I was told that there had been bad outbreaks of leafspot as a result; in others, that it had made no difference.

One Dominican grower who had several parcels of land in the Castle Bruce area and one inland "in the heights," two and a half miles from the nearest road, said the association did not even attempt to spray "in the heights," but in any case, leafspot infestation was not bad up there.

The fact that on the whole, leafspot control in the Commonwealth islands appears to have been satisfactory even though some bananas were seldom, if ever, sprayed suggests that extensive, mixed cultivations may have been less susceptible than intensive, purestand ones. In any case, control by the associations at uniform rates per pound of production does not appear to have entailed serious disadvantages for any category of growers, whatever their size or geographical location.

While the SLBGA and the DBGA provided more or less island-wide control of leafspot, their direct intervention in other forms of disease control was limited. Only one grower, in Dominica, drew attention specifically to his association's role in borer control, but the fact that borer damage was not usually mentioned may reflect the success of measures taken by the associations to inhibit their spread.

HURRICANE INSURANCE AND REHABILITATION

Wind damage is an ever-present threat to the Eastern Caribbean banana grower. A hurricane passing directly across an island may destroy its banana plantations almost completely, and at least nine months of production may be lost. The incidence of hurricanes is extremely erratic, and some islands have been spared the direct passage of a severe hurricane for as long as 50 years, but the crops of others have been devastated twice in successive years.

Although hurricanes generally occur only between July and September, destructive windstorms may occur at any season. Afflicted growers are deprived of income just when they need it most to rehabilitate their flattened plantations. Growers with no financial reserves, unable to repay debts incurred to buy fertiliser on credit, might be obliged to abandon the export banana industry if a high percentage of their crop were destroyed. Should a second devastating blowdown occur before farmers had had a chance to recover from its predecessor (as happened in Guadeloupe in 1963 and 1964 with Hurricanes Helena and Cléo), even growers of considerable substance might face ruin. In the 1950s, hurricane and windstorm damage was, with one or two exceptions (notably Hurricane Betsy, which devastated Guadeloupe in 1956), relatively modest. In the 1960s, it became far more severe, partly because more hurricanes passed through the area, but partly also because the buildup of nematode infestation in many areas weakened roots and made plants more vulnerable to wind. Failure to replant aging plantations so that plants became progressively shallower-rooted also rendered them more likely to fall.

In 1959, the growers' associations of all four islands in the Commonwealth Windwards entered into a joint scheme administered by WINBAN to insure both plant and ratoon crops against hurricane and windstorm damage. In 1960, an insurance ordinance was drafted, patterned on a Jamaican model, and this ordinance continued in force (with amendments in 1963) until 1968. Compensation to growers was based on the total weight of bananas they had delivered to their association in the year preceding the damage.

WINBAN's insurance fund during this period was obtained from a cess on all bananas accepted by Geest Industries: growers contributed 0.125¢ per pound and Geest contributed 0.25¢. Total liability was based on the total annual production of the four Commonwealth islands, multiplied by 2¢ a pound. Between July 1962 and July 1963, production was 120,026 tons, which resulted in the collection of an insurance cess of WI$1,008,218 and a total liability of $5,377,164. WINBAN carried the first 10 percent of total liability; 60 percent was reinsured with brokers in the United Kingdom (Lloyd's of London); and the remaining 30 percent was taken as a normal risk and not reinsured.

There were two forms of insurance: statutory insurance of ratoon mats, which was compulsory, and contractual insurance of plant mats, which was voluntary. Premiums for statutory insurance were deducted from the banana sales of the grower, and only plants from which a bunch had been harvested were covered. Compensation was calculated by multiplying the poundage of bananas delivered from the affected holding in the preceding four quarters by the assessed percentage loss of ratoon mats suffered by the holding, and multiplying the result by 2¢. In the case of contractual insurance, each plant mat might be insured for a premium of 3¢. If more than 20 percent of mats were damaged, the benefit payable for each damaged mat was 50¢. Damage was assessed by employees of the island growers' associations, who visited each holding for which wind-damage claims were submitted (Perryman 1964; WINBAN *News*, April–June 1967, 7).

Objections to the scheme were raised in various quarters. Initially, some farmers disliked the idea of paying premiums for an uncertain return, but the damage sustained in St Lucia, for instance, in 1960 (from Hurricane Abby) and 1963 (from Hurricane Edith) rapidly convinced growers of the merits of the scheme (Biggs, Bennett, et al. 1964, 52). However, growers complained that they had to wait too long for assessors to inspect their damaged holdings, which delayed the work of rehabilitation. Some said that the processing of claims was too slow and they had to wait months to receive benefits. For their part, the associations complained that the growers sometimes attempted to defraud them. The same holding might be registered by two farmers, both of whom might attempt to collect damage benefits (Romalis 1968, 200). A farmer with several parcels of land might register them under different names so that he could, for instance, claim for the blowdown of one acre as 25 percent of a four-acre holding, when in fact he had another undamaged parcel (Cools-Lartigue 1969, 18). In islands where dealers collected bananas from a number of small farmers, inaccurate or inadequate recording of the transactions could cause problems in the processing of claims (Perryman 1964).

Ultimately, however, the strongest objections came from the underwriters, who claimed to be paying out far more in benefits than they received in premiums. Without knowing the percentage of premiums absorbed by Lloyd's administration costs, it is impossible to judge the validity of this claim. Monplaisir (1966, personal communication) said that from 1961 to 1965, insurance companies had paid out £700,000 (WI$3,360,000) more than they had received; Cools-Lartigue gave a figure for the same period of WI$2,000,000 and a figure of WI$1,610,000 for the succeeding three years (1969, 16). From Persaud's *Abstract of West Indian Banana Statistics* it can be calculated that premiums paid on production from mid-1961 to mid-1965 must have totalled approximately WI$4,380,000 for statutory insurance only, while the cost of the scheme over this four-year period, including benefits paid and costs of assessing and processing claims, was WI$3,658,007, or WI$722,000 less (1966, 25,27). Over the same period, insurers sustained a net loss of about WI$35,000 on contractual insurance (26). Whatever the actual state of the matter, however, it was widely believed that as it stood, the insurance ordinance, on balance, favoured the growers.

In any event, when the ordinance expired in July 1968, the underwriters were prepared to renew it only on terms much less favourable to the producers. Growers were to bear the first 20 percent of liability, WINBAN the next 30 percent and the underwriters the next 30 percent. Under this plan, the underwriters' liability would have been for the top and safer layer (50 to 80 percent) of the risk, compared with 10 to 70 percent in the 1960–68 scheme (DBGA, Introduction of legislation, 1969). WINBAN initially rejected the plan, but it was ultimately accepted, for 1969 only, by the island boards of St Lucia, St Vincent, and Grenada. The DBGA withdrew and developed its own plan, which was passed into law in September 1969 as the Dominica Banana Industry Insurance Act of 1969. Its provisions were extremely complex, involving allocations of free fertiliser and cash benefits to growers who had lost more than 41 percent of their ratoon mats. If assessed losses were over 29 percent, growers were to receive a free allocation of nematicide and insecticide based on the acreage of bananas to be replanted. Regulations forbade the sale of free fertiliser allocations and their use on crops other than bananas. The Dominica Banana Industry Insurance Fund was to be established, financed by a cess on poundage, premiums paid for contractual insurance of plant mats, contributions from Geest Industries, and Dominica's share of the reserve funds of the WINBAN Insurance Scheme. The board might reinsure all or part of its potential liability if satisfactory terms could be obtained (Dominica 1969, 30–40).

Banana crop insurance was regarded as indispensible in the Commonwealth islands in the mid-1960s, and the DBGA in particular was anxious to organise it in an increasingly paternalistic way to ensure that the benefits were applied to rehabilitation. In the French islands, on the other hand, there was no banana insurance. In Guadeloupe, where hurricanes had been so frequent in the early 1960s that some growers had barely resumed production before being dealt another blow, ASSOBAG had investigated the possibility of insurance, but no French company would undertake it, and the conditions offered by Lloyd's of London were felt to be too draconian to be worthwhile (Mauréaux 1967, personal communication). The manager of SICABAM reported a similar experience. He felt that since insurance was too expensive, it should be subsidised by the French government; but the French government would never agree to subsidise premiums to a foreign insurance company (Léobon 1966, personal communication).

Farmers in the French islands did have access to some forms of assistance that were not available to Commonwealth farmers and that may have permitted them to be more critical of the hard terms offered by Lloyd's. If a hurricane in one island coincided with a period of overproduction in the other, fruit from the island with a surplus, or even from the Ivory Coast or elsewhere, might be sold in France using the devastated island's quota. Its association would retain some of the profits from such sales (Mauréaux 1967, personal communication). Moreover, if farmers lost 25 percent or more of their crop following a natural disaster, the state agricultural credit bank, the Crédit Agricole, was supposedly obliged to provide them with loans at a very low rate of interest: 3 percent, compared with commercial rates of 8 to 13 percent. The loans were subsidised by the treasury and borrowers were allowed six years to repay. Thirty percent of the "loan" was a gift from the state: that is, for every Fr100 borrowed, only Fr70 had to be repaid (Scholastique 1966, personal communication; Hazaël-Massieux 1967, personal communication). I was told in Martinique, however, that low-interest loans were not always forthcoming. In February 1966, 25 to 30 percent of the island's bananas had been blown down in a windstorm, and some growers had lost a very high percentage of their crop, but the Crédit Agricole had refused to give loans because the island was in a period of overproduction, and presumably would have had to destroy or dump part of its crop if it had not blown down (Léobon 1966, personal communication).

Other forms of assistance included the distribution of substantial amounts of free fertiliser in Dominica and free and subsidised fertiliser in St Lucia following hurricane damage in 1963 and 1964. This fertiliser was provided by the United Kingdom government and distributed by the island associations. As mentioned earlier, after Hurricane Inez in 1966, the DBGA instituted a carefully regulated scheme (HIR) to ensure not only that subsidies were used for rehabilitation, but also that rehabilitation was carried out in conformity with the association's guidelines.

Insurance and Land Use

The rationale for hurricane insurance is that it permits prompt rehabilitation of devastated banana plantations, so that production resumes rapidly enough to prevent markets being permanently lost to alternative suppliers. Insurance also serves the humanitarian role of providing a cash income for farmers who might otherwise be unable to meet essential current expenses and who might be forced into debt, possibly even at the risk of losing their land. Its effectiveness on either score in the Commonwealth Windwards of the 1960s is difficult to assess, since although Commonwealth banana growers were insured and French ones were not, other factors were at play that make comparison less than straightforward. On the one hand, the French farmers had access to credit at low interest. On the other hand, the frequency and severity of wind and hurricane damage varied greatly from island to island, and between 1960 and 1966, the French islands fared far worse than the Commonwealth islands.

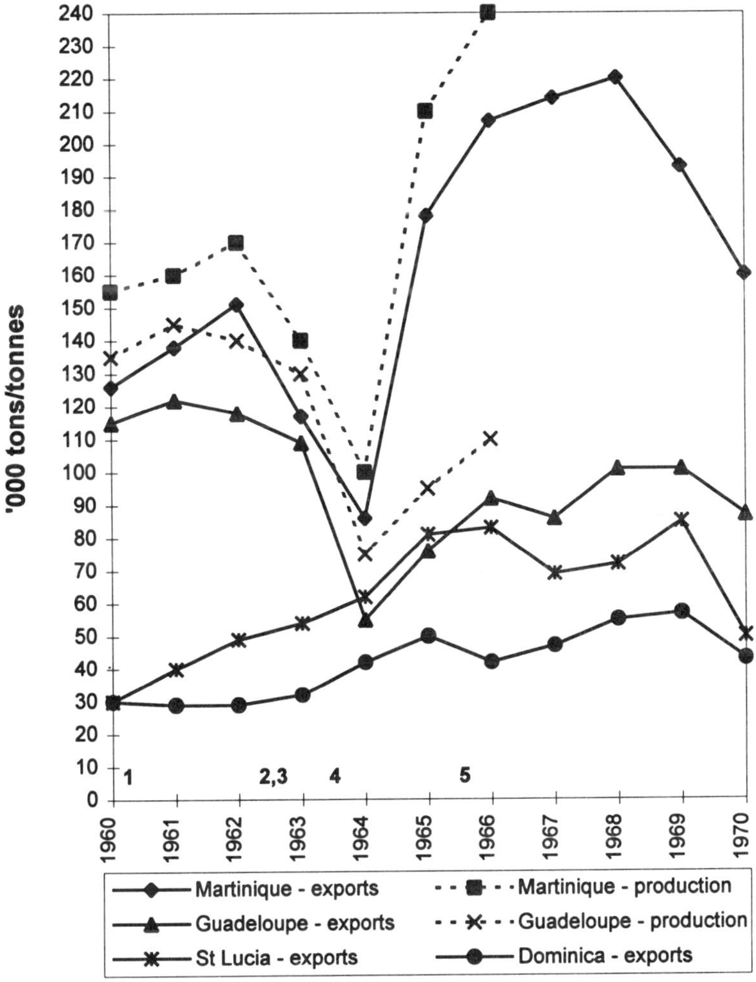

1. Abby - St Lucia
2. Edith - Guadeloupe - 60%
   - Dominica
   - Martinique - 100%
   - St Lucia
3. Helena - Guadeloupe
4. Cleo - Guadeloupe - 100%
5. Inez - Guadeloupe - 100%
   - Dominica - 40%

Figure 7.1
Martinique, Guadeloupe, Dominica, and St Lucia: Annual production, exports, 1960–70, and hurricane incidence

A consideration of all the circumstantial evidence suggests that, at least in the 1960s, although insurance conferred appreciable benefits on those who had it, it was not critical in restoring production to its former level. Figure 7.1, which gives annual production in each of the islands from 1960 to 1970, together with the dates of the hurricanes and the percentage losses they caused, shows that in general, whether it was insured or uninsured, production quickly regained and often surpassed prehurricane levels even after 100 percent devastation. In Guadeloupe, which suffered a quite unprecedented series of blows between 1963 and 1966, recovery was not immediate; by 1967, planters were so heavily in debt (by an average of Fr7,000 per hectare) that many were unable to afford enough of the materials necessary to keep their plantations in good condition. Production levels in the late 1960s were about 15 percent below those in the early years of the decade, and it was only government assistance in carrying debt charges that permitted this degree of recovery. Continued government support, however, enabled previous record export totals to be surpassed by the early 1970s (Menauge 1974, 105). Thus, even under circumstances as exceptional as those of 1963–66, no permanent damage was done to the industry. Under more normal conditions, even after the passage of a hurricane so severe that island production was reduced to nothing, prehurricane production levels could be achieved again within nine months in Martinique and eleven months in Guadeloupe (*La Banane* 1967, 1:11).

While ready access to other funds for rehabilitation meant that the large and medium-sized banana growers of the French islands could survive without insurance, what might have been the fate of the small growers in the Commonwealth islands if their bananas had been uninsured? It was feared in the early 1960s that if confronted with the loss of nine months' production, they might have abandoned the crop entirely without the encouragement of some financial compensation. This is questionable, however, since the small growers of Dominica and St Lucia were able to carry out the rehabilitation of their devastated holdings for a fraction of the amount expended per hectare by the medium-sized and large growers of the French islands. Moreover, growers who owed their associations substantial sums under the fertiliser credit schemes had little option but to replant and rehabilitate, since without resuming banana sales, most would have had no other way to pay off their debts.

If insurance was not critical for prompt rehabilitation after hurricanes, the question arises, what effect did insurance have on patterns and methods of land use? The responses to the 1966 survey give no reason to suppose that small growers' plantations were more vulnerable to wind damage than those of large growers. Nevertheless, there was a slight bias in favour of small growers, since their plants were often concentrated within a single valley or even on a single slope, and they were therefore more likely to suffer the 20 percent minimum damage required to qualify for compensation than was the owner of plantations with slopes exposed to wind from several different directions. Large growers might subdivide their estates into blocks for insurance purposes, but since the minimum size of the blocks was 40 hectares, they were still far less likely to qualify for a claim than a 1- or 2-hectare holding. One large St Lucian grower said he had made no claims from 1960 to 1966 (Moffat 1966, personal communication).

Evidently, farmers in windy or exposed locations were more vulnerable to damage than those in more sheltered spots, so that to some extent the sheltered farmer subsidised the exposed farmer. I was told that northeastern coastal locations and certain bottle-necked valleys in Dominica and St Lucia were particularly subject to wind damage. Compensation from insurance reduced the relative disadvantage of such areas in the Commonwealth islands, but the absence of compensation in Martinique had not prevented the north-eastern part of that island from becoming one of the foremost banana-producing districts.

If insurance reduced the relative disadvantage of windy locations, it must have had a similar effect on poor agricultural practices. Thus farmers who lost a relatively low proportion of their crop because they had propped plants effectively, invested in expensive nematode control, and replanted mats periodically to prevent ratoons from rising closer to the surface were subsidising, through their premiums, farmers who did not take these measures and consequently lost a far higher proportion of their crop to wind damage. In fact, farmers who replanted regularly were doubly penalised, since only ratoon mats were covered by statutory insurance: plant mats had to be insured contractually, and very few farmers opted to insure them. Some respondents to the 1966 survey said they did not uproot and replant their bananas after the recommended interval of three or four years because they could not collect insurance on fallen plant mats.

Farmers' attitudes toward insurance were coloured by their personal experience. In St Lucia, twelve farmers said they had made claims for bananas destroyed in hurricanes or windstorms, but only one said that he had been compensated satisfactorily. Three others had not made claims recently, one had never made a claim, and the remaining thirty-two who were interviewed made no comment about insurance. In general, the scheme seemed to work to the satisfaction of most growers and was not perceived as favouring any group or area at the expense of any other. When the time came to renegotiate terms, the St Lucian association was prepared to renew the agreement even on far less favourable terms, since it was perceived as essential for prompt rehabilitation after a disaster.

In Dominica, the insurance scheme was regarded much more critically. The interviews in 1966 were conducted in August, September, and October: the first thirty-six before and the last thirty-four after the passage of Hurricane Inez on 27 September. Damaging windstorms had also struck the island the previous February. Of the seventy farmers interviewed, twenty-seven had made claims for compensation that year. Four said that they had not received the amounts due to them, and six complained that the whole procedure was too slow, and actually held up the work of rehabilitation. One said that he had had to wait five months for WINBAN assessors to visit his holding. This complaint was probably an exaggeration, but even a delay of two or three weeks could cause the island as a whole to lose several thousand tons of production. Far more widespread were complaints that payment had been delayed up to seven months after damage had been assessed. Thus, just when fertiliser was most needed to rehabilitate cultivations, the money was not forthcoming. Although one northern farmer accused the DBGA of ignoring the North, in fact, complaints about slow settlement of claims came from several parts of the island.

It is possible that the main reason the WINBAN insurance scheme functioned less smoothly in Dominica than in St Lucia was that Dominica used a dealer system for collecting fruit, which complicated record-keeping and often made it hard to determine the ownership or control of specific holdings. One small grower who had received only two-thirds of what he felt was his due for damage sustained in the windstorms of February 1966 complained that all the money was taken by larger growers.

When the terms of the insurance agreement were renegotiated, the board of the DBGA decided that it was not, on balance, in the Dominican industry's interest to remain a party to it. The decision presumably reflected the negative feelings about the scheme expressed by many growers. However, it is interesting to note that, paradoxically, Dominica had derived a net benefit from the insurance scheme between 1961 and 1965: benefits of WI$1,040,000 were paid to growers, but premiums on exports totalled only WI$946,000.

On the other hand, St Lucia recorded a net deficit, having received benefits to growers of WI$1,380,000 and paid premiums of WI$1,713,000 (figures derived from Persaud 1966, 17). Moreover, although the DBGA withdrew from the WINBAN scheme, it did not abandon insurance altogether. It simply diverted the funds that would have gone to Lloyd's into a scheme of its own that was to provide compensation partly in fertiliser rather than in cash alone. Proponents of this scheme argued that it would ensure that benefits were used for rehabilitation, as intended, but critics claimed it was a ruse by some of the large growers on the board to increase the quantity of fertiliser used by tenants who grew bananas between the coconuts on their estates.

The impact of insurance in the 1960s is made more difficult to evaluate because after major hurricane damage, other rehabilitation measures almost invariably accompanied the payment of compensation for insurance claims. The Hurricane Inez Rehabilitation Scheme has been discussed above, but in addition, in 1963 and 1964 British government grants paid for the distribution of several thousand tons of fertiliser free or at subsidised rates. The value of the fertiliser distributed was approximately WI$752,000. This programme was probably as instrumental in ensuring that prehurricane production levels were quickly restored as was the payment of insurance claims, which amounted to approximately WI$900,000 (Persaud 1966, 15, 25).

Losses caused by more localised windstorms were often as disastrous for individual farmers as hurricane losses, but they rarely attracted outside attention and assistance. In September 1966, the passage of the notorious Hurricane Inez left many cultivations relatively unscathed, especially in the southern part of the island, but in February 1966, for instance, some Dominican farmers had lost up to 70 percent of their bananas in windstorms that received no international publicity. Thus, in Dominica insurance benefits were probably more instrumental in sustaining the morale and aiding the recovery of growers hit by moderate, localised but in some cases frequently recurring destruction, than in promoting prompt rehabilitation after a major disaster. Martiniquan growers, who lost 20 to 30 percent of their crop in the same February windstorms, received no compensation.

Overall, the WINBAN insurance scheme of the 1960s probably involved a net transfer of resources from farmers who took steps to reduce the vulnerability of their plants to wind damage to farmers who did not. Nevertheless, the provident and conscientious were the least likely to call for the ending of the scheme, since they required a much greater expenditure to restore their plantations when they were struck by major hurricane damage. There was no widespread perception that the insurance scheme favoured any class or category of growers at the expense of any other, and it is unlikely that it had much impact on conscious decisions about land use, although it did definitely discourage the uprooting and replanting of cultivations at regular intervals. This reluctance to replant not only produced mats that were less deeply rooted with each successive ratoon; it also prevented the alternation of bananas with pasture or other crops, as practised, for instance, in Martinique to reduce the level of nematode infestation.

Despite its drawbacks, the insurance scheme in the Commonwealth islands did make it less likely that farmers would be overwhelmed by crippling burdens of debt incurred for rehabilitation. The French system of long-term, low-interest loans with a 30 percent write-off for farmers who had suffered heavy hurricane losses positively encouraged indebtedness, on the other hand, since the greater the loan, the greater, in absolute terms, would be the write-off. This system also had a negative impact on agricultural practices, since heavily indebted farmers could not undertake desirable capital improvements. One of my informants in a periodically drought-stricken district of southern Martinique, for instance, had been forced as a result of Hurricane Edith in 1963 to abandon his plans for a dam and pumping system to irrigate his estate, even though the scheme was potentially profitable (Scholastique 1966, personal communication).

CONCLUSION

By the mid-1960s, Martinique, Guadeloupe, Dominica, and St Lucia all had banana growers' associations with the power to intervene in many aspects of cultivation. The extent to which they actually did so varied enormously from island to island. The associations in the Commonwealth islands were in most cases far more interventionist than those in the French islands.

The actions the associations took did not always have the results that were expected or intended. In the Commonwealth islands, considerable resources were expended on research and extension, but returns were very modest when gauged against the declared goal of increasing yields, even though ways of improving yields had been developed and many farmers were quite familiar with them. The idea that once farmers knew how to do so, they would produce the same quantity of bananas on a quarter of the acreage previously required proved illusory, at least in the short run. Although, on balance, hurricane insurance may have benefited small farmers at the expense of large ones, it may have been counterproductive, since it discouraged fallowing, rotation, and regular replanting, all practices that should have reduced windstorm damage.

On the other hand, universal leafspot control benefited everyone except, perhaps, growers in dry areas, who would not have had to spray frequently in any case. It was certainly highly advantageous to small growers in the rugged, wet interior and to all who grew bananas in mixed cultivation. Most critical, however, in permitting continuing participation in banana cultivation of small growers with very limited capital resources and no access to credit from banks or other sources, were the fertiliser credit schemes in the Commonwealth islands. This is not to say that had such schemes existed in the French islands, there would necessarily have been many more small growers there; other factors militated against this. Certainly, however, it would have been impossible on any island for farmers with small holdings to produce bananas acceptable for export for more than three or four years without chemical fertiliser, and many small farmers in St Lucia and Dominica would never have been able to purchase fertiliser without the help of their associations' credit schemes.

To some extent, then, the activities of DBGA and the SLBGA resulted in a net transfer of resources from large- to small-scale growers, from farmers in accessible lowland areas to farmers in rugged and remote inland districts, and from farmers with intensive, purestand plantations to farmers with extensive, mixed-crop cultivation. In some instances, it might have seemed that the feckless were being rewarded at the expense of the conscientious, but in fact, most of the co-operative initiatives undertaken by the associations benefited all classes of growers to some degree.

Large growers in the French islands, whose associations did not supply fertiliser on credit or organise disease control on a communal basis, were not able to obtain these essentials any more cheaply than were large growers in the Commonwealth islands. On the other hand, by not supplying communal disease control services or inputs on credit, the French growers' associations ensured that fewer small farmers would be able to participate in the export banana industry, especially where physical conditions were less than ideal. The difficulty, in many areas, of generating a cash income in any other way must have assured a more plentiful and reliable supply of labour to large-scale growers in Martinique and Guadeloupe than would have been available if their associations had facilitated the participation of more small growers in the industry.

8 Banana Growers' Association Intervention in Packing, Transport, and Marketing

The influence of differing association policies on the distribution and intensity of banana cultivation in the four islands meant that the associations were confronted with differing challenges when faced with the task of providing the most efficient means of conveying the fruit from the field to the dockside and from the dockside to the overseas market. Their procedures were described in broad outline in chapter 5, but when they are examined in detail, island by island, it is apparent that here again, growers' associations responded to the challenges that confronted them in characteristically different ways. Some attempted to reduce or eliminate locational disadvantages by providing collecting facilities that equalised costs for all growers. Some used their reserve funds for price support to try to ensure that growers' receipts never fell below their production costs. The problems posed by overproduction, which became critical at about the same time in French and Commonwealth islands, evoked various responses, and metropolitan marketing was carried on in two completely different ways. The issue of quality control had different implications for French and Commonwealth producers. And, most important of all, there were fundamental differences in shipping arrangements that could be exploited in various ways to benefit either the industry as a whole, or only specific sectors. The actions of the associations in all these spheres reflected divergent philosophies that can often be shown to have been inspired by the divergent interests of their constituent members.

FIELD TO DOCKSIDE

In the Commonwealth islands, the growers' associations undertook responsibility for ensuring that in all parts of the islands where bananas were grown, there were facilities to weigh and wrap the harvested stems and convey them to the reception stations in the ports of Castries and Vieux Fort in St Lucia and Roseau and Portsmouth in Dominica. In the mid-1960s, St Lucia's association was by far the most interventionist. The SLBGA had divided the island into 68 buying areas, each with its own buying team. For a day before each weekly shipment, the buying teams would service 159 sheds where stems of bananas could be weighed and wrapped. The teams, who were employees of the SLBGA, consisted of a selector, who was responsible for rejecting underweight, scarred, or damaged stems; a buyer; a paymaster, who made an immediate cash payment for the weight of fruit delivered, after deducting the association's cess and any payments due under the fertiliser credit scheme; a helper; and wrappers, who encased each stem in paper wadding and polythene tubing provided by Geest.

A typical buying area handled 500 to 1,000 stems a week. From buying point to exporting port, the SLBGA provided transport either in its own trucks or in vehicles rented for Banana Days. Private truckers were paid 2.25¢ per mile for every 100 pounds of bananas carried, or slightly more where roads were exceptionally rough or steep (Touche, Ross, et al. 1967). Prices paid at buying points were uniform all over the island.

Rather than selling their fruit to the association at buying points, growers with large quantities of stems might deliver them in their own vehicles directly to the port reception stations, where they were weighed on a weighbridge rather than stem by stem. Two hundred and forty growers, or 2 percent of the total, delivered their crop to the reception stations; but they accounted for approximately half the island's production (Touche, Ross, et al. 1967). Such growers received a rebate on their cess of 1.5¢ per stem to compensate for handling costs, and 2.25¢ per mile for every 100 pounds to cover transport costs (Monplaisir 1966, personal communication). They were also paid for fractions of a pound, whereas at buying points, each stem was assessed to the nearest pound (Romalis 1968, 79). They were reimbursed 2.5¢ a stem for wrapping, but this expense was met directly by Geest (Biggs, Bennett, et al. 1964, 25).

In Dominica, slightly different arrangements had developed. The DBGA maintained only 22 buying points, 13 of them clustered between Rosalie and Marigot in the central-eastern part of the island and within a mile or two of the coast. The remaining 9 were sparsely distributed, mainly on the leeward slope. To cover the cost of operating these buying points and transporting fruit from them to the port, growers selling their fruit there received a lower price than growers delivering to the reception stations in Roseau and Portsmouth: 0.68¢ per pound less in the southern district, 0.8¢ less in the northern district. (Batali and Salisbury, which were accessible only by sea until the 1960s, retained the designation of "reception station" throughout the 1960s, and growers delivering fruit there received the same price as that given at the Roseau Reception Station.)

Since the deduction at buying points was a flat rate and not differentiated according to distance from an exporting port, it was very disadvantageous for growers near the port to sell at buying points, and groups of small growers had begun to band together to truck their fruit independently to the reception stations. This practice caused difficulties in the administration of fertiliser credit schemes and hurricane insurance claims, so in 1961, the DBGA formalised and regulated the practice by setting up its dealer system. Under this scheme, the association issued licences to designated dealers (about 180 throughout Dominica), who were required to provide wrapping and weighing facilities, keep records for each of the registered growers in their group, and provide transport of an approved standard in their own or hired vehicles. They were paid for the total weight delivered at the reception station and paid the members of their group on the following day. Growers were paid only for the total of complete pounds of each stem selected, and not for fractions of a pound, but dealers were paid for the total poundage recorded at the weighbridge, and were entitled to keep the "overage" paid for accumulated fractions of a pound. They might also recover the incentive bonus of 0.25¢ a pound, provided certain conditions were met (Boyd 1967, personal communication). As in St Lucia, large growers generally transported their own fruit to the port in their own or hired vehicles. A minimum of 50 stems was required in vehicles using the reception-station weighbridge.

The DBGA had three trucks of its own to carry bananas from buying points to ports, but for the nine additional trucks it was obliged to hire, it paid from 1.09¢ to 5.66¢ per mile for every hundred pounds of bananas carried. Two cents was the usual rate, but much higher rates were paid to service areas with very poor or steep roads. The cost of transporting 100 pounds of bananas 28 miles from the most distant buying point to Portsmouth was 56¢; from the buying points close to Roseau it was only 17¢ and 21¢. These rates were comparable with the rates that large growers paid to private truck owners who transported their bananas (McQuillan 1968, 56). Even for the remotest growers, independently hired transport cost less than the buying-point discount, so that all but growers with a very small or erratic production had an incentive to arrange their own transport, individually or through dealers.

Unlike in St Lucia, where all growers received the same price for their bananas whether their holdings were one mile or ten from a port, in Dominica the growers bore the cost of transporting their fruit to port, producing a differential of up to 0.3¢ a pound between estates forty-five and six kilometres from Roseau, and up to 0.8¢ a pound between reception-station and buying-point sales.

Between field and dockside, the role of SICABAM and ASSOBAG was fairly limited. They were not involved in boxing bananas or in transporting them to port. While large growers could provide their own packing facilities and transport, growers producing less than about 300 stems a week were obliged to make other arrangements. Smaller growers were often grouped in cooperatives (SICAS) to handle their harvested fruit. An average SICA had between 100 and 250 members, generally relatives, friends, and neighbours living within a radius of three or four kilometres and cultivating an average of about one hectare of bananas each. A truck owned or rented by the SICA collected members' fruit, unwrapped, at the roadside near their holdings. It was the responsibility of the driver to decide whether the fruit was acceptable, and if it was, to weigh it and give the owner a receipt. The driver then transported it, unwrapped, to the SICA shed where it was washed, boxed, and then sent by truck to the exporting port. There, with bananas from other SICAS, it was handled by the Union des SICA (in Martinique) or FEDEG (in Guadeloupe). During periods of surplus production, the fruit of SICA members was still collected by truck, but it was taken unboxed to the port, where it was weighed and jettisoned. Transport costs at each stage were borne by individual growers: about 11¢ a stem for collection and carriage to the SICA shed and an average of 15¢ a stem (0.4¢ a pound) for carriage from shed to port.

SICABAM constructed its own cool-storage shed in Fort-de-France in 1966 with the idea that growers would be able to cut their fruit and bring it to the port any day of the week, rather than concentrating cutting on the one or two days before the banana boats called and clogging the port facilities with line-ups of trucks that might be delayed for lengthy periods in the hot sun. The shed had been completed in 1967, but at the time of my visit it was not yet being used for its intended purpose. Officers of both SICABAM and ASSOBAG spoke of installing conveyer belts to improve handling of boxed fruit between delivery at the quayside and loading into ships' holds. Although the associations were instigating this innovation, it was not clear whether they or the Compagnie Générale Transatlantique would be responsible for actually installing the belts.

Consequences for Land Use

St Lucia. The results of the idiosyncratic approaches of the four associations were as diverse as their policies. By providing buying sheds at frequent intervals along the roads wherever it was physically possible to grow bananas, the SLBGA minimized carrying distances for all growers in St Lucia, not just those in prime banana-growing areas.

If paid carriers had to be employed, the cost of transporting bananas from the field to the buying point might well represent the largest proportion of a grower's cost of production. For "heading," carriers were paid from 3¢ to 6¢ a stem (from 0.12¢ to 0.24¢ a pound) for distances of 400 metres or less, 30¢ (1.2¢ a pound) for distances of 1600 metres, and 40¢ or 50¢ a stem for longer distances. Among farmers with holdings more than two kilometres from the road, a widespread practice was to have their children carry out their bananas. Children were withdrawn from school on banana days for this purpose. In 1965, when average prices at the buying point were only 4.275¢ a pound, farmers would hardly have found it worthwhile to pay carriers to extract bananas from holdings more than two kilometres from the road, when this would cost them over 2¢ a pound for stems that might even then be rejected by the association's selectors. Indeed, Momsen's map (1969), which is based on her 1966 survey, confirms the impression that most bananas were grown within two kilometres of the road. Except in forest-reserve watershed areas or in areas where aridity made banana cultivation impossible, St Lucia's roads were lined on either side by a band of bananas, mainly in mixed cultivation, extending in places up to 2 kilometres from the road as the crow flies, but generally not more than half this distance. If carrying distance was a critical limiting factor, at least for those who had to pay carriers, then any reduction in the density of buying points was likely to add significantly to the costs of most growers. Eliminating buying points would reduce the costs of the association that had to maintain them, but it would also render export banana growing uneconomic for many farmers, since it would boost carrying costs from field to shed beyond the point at which the risk of rejection was still worth taking.

Table 8.1
Distance of St Lucian banana growers from nearest road, 1966–67

	Distance between holding and road (m)							
Survey informants	*0–*	*400–*	*800–*	*1200–*	*1600–*	*2400–*	*>3200*	*Total*
Number	23	5	6	2	2	2	1	41
Percentage	51.6	12.2	14.6	4.9	4.9	4.9	2.4	100

Source: Author's Survey, 1966–67.

The idea that access to buying points was a key factor in the distribution of banana growing in St Lucia was endorsed by a team of management consultants called in by the government in 1966 to examine ways of making the banana industry more efficient. The consultants proposed eliminating at least half the buying points, mainly those in more remote and marginal areas, where they expected bananas would be eliminated as a result (Touche, Ross, et al. 1967, 13). This proposal met with the approval of some large growers who imagined that excluding marginal producers would permit a reduction in their own cess contribution, but it was greeted in other quarters with scepticism and dismay. Not only was there concern for the economic hardship that would be inflicted on farmers who no longer had access to an SLBGA buying point close enough to make banana growing economically worthwhile; the elimination of too many such growers might also have reduced output to a level well below market requirements, so that the buyer, Geest, would have had to obtain supplies from alternative sources. Of these there was no shortage, and many of them could have easily undercut St Lucia's most efficient producers, threatening the future of any viable export banana industry in the island. As it turned out, the recommendations of the management consultants were applied only to a limited degree. There was some reduction in the number of buying points, but the SLBGA continued for the time being to service most parts of the island where bananas were grown.

At the time of the 1966 survey, the vast majority of growers sold their fruit to the SLBGA at the association's local buying points rather than transporting it by truck to the Castries or Vieux Fort reception depots and claiming the SLBGA allowance for transport costs. Among the forty-eight farmers I interviewed, only six delivered fruit to the reception depots. One of these was the manager of Dennery Estate, which was alone responsible for almost 16 percent of St Lucia's banana output. One large grower in the Errard Valley (the same grower who would not allow SLBGA's leafspot spraymen on his estate) claimed that he got a "better" (that is, less rigorous) selection at the port reception depots. The other four all came from the same district in the southeast and may also have had personal reasons for avoiding their local buying point. In general, however, there was remarkably little criticism of the buying points and their operation. In fact, about 6 percent of stems delivered to the buying points were rejected, but only two farmers complained that selectors were sometimes "capricious" or "whimsical," while one claimed cynically that the percentage of rejects varied according to the space available on the boats. Some farmers with weekly sales of over 300 stems sold at buying points, and the SLBGA reception officer for the south of the island, himself a medium-sized to large grower, said he made a point of selling his own fruit at the local buying point to reinforce the confidence of his neighbours in the system.

Dominica. In Dominica, where there was a larger area to be serviced, the DBGA had approached the problem of transferring fruit from field to dockside in a entirely different way. Some banana-growing districts were as far as 45 kilometres from the exporting ports (compared with a maximum of 30 kilometres in St Lucia), and cultivation was even less intensive: only 3.7 percent of the total banana acreage was in purestand plantings, compared with 14.5 percent in St Lucia, and island-wide yields averaged three tons per hectare, compared with six tons per hectare for St Lucia (Momsen 1969, 20,25). While in St Lucia in 1965, growers anywhere in the island received, on average through the year, 4.275¢ a pound for their fruit at buying point or reception depot, with compensation for transport costs to the depot, Dominican growers received a slightly higher average price, 4.402¢ a pound (Persaud 1966, 42), but with significant variations according to location. Thus, while growers very close to Roseau and Portsmouth might receive up to 0.127¢ a pound more than their St Lucian counterparts, growers 45 kilometres from the ports might receive up to 0.673¢ a pound less, especially if their low volume of production obliged them to rely on buying points.

However, I could find little evidence in 1966 and 1967 that this differential in receipts had been a critical factor in farmers' decisions about banana cultivation. As in St Lucia, bananas were being grown in every part of the island that had road access and appropriate physical conditions (and indeed in some areas that had only one or the other). Momsen's (1969) map shows that, in general, banana cultivation was more or less continuous in areas close to roads, and extended on either side of them for 500 metres to 2 kilometres, with isolated patches of cultivation as much as 3 or 4 kilometres as the

Table 8.2
Distance of Dominican banana growers from nearest road, 1966–67

	Distance between holding and road (m)							
Survey informants	*0–*	*400–*	*800–*	*1200–*	*1600–*	*2400*	*>3200*	*Total*
Number	23	12	5	3	6	3	5	57
Percentage	40.4	21	8.8	5.3	10.5	5.3	8.8	100

Source: Author's Survey, 1966–67.

crow flies from the nearest road. The distribution of banana holdings in my 1966-67 survey bore out this pattern (Table 8.2).

Rates for heading from field to roadside were less consistent than in St Lucia and may have been moderated to some extent by what the market would bear. One grower paid carriers 14¢ a stem for 300 metres; others paid 6¢ a stem for 800 metres. For 1600 metres, one grower paid according to size: 11¢ for a 5-hand bunch, 15¢ for 6 to 7 hands and 25¢ for an 8- to 10-hand bunch. For a distance of 2,400 metres, two growers cited a rate of 25¢, and for 3,200 metres, one gave 30¢. Fifty cents was paid for distances of 4.5 and 8 kilometres, while one Colihaut grower, with a holding 9 kilometres from the buying point, compensated his carrier by giving him the smaller of the two stems he carried out: this payment worked out to about 40¢ a stem, but was less at times of low prices.

Once the fruit had been brought to the roadside, it was conveyed to the ports in various ways. The most common method among those interviewed (57 percent) was to load the stems onto a truck or Land Rover, usually hired but in some cases (6 out of 32) belonging to the grower, and then to sell them in the owner's own name at the reception depots in Roseau or Portsmouth. Until 1966, growers with as few as 25 stems had sold at the depots, but in that year the minimum had been raised to 50 stems to reduce congestion at the ports. In order to have as large a load as possible or, at the very least, to meet the minimum of 50 stems, most of these growers harvested and sold fortnightly rather than weekly. One grower cut only at intervals of three weeks, and one at intervals of four weeks, but this practice was not desirable, since weekly harvesting was necessary if all stems were to be shipped at optimal ripeness.

McQuillan (1968, 56) ascertained the rates paid by estates in different parts of the island to truck their bananas to port. These rates corresponded closely with the rates cited by small, medium-sized and large growers in my survey in 1966. They ranged from 10¢ a stem (about 0.4¢ a pound) in the Bellevue area, 9 kilometres southeast of Roseau, to 16¢ a stem (about 0.6 cents a pound) in the Castle Bruce area, 40 kilometres from town. At most intermediate points the charge was 12¢ or 14¢. McQuillan converted rates per stem into rates per mile for 100 pounds, and noted that while this rate was as low as 1.61¢ for the most distant estate, it rose to 5¢ for estates close to Roseau. The average cost per mile for 15 locations with an average distance of 19 kilometres (13 miles) from port was 3.27¢ (56).

In the 1966 survey, I found that the second most popular means of disposing of harvested fruit, favoured by 21 percent of respondents, was through the agency of dealers. (Two respondents were themselves dealers.) More than half the respondents who favoured dealers had little choice, since their weekly production was less than 25 stems, and there were no DBGA buying points within several miles of their holdings. Most expressed no criticism of the arrangement, but one farmer who produced about 50 stems a fortnight said that he much preferred to take his own fruit to the depot and only used a dealer (his son, in fact) when he did not have the requisite 50 stems. One grower, who was also a dealer, complained that it wasted a great deal of his time. On the other hand, three Marigot growers who could have sold through a local buying point, and sometimes did, tended to favour the dealers because according to one, the buying-point staff were sometimes guilty of favouritism and arbitrary about rejection. According to another, while there was no financial advantage either way, dealing through a dealer saved time. The buying point was 5 kilometres from his holding, but trucks could come to within 3 kilometres, and the dealer's wrapping shed was more conveniently located.

Eighteen percent of respondents sold their fruit at DBGA buying points. In fact, this means of disposal was quite popular in those communities where it was available. All farmers interviewed in Colihaut used it, most of those in Castle Bruce, and, occasionally, some of those in the Marigot area. Surprisingly, a La Plaine farmer sold at the buying point even though he had his own Land Rover. In fact, at the most distant buying points, it was probably more advantageous, particularly for farmers with low bunch weights, to sell at 0.68¢ below the reception-depot price than to pay 16¢ a stem to a trucker to carry the bananas to port. Growers who regularly sold at buying points had no complaints about the selection process.

The remaining four percent of growers had informal arrangements for selling their very small production, either in groups or through other individuals. Such arrangements were regarded as unsatisfactory by the DBGA, and the dealer system had been developed to supersede them.

I was not able to determine when and how the 1966 distribution of buying points had evolved. Some buying points, at least, were certainly established after the introduction of the dealer system in 1961, since they were in locations not accessible by trucks until 1962. It was not clear, however, whether the DBGA had originally set up a comprehensive network of buying points. If so, it may then have closed most points nearer the ports when the financial advantage of selling directly to the reception depots caused most growers to bypass them. Alternatively, it may be that the DBGA originally left most growers to make their own transport arrangements, and set up buying points on the St Lucian pattern only in districts so remote that local entrepreneurs could not organise independent transport economically. Whichever was the case, the DBGA's more ad hoc approach to the collection of fruit did not appear, superficially at least, to have had much effect on the geographical distribution of banana cultivation. Although growers closest to the ports should have had an advantage of up to 0.8¢ a pound over growers who were most distant, some of Dominica's main banana-growing districts were on the eastern side of the island, as far as possible from Roseau and Portsmouth. Indeed, in his study of the relationship between transport costs and the character of estate agriculture in Dominica, McQuillan came to the conclusion that transport cost-differentials accounted for very little of the locational variation in volume or intensity of banana production (1968, 85).

A closer examination of the question, however, suggests that the differential impact of transport costs was not likely to be revealed by interviewing the farmers who were growing bananas, whether or not they were handicapped by high costs. It was farmers who had never started growing bananas, or who had stopped doing so, who might have been expected to provide the most significant information on critical cost levels. There was some evidence in the 1966 survey that farmers in the districts farthest from the ports did regard banana growing as only very marginally worthwhile.

Farmers in the Colihaut, Castle Bruce, Rivière Ciriques, and Marigot districts, in particular, complained about the very slender margin of profit left to them once they had sold their fruit to the association; high transport costs were their chief burden. In Colihaut, some farmers said they might give up banana cultivation and return to cassava as a cash crop. Two of the four interviewed reported declining production, and one of these, when revisited in 1970, had indeed gone out of bananas completely.

Along the Windward coast, there were several farmers who had holdings both near their villages and several miles away in the interior. In the 1950s and early 1960s, they had extracted bananas from their remote interior holdings where rainfall was always adequate and fertiliser not essential, but by 1966 they were cultivating only their more accessible plots. Holdings over three kilometres from the road were being abandoned, even though they were far more fertile and productive than holdings near the coast, where worn-out soils required substantial inputs of fertiliser and periods of dry weather were not uncommon.

In St Lucia, 30 percent of the farmers I interviewed in 1966 claimed their banana production was increasing; 66 percent said their production was stable; and only 4 percent that it was in decline. In Dominica, 64 percent claimed to have stable production, but only 13.5 percent were expanding, while 22.5 percent were decreasing their banana production. These percentages did not differ significantly for farmers interviewed before and after the passage of Hurricane Inez.

In St Lucia, even farmers with well above the minimum volume of bananas required for selling directly to the reception depots generally preferred to sell at the SLBGA buying points. In Dominica, however, the relationship between volume of production and means of disposal suggests that size imposed constraints on choice (Table 8.3). Only growers with too few bananas to organise a viable alternative were prepared to use the DBGA's buying points. With its more extensive, lower-density cultivation, it would have been more expensive in Dominica to set up and maintain a network of buying points as comprehensive and accessible to all growers as the network maintained by the SLBGA in St Lucia. Without such a network, relatively few Dominican growers could carry their fruit directly to the point of sale. Most had to make arrangements for jeeps or trucks to collect it at the roadside, and once they had done so, at a minimum cost of 10¢ a stem, it was usually more economical, provided there was sufficient volume, to carry fruit directly to the ports rather than to local collection points. Consequently, not more than about 15 percent of the island's production passed through the DBGA buying points and possibly 30 percent through the agency of dealers. While the Dominican arrangements had a certain flexibility that was lacking in the St Lucian system, and while they did ensure that all Dominican farmers whose holdings were not more than 2 or 3 kilometres from a road had access to the export banana market, the Dominican arrangements were less geographically egalitarian. In remote areas they rendered even more marginal those growers whose bananas had already cost up to 2¢ a pound to transport from holding to roadside.

Table 8.3
Disposal of bananas in Dominica, according to grower's volume of production

	Means of disposal					
	Reception depot	*Dealer*	*Dealer or buying point*	*Buying point*	*Other*	*Total*
Average production (stems per week)	82[a]	27	23	12.5	7	57
Number in sample	32	9	3	7	2	53

Source: Author's Survey, 1966–67.
[a]65 without largest producer.

Martinique and Guadeloupe. In St Lucia and Dominica, the economic structure of the banana industry made it feasible for farmers with a weekly (or fortnightly) output as low as 50 stems to deliver their fruit independently to the port reception depots. In Martinique and Guadeloupe, however, where SICABAM and ASSOBAG were not involved in this phase of the industry, a weekly production of about 300 stems was necessary for the viable operation of independent packing facilities and transport, and smaller growers were obliged to make their own cooperative arrangements, formal or informal. The organisation of SICAs in the French islands would seem at first glance to have much in common with the Dominican dealer system. Since membership in the DBGA was compulsory for all Dominica's banana growers, however, they were obligated to abide by the association's rules. SICA membership was voluntary, which made their regulations difficult to enforce. When members felt it would be more profitable for them to sell outside their SICA, many did so, getting immediate cash from *ramasseurs* who came with vans to the farm gate. When prices were high, agents of grower-exporters who, for one reason or another, could not meet the commitments they had made three months previously from their own production would attempt to make up the shortfall by offering tempting prices to SICA members. It was also claimed that in periods of surplus production, some growers continued to sell their fruit independently, contributing to the depression of prices, rather than delivering it to the SICA to be jettisoned. While this strategy brought the delinquent growers an immediate benefit, it undermined SICABAM's price maintainance strategy, as well as the credibility of the SICA in relation to SICABAM. When the SICA members were unreliable, the growers who did abide by the rules had to carry a heavier burden of overheads and fixed costs, and indeed, it was reported that SICAs in more peripheral areas, such as Deshaies in north leeward Guadeloupe, had collapsed when systematically undermined by *ramasseurs,* whose activities made it impossible for the SICA to supply its promised quota to the shippers. Eventually these SICAS lost their quotas (Nelson 1966, personal communication).

The failure of ASSOBAG and SICABAM to provide island-wide systems of collection for smaller growers was thus only partly compensated for by setting up local SICAS to arrange cooperative transport and marketing for their fruit. It is questionable, moreover, whether the network of SICAS was comprehensive enough geographically to permit all small farmers who might have wished to do so to participate in the export banana industry. SICAS were set up in the early 1960s with the assistance and encouragement of SATEC, almost exclusively in major, established banana-growing districts: from Vieux-Habitants in southwest Guadeloupe to Ste Marie on the east, and from Lorrain south and westwards to Rivière-Salée in Martinique. They consequently reinforced the existing pattern of banana cultivation, rather than encouraging new participation in nontraditional areas. Thus, while in the hilly area southeast of St Esprit, close to the exporting port of Fort-de-France, most farmers with holdings of 2 to 5 hectares grew export bananas and were relatively prosperous, none of the small farmers in this size-range that I interviewed in the Morne-Rouge area on the slopes of Montagne Pelée, 40 kilometres from Fort-de-France, was growing export bananas.

In any case, while the 15 SICAS were reasonably flourishing in Martinique in 1966–67 and had a total membership of about 1,600, which accounted for 10 percent of the island's production, in Guadeloupe, the 9 SICAS had only 500 members, of whom only 300 were classed as "active." They produced only 2 to 3 percent of Guadeloupe's export bananas. In Martinique it was claimed (somewhat optimistically) that *ramassage* (the unregulated purchase of bananas at the farm gate) no longer took place. In Guadeloupe, it was still common, so that banana cultivation was extremely speculative for small growers who might be obliged to sell their fruit below the cost of production or in times of surplus, might be unable to sell it at all. So anxious were the vested interests in Guadeloupe, the large grower-exporters, to discourage the development of effective cooperative associations of small growers that, in addition to subverting the SICAS' marketing arrangements, they also did their best to undermine any attempts to supply SICA members with inputs (such as fertiliser and packing materials) bulk-purchased independently at lower cost. Grower-exporters with vested interests in supplying inputs undercut SICA prices until these cooperatives could no longer afford to remain in business (Menauge 1974, 150).

DISPOSAL

Of the many factors that influenced the structure and pattern of Eastern Caribbean banana industries, the most critical were unquestionably those which related directly to the confidence farmers might feel that they would be able to sell their crop at a price at least marginally in excess of its cost of production. There were several ways in which associations could exert some influence on the price growers received for their fruit. They could lobby metropolitan governments to maintain quotas and tariffs that would prevent metropolitan markets from being overwhelmed by cheaper bananas from elsewhere; they could restrict the amount of their own fruit that reached the market, so that an oversupply did not lower price levels; they could seek alternative market opportunities; and they could redistribute their island's global receipts so that growers in the most favoured locations subsidised those in the least favoured areas. Above all, they could influence shipping arrangements in favour of one class of growers or another, in some cases to the extent that they could determine who might participate in the industry and who might not.

Relations with Metropolitan Governments

The economic position of Eastern Caribbean banana producers and the associations that represented their interests in their metropolitan marketplaces was becoming extremely weak by the mid-1960s. France and Britain could easily have obtained cheaper supplies from elsewhere, and the logic of the European Common Market, in which France was a founder-member and Britain an aspiring partner, suggested that they should do just that. From a moral point of view, however, it could be argued that the condition of extreme dependency in which the islands now found themselves was clearly the responsibility of the former colonial powers, which had indeed given the Eastern Caribbean banana industries every encouragement when it was in their interests to do so, and, consequently, they now had an obligation to see that these industries did not fail. For this reason, the Martiniquan and Guadeloupean associations, acting through the CNBA, and the Windwards' associations under the aegis of WINBAN, were able, by exerting sustained pressure on metropolitan consciences, to preserve their protected status throughout the 1960s and beyond. The French islands were in a particularly strong position, since in 1962 they had achieved an organised market that guaranteed them two-thirds of the French market. Martinique's quota was 52.73 percent of that share, Guadeloupe's, 47.27 percent.

The Commonwealth Windwards, on the other hand, had to compete on an equal footing with Jamaica, and until 1965, Jamaica's share of the United Kingdom market had been sufficiently commanding that Jamaica could afford to rebuff suggestions that the Windwards should be accorded a proportion of it. By 1966, however, Windwards production rivalled and threatened to overtake Jamaica's, and a Jamaica-WINBAN agreement was then signed, to run from 1 January 1967 to 31 December 1969. The two parties would cooperate to maintain an adequate supply of bananas on the United Kingdom market: 368,750 tons a year, 192,000 tons from Jamaica and 176,350 tons from the Windwards, according to a schedule apportioning weekly supplies from each area. There was to be joint promotion and advertising, and Cameroons bananas were to be kept out (WINBAN 1966). This was an arrangement between the Commonwealth Caribbean producers themselves, and although the British government did not object to it, it did not carry the force of the organised market agreement to which both the French government and the French Caribbean producers were parties.

However, even the French associations had only limited power to sustain the price of their members' fruit on the metropolitan market, because, unfortunately, bananas were one of the items in the national cost of living index on which statutory minimum wage rates were based. It was consequently a matter of government policy to maintain a ceiling price and to authorise the import of more fruit from lower-cost African producers if the ceiling was about to be surpassed.

Supply Management

In a protected market, the supplier of a commodity has an interest in matching supply as closely as possible with demand. Failure to provide adequate supplies is liable to provoke the government of the protected marketplace to authorise imports from alternative sources, which may be cheaper, better, or more reliable. Obviously this intrusion is not desirable. Oversupply, on the other hand, leads to falling prices. In the mid-1960s, the metropolitan markets of both groups of Eastern Caribbean banana producers were poised on the brink of saturation. Indeed, there were already seasonal surpluses. The associations of both the French and the Commonwealth islands were therefore increasingly preoccupied with developing strategies to prevent the flooding of their markets and ensure that prices remained at a satisfactory level.

The French Islands. After the organisation of the French market and the agreement to divide the Antillean quota in fixed proportions between Martinique and Guadeloupe, SICABAM and ASSOBAG had to set monthly tonnages appropriate to the demands of the French market. All growers who requested membership in their island associations had to be allocated a share of the available shipping space. Once space was requested, however, it had to be filled, or penalties were incurred. These penalties for *faux frêt* were reduced, although not eliminated, if one grower's shortfall could be counterbalanced by another's surplus. In that case, the association rather than the shipping company retained the penalty.

To ensure that shipping space corresponded as closely as possible with the quantity of fruit available for export and for which there was a market, growers were required to inform their exporters by at least the eighth day of each month, and exporters to inform SICABAM or ASSOBAG by the tenth, of their freight needs for the second month following the current one: for instance, requirements for March had to be submitted in early January. Growers were expected to base their estimates on the number or percentage of plants with forming, or "thrown," bunches three months prior to anticipated shipment.

So long as production did not exceed the demands of the French market and prices received on the quayside in France were above the minimum levels set by a CNBA protocol in 1963, the growers' associations had no further role to play in the transport and marketing of their members' fruit. If these conditions were not met, however, the associations had to intervene. They could seek markets in other countries, and on foreign sales they had a monopoly. Since banana prices in other markets were generally lower than those in France, growers whose fruit was diverted elsewhere were compensated out of SICABAM's equalisation fund, which was financed from a cess levied on all exported bananas.

When production began to surpass all export possibilities, SICABAM conducted a publicity campaign to discourage further expansion. It blamed newcomers to the industry, who had recently turned from cane to bananas, for flooding the market to the detriment of traditional banana growers. When this campaign proved ineffectual, an internal regulation was passed on 26 August 1965 imposing quotas on growers (*La Banane* 1967, 1:14). Under the regulation, steps might be taken to control exports proportionately, and if a decision was made to withhold fruit from sale because of low prices, total receipts were to be pooled and shared proportionately among those quota holders who had exported fruit. Unsold bananas were to be collected and either delivered free to schools and hospitals or destroyed. The purpose of this regulation was to make it extremely difficult for growers without quotas to enter the industry: if there was a glut they might be prevented from selling any of their fruit.

Finally, if as a result of hurricane damage, growers in one island were unable to supply their quota to the French market, their association was authorised to buy bananas from lower-cost foreign producers and sell them in France. The profits from this operation were to be shared among exporters in proportion to their usual exports.

The Commonwealth Islands. The Commonwealth associations did not control the rhythm of supply nearly as rigorously as SICABAM and ASSOBAG did, but they could exercise some discretion over the distribution of their receipts from Geest and thereby attempt to influence both overall production and timing. Geest paid the same basic price per pound to each of the four members of WINBAN, but it was up to individual associations to determine the price paid to growers and the amount of the cess withheld to cover association expenses. West Cameroon, which had formerly supplied Britain with 78,000 tons of bananas a year, fortuitously left the Commonwealth in 1963, so it was not until 1965 that overproduction became a serious problem. Before then, the associations encouraged their members to produce as much as possible, since Geest's contract required it to buy all fruit of acceptable standard. In 1965, however, winter surpluses drove the green-market price down from a high of £67.5.0 per ton to a low of £42.15.0, which translated into buying-point prices as low as 2.40¢ a pound. A costing survey in St Lucia had determined that there were some growers so favoured by infrastructure and natural conditions that they could have produced bananas profitably for buying-point receipts of only 2.50¢ to 3¢ a pound, but for the great majority, it was barely worth growing the crop if the price fell below 4¢ (Persaud 1966, 30). Concerned that many of its members might abandon banana cultivation, the SLBGA undertook to pay them no less than 4¢ a pound. Thus, while receipts to Dominican growers varied between 5.30¢ and 2.40¢ per pound, receipts to St Lucian growers were kept between 4¢ and 5¢ (46).

The SLBGA sustained the price level by drawing on reserves built up earlier in the decade, when prices had been higher and the SLBGA had retained a 2¢ cess. By the end of 1965, however, half the WI$1 million reserve of the SLBGA was used up, and it was becoming apparent that low prices might not be merely a temporary aberration (Monplaisir 1966, personnal communication). The associations, acting together through WINBAN, were forced to seek new terms from Geest, and in 1966, the company agreed to abandon the formula based on the green-market price and, instead, pay associations a fixed price of 5.13¢ a pound from October to March and 5.5¢ from April to September, with, in addition, an incentive bonus for good quality fruit. This agreement was linked with a commitment by the associations to deliver fixed quantities of fruit; Geest was no longer required to buy all they could produce, at all seasons (Monplaisir 1966, personnal communication). From the cess of 1.13¢ a pound levied by the DBGA and the SLBGA in 1966, 0.3¢ went into a winter surplus fund to pay growers for surplus production in winter that the associations could not ship. (In fact, however, there was no surplus that year).

Consequences of Supply Management

The results of association efforts to manage supply varied from island to island and were not necessarily the results expected or intended. In Guadeloupe, the ability of ASSOBAG or its forerunners either to keep production within quota limits or to deal with surpluses remained academic, since in 1963, 1964, 1965, and 1966 production fell well below the quota as a result of Hurricanes Edith and Helena (1963), Cléo (1964), and Inez (1966). The vice president of ASSOBAG, himself a large grower, was also an exporter and had a "group" (not a SICA) of twenty-five growers who produced small quantities of bananas and sold them through him. Some members of the group produced as little as 24 tonnes a year. When I asked him whether, in the event of a surplus, a standard percentage of each member's fruit would be held back, he replied enigmatically that owing to the succession of hurricanes, there had not been a surplus so far.

In Martinique, the situation was more critical, since the island produced considerably more than its quota. Efforts were made to sell Martinique bananas in foreign markets. From 1962 to 1966, small shipments were made by SICABAM to New York, to try to establish a toehold in the North American market. By 1965, however, prices there were so low that the disbursement of equalisation payments to growers whose fruit was sold in New York was proving ruinous to the Caisse de Péréquation, and by 1967, shipments to North America had virtually ceased (*La Banane* 1967, 1:13; SICABAM 1988, 23). An attempt was made in 1965 to sell Martinique bananas in the Federal Republic of Germany, but German importers were not keen to transfer their custom from their traditional Central American suppliers, with whom they had important and long-standing trading links, and the experiment was not a success. On the other hand, the Italian market did provide a viable outlet for some surplus Martiniquan fruit. The Italian government's desire to protect its traditional Somalian suppliers ensured that wholesale price levels were similar to those in France. In 1966, Martinique exported 29,000 tons of bananas to Italy (*La Banane* 1967, 1:13).

Certainly, exports of Martinique bananas to foreign markets rose substantially after the formation of SICABAM: from less than 3,000 tons in 1961 to almost 33,000 tons in 1966. Realistically, however, Martinique's high-cost producers could find only modest, temporary outlets for short-term surpluses in foreign markets; these did not offer a promising field for unlimited expansion.

SICABAM's attempts to maintain prices at as high a level as possible encountered resistance from various quarters. The French government policy of maintaining a ceiling price on bananas, which were a constituent of the cost of living index, meant that any move to drive up price levels by undersupplying the market was liable to be countered by the authorisation of higher imports from lower-cost African producers. Moreover, when prices fell to unsatisfactorily low levels in the summer of 1967 and SICABAM proposed that Martinique and Guadeloupe should cooperate to destroy their poor quality fruit in an attempt to revive price levels, ASSOBAG would not agree. It was, after all, in no danger of exceeding its quota.

Figure 8.1 shows the pattern of French banana imports during 1966, a distinctly different pattern from that in Britain (Figure 8.3, below). Evidently, demand for bananas in France in August, the month of lowest demand (when local fruits such as peaches were abundant) was only 60 percent of that in May, the month of peak demand. Monthly combined export totals for Martinique and Guadeloupe (Figure 8.2) showed a reasonably close correspondence with the totals to which they were theoretically entitled by their two-thirds share of the French market, at least until October when the impact of Hurricane Inez on Guadeloupean production was felt. The fact that a large part of Guadeloupe's deficit could be filled by greatly increased exports from Martinique suggests, however, that while SICABAM might have been able to control the level of exports, it had not succeeded in controlling the volume of production. It may have been difficult to convince growers of the need for restraint when hurricanes and windstorms in Guadeloupe had depressed production well below that island's quota levels in four successive years, providing a fortuitous outlet for Martinique's excess production. SICABAM felt complacency was unjustified, however. So anxious was it to protect the interests of its established members, or at least

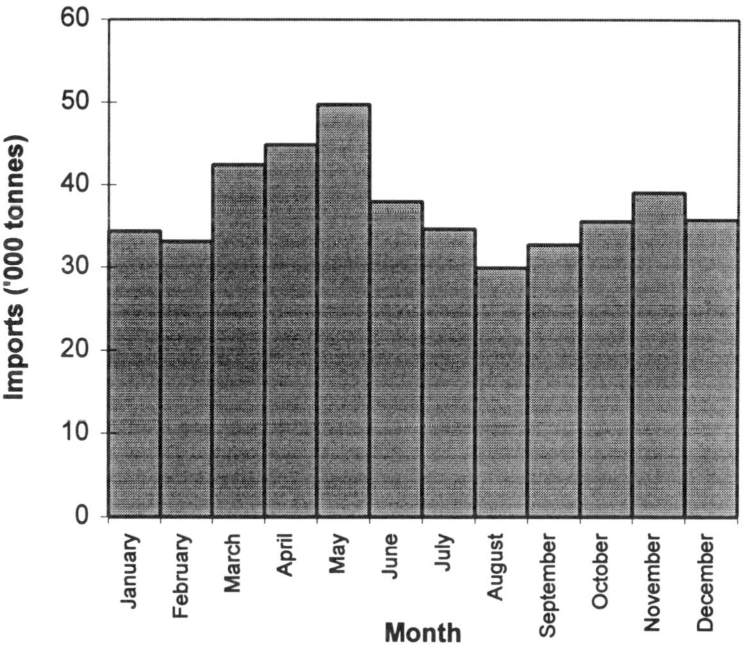

Figure 8.1
Monthly banana imports into metropolitan France, 1966
Source: *La Banane* (1967, 1:24).

members who were medium-sized or large-scale independent growers, that when the newly-formed SICA of Lareinty applied for an export quota in 1967 (the SICA was composed of farmers who had been allocated former cane land under the government-sponsored *Réforme Foncière*), SICABAM refused. SICABAM advised the SICA of Lareinty to apply to the Union des SICA for a part of their share. The Union also declined and the question had to be submitted to arbitration by the prefect.

If SICABAM and ASSOBAG, with their considerable power to control the rhythm of exports, did not seem to have been able to exert a very precise influence on the rhythm and volume of production, what was the case with the SLBGA and the DBGA, which served a far broader and more disparate clientele? By the mid-1960s, overproduction was a looming threat, but banana exports had become such an important element in the island economies that failure to produce the maximum that the market could absorb would have been regarded by many as gross negligence. This explains why the SLBGA was prepared to exhaust up to half its reserves in price

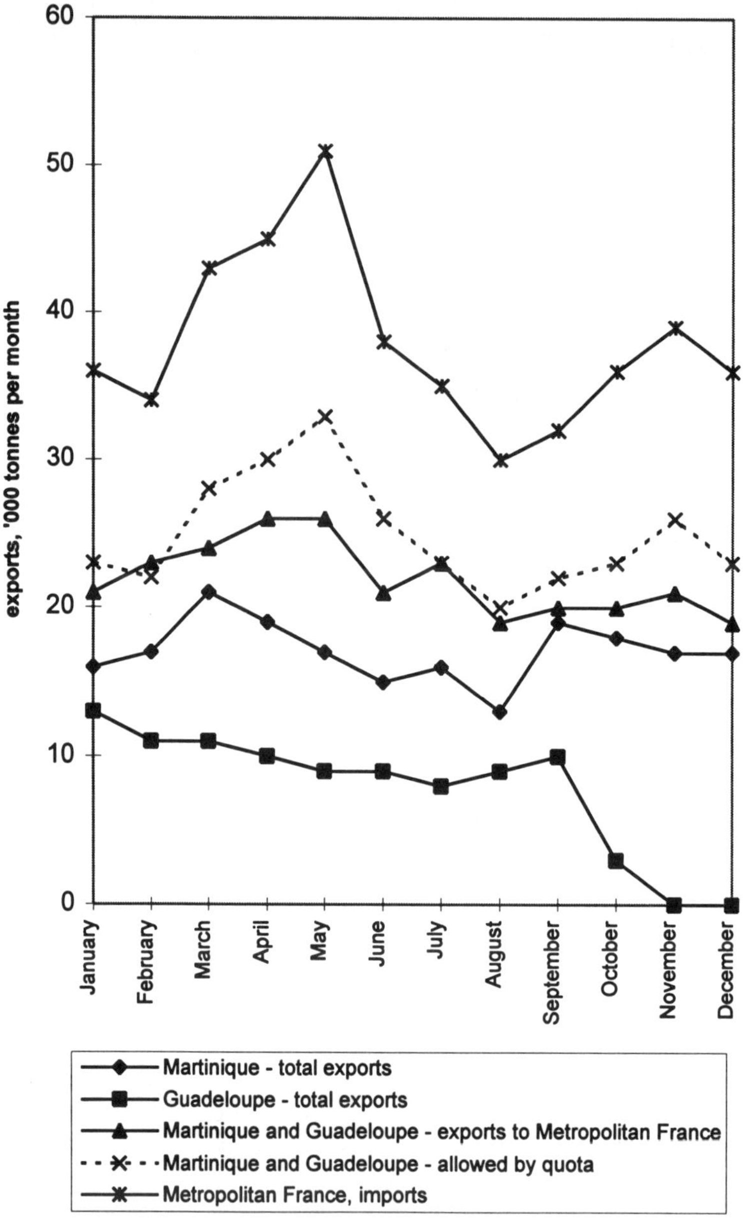

Figure 8.2
Martinique and Guadeloupe: Banana exports, 1966, actual and allowed by quota

support to ensure that its members did not abandon the crop, even though it had taken on major liabilities in the construction of a new headquarters in Castries and the introduction of aerial spraying. The success of this strategy is suggested by the fact that, as I mentioned earlier, very few St Lucian respondents in my survey of 1966 (only 4 percent) were planning to reduce their banana production, compared with 22.5 percent of the respondents in Dominica. Moreover, no one I interviewed in St Lucia expressed the degree of disillusionment with the industry that I encountered in Dominica. "At one time, bananas seemed to be the lifeline," remarked one Castle Bruce farmer, "but now my devotion is not with them again." Bananas were making him old before his time and he was working for nothing.

In the Colihaut district it was reported that many farmers were considering reverting to the production of cassava, even though they would have to buy new equipment for processing cassava into farine, since they had disposed of the old equipment when they had given up cassava for bananas. Bananas had never been particularly profitable in an area of such difficult communications as Colihaut, but in the late 1950s and early 1960s, the price to growers at the buying point had been up to 5¢ a pound, and on virgin soils, bunchweights averaged 30 pounds without fertiliser. In 1965, average bunchweights were only 18 to 25 pounds, so that if the buying point price fell below 2.5¢ a pound, the cost of carrying out harvested fruit exceeded buying-point receipts. Apart from farmers in the most marginal areas, several of whom were considering giving up bananas entirely and turning to an alternative crop (such as cassava, pineapples, limes, or bay), many Dominican farmers were reducing their dependence on bananas by interplanting more long-term tree crops, particularly citrus, even though the market for such crops was uncertain. St Lucian farmers, on the other hand, generally affirmed their faith in bananas and with one or two exceptions were reducing, rather than expanding, permanent tree crops such as cacao.

It was harder to find much evidence for the success of the summer bonus of 0.25¢ a pound, which was intended to encourage higher summer production. In any case, for 1966 any effect it might have had was obliterated by windstorm and hurricane damage. Figure 8.3 shows the monthly imports of bananas into the United Kingdom in 1965. Figure 8.4 shows exports from Dominica and St Lucia in 1965: actual and adjusted to take account of the overall rising trend in production. The export levels authorised under the 1966 agreement are shown as well.

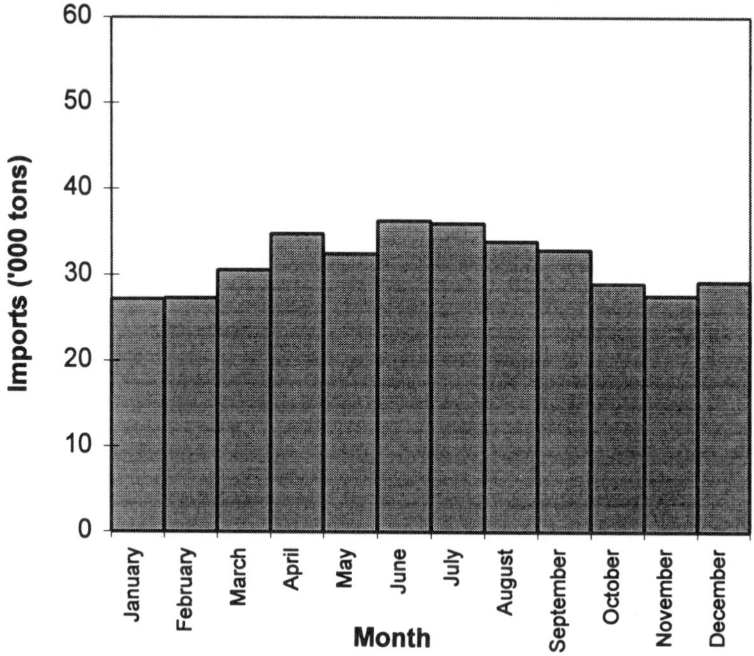

Figure 8.3
Monthly banana imports into the United Kingdom, 1965
Source: Persaud (1966, 54).

Figures for 1965 show some seasonal variation in monthly exports. In Dominica, 55.4 percent of the annual total was produced in the six summer months; in St Lucia, however, summer production only accounted for 50.8 percent of the total (Persaud 1966, 29). Unfortunately, the incentive effect, such as it was, of the summer bonus was outweighed by various other factors, both physical and economic. Particularly in St Lucia, where rainfall was generally lower and the dry season more pronounced, peak production would not naturally have occurred during the summer months. The timing of the harvest could be influenced in two ways: by planting time, which controlled the period of the first harvest (but since ratoons were harvested about six months later, much of the initial advantage was lost), and by judicious timing of fertiliser application.

Of 118 farmers that I interviewed in St Lucia and Dominica in 1966, only one, a large St Lucian grower, claimed to have taken any steps to achieve a summer maximum: he applied fertiliser in January and February to stimulate high summer production; but he had access to irrigation water. For farmers who

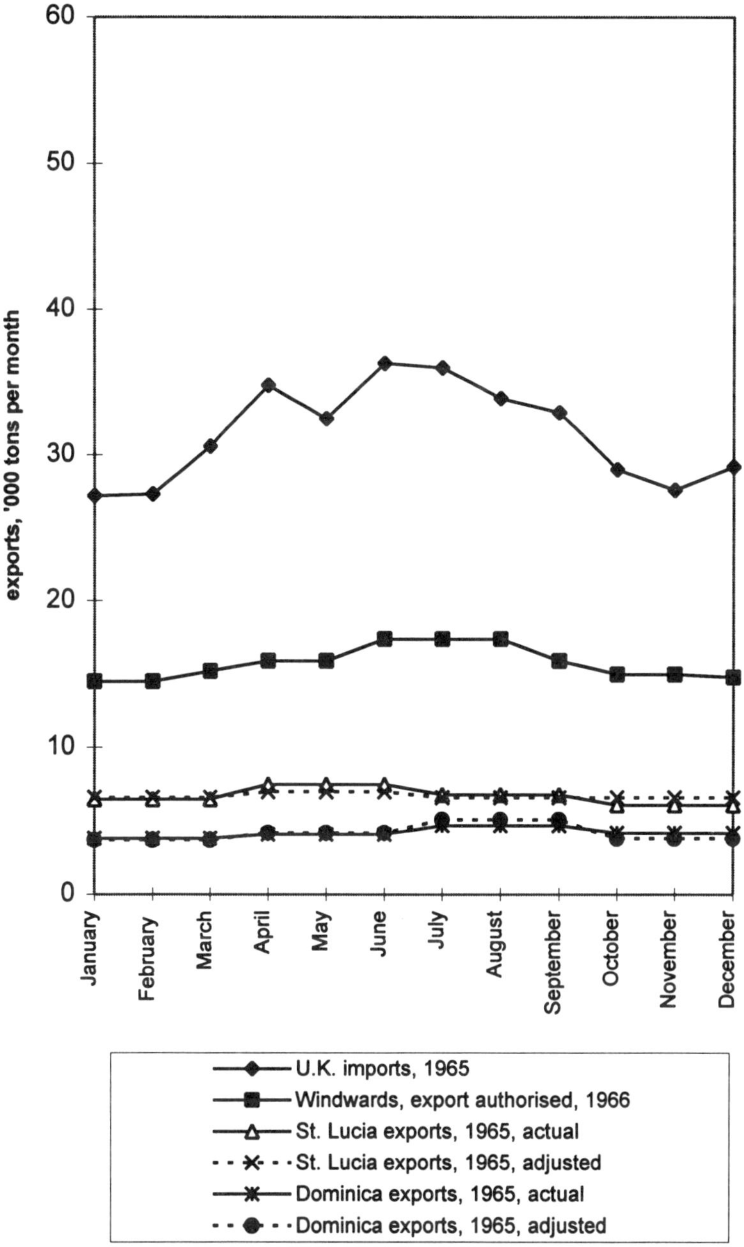

Figure 8.4
Seasonal rhythm of banana exports, Dominica and St Lucia, 1965, and total Windwards banana export authorised for 1966
Source. Persaud (1966, 29, 47, 54).

did not, dry-season fertiliser application would have been useless. One large Dominican grower that I revisited in 1970 was trying to achieve a summer maximum by planting at the appropriate season, but he found that ratooning intervals soon disrupted the pattern.

On a large estate belonging to Geest, it was claimed that while timed planting was a good idea in theory, in practice it was uneconomical to delay replanting until the optimal time. If this was so for Geest, how much more so for the mass of peasant growers who depended on the banana for a steady income throughout the year. Indeed, some recent studies have suggested that because of lower winter prices, some farmers tried to harvest more fruit in winter in order to sustain a stable monthly income, and particularly to have enough cash in the pre-Christmas period (Luu 1985, 70,81,89). Moreover, the risk of hurricane and windstorm damage made it much more prudent to try to distribute production evenly around the year. The farmer who delayed replanting to take advantage of summer high prices risked losing the entire crop just before it was ready to be harvested.

Apart from making agreements with other major Commonwealth producers not to oversupply the United Kingdom market, there was not a great deal that the Windwards associations could do outside the Caribbean to improve market prospects for their members' fruit. Per capita consumption in the United Kingdom was already high and offered only very limited prospects for expansion, no matter how much promotion and advertising were undertaken. Opportunities for finding alternative outlets for Windwards fruit were also very limited. In the first place, the associations were committed to keeping Geest supplied and could only negotiate with other buyers to sell surpluses that might not materialise. They could not divert bananas committed to Geest for the sake of securing temporarily higher prices elsewhere, or even to consolidate a tenuous foothold in a new market.

In the second place, there were very few attractive markets that offered any protection to the relatively high-cost Windwards producers, and without a tariff advantage, there was little reason why anyone would buy Windwards bananas in preference to cheaper Central American ones. Geest pointed out that even Eire, whose goods exported to the West Indies continued to enjoy Commonwealth preference, did not provide reciprocal protection for Commonwealth bananas. He proposed that overtures should be made through the Commonwealth Relations Office to the Irish government to persuade them to impose a tariff of £7.10.0 a ton on non-Commonwealth fruit (WINBAN 1966), but WINBAN did not have enough leverage for such an initiative to have much chance of success.

The Canadian market was also considered, since it did extend tariff protection to Commonwealth bananas and had winter prices higher than those in England. The protection amounted to only Can$11.00 a ton, however, and it was feared that any attempt by Commonwealth Caribbean producers to encroach on this market would be countered by retaliatory measures by United Fruit, which controlled the Canadian market and operated it as an extension of the United States market. A request to the Canadian government by WINBAN to negotiate quotas evidently met with no enthusiasm (Monplaisir 1966, personnal communication), and suggestions by the chairman of the SLBGA in 1967 that the Canadian government was anxious to see St Lucian bananas on the Canadian market (Atkinson 1967) must have been based on wishful thinking; unless they were simply part of a strategy to gain acceptance for intended changes in SLBGA operations that were regarded by many small growers with suspicion and distrust.

Quality Manipulation

If there was little scope for reducing production costs, the associations could at least try to enhance the competitive position of their members' fruit by encouraging or obliging members to take measures to improve its quality.

Since most fruit from the French islands was sold in the names of individual growers rather than SICABAM or ASSOBAG, there was a strong incentive for individuals to maintain the highest possible quality. In the case of exports to New York and trial shipments to West Germany, SICABAM did make an effort to see that only top quality fruit was shipped. This effort evidently paid dividends in New York, where Martinique bananas were said to have been well received, but not in Hamburg, where in the view of SICABAM management and French government officials, it had been a matter of policy to assert that Martinique bananas did not meet the exacting standards of the German market. This ruse permitted German importers to continue to obtain deferral of the implementation of Common Market provisions.

SICABAM proposed to strengthen the market position of Antillean bananas in France by collaborating with ASSOBAG to hold back poorer quality fruit, but Guadeloupe did not support the plan. Furthermore, a proposal by SICABAM management to sell all Martinique bananas under one label, with two recognised quality standards, proved unacceptable to the membership.

The Windwards associations were becoming increasingly concerned about quality control as total Caribbean production equalled and sometimes surpassed the capacity of the United Kingdom market to absorb it, and their bargaining position with Geest consequently became progressively weaker. In 1966 and 1967 nearly all Windwards bananas were still being shipped on the stem, and it was not until they were ripened and boxed that an assessment was made of their quality. By then, there was no way to identify and penalise the growers who were responsible for poor quality fruit. The associations did pay an incentive bonus for quality of 0.25¢ a pound to growers who complied with certain regulations regarding the transport of bananas, and as Geest expressed increasing dissatisfaction with the quality of Windwards fruit, they increasingly exhorted growers to address the problem and, especially, to take more care in handling the fruit. It was believed that the rough handling of unwrapped stems was largely to blame for their poor condition on arrival in the United Kingdom.

It was, however, difficult for the associations to take effective action. On the one hand, they could do little beyond offering minor incentives to oblige growers to adopt more stringent quality control techniques (the effects of rough handling were not apparent at the buying point), and on the other hand, they had no means of verifying the consistency of Geest's selection procedures. When boxed, Windwards bananas were divided into five grades: specials, bests, seconds, thirds, and loose. Between 1961 and 1965, the percentage of special and best grades declined from 70.77 percent to 43.79 percent. There is, however, no way of telling whether this decline represented a real deterioration in the quality of fruit or simply the raising of standards in an increasingly competitive market.

The overall downward trend in quality was clearly superimposed on strongly marked seasonal variations. Late-spring percentages of special and best grades were 20 to 30 points higher than midwinter percentages (Figure 8.5). The seasonal variation might have been directly related to climatic factors in the Caribbean, the North Atlantic, or in Britain, or it might have been influenced by price levels and anticipated receipts in the United Kingdom, and thus it might have been a function of seasonal climatic variation only at second hand. If the climate of the Windwards was responsible, it must be

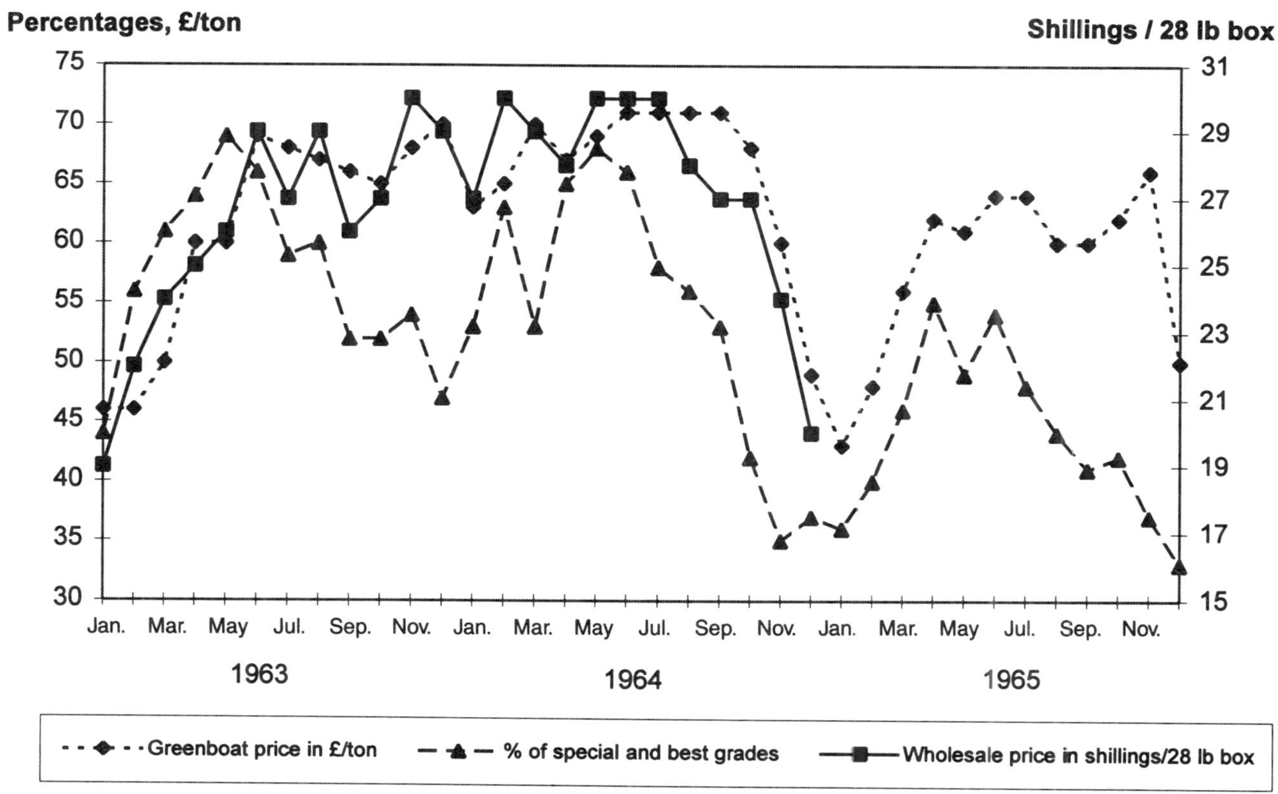

Figure 8.5 Fluctuations in United Kingdom banana price levels and the quality of Windwards bananas imported, 1963–65
Source: Persaud 1966, 48, 54, 57).

concluded that bananas grown wholly within the rainy season were less durable than those grown mainly in the drier season; but no positive relationship between high quality and low rainfall was suggested to me in the field, nor did I encounter any in the literature. It is true. however, that research in Guadeloupe in the 1980s did determine that bananas mature more slowly between the months of February and April (IRFA 1986, 43).

If the winter climate in Britain were the problem, it seems highly unlikely that Geest would not have taken measures to protect fruit from conditions that might adversely affect its quality. On the other hand, that there was some coincidence between trends in United Kingdom banana prices and the percentage of Windwards bananas graded "special" and "best" seems evident from Figure 8.5. The green-market price clearly moved in response to the wholesale price; but whether the wholesale price was influenced by the quality of fruit on sale or whether the percentage of fruit assigned to the superior grades was influenced by anticipated seasonal fluctuations in price level is not possible to determine. Perhaps neither was directly linked causally, or perhaps there was some overriding factor that influenced both price and quality. It may be significant, however, that Arthur, Houck, et al., writing about the structure of the contemporary Colombian banana industry, suggest that producer prices in Colombia remained relatively stable because exporters regulated supply by varying quality requirements rather than price (1968, 57).

Shipping Arrangements

The Commonwealth associations had relatively little control over shipping arrangements, since once it left the island their members' fruit belonged to Geest, the shipper, rather than the growers' association. By contrast, it was in the organisation of shipping arrangements that SICABAM and ASSOBAG had their greatest roles to play.

The Commonwealth associations were obliged to keep Geest informed as far in advance as possible of the quantity of bananas likely to be available and, more specifically, to give a firm estimate on the first working day of each month, accurate within 10 percent, of the quantity available for the third month therefrom (SLBGA 1964, 13). Geest was, however, obliged to buy all bananas of acceptable varieties and stem weight, and it does not appear that the company ever attempted to exact any penalty from the associations for incorrect estimates - if indeed there ever were any, except after the mass destruction of crops by windstorms or hurricanes.

Until 1965, the price received by the associations was based on the green market price of Jamaican bananas. The peaks and depressions in this index price were, however, modified by a freight escalator: when prices were high, Geest was authorised to deduct more for shipping expenses from the price paid to the associations than when prices were low. This provision was absent from the 1967 fixed price agreement.

The French associations, acting as intermediary agents between producers and the shipping company, were expected to play a far more active role than their Commonwealth counterparts. By 1966 they alone negotiated freight rates and shipping space with the sole shipper, the Compagnie Générale Transatlantique. The associations' role in allocating space among growers has been described in the discussion of supply management. Unlike the Commonwealth associations, the French associations were prepared to penalise growers or exporters who had failed to fill the space they had requested two months previously, even if the shortfall could be made up from another grower's surplus. It was proposed in 1966-67 that marketing should be streamlined and simplified by pooling all growers' fruit, possibly in two grades, and selling it in the metropolitan ports under a single brand name rather than individual growers' and exporters' labels. This innovation was, however, resisted by growers who felt that the current system ensured premium prices for their fruit, or at least gave their agents a chance to see that their fruit found a market before the fruit of smaller or less influential growers. Growers received payment for their bananas after they had been sold in France, two to three weeks after shipment. All shipping and handling charges were deducted from the payment, so a grower whose fruit failed to sell in France for whatever reason might receive a debit note.

While the French associations did not have much bargaining power with the shipping company, which had a monopoly of trade between the French Antilles and the *métropole*, they were able to secure for their members a ten percent reduction in overall shipping costs by instituting single freight contracts between the Compagnie Générale Transatlantique and SICABAM for all of Martinique's bananas and between the Compagnie and ASSOBAG for all of Guadeloupe's. The reduction was possible because the intervention of the associations greatly decreased the incidence of oversupply and underloading. Oversupply had previously resulted in wasted fruit that could not be shipped for lack of space; underloading had wasted money in penalties to growers when their production fell short of the tonnage for which they had contracted space three months earlier.

Although a single freight rate benefited growers and exporters already established in the industry, it was not much of an incentive for farmers to begin growing bananas for export. SICABAM calculated in 1965 that it would cost up to Fr412.77 to grow and harvest a tonne of bananas and transport them to the boxing shed. Expenses from the shed to the quay (including boxing and transport) would amount to Fr192.18, and loading, freight, and unloading, in addition to taxes and other shipping costs, would add a further Fr399.17. All these expenses had to be borne by farmers, whether or not they succeeded in selling their fruit in the metropolitan ports, unless they were prepared to take a chance on being able to sell it to a *ramasseur* for immediate cash at the farm gate. The choice for small farmers, then, was between trying to sell locally, with a substantial risk of losing much or all of their investment in cultivation and harvesting, or hoping to sell in the *métropole* through a SICA or private exporter. There, theoretically, imports were regulated to avoid oversupplying the market, so the risk of failing to find a buyer was much lower. Yet it was always possibile that the fruit would spoil en route and prove unsaleable on arrival. I was also told that small growers who could not afford to engage their own agents in the metropolitan port were particularly vulnerable, since they were in no position to verify whether it was indeed their own fruit that had remained unsold or the bananas of the exporters, who had simply attributed their own unsaleable fruit to small clients and disposed of the small clients' bananas as their own.

Moreover, a small grower was more likely than a large one to suffer a significant shortfall in percentage terms as a result of a localised windstorm. Since the intervention of SICABAM and ASSOBAG in regulating the shipment of members' bananas did not relieve growers of the responsibility for paying for all the space they had reserved three months previously, whether or not they had sufficient fruit to fill it, such a loss could prove doubly disastrous.

The most important consideration, however, was that most small farmers simply did not have the financial reserves to cushion them against bankruptcy. To participants in the banana industry, with its very high outlays before any returns were seen by the grower, bankruptcy or at least heavy indebtedness was an ever-present threat.

The result of the failure of SICABAM and ASSOBAG to insulate their members against devastating losses was that in each of the French islands, only two or three thousand farmers ventured to grow bananas for export, and these were mainly farmers with larger holdings in favoured locations. This was in marked contrast with Dominica and St Lucia, where almost the entire farming population grew and sold export bananas. In the French islands, of the 46 farmers I interviewed in 1966 and 1967, only 12 grew bananas for export (compared with 67 out of 70 in Dominica). Among the 34 who did not, all but 7 had holdings in areas in where banana cultivation was physically quite feasible, and at least 6 were in core banana areas.

One of these farmers, in the Bananier area of Capesterre *commune* in southeast Guadeloupe, gave some interesting insights into the way in which changing circumstances had led to dwindling participation in export banana production by small farmers. When the industry first gained importance, after the hurricane of 1928 had destroyed or weakened many tree crops, small proprietors had played a major role; large landowners with holdings in the flatter areas had stuck to cane. As bananas became more profitable (in the 1950s), large landowners switched, and monopolised the available shipping space, so that small growers wishing to export were obliged to sell their fruit to these large-scale operators. The larger landowners packed the small growers' fruit and sold it in their own name. The small growers normally received Fr 0.35 to Fr 0.40 a kilogram at the farm gate, but sometimes they were offered only Fr 0.10 a kilogram (less than WI2¢ a pound), and sometimes there was no sale at all. My informant had himself withdrawn from export bananas because exporting posed too many problems.

The weak position of the small grower - and any grower with less than five hectares in bananas was regarded as small in the French islands - and the problems and risks confronting those rash enough to try to enter or expand their stake in the export banana business were mentioned by most small farmers in banana-growing zones. A Goyave farmer in eastern Guadeloupe said that although his land was better suited for bananas than for cane, he had 5.5 hectares of cane and only 1 hectare of bananas, even though bananas were potentially much more profitable. He explained that he was dependent on *ramasseurs* to sell his crop and the market was too uncertain. It was generally agreed in Martinique in 1966 that bananas were the most profitable crop per hectare, certainly when compared with cane, ground provisions, or livestock. Banana profits per hectare were reckoned to be double or triple the profits for cane (Emélie

1967, personal communication), and yet small farmers in medium- to high rainfall areas such as Gros-Morne and Morne-Rouge often opted for livestock or cane, since they had been discouraged by previous disastrous experiences with bananas: heavy losses as a result of hurricanes, on the one hand, and gluts, on the other. Even the president of the Gros-Morne SICA, a farmer with a 10-hectare holding, had reduced his area of bananas from 7 to only 3 hectares since the passage of hurricane Edith, replacing it with cane, which he regarded as a less speculative crop.

There were instances locally of small farmers committing themselves to export banana production despite the risks involved: in Lorrain, for instance, in the northeast of Martinique, where the recent closure of the sugar factory meant that it was no longer easy for local farmers to dispose of the cane that had been their traditional cash crop. In the Ducos-Lamentin area, large sugar estates had been bought by the state, subdivided, and allocated to hundreds of small farmers, who were bound to pay for their land over a 20-year period. In principle, it had been intended that they should maintain their holdings in cane, but in practice, the returns from cane were too low for them to make an acceptable living and keep up their loan repayments to the Crédit Agricole, so they were obliged to try bananas and gamble on their chances of selling them profitably. Consequently, even though banana production was considered speculative for any one with less than a 10-hectare holding, since one *faux frêt* could spell ruin, there was a slight increase in the number of banana growers registered with SICABAM between 1963 and 1966: from 3,077 to 3,396 (*La Banane* 1967, 14; Léobon 1966, personal communication). Between 1966 and 1972, however, there was a sharp reversal in this trend: SICA membership in Martinique, which numbered 2,055 in 1966, had declined to 1,706 in 1970, 964 in 1971 and 846 in 1973. By 1973 the total number of growers had fallen to 1,497 (Burac 1975, 53,112,115; Léobon 1966, personal communication). The SICA of Gros-Morne, which had 210 members in 1966, had only 85 by 1970 (Fanon 1966, personal communication; Burac 1975, 55).

Trends in Guadeloupe were similar to those in Martinique. In 1964, there were estimated to be 1,740 banana growers in the *département*; in 1966, 2,850; and in 1970, 2,298 (*La Banane* 1967, 1:16; Menauge 1974, 61). While the overall number of growers declined by 19 percent from 1966 to 1970, the number of growers with less than a hectare of bananas fell far more drastically, by 32 percent (from 1,280 to 865) (Menauge 1974, 61).

CONCLUSION

In the production of bananas, a very sharp line could generally be drawn between the Commonwealth banana growers' associations, whose policy was to do whatever they thought was necessary to maximise production, and the French associations, whose policy was to interfere as little as possible and let growers make their own arrangements for obtaining credit, controlling disease, and learning about improved agricultural techniques. For the transfer of the harvested fruit from the field to the exporting port, the line was less clearly drawn. At one end of the spectrum was the SLBGA, which until 1967 tried to maintain a network of buying sheds accessible to all, even though in less favoured areas a buying team might process under 300 stems a week (Touche, Ross, et al. 1967, app. 1). At the other end of the spectrum were SICABAM and ASSOBAG, which took no part in conveying bananas from farm to port. The DBGA fell somewhere in between.

Although the lack of intervention by the French associations posed no transportation problems for large growers - and in Martinique some of the largest banana plantations were in the extreme northeast, as distant as possible from Fort-de-France - the evidence is that distance was a deterrent to small growers. They tended to be concentrated in areas not too far from the ports. In Dominica, growers who were distant from the ports were at a slight disadvantage, especially if their production was too low to permit them to sell independently at the port reception depot, and by 1966 many of the more marginal growers in Dominica were questioning their future in the industry; this was not so in St Lucia. When, in 1967, a change of the SLBGA policy resulted in the closing of many underused buying sheds, consternation among affected growers was extreme (*Voice of St Lucia*, 12 August 1967).

Of all the areas in which it was possible for growers' associations to pursue different policies, however, unquestionably the most critical was the system of marketing the fruit. It was the mission of the SLBGA and the DBGA to provide a market for *all* the bananas of export quality produced in their islands, and the SLBGA in particular felt obliged not only to buy all the fruit that was produced but to guarantee that no growers would ever have to sell at a price below the cost of production. In the French islands, there were no such guarantees, and the survival of the fittest, which largely excluded the smallest, was the prevailing orthodoxy.

The whole structure and location of export banana growing was most profoundly affected by the key question of who, ultimately, bore responsibility for the cost of transporting the bananas from where they were grown to the metropolitan port, and especially, who bore the shipping costs. Where banana growing entailed no risk for the farmer beyond that of losing his or her investment in cultivation and harvesting, the owner of even the smallest property might consider it worthwhile to devote some land and time to the crop. Where, on the other hand, the individual grower was confronted with liability for expenses that, at least in the short term, might easily exceed receipts, prudence excluded most farmers with holdings too small to assure them of a strong line of credit.

It might be argued that the differences in the way shipping and marketing were organised were due not so much to policy decisions by growers' associations as to the accident that a single importer, Geest, was prepared to deal with the entire Windwards production. In Jamaica, however, growers sold their fruit to the banana board at buying stations, but the board retained ownership up to the point of sale to wholesalers in the United Kingdom (Arthur, Houck, et al. 1968, 59). This arrangement did not render individual growers personally liable for shipping costs, and the export banana industry remained overwhelmingly the sphere of peasant growers: 33 percent of mats were on holdings of less than 2 hectares, and 73 percent on holdings of under 4 hectares (MacFarlane 1964, 48). In other words, what made the difference between the character of participation in French and Commonwealth islands were the associations' decisions whether the liability for the cost of transporting bananas to the metropolitan market should or should not rest with the individual grower.

Compared with the issues of responsibility for shipping costs and guaranteed markets, the actions that associations might take to discourage oversupply were a relatively minor matter, although locally important in Martinique in inhibiting newcomers' access to the industry. The options for finding new markets for excess production were very limited: SICABAM scored some modest successes, but the benefits of exporting anywhere other than to the carefully protected markets of France and the United Kingdom were so marginal that there was never any serious question of intentionally expanding production beyond the capacity of those two relatively safe markets to absorb it. The associations could, however, play a very important role in keeping prices at a reasonable level through negotiation with rival suppliers to metropolitan markets; unless they had presented a united front in the oversupplied markets of the 1960s, the banana producers of the Lesser Antilles might before the end of the decade have passed into history.

9 The Fourth Dimension

To revisit an area after a twenty-year hiatus and reappraise one's original conclusions in the light of subsequent developments may not prove an entirely reassuring experience. Taking advantage of the double-edged gift of hindsight, it is necessary to examine the ways in which the political, economic, ecological, and technological contexts of the Eastern Caribbean banana industries have evolved, before looking at changes in growers' organisations and assessing their role in land use in the four islands.

POLITICAL AND IDEOLOGICAL CONTEXT

By the mid-1960s, the transformation of French Caribbean colonies into *départements* of France was more or less a fait accompli. They sent *députés* to the French Assembly in Paris and shared most of the administrative structures of any metropolitan *département*. Social security provisions were progressively being aligned with those of the *métropole,* and while by no means all Martiniquans and Guadeloupeans were enthusiastic about the prospect of ever stronger economic integration and political assimilation within the French state, this was the destiny the Gaullist government favoured for the islands and promoted with relentless zeal. The Commonwealth islands, on the other hand, having made one false start along the road to independence as members of the short-lived Federation of the West Indies, were by 1967 semiautonomous "associated states," self-governing in all but defence and foreign affairs and seeking some viable regional economic and political framework within which they could move towards complete independence from Britain.

The 1970s brought little fundamental change in the political and social structures of the French islands; the impact of "Black Power" was mild compared with its effect in the anglophone Caribbean. Antillean *députés* in Paris, whether assimilationist, autonomist, or independentist, had little influence on the actual government of their islands, while a very substantial amount of power resided in the hands of the prefect, not normally Antillean, appointed by the government in power. He it was, for instance, who decided when the city of Basse-Terre was to be evacuated during the 1976 activity of the Soufrière volcano and, more controversially, when the evacuation was to end.

Meanwhile, the inexorable logic of interdepartmental mobility (allied with the incentive of substantial overseas allowances) brought ever-increasing numbers of *métropolitains* to Martinique and Guadeloupe, mainly civil servants and their families. There were reported to be 7,422 *métropolitains* in Martinique in 1967, 11,692 by the mid-1970s. They represented 3.4 percent of the total population but earned 25 percent of the total local income, were generally in the Antilles for periods of two to five years and were concerned with the promotion of French rather than Creole culture (Burton 1978, 21,30).

Meanwhile, the Commonwealth territories pursued economic integration within the Caribbean Free Trade Association (CARIFTA), which became, at least in theory, a common market (the Caribbean Common Market, or CARICOM) in 1973, but without corresponding political rapprochement. By the end of the decade the Commonwealth territories had opted for complete independence from Britain. St Lucia retained the Queen as nominal head of state, while Dominica became a "Commonwealth" headed by a president. Although the political parties voted into office in the mid-1960s remained in power throughout most of the 1970s, a significant social transformation took place on both islands as a result of Black Power movements. The continued existence of large expatriate-owned estates became socially unacceptable, and the labour required to work them became unmanageable or unobtainable. Consequently, several of the largest estates were subdivided into smallholdings and sold, sometimes, but not always, to those who had formerly worked on them (Bully 1988, personal communication). Tables 9.1 and 9.2 present what data is available on the evolution of agrarian structure from the 1960s to the 1980s. In both Martinique and St Lucia, there was a significant shift in the proportion of land in large and small

Table 9.1
Evolution of agrarian structure in Martinique, 1970–85

1970 (Centre-Nord only)		*1985*		
Size group (ha)	*Percentage of agricultural area used*	*Size group (ha)*	*Number of holdings*	*Percentage of agricultural area used*
0–3	23.7	<1	13,211	9.6
3–5	3.5	1–2	2,605	8.2
5–20	6.1	2–5	2,557	18.2
20–50	6.3	5–20	929	18.9
50–100	11.9	20–50	152	11.2
>100	48.5	>50	119	33.8
Total	100		19,573	100

Sources: Burac (1974, 5); Martinique (1985).

holdings. For Martinique, the 1970 figures are based on a part of the island only; but if they are representative, then the percentage of the agricultural area in holdings of less than 5 hectares rose from 27 percent to 36 percent between 1970 and 1985. In St Lucia, the percentage of the area in holdings of less than 10 acres (4 hectares) rose from 28 percent in 1961 to 35 percent in 1986, although as Table 9.3 shows, there was actually an absolute decline in the area of both large and small holdings. For holdings under 10 acres, however, the decline was only 10 percent, while the area in holdings over 10 acres fell by 42 percent.

It does not appear that this land redistribution took place as a result of any ideological bias or policy decision by the parties in power, which while they described themselves as "Labour" or "Workers' parties," were in fact run by middle-class politicians who had not previously shown much zeal for land reform. Nevertheless, the impact on the structure of participation in the banana industry was considerable, particularly in Dominica, where by 1987 there were only 15 growers producing over 100 tons of fruit a year, and 220 tons was the maximum (DBMC 1988). In contrast, Martinique's largest grower exported 10,314 tonnes in 1986 (Parmentier 1988, personal communication).

The election of a Socialist president in France in 1981 brought about a change of policy in the French islands. It was declared that the phase of *départementalisation,* which had been a period of assimilation and *uniformisation,* was to be succeeded by a new era

Table 9.2
Evolution of agrarian structure in St Lucia, 1961–86

1961			*1973–74*		*1986*	
Size group (acres)	*Number of holdings*	*Percentage of area in holdings*	*Number*	*Percentage of area*	*Number*	*Percentage of area*
0–4.9	10,414	17.7	8,558	14.2	8,770	21.3
5–9.9	1,365	10.3	1,082	9.8	1,191	13.4
10–24.9	571	9.1	475	8.9	560	13.4
25–49.9	183	6.8	199	8.8	98	5.6
50–99.9	63	5.0	58	6.0	35	4.0
100–199.9	38	5.7	19	3.7	17	3.9
200–499.9	33	12.0	28	11.3	17	8.4
500+	19	33.4	19	37.4	13	30.0
Total	12,686	100	10,436	100	10,701	100

Sources: St Lucia (1987, 11,13); WI Census of Agriculture, 1961 (1968), 181.

Table 9.3
Area of land-in-holdings in St Lucia, by size groups, 1961, 1973–4, and 1986

	Area in holdings (acres)			*Percentage change*
Size group	*1961*	*1973–4*	*1986*	*1961 to 1986*
0–	15,407	10,204	12,350	-20
5–	6,962	7,068	7,802	+12
10–	7,969	6,396	7,763	-2.5
25–	5,925	6,299	3,218	-45.5
50–	4,598	4,282	2,338	-49
100–	4,945	2,690	2,233	-45.5
200–	10,505	8,160	4,881	-53.5
500–	29,201	26,902	17,430	-40
Total	87,375	72,001	58,016	-33.5

Sources: West Indies Census of Agriculture, 1961 (1968, 181); St Lucia (1987, 13).

of regionalisation, associated with decentralisation. One of the first manifestations of the new policy was the election, in 1983, of *conseils régionaux*, intended to provide a synthesis between national and local identity. Planning and economic development had become the concern of the region, and there was a recognition of the distinctive nature (*spécificité*) of the *départements d'outre-mer* in the Republic, together with a much higher per capita state contribution for economic development than in metropolitan *départements*. Regionalisation, it was asserted, permitted the reaffirmation of three solidarities: with the Republic, with Europe, and with neighbouring countries, through projects of regional cooperation (France 1986).

While there were some tokens of the new regional solidarity, such as the renaming of a major Fort-de-France thoroughfare "Avenue Maurice Bishop" after the assassinated Grenadian leader, it is difficult to assess how far the changes in policy had produced a real transformation in the political climate of the French islands. One notable change was that economic and development priorities were no longer dictated by Paris-generated national five year plans, in which bureaucrats 5,000 miles away determined how many tonnes of pineapples or litres of rum should be produced, without any effective means of ensuring that their goals would be met. With priorities now being established at the regional level, it was possible to plan more realistically and take account of local factors that might be overlooked in Paris. Officials in the Direction Départementale des Services Agricoles (DDSA) in Martinique agreed that French government policy had become a little less *dirigiste*.

Table 9.4
Acreage of land-in-holdings in St Lucia, by administrative district, 1961, 1973–4, and 1986

	Acreage in holdings			*Percentage change*
District	*1961*	*1973–4*	*1986*	*1961 to 1986*
Castries	9,256	10,659	7,554	-18.5
Dennery	17,031	10,552	8,038	-53
Micoud[a]	10,499	11,301	12,416	+18
Vieux Fort	10,870	4,692	5,252	-51.5
Laborie	4,524	5,832	3,588	-20.5
Choiseul	2,855	2,016	1,941	-32
Soufriere	8,289	6,953	5,988	-28
Canaries and Anse-La Raye	11,459	8,044	6,084	-47
Gros Islet	12,614	11,952	7,154	-43
Total	87,375	72,001	58,016	-33.5

Sources: West Indies Census of Agriculture, 1961 (1968); St Lucia (1987, 13).
Note: "Land-in-holdings" is land held for agricultural purposes.
[a]And Praslin.

Nevertheless, when, in February 1988, the minister of agriculture in the Chirac government visited Martinique and Guadeloupe, the first such visit in fifteen years, DDSA officials, when asked what they had said to the minister when they met, reported that they had had little chance to convey any information: the minister spoke, and they listened. Moreover, there remained a very large number of *métropolitains* in the civil service, and there were few signs that they were particularly committed to the new regional approach. Their visits to neighbouring islands were rare, and contacts with opposite numbers in agricultural departments hardly existed. Even though French agricultural missions had been maintained for several years in St Lucia and Dominica, they did not appear to have stimulated fruitful liaisons. It was in fact quite difficult for St Lucian and Dominican nationals to obtain visas to visit the French islands, since the authorities feared that without stringent controls, the islands would be inundated by an influx of migrant workers.

During the 1970s, when a number of large estates were broken up in the Commonwealth islands, at least in part because of labour difficulties, the *réforme foncière* that had been initiated in the French islands in the previous decade had come to a virtual standstill when the government withdrew technical and financial support. It was claimed that pressure for land ownership was weakened by the high level of agricultural wages (Bachou 1988, personal communication). It was also suggested that in Martinique, at least, long-established *béké* (white Creole) families were not easily dislodged by passing phases of unrest and were still able to exercise a certain paternalistic hold over their work force (Morlet 1988, personal communication). Moreover, in 1972, the Crédit Agricole decided to stop financing farmers who were allocated holdings, because the lots allocated were judged to be too small to be economically viable, and the farmers who held them were incurring too many bad debts (Martinique DDSA 1985, 75). A further factor, according to one agronomist, was that the Communists opposed the land-reform programme, since they claimed it would not make any fundamental change in the socio-economic structure of Antillean society (Emélie 1988, personal communication).

In the 1980s, however, there was a revival of the *réforme,* with renewed government support. In Guadeloupe, about 1,000 hectares a year were being subdivided and leased on a 30-year basis, with some restrictions on how the land might be used. Agricultural department officers claimed that subdivision was proceeding more expeditiously there than in Martinique, where most of the land was owned by private individuals who could not easily be obliged to sell if they were reluctant to do so. In Guadeloupe the largest estates had belonged not to individuals but to sugar companies, which lacked an emotional investment in the land and, once the amount of cane being delivered to their factories fell below the minimum necessary for profitable operation, were not averse to selling. Company lands in the Capesterre area had all been sold in lots of 25 to 100 hectares (Bachou 1988, personal communication). However, the 1985 DDSA report on the state of agriculture in Martinique suggested that in fact Martinique had been at least as active as Guadeloupe in land reform: 1,500 to 2,000 hectares were changing hands each year, mainly in small lots (Martinique 1985, 75; see Table 9.1). Nevertheless, despite some land redistribution, there were still several banana plantations in both islands that were vast by St Lucian or Dominican standards.

One government initiative that was reported to be having some effect was the provision of start-up grants and loans on very favourable terms, to encourage young people under thirty-five to take up farming. According to a Crédit Agricole poster in 1988, holdings had to be at least 7 hectares, considerably larger than the land-reform farms of the 1960s.

If the 1980s brought some movement to the left in the French islands, there was a reaction in the other direction in the Commonwealth islands. Divisions within the more radical government that had replaced the twelve-year-old Compton administration in St Lucia in 1979 ensured that the Compton administration was back in power by 1982. In Dominica, the Labour Party was replaced by Eugenia Charles' Freedom Party, whose political agenda was heavily influenced by a concern to reassure potential donors of aid that Dominica would be a worthy beneficiary. By 1988, the success of both the St Lucian and Dominican governments in attracting foreign aid was evident in the burgeoning expatriate communities in both islands, which were more numerous than in the latter days of colonialism and far more cosmopolitan. In contrast with the French islands, where *la planification* had greatly declined in importance, many of the aid projects were far more prescriptive than the somewhat unfocussed schemes of the 1960s, which had been open to all who cared to take advantage of them. Indeed, agricultural policy as a whole had become more prescriptive, with the introduction, in Dominica in 1978, of "zoned project benefits," promoting particular crops only in those areas that the government considered appropriate.

In St Lucia, the prime example of a strongly focused agricultural development project was St Lucia Model Farms Limited, initiated in 1978. Geest's former banana estate in the Roseau Valley was in the process of being transformed into over 185 small holdings, with the assistance of loans from Geest, the Commonwealth Development Corporation (CDC) and St Lucian banks, and a grant from the European Development Fund. Candidates for holdings had to conform to rigorous selection criteria and grow the crops the company specified, in the manner and with the inputs that the company directed them to use.

There was some movement towards regional unity with the establishment in 1981 of the Organisation of Eastern Caribbean States (OECS)(Serbin 1990, 23). However, any island marginally more prosperous than the rest mistrusted any development that might expose it to immigration from less-favoured islands, and individual island governments usually insisted upon putting the interests of their own state ahead of those of the region as a whole. Consequently, the prospects for closer political ties, at least in the near future, did not look particularly bright.

THE ECONOMIC CONTEXT

If the political situation had evolved considerably over a twenty-year period, the economic situation for agriculture in 1988 was in

Table 9.5
Banana exports, Eastern Caribbean and Jamaica, 1965–93

Year	Weather	*St Lucia*	*Dominica*	*Total Windwards*	*Jamaica*	*Martinique*	*Guadeloupe*
		Thousands of tons				*Thousands of tonnes*	
1965	N	80.5	49.8	181.4	190.0	117.7	75.6
1966	N	83.7	43.4	177.6	200.3	232.7	91.8
1967	N	69.1	46.8	168.8	191.5	214.5	85.0
1968	N	71.4	54.8	183.6	153.2	221.9	111.5
1969	N	84.7	57.6	198.7	150.1	193.9	115.1
1970	SD	50.2	44.4	141.6	134.3	157.2	98.6
1971	D	45.0	38.3	126.2	125.8	165.7	117.8
1972	D	47.0	35.9	120.5	127.0	213.2	133.6
1973	SD	35.1	27.9	94.2	107.7	166.6	129.8
1974	D	44.1	30.9	105.3	71.3	206.6	134.3
1975	SD	31.6	27.0	90.4	70.2	183.9	126.1
1976	N	43.7	32.8	121.6	79.4	238.8	120.7[a]
1977	SD	39.6	30.7	111.3	80.1	246.6	116.6
1978	N	50.4	36.8	131.9	78.1	263.4	145.2
1979[b]	N	47.0	15.7	99.1	68.8	152.2	92.8
1980[c]	N	29.0	7.5	66.9	29.6	79.2	67.0
1981	W	43.4	26.5	110.5	15.6	166.3	126.6
1982	N	42.2	26.7	105.0	18.7	170.3	132.2
1983	N	53.5	28.2	117.4	20.9	166.8	–
1984	N	64.6	31.1	136.7	10.2	161.8	–
1985	N	80.6	33.3	162.0	11.0	170.8	–
1986	N	108.7	49.0	203.1	20.0	196.0	–
1987	N	90.0	64.5	199.5	39.0	–	–
1988	–	113.2	60.0	240.3	–	–	–

Table 9.5 (continued)
Banana exports, Eastern Caribbean and Jamaica, 1965–93

		St Lucia	Dominica	Total Windwards	Jamaica	Martinique	Guadeloupe
Year	Weather	*Thousands of tons*				*Thousands of tonnes*	
1989	–	125.6	50.3	250.2	–	–	–
1990	–	133.8	56.6	277.4	–	–	–
1991	–	100.6	55.5	225.6	–	–	–
1992	–	132.8	58.0	274.5	–	–	–
1993	–	120.1	55.5	238.7	–	–	–

Sources: SICABAM (1988, 23); *La Bananeraie Guadeloupéenne* (1984, 15); Geest Industries (1987); WINBAN (1992, 1994, personal communication).
Note: D=drought; N=normal; SD=severe drought; W=wet; –=not available..
[a]=Soufrière eruption; [b]=Hurricane David, 29 August, 1979; [c]=Hurricane Allen, 4 August, 1980.

many respects only too similar to the situation in 1967. In both sets of islands, a period of rising production was provoking mounting concern that the primary markets, still the United Kingdom and Metropolitan France, would soon be saturated. There were proposals to secure alternative markets to absorb surpluses. Ireland was again being considered by the Windwards, and there were fairly regular shipments to Italy from Martinique. Both sets of islands still enjoyed the protection of quota systems in their primary markets and consequently looked forward with very considerable apprehension to the end of 1992, when the full provisions of the Treaty of Rome were due finally to be imposed. The maladjusment between seasonal demand and seasonal supply was still to be resolved.

It should not, however, be supposed that the economic situation had remained static throughout the twenty-year period. In all the islands, but particularly the Commonwealth ones, the earlier trend of more or less steadily rising production had been broken by periods of stagnation and even decline (Table 9.5). In some cases, these periods were provoked by bad weather. There were several exceptionally dry years in the early 1970s, and two outstandingly violent hurricanes, David in 1979 and Allen in 1980. Both left a trail of destruction across at least three islands and caused unprecedented indebtedness in the banana industry.

Apart from climatic problems, however, production levels had been affected, especially in the Commonwealth islands, by the very marginal profits to be made from banana growing. A major blow was the tripling, in a single year, of the price of chemical fertilisers following the establishment of the OPEC cartel and the rise in world oil prices in 1973–74. The decline in Windwards and even more dramatically, Jamaican production (Jamaican growers had generally received a lower price for their fruit than their Windward counterparts) made it necessary for the British Government to grant import licences to bananas from African and Latin American countries. It was asserted that the superior quality of this fruit provoked dissatisfaction with the Commonwealth Caribbean product, and depressed demand for it.

Whatever the cause, consumption levels, which had been expected to continue rising until they reached the Swiss level of 9 kilograms per person per year, in fact declined substantially in both the United Kingdom and France during the early 1970s and only began to rise again in the 1980s. In France, consumption declined from 493,000 tonnes in 1972 to 420,000 tonnes in 1984 and rose to 430,000 tonnes in 1986 (Martinique 1985, 25; SICABAM, 1988, 25). In Britain, imports fell from 372,000 tons in 1965 to 322,000 tons in 1982 (Persaud 1966,

53; Thomson 1987, 14). It was suggested that bananas were perhaps regarded as a cheap, low-status fruit and that as incomes rose, banana consumption fell, but this rationalisation does not accord well with the high Swiss consumption of the 1960s.

The introduction of "boxing" in the Commonwealth Windwards in the early 1970s, which will be examined in the context of technological developments, brought about some changes in the economic relationships within the banana industry. Boxing was also accompanied by a new set of quality-control problems to which only the advent of "field packing" in the 1980s seems to have brought satisfactory solutions. Geest repeatedly complained about the poor quality of much fruit by the time it arrived on the supermarket shelves, and this quality problem may have been a major cause of lower demand in the 1970s.

The movement of international exchange rates, over which the producer islands had no control, had different effects in different islands. Since Martinique and Guadeloupe sold most of their fruit in France and all transactions were thus in francs, it might have been supposed that they would have been insulated from the effects of international currency fluctuations. An informant claimed, however, that the high value of the U.S. dollar in relation to the franc in 1985–86 was responsible for high Central American banana prices, which had encouraged Martiniquan growers to expand production (Morlet 1988, personal communication). The subsequent weakening of the dollar did not, however, appear to have had the reverse effect.

The Commonwealth islands were in a completely different situation. Since 1976 their currency, the Eastern Caribbean dollar, had been tied to the U.S. dollar. Banana prices were, however, negotiated in pounds sterling, based on a green wholesale price that in 1986 was buffeted upwards and downwards by events as diverse as, for instance, strikes in Panama, the Chernobyl disaster, an embargo on South African apples, and a cold, wet spring. As a result of the rise of the pound against the U.S. dollar, prices to Windwards associations rose substantially in 1986 and 1987: from EC38.87¢ a pound in the first quarter of 1985 to EC55.99¢ a pound in the fourth quarter of 1986 (WINBAN 1987, 23).

The Convention of Lomé, first signed between the European Economic Community (EEC) and the so-called ACP (African, Caribbean, Pacific) countries in 1975, and renewed twice subsequently to run until 1990, did not materially alter the relationship between the Eastern Caribbean banana producers and their marketplaces, but it did make this relationship somewhat more complicated (Martinique

1985, 26). In the 1960s, the metropolitan French market was divided simply between the French West Indies, which had two-thirds, and former French African possessions, which had one-third, while the British market was divided almost equally between the Windwards and Jamaica, with a small quota allocated to Canaries bananas. Although the Lomé accord did not expose the Eastern Caribbean producers to competition from low-cost Latin American producers, it did open the British market to several additional ACP countries, such as Surinam, Belize, and various African states. By 1988, the tariff that had originally provided a sheltered market for Commonwealth production was irrelevant, but "dollar" bananas, including those from Nicaragua, might enter the United Kingdom only if ACP fruit could not supply the market. Decisions as to when to licence imports of dollar fruit were made by the Banana Trade Advisory Committee, a body made up of representatives from the Windwards and Jamaica, three importers (including Geest and Fyffes) and a United Kingdom Board of Trade representative.

The arrangements for orderly marketing in the United Kingdom in the 1980s had much in common with the arrangements that had existed in France since 1962, when the Comité Interprofessionnel Bananier had taken control of the organisation of the market, succeeded in 1970 by the Groupement d'Intêret Economique Bananier (GIEB), which controlled licences. Its role was to keep the market correctly supplied while keeping prices at a level that was satisfactory for producers and others in the industry. Its ultimate objective was a weighted mean annual price at the *wagon départ* stage, determined jointly by GIEB and the Ministry of Finance (Martinique 1985, 24). It is not clear whether the British arrangements were modelled on those in France or whether they developed independently in response to a similar situation.

The expansion of the EEC meant that besides having access to the Italian market (by 1988, Martinique was making substantial shipments to Italy, and the Windwards, more modest ones), the Eastern Caribbean producers had some hopes of penetrating the Greek and Portuguese markets. On the other hand, the possibility that after 1992 they might have to compete even in the United Kingdom and French markets with imported "dollar" bananas was creating an atmosphere of considerable foreboding. In the Commonwealth islands, there were some people who felt that provided quality could be maintained and production costs kept down, they might be able to retain their share of the market. Indeed, Margaret Thatcher had given the Windwards assurances that they would still be protected after 1992 (Cadet 1988, personal communication). In the French islands, where the daily agricultural wage was five times the wage in Dominica and St Lucia (but it should be noted that it may have bought twice as many hours of labour), there was little faith in the industry's ability to survive competition. It was, however, felt that in order to avoid the social disruption that would inevitably result from the destruction of the Antillean banana industries, the French Government would almost certainly take some action to ensure that the worst did not happen.

The conversion of Geest into a public liability company in 1986 was a development whose implications for Windwards growers were hard to assess. The four growers' associations applied to purchase £330,000 worth of shares in the company, about one percent of the shares issued, thus giving themselves a modest stake in shipping, importing, and ripening. Geest assured WINBAN that the change in the company's status would not alter its relationship with the banana industry, but it was anticipated that in future business dealings, Geest would "nevertheless be expected to be more conscious of its obligations to its shareholders" (WINBAN 1987, 12). This remark implied that as a private company, Geest had sometimes put growers' interests ahead of profits. It was pointed out, for instance, that Geest boats had continued to load Grenadian bananas even when the amount of fruit available for shipment from Grenada was less than the amount that had to be left back as surplus in the other islands (Leonce 1988, personal communication).

The economic situation of both French and Commonwealth islands in the 1980s was affected by various aid programmes and initiatives. In the French islands between 1972 and 1977, a Fonds d'Organisation et de Recherche des Marchés Agricoles (FORMA) subsidy had been granted to modernise the *stations de conditionnement* (Martinique 1985, 23). In 1988, the Office de Développement de l'Economie Agricole des Départements d'Outre-Mer (ODEADOM), the successor to FORMA, was providing funds for the modernisation of boxing sheds (Parmentier 1988, personal communication).

In the Commonwealth Islands, there were injections of British government aid to finance rehabilitation and revival schemes both after the drought years of the early 1970s and the hurricane years of 1979 and 1980. In addition, European Development (STABEX) Funds were received under Lomé II. United States aid received in Dominica between 1984 and 1986 was used to cover the cost of leafspot control for two years, permitting the DBMC to build up its reserves, while in 1985-86, money remaining from the British Government's £5 million Independence Package was used to subsidise inputs provided under the British Banana Expansion Programme

(DBMC 1987, 2). In 1985 and 1986, the DBMC was in a position to offer starter credit facilities, which were thought to have brought in many new young growers (Scotland 1988, personal communication).

Thus, looking only at the reference points of 1966–67 and 1988, one may have the illusion that nothing much had changed in the economic predicament of the Eastern Caribbean banana industries. A brief survey of the intervening period gives a different picture. The industries had in fact passed through many vicissitudes, and it was more or less by chance that the problems of overproduction and the implementation of the next stage of EEC provisions were again the foremost economic preoccupations in the four islands.

THE ECOLOGICAL CONTEXT

In the course of over twenty years, ecological conditions in the Eastern Caribbean have altered in various ways, in some cases irreversibly. Some of these changes were brought about by exceptional climatic events, while others developed as a result of persistent banana monoculture, or simply by chance.

In Martinique, Guadeloupe, and St Lucia, hurricanes had been fairly routine in the 1960s, and the hurricanes of the subsequent twenty years did not profoundly affect the natural or planted vegetation of the islands. In Dominica, however, Hurricane David in 1979 was the first major hurricane to pass over the island for two generations, and it wreaked unprecedented damage on forests and crops. In the French islands, the frequent hurricanes of the 1960s were blamed for the scarcity of citrus trees, but paradoxically in Dominica in 1988 it was suggested that "David" had actually provoked an increase in fruit tree planting. Farmers there had been struck by the fact that while their bananas had been entirely destroyed, half of the island's citrus trees had survived.

A minor eruption of the Soufrière volcano in Guadeloupe in 1976 had a significant impact on that island's banana industry. In fact, the volcanic activity was very slight and deposited not more than a few millimetres of ash over a radius of 3 or 4 kilometres on the leeward slopes of the volcano. In anticipation of a major eruption, however, the commune of St Claude was evacuated and its banana plantations neglected for three months. According to one DDSA agronomist, it never regained its former importance as part of the heartland of Guadeloupe's banana zone, since frustrated owners of St Claude estates began to buy land in Trois-Rivières and Capesterre. There was some incentive to do this in any case, since mechanisation was more feasible on the gentler windward slopes, and the quality advantage possessed by the "mountain" bananas of St Claude, which had been important when fruit was shipped on the stem, was irrelevant once boxing had become universal. Without the provocation of the 1976 eruption, however, the trend to abandoning banana growing in St Claude in favour of lower, flatter, and drier windward areas might not have become so significant or progressed so rapidly (Bachou 1988, personal communication).

In both Martinique and Guadeloupe, agronomists reported that in areas where bananas had been grown intensively for twenty years or more, soils were exhausted and, even with heavy inputs of chemical fertiliser, were less productive than they had once been. Formerly, the northeastern slopes of Montagne Pelée in northern Martinique had been the highest-yielding zone in the island, but by 1988 yields were higher south of Lorrain, particularly on land that had become available for bananas only recently as the perimeter of irrigation was extended (Morlet 1988, personal communication). Soil exhaustion was also cited as a problem in Guadeloupe. In both islands, failure to leave an adequate fallow period had led to a very high level of parasitism in the soil and a serious loss of organic matter.

Remedies were being sought. In Martinique, a pineapple-banana rotation was quite widely practised, while in Guadeloupe, *bagasse* (crushed cane-residue) and sewage residue were being studied as possible replacements for lost organic matter (Bachou 1988, personal communication). Nevertheless, despite twenty years of research and an ever-increasing level of chemical inputs, yields remained, on average, the same as those recorded twenty years earlier: 25 tonnes per hectare in Martinique and 20 tonnes in Guadeloupe.

While the loss of organic matter was mentioned as a serious problem only in the French islands, infestation with insect and fungal pests was a major concern throughout the region. In 1967, I was told that at least on areas of heavy clay soils in the southeast of Guadeloupe, nematode infestation was not a problem, and no treatment was necessary. In 1988, however, anti-nematode measures were said to be essential everywhere. Fungi of various kinds menaced bananas in the field as well as in the box (Piloquet 1988, personal communication), and a Martinquan farmer that I revisited after twenty years complained that new diseases were constantly appearing, the latest being a *cochenille* that thrived in humid conditions and caused brown scarring on fruit, making it unsaleable (Scholastique 1988, personal communication). This may have been the lachnopus weevil, which was becoming a serious problem in northeast Dominica in the mid-1980s. Affected farms suffered average losses of approximately 23 per cent in rejected fingers (WINBAN 1987, 56).

Potentially the most serious menace to the region's banana industries was, however, Moko disease. Present in Grenada since the early 1980s, this disease probably prevented that island from sharing the spectacular increase in production that the other three Windward Islands experienced between 1983 and 1987.

Thus, the ecological changes that had taken place in the Eastern Caribbean between 1967 and 1988 were mainly negative: the impoverishment of soils, the proliferation of pests and diseases, and a reduction in the area available for banana cultivation as a result of natural disasters.

TECHNOLOGICAL DEVELOPMENTS

Despite some deterioration in the physical conditions for banana cultivation in the Eastern Caribbean, the level of production in 1987–88 was almost as high as it had ever been in the French islands, and in Dominica and St Lucia it had exceeded the previous peak of the late 1960s. This production was possible because of various technological developments, particularly in the sphere of disease control. Research at IFAC (later the Institut de Recherches sur les Fruits et Agrumes, or IRFA) in Guadeloupe and at the WINBAN research facility in St Lucia was concerned primarily with developing and testing more effective forms of chemical control for leafspot and nematode infestation and, if effective products were available, with determining the most efficient and economical ways of using them to keep input costs as low as possible.

During the 1960s, leafspot was controlled by oil sprays. Between twenty and thirty-six spray cycles a year were necessary for satisfactory control. In the early 1970s, however, it was discovered that better control could be obtained if a benzimidazole fungicide was added to the spray oil, and thereafter, less frequent spray cycles were necessary. If a careful watch was kept on climatic conditions and the build-up of leafspot infestation, spraying could be carried out only when and where necessary, instead of at regular intervals (*La Bananeraie Guadeloupéenne* 1984 24). Thus, in Martinique in 1986, only 5.5 cycles were run (SICABAM 1988, 8), in Dominica, 9 cycles (DBMC 1987, 6). Even as solutions were developed that gave growers some cause for optimism, however, new problems appeared to undermine that optimism. In 1981, it was found that leafspot in Guadeloupe was becoming resistant to Benilate, the benzimidazole fungicide, and it became necessary to use triazole fungicide, which was almost twice as expensive (*La Bananeraie Guadeloupéenne* 1984, 21).

By the mid-1970s, products assuring effective control of nematodes were on the market, and thereafter a succession of new nematicides became available, developed by the major transnational chemical companies and tested locally. In St Lucia, it was claimed that they were so effective that they had virtually eliminated the need for periodic uprooting and replanting of old banana fields (St Hill 1988, personal communication). In the French islands, replanting after two or three ratoons was still customary, since it was uneconomical with expensive labour to carry out agricultural operations in fields where plants were not all more or less in the same phase. Nevertheless, nematode control added considerably to the cost of production (Fr 7,000, the equivalent of EC$2,660 per hectare for Nemacur (GIPAM estimate, 1987); EC$825 per hectare for Furadan (St Lucia 1986).

In addition to improvements in chemical methods of disease control, there were infrastructural improvements that brought undoubted benefits to many growers. In all four islands, there was a considerable investment in road building. In the French islands there were excellent main roads reaching all the traditional banana-growing areas, and feeder roads had also been extended. Indeed, roads now reached so far up some of the leeward valleys in Guadeloupe that it was possible for vanilla growers to drive up each morning to fertilise their plants (Bachou 1988, personal communication). In St Lucia, the main east-coast road between Castries and Vieux Fort had been widened, straightened, and realigned to avoid passing through villages. In central and southern leeward areas, however, communications remained much as they had been in the 1960s. In Dominica, there had been a major effort at road improvement following the devastation caused by Hurricane David in 1979, and here, too, feeder roads had been much developed; but while road building in the Carib Reserve area had made that part of the windward coast more accessible, the southeastern corner of the island was still relatively isolated.

There had been substantial changes in methods of handling bananas over the twenty years. In 1967, boxing was customary in the French islands, but had hardly begun in the Commonwealth islands. In 1980, a major new reorganisation took place in Martinique and Guadeloupe when the shipper, now known as the Compagnie Générale Maritime (CGM), decided to containerise all its Antillean traffic. Bananas were henceforth shipped and sold in 20- or 40-foot containers, each of which had to contain fruit of uniform quality.

The 40-foot containers held 21 tons of fruit, the 20-foot containers, 10.6 tons (600 boxes) (*La Bananeraie Guadeloupéenne* 1984, 21–22).

Containerisation created two classes of growers: growers who produced more than ten tonnes a week and who could therefore fill one or more containers a week (shipments were now weekly) and growers who produced under ten tonnes a week. Growers in the first class filled containers at their own *stations de conditionnement* on their plantations, from which the bananas were driven directly to the exporting port. Growers in the second class had to bring their fruit, boxed, to a *centre d'empotage,* where it could be loaded into containers with bananas of similar grade. In Guadeloupe, 70 to 75 percent of production went directly from the plantation to the port, 22 percent in 40-foot containers. The remainder was put into containers at one of Guadeloupe's two *centres d'empotage,* at Trois-Rivières and Ste Marie (north of Capesterre). Basse-Terre was no longer the exporting port; all container traffic was shipped from the port of Jarry, on the outskirts of Pointe-à-Pitre (*La Bananeraie Guadeloupéenne* 1984, 22).

It was claimed that containerisation had improved the quality of fruit when it arrived in the *métropole,* since handling had been reduced, much of the transport within the island was within the protection of containers, and where packing facilities were equipped with electricity, the isothermal containers could be refrigerated immediately. On the other hand, smaller growers who could not fill a weekly container (they would have needed at least 12 hectares of bananas) were at a considerable disadvantage, since their fruit still had to be transported about the island in vans, and metropolitan buyers were said to prefer containers of fruit that had come from a single estate, since it was more likely to be of uniform quality (Morlet 1988, personal communication).

In the Commonwealth islands, the changeover from shipment on the stem to boxing did not begin in earnest until 1969 and was not complete until 1972. Those farmers (the great majority) who did not produce enough fruit to justify operating their own boxing facilities transported their bananas to boxing sheds run by growers' associations or cooperative groups of farmers, where "hands" of bananas were cut off the stems, washed in fungicide, and packed in cartons to be transported by truck to the exporting port. Dominica had about a dozen DBGA boxing sheds and a similar number of cooperative plants, widely distributed throughout the island (DBMC 1986, 4a). This system remained in operation for about fifteen years. It had the advantage for growers that there was no longer a minimum stem weight. However, bananas generally had to be transported farther to the more sophisticated, but more sparsely distributed, packing plants, and the importer, Geest, complained ceaselessly about the poor condition of much of the Windwards fruit when it arrived in the United Kingdom. Consequently, WINBAN expended much effort on research to develop more satisfactory methods of handling bananas.

In the mid-1980s the old system of boxing, known as "wet-packing," was replaced by "field packing." Under this system, farmers cut, dehand, and box green bananas in the fields. The fungicidal dip is replaced by the "crown pad," which is placed over the cut stem to inhibit the development of mould, and when bananas are packed immediately after harvesting, the need for washing (and thus a water supply at the packing point) is eliminated. Depending on the quantity of fruit harvested, the growers might transport their boxed fruit either to the port reception depots or to an inland buying depot (IBD), of which the SLBGA had twenty-one and the Dominica Banana Marketing Corporation (DBMC), heir to the DBGA, twelve (DBMC 1987, 6; St Hill 1988, personal communication). Only growers, or groups of growers, with at least seventy-two boxes a week or fortnight might deliver directly to the port, since this was the quantity required for a one-ton pallet. In 1986, 75 percent of Dominican production went straight to the port and only 25 percent was sold at IBDs (DBMC 1987, 6).

The introduction of field packing in the Windwards was associated with a great improvement in the quality of fruit shipped, and it might have been anticipated that it would have replaced wet packing in the French islands, since it does not appear to be incompatible with containerisation. However, the French market is accustomed to receiving boxed fruit with the hands already cut into clusters of four or five bananas, and this practice would require the use of too many crown pads.

In the French islands, there has been a considerable extension of irrigation since the 1960s. In Guadeloupe, in addition to government schemes in the leeward valleys of Baillif and Vieux-Habitants, there have been several private schemes in Capesterre and in the northeast in Lamentin and Ste Rose. It was claimed that irrigation added very little to the cost of banana cultivation (Bachou 1988, personal communication). In Martinique, the creation of a reservoir east of Fort-de-France has permitted the irrigation of a large area of the south-central part of the island. The Commonwealth islands have not carried out any major irrigation schemes, despite the fact that bananas are still grown in areas where rainfall is quite often insufficient for their satisfactory cultivation. However, in 1988, the irrigation of northeastern Dominica, possibly with Israeli assistance, was under discussion.

In Martinique and Guadeloupe, it seemed that the undoubted technological advances of the past twenty years had just about kept pace with the proliferating ecological problems. In St Lucia and Dominica, problems and solutions had been less well synchronised. The high cost of applying chemical remedies to ecological ills and the failure to resolve the problem of quality led to an absolute decrease in banana production during the 1970s; field packing and more effective disease control measures coincided with a resurgence in production in the mid-1980s.

THE EVOLUTION OF THE GROWERS' ASSOCIATIONS

The institutions controlling the banana industries of the four islands in 1988 differed in many ways from those of the mid-1960s. In most cases, their formal structure and constitution had been altered, sometimes radically, and in every case their roles and activities had changed.

St Lucia

The major change in status of St Lucia's association took place as early as 1967 and was alluded to briefly in chapter 6. Under the terms of the St Lucia Banana Growers' Association Act of 1967, the independent association entirely controlled and run by growers ceased to exist and was superseded by a statutory body over which the government had a large measure of control. If in the opinion of the relevant minister, the board of the new association defaulted in the performance of its duties or abused or exceeded its powers, the minister might direct the board to regulate its affairs to comply with the provisions of the act, and if it failed to do so, Cabinet could dissolve the board and a ministerial appointee would exercise the board's powers. The board of directors of the association was to consist of nine members, of whom three were to be appointed by the minister and six elected for a two-year term by the annual conference of delegates (one delegate representing each district branch). The six were to be elected from nominees put forward by branch members from among "eligible growers." The chairman of the board was to be elected by the board from among the six elected members.

The House of Assembly might by resolution increase or decrease the number of directors but not change the proportion of those elected and nominated (St Lucia 1967, 56–72). While every grower with 200 or more plants was eligible for membership in the new SLBGA, only those producing at least 1000 stems a year, a small minority of growers, were eligible for membership on the board. Of the six elected board members, two were to be "small" growers (selling between 26,000 and 124,000 pounds annually), two, "medium-sized" growers (selling between 124,000 and 624,000 pounds annually), and two, "large" growers (selling over 624,000 pounds annually).

In effect, not only did the act of 1967 ensure that the board would never again be dominated by small growers, it also guaranteed that the great majority would play no further part in directing the association's affairs. The only power they did retain, and that indirectly, through the delegates each branch sent to the annual conference of delegates, was the power not to renew the mandate of a director with whom they were dissatisfied after a two-year term in office. While it might be argued that it would have been imprudent to have left the destiny of the mainstay of St Lucia's economy in the hands of growers whose stake in it was so small that their individual production was less than 12 tons of fruit a year, which could be grown on half a hectare, nevertheless it seems hard to justify the complete denial of direct representation on the board to the producers of at least a third of the bananas St Lucia exported (this figure is an estimate derived from 1961 census figures).

Directors might not be members of the state legislature or hold places of profit in the association. Salaries above WI$6000 required ministerial approval, and the amount of the cess could only be varied with Cabinet approval. If, however, the association made a profit, it might set aside such sums as it thought fit for general or special funds or for such purposes as it might determine (St Lucia 1967, 68–76).

The act of 1967 was still in force in 1988. In 1979, it had been amended to increase the size of the board from nine to thirteen directors, of whom six were to be elected by the conference of delegates and seven appointed by the minister. The chairman might be chosen from among either elected or nominated members, and parliament might increase or decrease the number of directors by resolution (St Lucia 1979, 285–7). Although this amendment was passed by the Labour government and according to Demacque was aimed at broadening the participation of the small grower (1983, 101), it retained the requirement that the elected directors should be drawn equally from the ranks of large, medium-sized, and small growers, and it failed to extend representation to the mass of really small growers. In any case, it was ignored by the UWP government on its return to power, and in 1988 there was still a nine-member board with six elected members.

By 1988, the focus of the SLBGA's mission had shifted from trying to put the maximum possible quantity of fruit on the market to trying to ensure that St Lucia's bananas were able to meet the increasingly demanding quality requirements of the United Kingdom marketplace. The SLBGA continued to support WINBAN's research programme, which in addition to developing improved varieties and improved agronomic practices and methods of disease control, was seeking ways to upgrade techniques after harvest. The association played a much greater rôle than previously in extension. Thirty-two fruit-quality officers, six area supervisors and two coordinators were advising and demonstrating to members in programmes to improve drainage, pesticide application, sanitation, harvesting, and packing. This service, which was independent of the agricultural department, was begun in 1980, and by 1988 had incorporated former leafspot control officers (St Hill 1988, personal communication; SLBGA 1986, 28).

The range of inputs regarded as essential for the successful cultivation of export-quality bananas was much broader in 1988 than in the 1960s. A "typical middle-of-the-road farmer" was estimated to use three-quarters of a ton of chemical fertiliser per acre (two tons per hectare approximately), double or triple the 1965 average (St Lucia Development Bank estimate, 1986; Persaud 1966, 15). Nematicides were indispensable, and farmers also needed weedicides, blue diothene sleeving, twine, boxes, crown pads, and mist blowers. All of these items were supplied by the association and paid for by a cess on growers' sales. The introduction of computers facilitated the management of farmers' accounts for the purchase of inputs on credit (SLBGA 1986, 24,28).

The SLBGA owned two aeroplanes and provided aerial spraying for leafspot control to all members. This was supplemented by ground spraying, which had been carried out by the growers themselves since about 1983. It was claimed that grower-spraying had given better control, but the claim was hard to substantiate since the change in practice had coincided with the introduction of field packing and an insistence on improved management practices, such as better weed control (St Hill 1988, personal communication).

At some point during the 1970s, the SLBGA had ceased to arrange for the insurance of growers' banana crops, so that rehabilitation after the devastation of Hurricane Allen in 1980 had had to proceed without this source of compensation. In November 1987, however, a new insurance scheme was inaugurated. Growers contributed a premium of 1.6¢ per pound of bananas sold and received compensation for losses over 20 percent. The scheme was underwritten by WINBAN itself (St Hill 1988, personal communication).

Marketing arrangements in the Commonwealth Windwards since the introduction of field packing have been described earlier in this chapter. In St Lucia, field packing began experimentally in 1981, and the new system was in full operation by 1984. The SLBGA owned four or five trucks and hired others both to deliver inputs and to pick up boxed fruit from small growers all along the roadsides and transport it to the IBDs and thence to the ports. Members of field-pack groups had to pay to truck their fruit to the group's depot, but from there to the port they, like individual growers with over seventy-two boxes, were compensated at a rate of 9¢ per mile for every 100 pounds. Either at the IBD or at the wharf, a premium of 3¢ a pound was offered for fruit that met certain quality norms. Each box carried the grower's identification, and if the fruit was found unsatisfactory on inspection, the premium was not paid. Although there was apparently no pecuniary advantage in bypassing the IBDs and delivering directly to the wharf, growers were said to prefer it because it entailed less waiting about and, since only growers whose packing standards met certain criteria were granted permits to deliver to the wharf, it carried greater social prestige (St Hill 1988, personal communication).

Growers were paid one week after delivery. The SLBGA bought all bananas produced by its members that were of acceptable quality (standards were set by the fruit-quality monitoring committee), but when the United Kingdom market was oversupplied, it held back a proportion and shipped only the best fruit, to try to ensure that prices were not depresssed (Leonce 1988, personal communication). The amounts to be held back were negotiated between the four members of WINBAN. The associations were not paid by Geest for "leftback" fruit, so the amount per pound to be distributed to growers was reduced by the amount not received for fruit that was not shipped. In 1987, "leftback" fruit represented 7.7 percent of St Lucia's total production (WINBAN 1988, 1). The association had been deducting 3¢ or 4¢ a pound from payments in summer, when prices were high, to build up reserves so that it could subsidise winter prices, although in February 1988, they were intending to discontinue this practice (St Hill 1988, personal communication).

In 1987, St Lucian growers received an average of 30¢ a pound for their bananas. The price varied between 25¢ and 38¢ owing to fluctuations in both the green wholesale price and the sterling exchange rate. The SLBGA's directors decided the price to growers weekly, ensuring that it never fell below the estimated average break-even price of 18¢ a pound (Nathanial 1988, personal communication). From 1¢ to 10¢ a pound was deducted from this growers' price to cover the cost of items such as fertiliser and nematicides (St Hill 1988, personal communication). The growers' price represented the amount remaining from the association's sales to Geest after the deduction of a cess to cover administrative and other expenses (Table 9.6) and the withholding of an amount determined by the board for price stabilisation. In 1988, the SLBGA passed on a higher price to its growers than did the DBMC, which had a substantial burden of debt (St Hill 1988, personal communication). Tables 9.6 and 9.7 give a comparative breakdown of receipts obtained by participants in the various stages of the banana industry within and beyond the Eastern Caribbean.

In some respects, the role of the SLBGA was even more paternalistic and invasive in 1988 than in 1967. Pressure to use purchased inputs was much stronger and supervision of growers much closer. On the other hand, while the principle of providing all services to all growers on an equal basis had clearly not been abandoned, there was a tendency for farmers to take individual responsibility for an increasing range of operations that had previously been largely or wholly the concern of the SLBGA: spraying for leafspot from the ground and the packing and transport of fruit from the districts where it was grown to the exporting port. There did not seem to be much opposition to these developments. Indeed, growers were said to have taken the initiative in assuming responsibility for leaf-spot control and transporting their own fruit to port. Although field packing had been imposed by the association, it appeared to be popular since it left a higher share of the sales price in the growers' hands. The actual impact of these changes will be considered in the last section of this chapter, but the possibility has to be borne in mind that although the growers who remained in the industry were apparently enthusiastic about the transfer of responsibility to individual growers, those who had not benefited from it might have left the industry.

One aspect of the industry in which problems had been identified in the 1960s and yet not effectively remedied even in 1988 was the control or at least the prediction of the rhythm of production. Production was generally highest in November and December, when United Kingdom demand is lowest, and lowest in May and June, when United Kingdom demand is highest. It had been proposed that the SLBGA should discourage this production pattern by ceasing

Table 9.6
Breakdown of average receipts, deductions and, payments, SLBGA, January to September 1987

	EC¢ per pound
Fruit sales to Geest: SLBGA received	61.95
Cost of fruit purchased: cash to grower + inputs (inputs = fertiliser, pesticides, herbicides)	-35.25
	26.70
Operating Expenses	
(a) *Administrative cess deductions*	
Administration and general	1.22
Field operations	.52
Buying and distribution	.23
Disease and pest control	1.81
Transport and maintenance	.46
WINBAN contributions	.57
	4.81
(b) *Other specific deductions*	
Packaging materials	9.48
Sleeving allowance	.76
Inland buying depots	1.22
Transportation of fruit	1.70
Boxing allowances	1.79
Export tax	.25
Field pack bonus	3.03
Field pack and deflowering incentive	1.02
	19.25
Residue from sale to Geest	26.70
Association's operating expenses	19.25
Balance retained by SLBGA for reserves	7.45

Source: Nathanial (1988, personal communication).
Note: Green Wholesale Price
£475 (week 1) =82.96 EC¢/lb.
£535 (week 10) -
£520 (week 38) =101.12 EC¢/lb.
Sterling
EC$3.9123 (week 1)
EC$4.5139 (week 18)
EC$4.3561 (week 38)

Table 9.7
Distribution of banana trade receipts, in EC¢ per pound

Source	*Grower*	*Association*	*Shipper*	*Handler*	*Ripener*	*Retail*	*Inputs*
1a (percentage)	17	23	15	7	12	26	-
1b (EC¢/pound)	27.6	37.4	24.5	11.4	19.4	42.4	-
2 (EC¢/pound)	31–39	19–27	16				
3 (EC¢/pound)	31.13	29	(	34)		-	-
4 (EC¢/pound)	35.25	26.7	(	36)		-	-
5 (EC¢/pound)	64	4.0	26	6	-	-	18
6 (EC¢/pound)	63.5	5.5	22	6	-	-	17.5

Sources: (1) Simpson (1988), (Commonwealth Windwards); (2) WINBAN (1987); (3) DBMC (1987); (4) Nathanial, St Lucia, 1987 figs.; (5) SICABAM, (1987a); (6) GIPAM (1987b)
Note: "Shipper" may sometimes include loading or unloading costs; Ripener = ripener, packager, and distributor; Inputs = fertiliser, herbicides, pesticides and packaging materials.

to use its reserves to augment winter prices, but it had not yet taken this step. Furthermore, the SLBGA had no system of production forecasting and was unable to predict weekly shipping requirements, so that sometimes fruit for which there would have been a market was left back for lack of space, and it still had to be paid for by the association (SLBGA 1986, 29). Since the association, rather than Geest, now bore the cost of the bananas that could not be shipped, it is perhaps surprising that a more aggressive approach had not yet been taken to resolve these problems. This may, however, have been because surpluses had reemerged as a significant issue only fairly recently.

Dominica

In Dominica, the banana growers' association had always been a statutory body. Although its general constitution was otherwise very similar to that of the pre-1967 SLBGA, there was no major change in the existing Banana Ordinance until 1984. The DBGA was controlled by growers; in the 1960s, large growers dominated the board of directors, but by 1980, the DBGA was controlled by small farmers. It was at about this period that pressure for change in the organisation of the banana industry seems to have become manifest. The association was reported to have been EC$3 million in debt as a result of mismanagement; credit had been given freely, and growers had failed to repay (Scotland 1988, personal communication). Considering that the association had been operating a compulsory fertiliser cess scheme since 1971 and that the devastation of Hurricane

David in 1979 had reduced banana shipments to virtually nothing for the following nine months, its poor financial situation seems unsurprising. Nevertheless, the Freedom Party government, elected in 1978, evidently decided that the time was ripe for reorganisation, and made plans accordingly.

Eguchi, who was carrying out fieldwork in Dominica in 1982–83, gives a contemporary account of the situation. It was reported that by 1981, the DBGA's debt was EC$18 million, and the government proposed to replace the association with a new company that would be fully commercial and controlled by the government. According to local newspaper accounts, when it was established and operating efficiently, it was to be converted into a joint stock company in which producers would be able to purchase shares (*New Chronicle*, 27 November and 18 December 1982, quoted in Eguchi, 1984, 192). Concern was aroused among many small farmers, however, that large-scale farmers and estate owners would take over all the shares. The Prime Minister, Eugenia Charles, had said that "the biggest problem of the banana industry is that growers do not see themselves as part of the industry," but in fact, Eguchi claims, there was no clear explanation at the peasant level of the details of the proposed new company. Moreover, it was believed that pressure for the reorganisation came from the United States Agency for International Development (USAID), which had agreed conditionally to fund one-third of its cost, and the possibility of excessive control by the United States was also a cause of concern (Eguchi 1984, 192).

In June 1984, legislation was passed replacing the original DBGA with two new institutions: the Dominica Banana Growers' Association (DBGA) and the Dominica Banana Marketing Corporation (DBMC). The status of the new DBGA was reduced to that of an advisory body, or, more accurately, a pressure group. Membership was open to all persons who had sold one ton of bananas in the previous year (unless prevented from doing so by factors such as hurricanes, lack of shipping space, or the need to replant their banana lands) and had paid an annual fee of EC$5.00. (In 1988, the minimum requirement was one-quarter of an acre of bananas or the purestand equivalent (Didier 1988, personal communication)).

District branches of the DBGA were to be established with 20 to 250 members. The branches were to promote measures for the well-being of local growers and for the industry generally, and they were to submit resolutions on such measures for the association to consider and implement. A central committee comprising the presiding officers of the district branches was to manage and control the association, and annual general meetings were to be held at which the members of the central committee and two delegates from each branch might be present and vote. Other association members had the right to attend but not to participate.

The annual general meeting was to receive and consider the association's budget and accounts, the accounts of the corporation, and reports from the branches and the executive secretary. It was to receive and consider and, if necessary, vote on proposals for nominating one person to be appointed as growers' representative on the board of the marketing corporation. (The association was to have three nominees on the board, each serving a three-year term.) The executive secretary, to be appointed by the Minister of Agriculture, was to be the association's chief executive officer, responsible for day-to-day administration of the activities of the association and for liaison with the marketing corporation. The objectives of the association were to promote growers' interests and, particularly, to present their views to the government and the marketing corporation. The DBGA was also to establish an office for the dissemination of information to members, to arrange demonstrations and field days, and to award prizes to encourage efficiency in the banana industry (Dominica 1984b, 84–92). The executive secretary himself defined the association's role more succinctly as being to ensure that growers received a satisfactory price from the corporation, which was wholly responsible for marketing, to see that the farmers had access to credit, and to press for the provision of more feeder roads (Scotland 1988, personal communication).

The body with all the real power for conducting the affairs of the banana industry was the Dominica Banana Marketing Corporation (DBMC). Its objectives were to promote the well-being of the banana grower and to ensure the financial viability of the banana industry. The board responsible for pursuing these ends was to consist of nine members: three DBGA nominees, the executive secretary of the DBGA, three members of the business community (at least one from the banking sector) on the nomination of the minister, and one member representing the Ministry of Agriculture and another the Ministry of Trade, each on the nomination of the minister. The chairman and deputy chairman of the board were to be appointed from the nine members by the minister, who might at any time terminate such appointments. The minister was to decide which of the DBGA's first three nomineees should retire at the end of one year and two years respectively, membership being for three years but with one of the three appointees being renewed or replaced annually. The day-to-day business of the DBMC was to be conducted by a general manager, appointed by the minister after consultation with the board. All existing employees of the original DBGA were to become employees of the DBMC (Dominica 1984a, 73–7). Thus, control of Dominica's banana industry was henceforth to rest firmly in the hands of the government, with only a consultative role being reserved for growers.

The DBMC was to be the sole purchaser of bananas for export to countries outside the Caribbean. In setting out its duties, emphasis was laid on its obligation to carry on its business operations in a cost effective and commercial manner and to encourage and facilitate the participation of private enterprise in all sectors of the banana industry. It was to secure the most favourable arrangements for the industry for the purchase, sale, handling, storing, transporting, exporting, shipping, packing, processing, and marketing of bananas. It might provide, directly or indirectly and by licence or other means, processing facilities, disease-control services, technical services, and input services, and it might specify the grades of bananas to be purchased and the prices to be paid for them (Dominica 1984a, 78–9).

In fact in 1988, DBMC was conducting the business of the banana industry in Dominica in a manner very similar to the SLBGA's operations in St Lucia. The organisation of extension and leafspot control differed in detail: the two services remained separate in Dominica, and ground spraying was still carried out directly by the DBMC, which had seventy-three leafspot officers and twenty-four extension staff (Scotland 1988, personal communication). Inputs were financed by a standard prepaid cess of 8¢ a pound. From the balance in their accounts, farmers decided how much fertiliser, nematicide, and so on to order, and refunds from the cess fund were paid periodically to farmers with high yields. Price support was on an ad hoc basis (Didier 1988, personal communication). In 1986, the DBMC had received an average of 59.10¢ a pound for banana sales to Geest and distributed 31.17¢ a pound to growers, thus retaining 27.93¢ a pound to cover operating and administrative expenses and loan or debt repayments (Table 9.6 above). The SLBGA retained 26.7¢ a pound in 1987, but the DBMC's heavy burden of loan repayments, amounting to 6¢ a pound in 1986, may explain its higher expenses (DBMC 1987, 6,7).

Field-packing arrangements were much the same as in St Lucia. A minimum delivery of seventy-two boxes was required to sell at the wharf. Eguchi mentions that in 1983, when the system was being phased in, growers had to fulfil fairly rigorous requirements to participate: they needed a minimum of three acres of bananas on flat land near a road (1984, 144). By 1988, however, there was no mention of these conditions. The network of IBDS was less dense than in St Lucia; Dominica had only twelve depots compared with twenty-one in St Lucia, although Dominica was considerably larger. Eighty percent of growers delivered directly to the wharf, many in field-pack groups, and received a mileage allowance to compensate for transportation costs. It was hoped that the IBDS could be eliminated, since they were expensive to run and were a source of holdups and confusion when boxes were inspected, unpacked, and repacked (Scotland 1988, personal communication).

In 1966, the contract for banana purchases between Geest and the island associations or boards was available as a published document, but by 1988 it no longer appeared to be available, and my attempts to obtain details of the current contract proved abortive. However, the WINBAN economist described it as a cost-plus contract, favourable to the grower when prices were rising, unfavourable when prices were falling (Thomas 1988, personal communication).

Martinique

I was told in Martinique in 1988 that SICABAM was in essence unchanged since the 1960s, although the range of functions in which it was involved had been somewhat expanded. As the manager of the Guadeloupean growers' association, ASSOBAG, pointed out, however, SICABAM had in fact been changed from a producers' group to a *société anonyme.* This status entitled shareholders to a share of the company's profits (Piloquet 1988, personal communication), although according to SICABAM's annual report, no dividends had been declared since the change in status in 1980. The annual surplus had in fact been returned to growers as a rebate (SICABAM 1988, 9). Moreover, the shareholders were still the growers themselves. Shares were allocated according to the tonnage exported, and the number of votes assigned to each shareholder was proportionate to the number of shares held.

Before 1985, IRFA (previously IFAC) carried out extension work for the banana industry. In 1985, IRFA changed its focus, and SICABAM subsequently developed its own agro-technical service, with twelve field staff, two economists and three development experts. The company also bought inputs such as fertiliser and plastic sleeving in bulk, stocked them, and sold them to farmers. Credit, however, had to be obtained from the banks or through the SICAS, which advanced inputs to their members and made deductions from their sales (Parmentier 1988, personal communication). From 1975 onwards, SICABAM had taken charge of aerial leafspot spraying. Planes and helicopters were used, but SICABAM did not own them itself, although the company that it employed worked entirely on Martinique's banana plantations. A cess was levied to cover the cost of aerial spraying as well as the oil for supplementary ground spraying, but as in St Lucia, labour was supplied by the grower (Morlet 1988; Parmentier 1988, personal communications).

Members of SICABAM still sold their fruit individually through an agent in metropolitan France, with the grower's *marque* and the exporter's *contremarque* on each box. If fruit in a container was found to be unsatisfactory when unpacked, the buyer would not pay for it (Parmentier 1988, personal communication). The French market price to growers was generally maintained within narrow limits set annually by agreement between the Antillean producers' groups, the Ministry of Agriculture, and GIEB (representing all sectors of the industry in France), after consultation and consideration of costs of production. The target price fixed for 1987 was Fr 5.22 per kilogram *wagon départ* (SICABAM 1987, 6), and the actual average price received was Fr 5.25 per kilogram (Parmentier 1988, personal communication). (The *wagon départ* price may be regarded as roughly equivalent to the green wholesale price in Britain, and Fr 5.25 per kilogram would have been approximately £528 a tonne). Export sales to foreign countries were made by SICABAM rather than through exporters, and SICABAM operated an equalisation fund to compensate growers whose fruit had had to be sold abroad at prices lower than those in France.

Each grower had a quota, and while eleven SICAs were members of SICABAM, quotas were allocated to their participant growers on an individual basis rather than to the SICA as a unit. When there was a surplus and fruit had to be held back, shipping quotas were assigned on the basis of the previous three years' production. Since Martinique habitually oversubscribed its quota of the French market and since by the mid-1980s, Guadeloupe and France's African suppliers were starting to fill theirs, it was risky for Martiniquans to start growing export bananas or greatly expand production. Quotas went with holdings and were bought and sold with them (Morlet 1988; Parmentier 1988, personal communications). The practice of *ramassage* was unheard of, although the SICAs, which grouped most of the small growers into local cooperatives, still had difficulty in forecasting anticipated production by their members three months hence.

Growers generally used their own vehicles to transport fruit to the port or to SICABAM's two containerisation centres at Ste Marie and Lamentin. Transport costs were said not to be regarded as a major expense in relation to total production costs, so distance was not a factor in the location of banana cultivation (Parmentier 1988, personal communication). As in the 1960s, SICABAM as such had no metropolitan ripening facilities (Morlet 1988, personal communication).

There had, however, been one startling development in the organisation of Martinique's banana industry. In 1980, two or three growers dissatisfied with the way SICABAM was being run broke away and formed the Groupement d'Intérêt des Producteurs Agricole de la Martinique (GIPAM), a rival producers' group. Various explanations were given for the schism. According to the director of GIPAM, the main issue was marketing. The breakaway group felt that with individuals selling their fruit in their own name, there were too many intermediaries (exporters, and agents in France), and this led to unnecessarily high costs. GIPAM was formed, therefore, to export and sell all its members' fruit through a single agency, with all members receiving the same price for fruit of a given category. Under the old system, prices to different growers might vary by as much as Fr.15 or Fr.20 a kilogram (EC4¢ a pound). GIPAM members received a higher price for their fruit because of the elimination of intermediaries. Nevertheless they retained responsibility for their produce until it was sold. Each box bore the grower's *marque,* and if it was spoilt or unsaleable, the grower was not paid (Pompignan 1988, personal communication).

The manager of ASSOBAG had a slightly different perception of GIPAM's raison d'être. He suggested to me that some Martiniquan growers had become frustrated with SICABAM's reluctance to do what ASSOBAG was already doing, namely, buying inputs wholesale to supply to growers (Piloquet 1988, personal communication). This opinion was endorsed by a senior member of Guadeloupe's agricultural department who asserted that SICABAM had been controlled by grower-exporters who also imported fertiliser and other inputs and often had interests in European banana-importing companies. Needless to say, they were not keen to see any of these functions taken over by SICABAM.

The structure of GIPAM resembled that of SICABAM. It was run by a *conseil d'administration,* or board of directors, who appointed the chief executive officer, the *directeur.* There were 150 members with 150 votes in 1988, but the members held different numbers of shares (SICABAM had 137 voting members representing 1160 growers) (Parmentier 1988, personal communication). In principle, anyone who applied might become a member. However, the *directeur* suggested that banana production was unlikely to be profitable for any farmer with less than four hectares in the crop. No SICAs had joined GIPAM since SICAs were already somewhat analogous organisations that sold members' fruit in common. Membership in GIPAM continued to grow slowly, but many of those who might have liked to join were inhibited from doing so because they were bound to "the traditional channels" by debt. Unlike SICABAM, GIPAM was mandated to involve itself in the cultivation and marketing of other fruits besides bananas. Although bananas were overwhelmingly its prime concern, it also shipped limes and avocadoes (Pompignan 1988, personal communication).

Apart from undertaking the marketing of members' fruit directly, GIPAM performed many of the same functions as SICABAM. It had its own four extension staff and was responsible for arranging leafspot control for its members. It sold inputs to growers (fertilisers, nematicides, and boxes), on credit if necessary, and it was building a large warehouse to stock these items. It undertook the transport of fruit from boxing shed to containerisation centre and employed contractors to haul the fruit, since GIPAM owned no trucks. It was emphasized, however, that the cost to the grower varied according to distance, since it was not part of GIPAM's policy to distort the pattern of real costs. Indeed, although the group was formed in order to cooperate and benefit from economies of scale, stress was laid on the need for all growers to feel personally responsible for their own production. A cess of Fr280 per tonne was levied (SICABAM levied Fr201) to cover the cost of services and administration, but inputs were not covered by a cess. GIPAM did not have interests in ripening facilities, supposedly because such vertical integration would have made it difficult to determine the appropriate price to pay growers (Pompignan 1988, personal communication).

To some degree, both the Martiniquan associations had become more like their counterparts on neighbouring Commonwealth islands as it had become economically expedient to provide increasing numbers of services to members on a common basis. GIPAM had moved further in this direction than SICABAM. How far they were influenced by the experience of their neigbours is not clear. They, too, were intensely conscious of the need to improve the quality of their fruit if they were to survive the chill winds of competition that might strike them after 1992. However, although they were aware of the claims made for the success of field packing in improving quality in St Lucia and Dominica, they dismissed any suggestion that it was even worth considering in the Martiniquan context. Such a system might be suitable for the very small growers of the Commonwealth islands, but it would be quite incompatible with containerisation. It was not, after all, until 1975 that SICABAM organized communal leafspot spraying, almost 20 years after it had begun in the Commonwealth islands to the north and south. Moreover, spraying was still subcontracted in Martinique. In 1988, it cost Fr85 per tonne of bananas harvested, no less than in the Commonwealth islands, despite their lower yields per hectare. An indication of the extent to which the Commonwealth associations provided services for members compared with SICABAM and GIPAM is given by their respective cesses: Fr980 per ton for the Commonwealth associations, Fr201 per tonne for SICABAM, and Fr280 per tonne for GIPAM. Moreover, it must be borne in mind that salary levels were far higher in Martinique.

Guadeloupe

The status of ASSOBAG, Guadeloupe's growers' association, had remained unchanged since 1967, and no dissident groups had broken away from it. It was suggested that there had been no schism-provoking conflicts in Guadeloupe's organization because it was not controlled by growers who were also exporters of bananas and importers of inputs. Generally in Guadeloupe, exporters were not growers. Furthermore, unlike the Martiniquans, Guadeloupeans did not have interests in importing companies in Europe (Bachou 1988, personal communication). This was a dramatic change from the state of affairs in the early 1970s, when there were over 120 grower-exporters, many of whom also imported inputs and some of whom did have interests in metropolitan ripening facilities (Menauge 1974, 135, 144).

The change appears to have coincided with the advent of containerisation and the transfer of all banana shipping to the port of Jarry near Pointe-à-Pitre. In this context it is interesting to note that the four-month evacuation of Basse-Terre in 1976 during a series of minor eruptions by the neighbouring Soufrière volcano was widely perceived by its citizens as an unnecessary exercise, a conspiracy by the administration and Pointe-à-Pitre interests to undermine Basse-Terre's economic position and direct all ocean trade to the rival port (Loubat and Pistolesi-Lafont 1977; Farrugia 1977). Whether ulterior motives or simply an excess of caution were to blame, the evacuation certainly weakened Basse-Terre, and by 1988 its port was virtually dead.

The mandate of ASSOBAG in the 1980s was wider than it had been in the 1960s. It was still charged with looking after growers' interests in such a way that their income was safeguarded at every level. It was charged with negotiating shipping contracts, with regulating exports according to Guadeloupe's quota, and with finding and making sales to foreign markets should the monthly quota be exceeded. In addition, however, it had become responsible for setting up banana development plans, for the dissemination of agrotechnical information, the provision of inputs on the most favourable terms possible, the control of leafspot disease, and the containerisation of the boxed fruit of growers whose production was too small to fill a container on their holdings (*La Bananeraie Guadeloupéenne* 1984, 16).

In February 1988, plans were under way for ASSOBAG to market all its members' fruit in metropolitan France, as it was already doing in the United Kingdom and Italy, in a manner similar to the practice of GIPAM: that is, all growers would receive the same price unless boxes of fruit carrying their identifying *marque* were found to be defective on arrival. In that case, they would receive nothing for them (Piloquet 1988, personal communication). The ten exporters who then sold all the island's bananas in France, including those from the twelve SICAS, would presumably be eliminated.

ASSOBAG first took responsibility for extension services in 1968 (Menauge 1974, 160). According to the director in 1988, it was felt that the DDSA were not really interested in bananas: sugar was more important politically. By 1984, ASSOBAG's Services Agrotechniques had a staff of sixteen and two secretaries. They produced a bimonthly magazine, conducted training sessions and advised growers on techniques of harvesting and transport that would improve the quality of exported fruit. In France, as in Britain, the quality of Eastern Caribbean fruit had become an issue after imports of Latin American fruit had been permitted following Hurricanes David and Allen. (*La Bananeraie Guadeloupéenne* 1984, 18–20).

In 1984, ASSOBAG levied a cess of Fr35 per tonne of bananas exported. This was used either to repay debts incurred for phytosanitary chemicals, chiefly nematicides, distributed on credit after the hurricanes, or to reduce the direct purchase price of such inputs. Individual growers' accounts were audited every six months, and rebates were given to those who had built up too much credit. Those who had fallen too far into debt were prevented from receiving further material on credit until their accounts were deemed to be in a satisfactory condition (*La Bananeraie Guadeloupéenne* 1984, 21). In 1988, however, ASSOBAG was selling inputs for cash only and gave no credit (Piloquet 1988, personal communication).

Leafspot control was carried out by ASSOBAG, which had owned and operated its own planes since 1982. It was claimed that the association's close ties with IRFA had enabled it to provide the most advanced control in the region, and it did so at a cost of Fr70 per tonne, compared with Fr85 in Martinique, despite higher yields per hectare in Martinique (Piloquet 1988, personal communication).

The advent of containerisation in 1980 was potentially disadvantageous to many Guadeloupean growers. The new container port at Jarry was outside the traditional banana-producing zone and more distant than Basse-Terre for the majority of growers. Moreover, those with less than a full container (10.6 tonnes) for each shipment could no longer deliver direct to the port but had to assemble their boxed fruit at containerisation centres, with the additional cost of a two-stage journey. To compensate, ASSOBAG collected a cess of Fr10 a tonne from all growers. The cess financed an equalisation fund from which ASSOBAG could subsidise transport for growers distant from Pointe-à-Pitre. ASSOBAG rented vehicles to haul containers from the centres to the port, since it had no vehicles of its own (Piloquet 1988, personal communication).

Although ASSOBAG appeared to be slightly more interventionist in its philosophy than SICABAM and, with its transport subsidy, more egalitarian than GIPAM, in fact ASSOBAG'S cess of approximately Fr200 per tonne was very close to the cess of its chief Martiniquan counterpart. ASSOBAG'S proposed move to selling as a group rather than as individuals seemed progressive but was still no more than a proposal. A similar move had after all been proposed by SICABAM for Martinique as early as 1967. It was suggested in Guadeloupe that Martiniquans were more individualistic (by implication less co-operative) than Guadeloupeans, but ASSOBAG'S apparently more progressive attitude toward group selling may have had more to do with the fact that Guadeloupe had never exceeded its quota than with any fundamental difference of temperament: ASSOBAG had never had to make controversial decisions about the disposal of surpluses (Piloquet 1988, personal communication).

As the combined production of the French islands rose above the capacity of the French market to absorb it, there were signs of friction between their growers' organisations. In February 1988, it was asserted in Guadeloupe that Martinique was shipping more than her agreed tonnage and risking depressing price levels; but there appeared to be little ASSOBAG could do but protest.

TWENTY YEARS ON: THE IMPACT OF ORGANISATIONAL CHANGE ON THE CHARACTER AND INTENSITY OF LAND USE

After 20 years, what was different in the banana industries of the four islands, and how far were organisational changes responsible?

In all four islands, there had been changes, some trivial, some profound. In some cases, the zones of most intensive banana cultivation had shifted and the relationship of bananas with other crops had changed. The structure of participation in the banana industry had altered, as had yields and production totals. An island-by-island analysis reveals some general trends as well as developments peculiar to local circumstances.

St Lucia

There are detailed quantitative data on the location of banana production for two years: 1961 and 1986. Table 9.8 has been constructed from these data to show what proportion of the island's bananas were grown in each administrative division, bearing in mind that the total export was 40,000 tons in 1961 and 108,000 tons in 1986. Also shown on Table 9.8 is the percentage of the island's total land-in-holdings in each district.

Several interesting observations may be made about the pattern revealed in Table 9.8. In the north and west of the island, each district's share of the land-in-holdings has remained fairly stable. In the south and east, however, there has been a considerable change, with a moderate decline in Dennery and Vieux Fort and a dramatic rise in Micoud.

Figures for 1961 show a moderately good correlation between land-in-holdings, percentages of the island's banana trees, and percentages of stems cut, except that the dry southwestern districts have a relatively low proportion of bananas in relation to their area, while Dennery's proportion is extremely high.

By 1986, the relationship between shares of land-in-holdings and shares of banana production had apparently become much more erratic. Both Castries and Micoud had a much greater share of banana production than of land-in-holdings; Soufrière's share was disproportionately small; and Anse-La-Raye showed a large decline. Dennery, although still an area of relatively high production, showed a much smaller discrepancy than in 1961.

At first glance, it appears that production has shown a relative rise in districts close to the two ports and a relative decline in the districts farthest away. On closer examination, the situation proves less straightforward. It seems probable that much of Castries' apparent gain and Anse-La-Raye's apparent loss were on paper only. In 1961, the entire Cul-de-Sac and Roseau Valley estate lands then belonging to Geest were presumably enumerated as being in Anse-La-Raye, where the headquarters of the estates were located, whereas

Table 9.8
Location of banana production in St Lucia in relation to each district's share of land-in-holdings and fertiliser use, 1961 and 1986

	Land-in-holdings		*Banana trees*		*Production*		*Bags of fertiliser used*
	(percentages)						
District	*1961*	*1986*	*1961*	*1986*	*1961*[a]	*1986*[b]	*1986*
Gros Islet	14.4	12.3	9.0	8.0	10.9	32.0[c]	6
Castries	10.5	13.0	17.4	25.0	14.6		26
Anse-La-Raye & Canaries	13.1	10.8	12.0	6.0	13.4	4.5	8
Soufrière	9.5	10.3	6.5	2.0	5.9	1.0	2
Choiseul	3.2	3.4	0.7	0.5	0.5	0.6	1
Laborie	5.2	6.2	2.0	4.5	1.2	1.0	3
Vieux Fort	12.4	9.0	6.0	7.5	2.6	9.0	6
Micoud-Praslin	12.2	21.4	13.3	27.0	9.7	27.0	26
Dennery	19.5	14.7	33.1	19.0	41.1	24.0	21
St Lucia	100	100	100	100	100	100	100

Sources: Derived from WI Census of Agriculture, 1961 (1968, 182,186); St Lucia (1987, 18,46); SLBGA, (1987a).

[a]Stems cut.

[b]Amount sold (lbs.)

[c]Includes Castries.

most of their banana lands were actually in the quarter of Castries. (The 1961 census records no estates of 200 acres or more in Castries). By 1986, most of Cul-de-Sac had been subdivided and sold and so would have been enumerated within Castries.

If there is no evidence for the intensification of production close to Castries, the decline of Dennery can also be explained by factors other than its degree of accessibility to a port. In the 1960s, a single former sugar estate, Dennery, had over 400 hectares of bananas in the Mabouya Valley and produced more than 12,000 tons of fruit a year. In the mid-1970s, difficulties with the labour force and problems of pilferage in the peripheral areas of the estate caused the management to consolidate operations in the valley bottomlands, and the marginal areas went out of cultivation. The owner, a St Lucian white Creole, stopped investing in the estate and subsequently sold it to the government, after which much of it was subdivided. By 1988, it was the object of a development project that involved 2000 families and was intended to rehabilitate the lands that had gone out of cultivation (Vermeiren 1988, personal communication). Since the valley was subject to both droughts and flooding and since it had benefited from a quite extensive drainage and irrigation infrastructure in the 1960s, it is not surprising that neglect, abandonment, and subdivision had reduced the district's proportional share of the island's production.

The dramatic increase in Micoud's share is less easy to explain. Since growers are compensated at a set rate per mile for the distance they bring their fruit to the wharf, there really seems no reason why growers close to Vieux Fort or Castries should enjoy any particular locational advantage. There has, however, been a substantial improvement in communications in inland Micoud since the 1960s. New roads and feeder roads have been built in the interior, opening up land to an altitude of 350 metres above sea level (OAS Land Use and Vegetation Map, 1984). In Soufrière, on the other hand, there did not appear to have been much extension of the road system. Indeed, in some parts of the inland southwest, roads shown on the map of 1964 as "secondary roads" have been downgraded on the map of 1984 to "other roads and tracks." It may be that deteriorating communications, at least relatively speaking, have proved too discouraging to former banana growers in this exceptionally rugged area. Over the island as a whole, 53 percent of those listed as "growers" actually made sales in 1986, but in the Soufrière district, only 21 percent did so (SLBGA 1987a).

While shifts in the regional distribution of banana cultivation cannot be directly attributed to the activities of the SLBGA, there has been an island-wide withdrawal from land inaccessible by road. It was generally agreed that it was not really feasible for a farmer to carry boxed bananas on foot for long distances since the longer the journey the greater was the risk that the fruit would be battered and bruised. Eight hundred metres was considered about the limit, and while individual instances were cited of farmers who still headed fruit four kilometres from holdings in the interior, three boxes at a time, this was now exceptional. In 1966, the average distance from the road of the holdings of the 48 growers I interviewed was 0.5 miles (0.75 kilometres). The average distance of the 14 of those original growers who were still listed as active in 1986 was only 0.23 miles (0.34 kilometres). This is assuming that they still farmed the same holdings and that these were still at the same distance from a road. The extension of the road system may well have reduced the distance for at least some of them.

Even though there was a significant expansion in the road network over the twenty-year period, it seems probable that the bulk of St Lucia's banana production is now concentrated in a much smaller area than in the 1960s: in a band along the roads extending not much more than 800 metres on either side of them. There is no recent survey of the kind conducted by Momsen in 1965 (Momsen 1969), but the 1986 census recorded 5300 hectares in bananas, which is consistent with the claim of the SLBGA that average yields are now about 21 tons per hectare (St Hill 1988, personal communication). Just how far this concentration and consolidation are attributable to the SLBGA is hard to assess. The trend is certainly in line with current policy, and indeed with the policy favoured by the UWP government when it radically restructured the SLBGA in 1967. When boxing was introduced in the early 1970s, the dense network of buying points was replaced by a much sparser network of boxing plants. Yet even today in Martinique, "wet-pack" boxing is carried on at sheds with a weekly throughput of only six tonnes. On this scale, St Lucia could have supported 170 boxing sheds: a network as dense as the buying points; but the change in packaging technology was used as a pretext for reducing the number of points of sale to 30, and the inland buying depots that have now replaced the boxing plants number only 21 for the whole island.

The effect of the consolidation of servicing points must have been to reduce the viability of holdings located far from roads, in many cases to the point where their owners felt it no longer worthwhile to continue banana production. Certainly, between 1965 and 1972, the overall number of growers was greatly reduced: from 12,479 (Persaud 1966, 12) to 6,102 (SLBGA 1986), presumably largely because the

Table 9.9
Banana growers in St Lucia, numbers and production percentages in each size class, 1972 and 1986

Class[a]	*Number*	*Production, 1972 (%)*	*Average tonnage*	*Number*	*Production, 1986 (%)*	*Average tonnage*
Large	5	27	2358	12	5	452
Medium	36	9	118	265	23	94
Small	536	30	26	2009	49	26
Growers	5525	34	2.9	4532	23	5.5
Total	6102	100		6818	100	

Sources: *Banana Commission Report, 1980*, quoted in Demacque (1983, 116); SLBGA (1987b).
[a]Large = >278 tons/year; medium = 56–278 tons/year; small =11.6–56 tons/year; growers = <11.6 tons/year.

most remote farmers were discouraged. Since the most remote included a disproportionate number of the smallest, the composition of participation in the industry changed substantially over the period. Unfortunately, there was no classification of growers by production in the 1960s, but from the 1961 census data it can be estimated that perhaps almost half of St Lucia's production at that time was contributed by growers who produced less than 11.6 tons a year: growers who after 1967 could not participate directly in SLBGA decision making. Table 9.9 shows numbers and production percentages for growers in each category in 1972 and 1986.

In 1972, only 10 percent of St Lucia's banana growers were eligible to sit on the board of directors of the SLBGA. The remaining 90 percent now produced only a third of the island's production, which was in any case little more than half the 1966 total. With the elimination of half the island's growers, most from the lowest end of the production scale, the profile of grower participation moved sharply towards the Martinique-Guadeloupe pattern, in which the industry was dominated by a few large growers. Contemporary observers offered no explanation for this change. It coincided, more or less, with a succession of droughts and unsatisfactory price levels, and in retrospect these factors were evidently considered an adequate explanation for the decline – this despite the fact that production levels in Martinique, located between Dominica and St Lucia, did not show closely comparable fluctuations. (See Table 9.5, above).

If regional drought had really been the main cause of depressed production, it is surprising that a shortage of bananas would not have enabled WINBAN to negotiate better prices. In fact, however, the introduction of wet-pack boxing, which was accompanied by a sharp decrease in exports in all four Windwards, seems more likely to have been the critical factor.

The introduction of wet-pack boxing permitted a restructuring of buying operations that was very detrimental to small growers with holdings far from the road. Even if they were compensated for the expense of transporting fruit the extra distance to the boxing plants, they were compensated only for fruit accepted. In 1965, the rejection rate at buying points had been under 5 percent (Monplaisir 1966, personal communication), but now with a rejection rate of 30 to 40 percent (Demacque 1983, 42), even farmers who had invested nothing in inputs might easily be faced with expenses that exceeded their receipts. Fruit that had been headed several miles over rough and muddy tracks was particularly liable to be rejected. It is interesting to note that despite the elimination of so many small, remote growers, Geest continued to express dissatisfaction with the quality of Windwards fruit right until the introduction of field packing. It is now suggested that quality problems in the 1970s were at least in part attributable to rough handling by disaffected labour on the large estates.

It might have been anticipated that the shift towards fewer and larger growers would have continued as large growers took advantage of opportunities to modify the industry's operations in their favour. In fact, they were overtaken by forces far more potent. Labour unrest led to a slump in estate production, and within the next decade, the three largest estates (Dennery, Cul-de-Sac, and Roseau) and several others were sold and subdivided. By 1986, the profile of participation in banana cultivation was quite different from the profile in 1972 (See Tables 9.9 and 9.10). While part of the increase in numbers of farmers producing over 11.6 tons a year may have been due to the subdivision of very large estates into only fairly large ones, much of it must be attributable to increased production by farmers formerly in the category of "growers", which in this context refers to all those producing less than 11.6 tons of bananas a year.

The sociopolitical upheavals of the 1970s presumably convinced those responsible for the well-being of the banana industry that its future lay not with the large estates, but with the small grower who was not entirely dependent on hired labour. Demacque noted that in 1978, only 25 percent of growers with holdings under 10 hectares made use of agricultural credit. A further 29 percent did not need it, but 25 percent were ignorant of the procedure for obtaining credit, 13 percent feared they would be unable to repay, and 10 percent lacked the security to obtain loans (the remainder cited "other reasons") (1983, 77). By 1988, as a result of effective extension work by the SLBGA's own extension personnel and the provision of inputs on credit as a matter of course, nearly all growers were said to be using at least the minimum recommended amounts of fertiliser and nematicide. Certainly, the 1986 census figures show a very close correspondence between percentages of bags of fertiliser used and percentages of the island's bananas produced in each district (Table 9.8, above).

When field packing was first introduced in 1981–82, it was viewed with some apprehension by small growers, some of whom doubtless feared that it might be another ploy to marginalise them and squeeze them out of the industry. In fact, the advantages of field packing outweighed the anticipated drawbacks. Handling of unboxed fruit was reduced by 75 percent (SLBGA 1986, 27) and the rejection rate was brought down to an insignificant level. In St Lucia, as in Dominica and St Vincent, production climbed steadily as field packing was phased in. While most of the increased production was the result of established growers selling more fruit, there was some recruitment of new growers (or return of old ones). Luu, working in southwest St Lucia in 1984–85, encountered farmers who grew small quantities of bananas simply because this gave them access to fertiliser that would otherwise have been difficult to obtain on credit (1985, 72). Table 9.8 (above) tends to support the idea that this may have been a fairly widespread practice, since in the five southwestern districts, the percentage of total fertiliser used was two or three times the percentage of total banana production.

While it seems unlikely that there will ever be a return to the pattern of the mid-1960s when everyone who had access to a piece of land, no matter how remote, grew bananas on it, as Table 9.9 (above) shows, there has been some expansion in grower numbers since the difficult days of the early 1970s. There has also been a substantial rise in the proportion of growers eligible to hold office on the board of the SLBGA. This trend is likely to continue if production rises further and grower numbers remain stable. Between 1985 and 1986, despite an increase in production of 27.5 percent, the number of growers remained almost constant. There were 6,843 growers in 1985, of whom 681 dropped out of the industry in 1986, and 6,818 growers in 1986, of whom 656 had not sold bananas the previous year (SLBGA 1987a).

Unfortunately, it is impossible to make direct comparisons between the proportion of bananas produced on holdings of different sizes in the 1960s and the 1980s, since growers are not classified

Table 9.10
Banana production in St Lucia, by holding-size group, 1961 and 1986

Size group (ha)	*Stems cut, 1961 (%)*	*Bags of fertiliser used, 1986 (%)*
<2	33	42
2–4	18	24
4–20	22	20
20–40	2	1
>40	25	13
Total	100	100

Sources: Derived from WI Census of Agriculture, 1961 (1968, 186); St Lucia (1987, 57).

by holding-size group in the 1986 census. On the grounds, however, that quantities of fertiliser used, for which the 1986 census does contain a classification by holding size, can now be taken to provide a reasonably good reflection of production percentages, the statistics for fertiliser have been used to make an indirect comparison (Table 9.10).

Over the twenty years, SLBGA policy has swung first away from and then back towards the interests of the small grower. It would seem that the post-1967 oligopoly controlling the industry was prepared initially to eliminate most small growers on the grounds that only the survival of the fittest would guarantee the industry's health. When, on the contrary, the industry went into a slump from which it showed few signs of recovering, growers' dissatisfaction with the functioning of the SLBGA led to the appointment, in early 1980, of a commission of enquiry. The commission determined that the post-1967 directorate had not addressed itself to the expansion of productive activities, had dealt flippantly with vital questions raised by growers regarding fertiliser, feeder roads, aerial spraying, and qualification for delegate status, and had been guilty of gross irregularities and misuse of funds (Acosta and Casimir 1985, 49–50). As a result, the board, now with seven government appointees and six elected directors, began to pursue a more interventionist role. Its efforts were, however, directed towards intensifying production in existing locations and by existing participants, rather than returning to mass participation and extensive cultivation on the scale of the 1960s. The resumption of banana growing in areas of marginal rainfall, a phenomenon that appears from SLBGA records of 1987 to have been of fairly minor significance, was singled out for criticism in WINBAN's annual report of 1986 (WINBAN 1987, 2–3).

Dominica

In Dominica, the main zones of banana production remained much the same in the 1980s as in the 1960s. About a third of the island's bananas came from the northeastern parish of St Andrew and a quarter from the Layou Valley area, including much of the parish of St Joseph. Between 1961 and 1986 there was a decline in the share of production of most of the leeward parishes (from 22 to 7 percent) and a rise in the share of the central and southern windward parishes (from 17 to 27 percent) (DBMC 1987, 4). Windward communications had been greatly improved after 1961, which would account for their increased share. Feeder roads had been extended into areas where large quantities of bananas were already being grown or where land was suitable but not accessible, such as in the Carholm and New Venture districts of the Layou Valley (Bully 1988, personal communication). However, it had not been worthwhile to build roads for miles up the narrow leeward valleys, so that hardly any bananas were now sold from areas such as the heights of Colihaut (Scotland 1988, personal communication).

While the distribution of the main zones of production remained somewhat more stable in Dominica than in St Lucia, the number and profile of participants in the industry evolved in a similar, if slightly less dramatic, manner. In the 1961 census, there were 7,292 banana growers. They can be classified by the size of their holdings but not by their level of production, although from average grower-tonnages in each holding-size class, it is possible to gauge the approximate percentage contributions of different classes of growers defined according to St Lucian criteria (Table 9.11). In 1966 there were estimated to be about 9,300 growers (Persaud 1966, 12); in 1975, 6,000 (Williams 1975, 61). There were 5,388 in 1984, 5,021 in 1985, 5,063 in 1986, and 5,998 in 1987. Tables 9.11 and 9.12 show the profile of participation in 1961, 1985, and 1987.

The generally cited reasons for the sharp decline both in participation and production in the early 1970s were weather problems, especially drought, low prices, and difficulties in meeting Geest's quality requirements. While all these factors no doubt contributed to the industry's problems, the introduction of boxing, which coincided with the decline, seems likely, as in St Lucia, to have been a more critical factor. An anthropologist who worked in Dominica in the early 1970s and investigated reasons for the widespread sense of alienation expressed by growers towards the DBGA saw the introduction of an inappropriate and unpopular boxing system as one of the prime causes.

Table 9.11
Profile of participation in banana production in Dominica, 1961

Holding-size groups (ha)	*Production(%)*	*Average tonnage*	*Tons/year/grower*	*Production (%), estimated*
0–0.4	4.2	0.64	<10	58
0.4–2	21.2	1.52		
2–4	20.1	4.03		
4–10	9.2	5.2		
10–20	3.7	8.09	10–50	6
20–40	5.9	23.03		
>40	35.7	100.43	>50	36

Source: Derived from WI Census of Agriculture, 1961 (1968,102).

Table 9.12
Profile of participation in banana production in Dominica, 1985 and 1987

Annual tonnage	*Number of growers*		*Production (%)*		*Average tonnage*		*Average area in bananas (ha)*
	1985	*1987*	*1985*	*1987*	*1985*	*1987*	*1987*
<10	4,064	4,014	29	22	2.45	3.56	0.67
10–50	878	1,816	54	60	20.88	21.47	2.83
>50	79	168	17	18	74.39	69.64	3.66
Totals	5,021	5,998	100	100	6.8	10.8	0.97

Source: DBMC (1986,4); DBMC (1988).

When the decision was made in 1970 to start boxing, the association hired outside management consultants to advise on the best way to set up the new system (Baker 1994, 151). The scheme they proposed, which used twelve regional boxing plants, was similar to that employed on large estates in relatively flat areas of Central America and resulted in increased transportation of unpackaged bananas, with a consequent increase in mechanical damage to fruit and a deterioration in quality. By the time of the changeover to field packing, there were twenty-four boxing plants, half operated by the DBMC and half by cooperatives. Many farmers would have had to transport their fruit several miles by road to the nearest plant, and while the DBGA paid for transporting fruit from plant to port, the growers bore the cost of transport to the plant, based on the number of bunches they were sending (Eguchi 1984, 86). As in St Lucia, there was reported to have been a 30 to 40 percent rejection rate at the boxing plant (Marie 1979, 28).

In Dominica, production and grower numbers fell by about a third in the early 1970s, compared with almost half in St Lucia. The impact of the change to boxing in Dominica may have been reduced by the fact that Dominica had never had a dense network of buying points, and many growers were already accustomed to organising their own transport. Moreover, with uniform boxing-plant prices, growers distant from the ports were no longer at a relative disadvantage. There is no evidence that it was government policy to drive out marginal growers, whereas since 1966 the St Lucia government had been anxious to drive them out and implement the management consultants' recommendations for "rationalising" their banana industry.

On the ground, the reduction in grower numbers in Dominica also translated into a concentration of banana cultivation near the roads. Eguchi comments on the tendency for farmers in St Patrick's parish to give up working their remote interior lands and to grow their bananas on naturally unsuitable but accessible land, land made "suitable" with fertiliser (1984, 196). According to the DBMC's operations manager, by 1988, no one headed bananas more than half a mile to the road (Didier 1988, personal communication). The superintendant of agriculture suggested a limit of half an hour for heading bananas, although older farmers might still walk up to three hours to their provision gardens (Bully 1988, personal communication).

Tables 9.11 and 9.12 (above) show that since the 1960s in Dominica, even more than in St Lucia, not only was there a reduction in the proportion of fruit grown by the smallest growers, those who produced under 10 tons a year and yet in 1961 accounted for almost 60 percent of production, there was also a drastic decline in the contribution of the large estates. In 1988, the largest single grower in the island produced about 220 tons, which was insufficient for a grower to qualify as a "large grower" in St Lucia. Labour management problems in the early 1970s were cited as the cause of the breakup of the large estates, and their subdivision put much of Dominica's best and most accessible land in the hands of small farmers, often former estate workers (Didier 1988; Bully 1988, personal communication).

Whatever impact the termination of the old grower-controlled DBGA and its replacement by the government-dominated DBMC might have had has been largely masked by the contemporaneous introduction of field packing and the subsequent rise in prices to growers as a result of the decline in value of the dollar relative to sterling. Between 1984 and 1988 there was reported to have been a 30 percent expansion by growers already in the industry, in addition to a large influx of new growers, many of them young, brought in by the DBMC's offer of credit facilities for new growers (Scotland 1988, personal communication). A typical case was the owner of an estate of approximately ten hectares who had neglected his bananas to the extent that only three or four tons had been produced in 1987. By 1988, he was planning to rehabilitate the bananas and start selling significant quantities again.

The scarcity of the agricultural labour supply imposed certain constraints on the ability of the marketing board to pursue policies likely to modify the structure of participation in the banana industry. Forty-four percent of Dominica's bananas were grown in 1987 by farmers producing under 20 tons a year: in Guadeloupe 20 tons was the average yield per hectare, which required a single worker for its cultivation. It was claimed that in Dominica in 1988, most bananas were grown by family labour, with some use of exchange labour groups for harvesting and field packing (Bully 1988, personal communication). Most of those involved in agriculture were now landowners, so that there was almost no pool of labour to be employed on other people's estates (Scotland 1988). While wages were extremely low compared with wages in the French islands (EC$15 to EC$20 a day compared with EC$135, including social security contributions), a "daily" wage purchased a very variable amount of work, sometimes only three hours, as against a standard eight hours in Martinique or Guadeloupe (Didier 1988, personal communication). Thus DBMC policies had to take account of the fact that in Dominica for the foreseeable future, production was likely to be dominated by the small grower who was independent of hired labour. The contemplated elimination of the IBDs, for example, would presumably not be practicable if it drove the thousands of growers who used them and produced 20 percent of the island's bananas out of the industry.

Martinique

In St Lucia and Dominica during the period from 1966 to 1988, there was a drastic decline followed, much more recently, by a spectacular rise in banana production. There were only relatively minor adjustments in the regional pattern of banana growing, and the small grower with an average annual production of about 20 tons on 2.5 hectares emerged as the backbone of the industry. There was, simultaneously, a sharp reduction in the role of both the very small and the very large grower. Over the same period in Martinique, indeed in both the French islands, the pattern differed in virtually every respect. Except in years when production was severely affected by hurricanes, volcanic eruptions, or protracted droughts, production remained fairly steady, and the estimated area in bananas in Martinique fell by only 20 percent, from 10,000 to 8,000 hectares (SICABAM 1988, 24).

In the mid-1960s, the northeast, from Lorrain northwards, was the banana zone par excellence, while farther south in Ste Marie, Trinité, and central Martinique, cane still contended with bananas for supremacy. By the 1980s, however, the centre of gravity of the banana industry had shifted southwards toward the greatly extended irrigable zone, and the overworked pumice soils of the northeast were given some respite with fallow years or banana-pineapple rotations (Morlet 1988, personal communication). There was also a movement from the more rugged inland districts to the gentle, easily mechanised slopes near the Atlantic coast (Burac 1975, 121). Finally, the largest growers, those with over twenty hectares in bananas, had expanded their share of the total banana acreage at the expense of the medium and smaller growers. While in terms of their share of the total acreage, the medium and small growers had suffered only a very small decline, the actual number of growers in the "small" category - under 5 hectares - had fallen to half its former level. Moreover, this was not a class that had been unproductive: in 1964, such growers had average yields of about 21 tonnes per hectare. Really small growers, in the St Lucian or Dominican sense of the term, had nearly all been eliminated before the mid-1960s.

Except for the smallest growers, the most remarkable aspect of the profile of participation in Martinique's banana industry has been its stability. The continuing deterioration in the position of the very small grower, which reached catastrophic proportions in the late 1960s, is understandable given the nature of Martinique's marketing procedure with its potential for inflicting heavy losses on the unlucky or the poorly organised. Moreover, the SICAs, which were umbrella organisations created to look after the interests of the smallest growers, went through a period of crisis in the late 1960s after the government withdrew support for the SATEC personnel who had been providing subsidised technical and managerial assistance. SICA membership declined from 1,591 in 1968 to 846 in 1972 (Burac 1975, 114,128-30).

Coupled with rising production costs and increasingly stringent

Table 9.13
Structure of the banana industry in Martinique, 1960s, 1970s, 1980s

	Size groups (ha)							
	0–1	*1–2*	*2–5*	*5–10*	*10–20*	*20–50*	*50–100*	*100+*	*Total*
AREA (%)									
1963			29[a]		19[b]			52[d]	8,500 (ha)
1986			27[a]		16[b]			57[d]	7,850 (ha)
1988			29[a]		17[b]			54[d]	7,567 (ha)
NUMBER OF GROWERS									
1963	1,860	505	428	120	63		101[d]		3,077
1972		846[c]	404	92	42	77	41	2	1,497
1986			1,050[a]		130[b]		95[d]		1,275
1988			1,043[a]		135[b]		87[d]		1,265

Sources: *La Banane* (1967, 14); Burac (1975, 115); SICABAM (1988, 24); Parmentier (1988, personal communication).

[a]Total for size groups of 0–1, 1–2, and 2–5 ha.

[b]Total for size groups of 5–10 and 10–20 ha.

[c]Total for size groups of 0–1 and 1–2 ha.

[d]Total for size groups of 20–50, 50–100, and 100+ ha.

quality requirements, the withdrawal of subsidised personnel was seen by many SICA members as a ploy by the government, in league with the big planters, to exclude them from the banana industry. The share of the SICAs in Martinique's banana export fell from 10.9 percent in 1965 to 5 percent in the early 1970s (Burac 1975, 128,130). In 1972, the government and SICABAM felt impelled to take steps to halt the decline of the SICAs by providing funds to rehabilitate 1500 hectares of plantations and guarantee a reserved quota for the SICAs rising to 10.5 percent of exports in 1975 (Burac 1975, 132). By 1988, the Union des SICA was responsible for 15 percent of production and had 800 members (Parmentier 1988, personal communication). Evidently, it was possible to take action to improve the condition of those remaining in the industry, but not to bring back those who had left it.

One potential setback that the banana industry in Martinique was fortunate to have escaped was the establishment of a network of central boxing plants. In 1969, SICABAM embarked with government support on a programme to construct twenty-five large central boxing plants to pack fruit for all classes of growers. The project was abandoned, however, after unsatisfactory results with the first pilot plant. Dissatisfaction arose in part because it was impossible to keep different growers' lots separate, but transporting unwrapped bananas over long distances also created problems, since it damaged the fruit and tied up so much capital in vehicles that projected economies of scale were not realised. Instead, SICABAM applied for funds to modernise the existing packing sheds and to construct 150 additional sheds for small growers, a plan that was approved in 1972 (Burac 1975, 9–120).

There were two reasons why Martinique's large growers were able to flourish and even expand production in the 1970s at a time when their Commonwealth counterparts were falling behind. In the first place, because of their involvement in all sectors of the island's economy, they had the resources to invest in modern equipment and land that could be mechanised. When small farmers were obliged to quit as they built up intolerable burdens of debt, the large growers were able to take over their quotas (Burac 1975, 121). In the second place, Martinique was not affected by the labour crisis to nearly the same degree, perhaps because, it was suggested, the long-established and closely knit white Creole *béké* families of Martinique had been more tenacious and less easily discouraged and had continued to command a degree of traditional loyalty from their workers (Morlet 1988, personal communication). However, the payment of wages at the same level as those of agricultural workers in metropolitan France may have been a more critical factor. In any case, in 1988 there was said to be no shortage of labour in any region (Parmentier, personal communication). Moreover, while it was very difficult to find agricultural labourers to work on estates in Dominica or St Lucia, there were said to be hundreds, if not thousands, of migrant workers from these islands cutting cane in Martinique and Guadeloupe.

The relative stability of production levels and the structure of participation in the banana industry of Martinique reflects the essentially conservative nature of its growers' organisations. When SICABAM did expand its sphere of action over the past twenty years, it did so largely in response to the exigencies of technological developments, rather than through any desire to take initiatives that might disturb the status quo. Thus, SICABAM assumed responsibility for leafspot control, for instance, only after the development of new techniques that could be used effectively only if a single authority was in charge of spraying island-wide. The formation of GIPAM, with the desire of its members to rationalise marketing procedures, followed closely upon the switch to containerisation; it does not appear that the new organisation was particularly interested in accommodating smaller growers. Indeed, while the island's largest growers remained with SICABAM, so did the smallest. In 1988, the average GIPAM member had 13.6 hectares of bananas, more than double the 5.3 hectares of the average SICABAM member. The director of GIPAM told me that it was impossible to grow bananas profitably with less than four hectares in the crop (Pompignan 1988, personal communication); while the head of SICABAM's agro-technical service said that nine hectares was really the viable minimum that permitted a grower to fill a 10.6-tonne container each week or so and avoid the problem of transporting boxes of uncontainerised fruit around the countryside or having to ship the fruit of several growers in the same container, which was said to be unpopular with buyers (Morlet 1988, personal communication). While it might theoretically be possible to manage the harvesting of bananas from a 9-hectare plot so that a container could be filled two weeks out of three, it would certainly require both skill and luck. Possibly, SICABAM regarded a 9-hectare minimum as desirable for bureaucratic reasons, rather than as necessary for viability. The one grower interviewed in 1966 who could be traced and reinterviewed in 1988 had in fact reduced his area in bananas from 35 hectares to 6.5 hectares, with a weekly yield of four to five tonnes. Land that had formerly grown bananas was now being used to raise livestock. It would be rash to generalise from a single case, but evidently he did not regard the container load as the weekly minimum for viability.

Table 9.14
Location of banana plantations in Guadeloupe, 1964–1987

	Percentage of total banana acreage				
Communes	*1964*	*1966*	*1970*	*1984*	*1987*
Trois Rivières	17	17	18	15	19.5
Gourbeyre	16	11	12	8	
St Claude	16	20	19	9	12.5
Baillif	7			4	
Vieux Habitants	5			2	
Bouillante	3	16	12	1	
Pointe-Noire	1			1	
Deshaies	–			–	
St Rose	–			3	12
Lamentin	–			1	
Moule	2	8	5	–	
Vieux Fort	1			–	
Petit Bourg	4			2	
Goyave	2			4	56
Capesterre	28	28	36	51	
Total	100	100	100	100	100

Sources: La Banane (1967, 17); Menauge (1974, 18); *La Bananaraie Guadeloupéenne* (1984, 11); Guadeloupe (1987, 46).
Note: Blank spaces beneath a figure indicate that the figure represents the percentage for a group of communes or zones: for example, for 1987, 19.5 is the percentage for Trois Rivières and Gourbeyre.

Guadeloupe

As in Martinique, both production levels and the acreage occupied by bananas remained fairly stable over the twenty-year period, except when natural disasters intervened. Guadeloupe consistently produced between 110,000 and 140,000 tonnes of bananas a year, just below its quota of 155,000 tonnes. The area in bananas, mainly pure-stand but perhaps 20 percent mixed, was variously estimated at 6500 to 9000 hectares. In 1987 it was 7600 hectares (*La Banane* 1967, 1:17; Guadeloupe 1987:46).

Also as in Martinique, while the acreage remained stable, the areas in which the bananas were grown shifted significantly. This is documented in Table 9.14 for certain years on a commune-by-commune basis, and for others, on a zone-by-zone basis, grouping sets of communes (unfortunately not always the same ones). Most striking is the increased importance of Capesterre and the decline of St Claude and its neighbours. In the early 1960s sugar was still the chief crop on the gently sloping plains of Capesterre, and the best quality bananas, which is to say the most durable, were those grown inland, in the heights. By the late 1960s, boxing had made durability less important, high labour costs made at least some degree of mechanisation desirable, sugar was disappearing from Capesterre, and even when rainfall was suboptimal, irrigation added less to costs than did the longer growing cycle and higher labour costs in the rugged interior. Sugar company lands were sold in lots of 25 to 100 hectares, often to growers who already had large holdings in the heights of St Claude and Gourbeyre. This tendency was given a further boost in 1976 when the Soufrière volcano showed signs of activity. Surrounding areas were evacuated for four months and the banana plantations were neglected for much of this time. They were also damaged by ash falls (Bachou 1988, personal communication).

Banana production in the leeward coast communes, which was as much as 16 percent of the total in 1964, had declined to 8 percent by 1984. The steep-sided valleys were now considered too rugged, and while the extension inland of feeder roads had made them more accessible, it had also rendered vanilla cultivation a viable option once more. On the other hand, some bananas were now being grown in Lamentin and St Rose in the northeast. They required some irrigation, but the land was gently sloping (Bachou 1988, personal communication).

It should be emphasised, however, that while there has been a major shift in the centre of gravity of banana cultivation, the main concentration remains in the southern part of the island, and it remains in the same hands, despite the shift of the exporting port to Pointe-à-Pitre. The soils of the northeast were said to be poor for bananas (Piloquet 1988, personal communication), and large areas of Petit Bourg and Goyave that would probably have been planted in bananas had they been in Dominica were in rough pasture or left fallow. However, it seems likely that ASSOBAG's policy of equalising transport costs for all members helped to maintain most banana production within the communes where it had traditionally been important. The soils of the northeast may have been less than ideal, but opinions on what constitutes the ideal banana soil change. In 1967, the rusty-brown halloysitic soils of Trois Rivières were said to be the best because of their excellent physical and chemical properties and low level of nematode infestation. By 1988, they were as badly affected by nematodes as any other soils, and it was the allophane soils of Capesterre that were the most highly esteemed (IRFA 1987, 79).

Table 9.15
Structure of the banana industry in Guadeloupe, 1960s, 1970s, 1980s

	Size group (ha)					
	0–5	*5–10*[a]	*10–20*	*20–100*	*100+*	*Total (ha)*
AREA (%)						
1960	42	(	30	)	28	9,000
1966	34	(18.5	)(	45.5	)	9,000
1970	36	(16	)(	48	)	8,500
1984	34	8	14	(44	)	7,500
NUMBER OF GROWERS						
1960	c.3,600	(	230	)	9	3,950
1966	2,605	(169	)(	76	)	2,850
1970	2,090	(142	)(	66	)	2,298
1984	1,187	81	68	(64	)	1,400

Sources: Lasserre (1961, 2:659,684); Menauge (1974, 53–4,61); *La Bananaraie Guadeloupéenne* (1984, 14).
Note: Brackets indicate range of hectare class size.
[a]The figures for 1966 and 1970 are based on 0–6 hectare classes.

Table 9.15 shows the evolution of the structure of the industry in Guadeloupe. The pattern of evolution is fairly similar to that of Martinique (Table 9.13). Size-group boundaries differ for different years, but it is clear that most of the erosion in numbers was from farms smaller than 5 hectares. The number of farms larger than 20 hectares remained remarkably stable. While the percentage of the total area in bananas in the smallest group (under 5 hectares) declined by 8 percent, the average size of banana holdings in the smallest group rose from just below 1 to over 2 hectares. Menauge (1974) investigated the decline in grower numbers between 1966 and 1970, and was able to determine that most of those who had dropped out (519 out of 556) had had less than 3 hectares in bananas.

Menauge thought that small farmers had abandoned export banana growing largely because of the series of hurricanes that had devastated Guadeloupe's bananas four times between 1963 and 1966 and had left growers with a crushing burden of debt. By 1970, the industry was in such a critical state that the government agreed to provide financial assistance, both to service debts and to help fund a programme to breathe new life into the industry. This programme was set in motion in 1971, and by 1972 production was already passing the previous record levels of the early 1960s (Menauge 1974, 104–5,175).

While ASSOBAG, with its recently formed Service Agrotechnique, doubtless played an important role in this revival, it is clear from the responses to Menauge's survey of growers' opinions of ASSOBAG that its activities were relevant only to a small minority of growers, chiefly larger growers. Seventy-seven percent of growers with less than 3 hectares of bananas had no opinion at all of ASSOBAG; they did not know what it was and often were not even aware of the way their local SICA operated (Menauge 1974, 169–70). Such a lack of awareness of the DBGA or the SLBGA by any class of grower would have been inconceivable. Menauge found that the proportion of growers without opinions declined as the area of their banana cultivations increased and that large growers were more likely to be satisfied than smaller growers, who felt they were not kept well informed and that their complaints were not heard. Growers of all sizes deplored the influence exercised by exporters in the affairs of ASSOBAG. Among those who had an opinion, however, the majority saw the association as a positive force, because it provided a powerful and united front in negotiations with Martinique and with metropolitan agencies and because it was successful in obtaining subsidies and in protecting production by waging an effective campaign to keep leafspot and borers under control (Menauge 1974, 170).

In other words, while ASSOBAG was a force to be reckoned with, its role was not to help the marginal producer, and it did little to protect the small grower. Asked whether he, too, regarded 9 hectares as the lowest threshold for a viable banana holding in the future, the director of ASSOBAG was noncommittal. With each round of climatic disasters, more small farmers fell by the wayside, whereupon ASSOBAG instituted another renewal programme that resulted in increased production by those who remained in the industry. This happened after the hurricanes of 1979 and 1980: land dropped out of cultivation in some areas, and elsewhere yields declined because growers' debts had become too large for them to afford appropriate levels of inputs.

After ASSOBAG's 1985 renewal campaign, acreages had begun to rise again (Bachou 1988, personal communication; Guadeloupe 1987, 44–6). There was said to be an influx of young farmers into the banana industry, attracted by the very favourable grants and loans that the government made available to first-time farmers through the Crédit Agricole. Since the scheme began in 1985, ASSOBAG had recorded 150 new young growers, but it transpired that many of these farmers were simply taking advantage of the scheme to take over their fathers' holdings (Piloquet 1988, personal communication).

Unlike its Commonwealth neighbours, Guadeloupe did not experience particularly severe labour unrest in the 1970s, since high wage levels defused discontent. Consequently, difficulty in maintaining a reliable work force did not become a factor leading to the break-up of large estates. By 1988, however, despite high unemployment, labour was said to be hard to obtain throughout rural Guadeloupe. Agricultural labourers from Dominica were employed in the banana industry, but their numbers were unknown. Most came illegally and were expelled if caught (Piloquet 1988, personal communication).

SICABAM had firmly discouraged the practice of *ramassage* in the 1960s, and it was apparently unknown in Martinique in 1988. ASSOBAG had been more tolerant, however. *Ramassage* was still widespread in Guadeloupe in 1970 (Menauge 1974, 150), and even in 1988, it was not unheard of (Bachou 1988, personal communication). Presumably, then, a few very small growers were still involved in banana production, but on an official level, they hardly seemed to exist.

CONCLUSION

I shall consider the question of how far growers' associations *could* shape the destiny of the industry they were formed to protect and promote in the concluding chapter. Here I have asked how far they *did* do so in the Eastern Caribbean between the 1960s and the 1980s. In chronicling both the changes in the growers' associations and the changes in the location of export banana cultivation and the profile of banana growers, I have attempted to understand how these relate to each other. More often than not, they have been consistent with the interests of those who currently controlled the growers' associations. In both St Lucia and Dominica the government is now, ultimately, in control. In each case it is reputed to draw its main support from the would-be upwardly mobile, rather than from those who are at the bottom of the socioeconomic ladder and expect to remain there. In Martinique and Guadeloupe, the associations are controlled by a small group of wealthy planters who are prepared to take concerted action when necessary to ensure the survival of the industry but who have no particular mandate to protect the interests of growers too small to be represented on the boards of the associations. The smallest growers must place their interests in the hands of the SICAs, the strength of whose influence depends ultimately on the complexion of the government in Paris.

10 Conclusion

This book is the account of an exploration of the role that locally organised institutions may play in modifying the possibilities afforded by physical resources and international economic dispositions. Its purpose is to contribute to the understanding of how patterns of agricultural land use evolve, sometimes seemingly in defiance of all rational expectations. In default of two regions sufficiently congruent in all but institutional structures to offer ideal conditions for hypothesis-testing, four Eastern Caribbean islands of broadly comparable physical endowments and economic relationships were chosen as an area for study, since in the 1960s they afforded possibilities for a variety of permutations of lateral comparisons. In the 1980s, the opportunity to make temporal comparisons added a further dimension to the study.

Even when the exploration of the topic was largely restricted to a narrow time span, the conclusions to be drawn from it were by no means straightforward. The addition of a temporal dimension, while illuminating some areas, has only compounded the complexity in others; nevertheless, some progress can be claimed in disentangling causes and effects. The conclusions that emerged can be considered in the light of five main questions. First, to what extent, in the Eastern Caribbean context, have banana growers' associations been able to determine or modify the location and intensity of land use? Second, what is the relationship between such institutionally induced land use modifications and the membership profiles of the associations? Third, were the growers' organisations the product of conscious policies or were they a spontaneous response to a perceived need or threat? Were the forces that animated them primarily ideological or pragmatic? Fourth, did the institutional structures in the Eastern Caribbean reflect different national traditions and philosophies in their constitutions and modes of operation? Fifth and finally, will such institutional structures as growers' associations and marketing boards be able to exert any influence over land use decisions in the years to come? In drawing together all these themes, I shall consider the value of this type of analysis, both for explaining existing land use patterns and for predicting patterns that, under certain conditions, might come to be.

As a background to this discussion, some points that emerged from the study are worth bearing in mind. A piquant lesson to be learned from an investigation drawn out over many years is the danger of overestimating the ability of informants to recall events and, especially, dates with accuracy. Informants tend to contract the time that has elapsed between what they perceive as causal events and the developments that they believe have flowed from them. Sometimes events are reordered to ensure that the supposed effects follow rather than precede the supposed causes, and informants nearly always assume that the events in question were more recent than they actually were. The experience of 1988 caused me to reexamine with a more critical eye some of the information about events in the 1950s, 1940s, and earlier that I gathered in the 1960s. It also reinforced my appreciation of the advantages of a long-term involvement in a research area, already well-awakened by the detection of various errors in statistical records that would have been apparent as anomalies only to those with an extended knowledge of the trends.

If recognition of the value of a long-term perspective was enhanced by my own experience, the desirability of pursuing such a study in breadth as well as in depth was made no less manifest. Often, in works consulted that related only to one island or were restricted only to the French or only to Commonwealth islands, authors attributed responsibility for certain developments to purely local causes such as hurricanes or droughts when in fact similar developments had taken place in areas untouched by these misfortunes. Similar events were sometimes credited with having provoked diametrically opposite responses. For instance, in Guadeloupe in the 1960s, it was said that the dearth of citrus trees was the result of the hurricane of 1928, which had been so destructive of orange and grapefruit trees that farmers had not considered it worth reestablishing these long-term crops and preferred instead to plant bananas, which, if blown down, could be replanted and bearing within a year. In Dominica, however, the devastating hurricane David of 1979 was reported to have had precisely the opposite effect: farmers noted that while all bananas had been lost, only half the citrus trees had been destroyed. Accordingly, in the years that followed they planted fewer bananas and more citrus trees. Similar causes may provoke dissimilar effects at different periods and in different circumstances. Yet such contrary explanations do indicate a need to reappraise interpretations that may be regarded as quite plausible within the context of a single island.

It might be imagined that between four neighbouring islands with common agricultural interests (and even, to some degree, with a common language, Créole), the diffusion of mutually relevant ideas and information could almost be taken for granted. Both in 1966–67 and in 1988, however, it became evident to me that it could not. This discovery emerged particularly in discussions with banana industry personnel in the French and Commonwealth islands regarding the timing of the rhythm of production to harmonise with peaks and depressions in demand and prices. Since the 1960s, growers in the French islands have been required to notify their island associations of their anticipated production three months hence, a not especially onerous requirement on an orderly plantation, provided that regular records are kept of "shot" bunches. In 1988 an association officer on one of the Commonwealth islands complained to me that it was difficult to predict how much shipping space would be required before the fruit actually arrived at the port: it was evident that he was quite unfamiliar with the French system of mandatory forecasting. Comparable instances could be cited of French unfamiliarity with Commonwealth practices. Thus, it cannot be assumed that failure to follow a practice necessarily means that it has been considered and rejected as inappropriate.

A last general point to be borne in mind is that the history of banana cultivation in the Eastern Caribbean has not been one of inexorable, unilinear progress. There is not now, and never has been, general agreement about the "best" way to grow, harvest, and transport bananas. In the French islands, mixed-stand plantings of bananas and tree crops were regarded as an aberration, an unfortunate relic of the past. In Dominica, such combinations were seen as advantageous and were encouraged. Regular replanting was considered de rigueur in the French islands, but generally unnecessary, if not undesirable, in St Lucia and Dominica. By 1966, boxing, which was carried out in hundreds of widely distributed packing sheds, had superseded the wrapping and shipment of bananas on the stem in the French islands, but boxing was declared to be inappropriate and unacceptable to Geest in the Commonwealth islands. Nevertheless, by 1972, reportedly at Geest's instigation, the Commonwealth islands had converted entirely to boxing, using a highly centralised system that had been rejected by Martinique as unsatisfactory. Ten years later, the Commonwealth islands began to phase out centralised boxing and introduce field packing, while the French islands had meanwhile determined that containerisation, preferably on the estate, was both an inevitable and a beneficial innovation.

The fact that there was never any set of methods generally accepted as being the most satisfactory meant that there was considerable latitude for institutional manipulation. Growers' associations could promote methods and pursue strategies that accorded with their philosophies and were in the interests of whoever had the power to determine their policies, and at least in the short run, there was little risk that the choices they had made could be proved demonstrably wrong. Had there been a single, clearly superior course of action, one that was guaranteed to maximise benefits to the banana industry as as whole, the role of the associations would have been very circumscribed. They would have been open to criticism if they had deviated from the obvious path.

With these points in mind, the five questions outlined in the introduction to this chapter can be addressed.

ASSOCIATIONS, LAND USE, AND PARTICIPATION IN THE INDUSTRY

In the early chapters of this book, it was shown that while by world standards, the volcanic islands of the Eastern Caribbean did not offer ideal physical conditions for large-scale banana cultivation, yet in each of the four islands studied, there was enough suitable land to make export banana production perfectly feasible. While the proportion of land appropriate for bananas varied somewhat from one island to another, the range of physical conditions was broadly similar in all four. Economic conditions did impose certain constraints, but left the way open for a substantial level of banana production in all the islands, and because the agrarian structures were sufficiently similar on three of the four islands, they did not offer a plausible alternative explanation for interisland land use differences.

After a detailed analysis of all the local factors that might have been responsible for regional variations in land use choices, I was led to the conclusion that while these local factors were often of considerable significance, they could not adequately explain why, in the French islands, banana cultivation was far more concentrated geographically than in their Commonwealth neighbours, nor why bananas were grown intensively in pure stands rather than extensively, in mixed cultivation. Local factors could not account for why bananas were grown mainly on medium and large holdings in the French islands, whereas in Dominica and St Lucia, a quarter to a third of production came from holdings of less than two hectares, and well over half from farms whose annual production was less than ten tons.

Since there were obvious differences in institutional structures and since there appeared to be no other factors that could have produced these major dissimilarities in the character of land use, the nature and effect of the involvement of banana growers' associations in various aspects of the banana industry were scrutinised, both qualitatively and, where possible, quantitatively. I concluded that by shifting resources from one group or class of farmers to another, it was possible for associations to make adjustments to production costs that might be of critical significance to marginal producers. Even more important was the role played by the associations in marketing their members' fruit. By ensuring - or failing to ensure - the sale of their export bananas at a price that did not expose farmers to the risk that the cash expenses required to put their fruit on the market might exceed their ultimate receipts, the associations could alter the whole land use pattern of their island.

So long as they had a 95 percent or better chance that their bananas would be sold, small farmers in Dominica and St Lucia were prepared to grow at least a few mats, even if the margin of profit was remarkably slender and the return on labour invested very low. Lacking other means of obtaining cash, they were able to rely on their growers' associations to accept almost any and every stem of bananas they could deliver and pay them immediately, or at least within a week. There was evidence that in the 1950s, before production by large growers and by franc-zone African producers rose to the point where there was a constant risk that supply might outstrip demand, many thousands of small farmers in Martinique and Guadeloupe also found it worthwhile to grow export bananas, the smallest relying on *ramasseurs,* the agents of the big grower-exporters, to buy their fruit for cash at the roadside. Once there was a possibility that the *ramasseurs* might fail to call, or might offer prices well below the cost of production, most of the really small growers dropped out of production for export.

While the associations in the French islands did intervene on their members' behalf to negotiate more advantageous conditions for ocean transport, they did nothing to shield growers from the daunting possibility that they might have to pay ocean freight costs on fruit that failed to find a buyer at the metropolitan port. Small growers with limited financial resources simply could not afford to take such a chance.

By the 1970s, even the banana growers' associations in the Commonwealth islands no longer guaranteed a market for all growers' fruit, and with a 30 to 40 percent rejection rate at the boxing centres, thousands of the most marginal small growers dropped out of production as they had done in the French islands a decade earlier.

In the French islands, elimination of the smallest growers, whose holdings tended to be located in the steep, mountainous interior, resulted in the concentration of banana cultivation in fairly compact zones on the more gently sloping areas, where properties were generally larger. In the Commonwealth islands, the growers who were eliminated in the wake of the introduction of centralised boxing were not necessarily the smallest, but they tended to be the most remote from roads.

While the survival of thousands of farmers in the banana industry of the Commonwealth islands depended on the policy of their associations regarding guaranteed markets, other forms of intervention by the associations were of more limited significance. Leafspot control financed by a common cess on production clearly represented a subsidy of high-rainfall and mixed-crop producers by low-rainfall and purestand producers. Fertiliser credit, while not necessarily subsidising any particular group, permitted sustained banana cultivation by farmers whose resources would otherwise have been inadequate for them to buy essential inputs, and these were mainly small farmers. Island-wide buying points also favoured the small and remote.

In the French islands, on the other hand, it was mainly larger growers who benefited from their associations' efforts to persuade the French government to ease the burden of indebtedness brought upon them by successive devastating hurricanes. Moreover, the target selling price established by negotiation between growers' associations, the French government, and those with importing and ripening facilities in France, was established with reference to production costs based on yields attainable only by farmers with fairly good land, operating on a fairly large scale. In the Commonwealth islands in 1966, WINBAN persuaded Geest to accept the break-even costs of the marginal small grower as the minimum price to be paid.

The associations, then, by influencing who might participate in the industry without fear of financial disaster, exercised a primary role in determining the location of banana production within each island. Their other interventions, while significant locally and affecting intensity of cultivation, were less critical in the majority of farmers' decisions to grow, or not grow, bananas. They were of an order of importance similar to such factors as the distance of a holding from a motorable road.

INSTITUTIONALLY INDUCED LAND USE MODIFICATIONS AND MEMBERSHIP PROFILES OF THE ASSOCIATIONS

According to whose interests are being served by an institution such as a banana growers' association, banana cultivation may be widely dispersed throughout an island, concentrated in a highland interior, or restricted to valleys and coastal lowlands. It may also be limited to zones close to feeder roads, or extend for miles into areas accessible only on foot. In the Commonwealth islands in the 1960s, thousands of growers, large and small, had, at least in theory, an equal voice in how their associations were run, and services were provided to all growers on an equal basis. In these islands, bananas were grown almost everywhere their cultivation was physically possible, and especially in the rugged, well-watered interior, sometimes as far as eight kilometres from the nearest road. In the French islands, large grower-exporters numbering a few dozen at most dominated the growers' associations, and there was a decline in banana cultivation in the rugged interior, while an increasing proportion of export bananas were grown on lowland areas where mechanisation was possible. Few bananas were grown more than a kilometre from the roadside. By failing to provide small farmers, whose holdings were mainly in more rugged areas, with the assurance that there would be a market for their crop, the associations made it inevitable that export banana cultivation would disappear from most of these areas.

This correspondence between the structure of growers' associations and the spatial distribution of banana cultivation that results from their activities emerges clearly in all the islands in the 1960s and appears to be confirmed by the modifications that occurred in the pattern of banana cultivation in St Lucia after the restructuring of the SLBGA in 1967. In Dominica, the relation of the evolution of land use patterns to the institutional structure becomes more problematical in the 1970s, since the structure of the DBGA did not change, but the centralised boxing system it instituted was similar to that introduced by the SLBGA. The changeover to boxing in Dominica was likewise attended by the abandonment of export banana production by thousands of marginal growers, especially those with holdings distant from the roadside. One possible reason for the decision of the DGBA is that the change to boxing was initiated earlier in St Lucia, and the DBGA may have felt unable to introduce a different system that might have been stigmatised as less modern. It must be borne in mind, moreover, that the board of the DBGA was at that period still controlled by large growers, and it may not have been reluctant to take advantage of a change in technology that might drive the most marginal growers out of production, since these might then become available to work on large estates.

Two different ways may be distinguished in which the spatial distribution of a particular form of land use may be affected by institutional policies: facilities may be provided or withdrawn in certain types of areas, such as dry, mountainous or remote areas; and marketing possibilities may be provided or denied to a whole class of growers, resulting indirectly in the expansion or contraction of the crop in question in those areas where that class of farmer predominates. In St Lucia and Dominica in the 1960s, nearly all farmers were banana growers, to a greater or lesser extent. In the 1970s, some farmers ceased to grow bananas and many erstwhile banana growers ceased to be farmers, and by 1982–83, Eguchi remarked on the increasing social polarisation between those with good land and those with poor (1984, 207). Accessibility rather than innate fertility was the primary criterion of "good" land.

Not only may the spatial distribution of a crop at a specific time be influenced by the character of those directing its growers' organisation; the stability of land use patterns over time may also be affected. Smallholders, many of whom do not even have a clear title to their holdings, are usually obliged to remain in situ and adapt themselves and their land to the changing demands imposed by the cultivation of their chosen crop. Large landowners, on the other hand, may sell land that no longer suits their requirements and buy or lease holdings elsewhere. Frequently, large landowners already had holdings in different districts with different physical characteristics. Thus, in Martinique and Guadeloupe, the pattern of banana distribution was quite volatile, and there was a major shift from elevated areas producing slow-growing, durable fruit to low areas of gently sloping mechanisable land.

In the 1960s, the already stable pattern established in the Commonwealth islands was reinforced by banana growers' association-run insurance schemes, which discouraged even rotation with other crops. By the 1980s, these schemes had lapsed, and while there was nothing as dramatic as the large-scale rotation of cane and bananas practised in northeast Guadeloupe in the early 1960s, or the rotation of bananas and pineapples in vast fields in northeast Martinique, Eguchi observed that on smallholdings, a rotation of bananas and ground provisions was not unusual (1984, 82).

There was also a major difference in the intensity of banana cultivation in the two sets of islands and a vast disparity in average yields per hectare, which arose largely from the prevalence of mixed cropping and low level of fertiliser use in the Commonwealth islands. While mixed cropping resulted from the cultural preferences of small farmers and low levels of fertiliser use from their lack of funds, the resultant pattern was reinforced by the banana growers' associations' willingness to provide comprehensive services such as leafspot control in ways that did not discriminate against farmers with low yields. In the French islands, banana cultivation could remain profitable for the dominant group of large planters only if they kept labour costs to a minimum. This required high-yielding purestand plantations, and they had no interest in providing subsidised services to growers who might have opted for less intensive styles of production.

As a rule in the Eastern Caribbean, growers' associations have been established to protect the interests of the growers of a particular crop, and if they have been really successful at doing that, it has often been at the expense of attempts to diversify and broaden the base of the agricultural economy. This has been especially so in Dominica and St Lucia, where by originally ensuring a guaranteed market for bananas for all growers, large and small, the DBGA and the SLBGA fostered such a momentum for this one crop that it became the automatic choice of any farmer desiring to enter the cash economy. Thus, over the past two decades, bananas have become even more dominant in the agricultural landscape, despite periodic initiatives aimed at diversification.

In the French islands, on the other hand, the banana growers' associations have been far less monolithic and all-embracing and consequently not so inhibiting. The small farmers who have been excluded from banana exporting have been obliged to seek alternative cash crops, while some of the large growers, conscious of the precarious future of Antillean bananas in Europe, have started experimenting with alternatives such as limes and avocadoes. Their established links with metropolitan fruit importers have doubtless facilitated this development, but in addition, GIPAM, although primarily an organisation run by and for banana growers, was also mandated to deal with other agricultural products and in 1988 was exporting limes and avocadoes.

Between 1975 and 1984, over 500 hectares of limes were established in Martinique. It was intended that limes would win over 20 percent of the French acid citrus market by displacing Mediterranean lemons (Martinique 1985, 33–5; Emélie 1988, personal communication; Pompignan 1988, personal communication). By contrast, in neighbouring Dominica, which in the 1960s had had over 1000 hectares of limes and had counted lime products as its second most important export, the lime industry was said to be in a state of decline from which recovery seemed doubtful. It is probably no coincidence that the initiative to branch into new crops was taken by GIPAM, a small organisation said to have attracted more of Martinique's younger growers and with a reputation for dynamism and flexibility, rather than by an old-established and more conservative organisation like SICABAM.

While positive correlations can be confirmed between the activities of growers' associations and their impact on land use, it is harder to test hypotheses about the effects of membership characteristics on the policies of an association. It is only to be expected that those in control will do their best to see that their own interests are promoted, or at least not compromised. One can anticipate, then, that an association dominated by large growers will have different priorities from one controlled by small growers, and indeed, there seems to be a good deal of circumstantial evidence for this assumption. On the other hand, it is not always possible for the decision makers to assess correctly what is in the best long-term interest of their confreres, and they may be inhibited for political reasons from adopting policies that could be seen as flagrantly self-interested.

Thus, while possible and even probable relationships may be identified between on the one hand the character of an institution's membership in terms of, say, wealth or age, and on the other, the location, stability, and intensity of various types of cultivation and the diversity of crops, irrefutable proof of such relationships is rarely forthcoming. Nevertheless, when associations controlled by large grower oligarchies routinely follow strikingly different policies from those whose directors depend on the votes of many thousands of small producers and when changes in the profile of those in control have been succeeded by radical changes in association policy, it would seem reasonable to put the onus of proof on those who would claim that this pattern was pure coincidence.

BANANA GROWERS' ASSOCIATIONS: IDEOLOGY OR PRAGMATISM?

The banding together of a group of producers of an agricultural commodity to protect or promote their own interests is largely a twentieth-century phenomenon. Before this century, it was unusual for farmers to engage in overseas commerce if the scale of their enterprise was too small to sustain the expense of protecting their own interests at long range. The emancipated slaves who became smallholders in the West Indies were involved mainly in the production of provision crops and fruits for their own subsistence, and any surpluses were sold in local markets. Those who produced cash crops such as cane or limes had no alternative but to sell them to local factories for processing before they could be exported.

The need for some sort of intermediary organisation seems to have arisen when products requiring little or no further processing beyond that carried out by the farmer began to be produced for export by growers who were too small to maintain any direct liaison with their distant markets. They were at the mercy of commercial intermediaries, and to ensure that they were not exploited, the formation of some form of co-operative association appeared to be a logical response. Even from the point of view of the buyer, there would have been some advantages in dealing directly with a single body representing all growers.

While the case for growers' organisations seems reasonable on all sides, writers about the development of such bodies have often seen sinister political implications in their establishment. For example, Bauer, writing in 1954, disapproved of the statutory produce marketing boards set up in British West Africa in the late 1940s, because he saw them as agents of state interference and state control in what he regarded as a perfectly satisfactory free-market system, with import-export merchant companies run by expatriates and employing commercial intermediaries to deal directly with farmers (Bauer 1954, 138,141,151–53). He did not see the stabilisation of producer prices as necessarily desirable, and he claimed that producers were paid below world prices so that in effect, the boards with their monopolies operated a form of taxation (138).

In the Caribbean context, however, it has been suggested the postwar development and expansion of banana cultivation in the Windward Islands was largely a calculated response on the part of the colonial administration and allied business interests to the threat to social peace posed by economic discontent and increasing trade union organisation and agitation (Thomson 1987, 4,5,28). Not only was the industry protected by special tariff and quota arrangements, but WINBAN, which was set up in 1958 ostensibly to represent growers' interests in negotiations with Geest, was in fact, according to Thomson, created as a stratagem to preserve British interests in the islands. While it was acting on behalf of growers, it was also bound to adopt a subservient attitude toward Geest, since the company might look elsewhere for supplies if its profits were not sustained (Thomson 1987, 35).

On the one hand, then, some commentators see any government action to channel the marketing of agricultural commodities through institutions in which producers are represented as an insidious introduction of socialist modes of economic organisation into Britain's colonial possessions, a policy for which they doubtless hold the Labour government of Clement Attlee to blame. On the other hand, there are those who see the fostering of such institutions as just a facet of an equally insidious attempt, presumably receiving its ideological impetus from Churchill's Conservative government of the early 1950s, to create "a collaborative class of petty capitalists" (Thomson 1987, 5).

The evidence that either of these forces inspired the genesis of growers' organisations in St Lucia and Dominica is weak. The banana growers' associations of the 1950s and 1960s appear to be greatly expanded models of the prewar prototypes that were set up initially by colonial governments to protect growers' interests in relation to the company that had a de facto monopoly on the purchase of the island's export bananas. While their constitutions permitted a very wide membership, it is unlikely that anyone anticipated in the early 1950s that within a decade the mass of peasant growers might not be content to leave control of the associations in the hands of a narrow group of prosperous and influential planters and professionals.

There is also no real reason to suppose that the British Labour government granted protection to Caribbean banana producers primarily to further the development of banana production as "a plausible vehicle for social stabilisation through the promotion of small-scale (as well as large-scale) private enterprise" (Thomson 1987, 4). It is much more likely that they simply wished to develop a non-dollar-area source of supply of a popular fruit of which the British public had been deprived since 1939. If this incidentally also provided a source of cash income to Caribbean peasant farmers, then that would undoubtedly have been regarded as a fringe benefit and one that was certainly in line with government policy that colonies ought to be self-financing (Hart 1982, 43).

Likewise in the French islands, while the government of the early 1960s encouraged the formation of a single growers' association in each island, there is no evidence that this was part of an attempt to promote either socialism or capitalism; it was first and foremost an attempt to get growers to respond in a coordinated fashion to the challenges posed by oversupply of the market; an attempt that in Guadeloupe was frustrated for several years by a conflict between rival groups of large growers over the location of the projected new docking facilities for the banana boats of the Compagnie Générale Transatlantique (Menauge 1974, 164).

A more ideologically inspired creation was the SICA, designed to protect the interests of small growers within the industry. SICAs were encouraged during the 1960s with administrative and technical support provided by the government. Any strong government commitment to either the all-island association or the small growers' cooperatives was, however, belied by its laissez-faire approach toward them, so that in Guadeloupe there was no single unified growers' association until four years after the agreement to share the French market on a quota basis, and the SICAs had to fight their own battles for a share of their island's quota, or even, when deliberately undermined by hostile exporters, for their very existence. The administration in the French islands was in any case limited in its ability to take action to address needs that were specifically Martiniquan or Guadeloupean by the fact that they had to operate within the constraints of legislation designed to apply to all regions of France.

If the origins of the growers' associations owed more to circumstances than to ideology, these bodies certainly did not remain free of political intervention or manipulation. By the 1960s, bananas had assumed such a dominant role in the economy of St Lucia and Dominica and employed such a large proportion of the population that the presence of the associations was in many ways more strongly felt than that of the government. In 1966–67, the SLBGA built a headquarters far more impressive than any government building. Elections were fought on the issue of whether governments should be empowered to exercise greater control over banana growers' associations, and politicians who had come to power on a platform of opposing government interference in growers' associations did not hesitate to pass sweeping legislation to curtail the powers of the associations when these were not in accord with the governing party's policies for restructuring the industry. In the 1960s, the alleged reluctance of foreign banks to extend credit to the SLBGA until it had carried out drastic "reforms" advocated by foreign management consultants with no expertise in the area of tropical agriculture was used by one government as a pretext for entirely restructuring its island association. A democratically run body operating in the interests of the majority of growers was replaced by one representative of a small minority, which had different priorities. In the event, members of the old board alerted public opinion to the potentially disastrous consequences of some of the proposed "reforms", and they were not fully implemented. Nevertheless, following this government intervention modifications were made in the industry's operations that had a lasting impact on the island's land use patterns.

In the 1980s, the United States Agency for International Development (USAID) offered funds to Dominica's government to help reorganise its banana industry along lines more consistent with a Reaganite view of free enterprise. Once the reorganisation had taken place, the new growers' company was to be privatised (Eguchi 1984, 192). The Prime Minister reportedly declared that there was "no room for politics in bananas" (quoted in Thomson 1987, 73). Although strong opposition forced the government to retreat from the full implementation of the plan, legislation was passed to put direct power over marketing and many other aspects of the banana industry in the hands of the government rather than the growers. As yet, however, government control has not resulted in the complete elimination of grower representation as has been the case in Ghana, for instance, where by 1973 the Ghana Cocoa Marketing Board had ceased to be solely a marketing agency and had become "an instrument of the government for purposes of national development and mobilising support for the party in power" (Arhin 1985, 49).

In Martinique and Guadeloupe, the political frame of reference was quite different. Banana growers formed a small proportion of the entire electorate, and in Guadeloupe, at least, they complained that the administration accorded more political weight to the cane industry. In any case, since export banana cultivation was dominated so overwhelmingly by larger growers, its institutions were an unlikely arena for conflict and rivalry between different classes of growers. Such internal conflicts as did occur were generally over technical issues and were attributed to differences of opinion between the young and dynamic and older, more conservative elements: the schism in SICABAM that led to the formation of GIPAM is a case in point. As Menauge makes clear, small growers in Guadeloupe were barely aware of the existence of ASSOBAG (1974, 169–70).

There was some friction between the administration and the growers' associations, but again, it usually concerned technicalities. In 1970, the French government set up a new organisation, Le Groupement d'Intérêt Economique Bananier (GIEB), to ensure the smoother operation of market supply mechanisms. All branches of the banana trade were to be represented. ASSOBAG refused initially to join, fearing that it would be at a disadvantage in quota allocations. They were to be determined with reference to current production levels, but Guadeloupe's production was temporarily depressed as a result of the passage of Hurricane Dorothy. The government, however, delayed making hurricane compensation payments to growers until ASSOBAG agreed to participate in GIEB (Menauge 1974, 172).

When changes did occur in both the constitutional structures and the spheres of operation of the French growers' associations, they were generally provoked either by an economic crisis, such as the threat posed by the projected removal of tariff barriers for bananas within the ECM, prices lagging behind rising production costs, or indebtedness arising from hurricane damage, or by a technological development that required greater cooperation between growers: coordinated leafspot control and containerisation are examples. Thus, while politics and ideology drove the Commonwealth banana growers' associations in the direction of the French models, circumstances and pragmatism set the French associations on a path of convergence with their Commonwealth counterparts.

In recent years, commentators on the Windwards banana industry have tended to characterise it as the perpetuation of a neocolonialist conspiracy, the conspirators being the United Kingdom and Eastern Caribbean governments, Geest, and the growers' associations. Their combined activities are alleged to have locked small farmers into the production of a low-priced export with a doubtful future, preventing them from diversifying and producing more food crops for local consumption (Demacque 1983, 108,110; Crang 1986, 40,59,86; Thomson 1987, 84–5; Simpson 1988, 6; Trouillot 1988, 144–5,149,157,160,295). Critics have also suggested that capitalist exploitation has diverted an undue proportion of the profits of the Windward banana industry into the hands of Geests. It is, however, extremely difficult to determine either the true amount of profit the company has made out of bananas over the years in relation to its investment, or indeed whether, given the risks of the banana trade and the alternative opportunities for investment that were available, this profit was really exorbitant. By manipulating the statistics, it would be quite easy to represent Geests as either robber barons or philanthropists. For instance, those fortunate enough to have owned or acquired Geest shares in 1986 when the company went public could in theory have made a 50 percent return on their investment twelve months later, although, presumably, if too many of them had attempted to sell their shares at that point, their market value would have rapidly declined. In 1990, on the other hand, shareholders had to be content with a far more modest return of about 10 percent (calculated as the increase in share value plus the dividend paid per share). This return was less than they would have received if they had left their money in the bank (Geest PLC 1990,1991,1992).

Another putative indicator of the degree to which third world producers are being exploited is the percentage of the final retail price of their produce that remains in the producing country and, in particular, in the hands of the grower. Thomson, quoting an admittedly rather antique source, suggested that world-wide, banana-exporting countries retained about eleven percent of the final retail price of their produce (Thomson 1987, 13, citing Ellis 1975). Simpson (1988), in the booklet *Whose Gold?*, published explicitly as a critical examination of Geest's involvement in the banana trade, gives a figure of 40 percent for the Windwards (16–18). From this figure one would presumably deduct the value of imported inputs, which would mean that a net sum of about 27 percent of the final retail price remained in the producing islands. Simpson's breakdown of the percentages of the retail price accruing to growers, associations, transporters, handlers, ripeners, packagers, distributors and retailers is based on estimates from Geest, but her percentages are in accord with figures I obtained in 1988. Moreover, despite the quite dissimilar structure and organisation of the French Antillean banana trade, the *wagon départ* price received for French bananas was close to the roughly comparable GWP price of Commonwealth Windwards bananas. A similar proportion was retained in the islands and a similar amount was spent per pound on imported inputs (fertilisers, pesticides, herbicides, and packing materials; see Table 9.7, above). So far as it is possible to judge, transatlantic freight rates appear to be slightly lower for Windwards than for French bananas.

In other words, while the returns to the average small grower for the fruits of his or her labour have certainly been rather modest, to attribute this primarily to exploitation by Geest and to suggest that the Windward banana growers' associations had connived in such exploitation reflects a somewhat unrealistic view of the modalities of conveying a perishable tropical crop to a temperate market. It seems gratuitous to charge growers' associations with excessive caution in negotiations with Geest when a miscalculation on their part could bring about the collapse of the industry. If the Windwards banana trade was so patently weighted in favour of its capitalist shareholders, it is surprising that island growers' associations did not commit themselves more heavily when Geest went public in

1986. The DBMC, for instance, purchased EC$84,000 worth of Geest shares; a conservative gesture of confidence in the industry by a corporation whose operations that year generated an increase in available funds of EC$5.2 million (DBMC 1987, 9–10).

Those who reproach WINBAN and the island growers' associations for their failure to secure a larger proportion of the retail price of bananas for the growers seldom make any reference to the predicament of Central American banana producers. Traditionally, the industries of "banana republics" such as Honduras were classic models of vertical integration, dominated by one or two huge companies that owned the plantations on which the fruit was grown, the ships in which it was transported, and the wholesale distribution facilities in North America. "Independent" ripeners could be discouraged from purchasing fruit from alternative sources by the threat that should the alternative sources falter, they would be denied access to any further company supplies, or that they might be the victims of protracted price wars that they could not hope to win. Needless to say, under this arrangement, the rewards yielded to those who actually laboured in the fields to grow the bananas were minimal. Moreover, it is doubtful whether they are any better off under the system that has succeeded it.

In the early 1960s, United Fruit and Standard Fruit began to divest themselves of their vast landholdings in Central America. Not only was there a risk of losing them to nationalisation in the wake of Cuban-style revolutions; it had also been determined that the companies could extract higher profits from the trade if the risks inherent in cultivation were born by local growers rather than the companies themselves. Under the new system, growers may be guaranteed a certain percentage of the purchase price, generally less than 25 percent (from which the expenses of cultivation must then be deducted), but they are not necessarily guaranteed a market. The buying company provides credit, technical advice, planting material, fertiliser, farm machinery, chemicals, aerial spraying, irrigation equipment, and plastic wrapping and boxes, often advancing the guaranteed percentage to farmers in the form of loans to enable them to pay for these items (Barry, Wood, and Preusch 1983, 17). This is a prescription for indebtedness, and ensures that the farmers' scope for any independent initiative is severely restricted. Growers' associations have no place in such a system.

Most critics have failed to explain why, if the cultivation of export bananas in the Windwards is so unrewarding, farmers have not abandoned it for more appropriate and less exploitative alternatives. Indeed, the critics are generally vague about what the alternatives might be. Under the circumstances, the stigmatization of banana growers' associations as capitalist pawns seems unconstructive. Until organisations with equal dynamism are set up to produce dependable and profitable market opportunities for alternative crops, putting the banana industry in jeopardy is a luxury the Windwards can ill afford.

INSTITUTIONAL STRUCTURES AND NATIONAL TRADITIONS

In the 1960s, it seemed reasonable to speculate that the differences in the growers' associations in the two sets of islands might stem from long-standing and deep-rooted cultural differences, and it was not hard to assemble evidence to support this theory. It seemed a valid generalisation, for instance, to say that the French administration favoured planning, with the application of specific, circumscribed solutions to specific problems, whereas the British preferred blanket solutions, and favoured schemes rather than plans.

Thus, for instance, in Guadeloupe in 1966 there was a plan for the development of the leeward coast that specified in detail, according to identified needs, how many hectares of land were to be irrigated in each valley and what crops or livestock were to be established there (France 1966, 294). In Dominica, however, when there had seemed to be a potential market for expanded citrus production in the early 1960s, the British government had simply allocated funds for a citrus development scheme that supplied free citrus plants of approved varieties and subsidised fertiliser to any farmers who met certain minimum conditions, no matter where they lived. Banana growers' associations in the Commonwealth islands operated on similar principles: they provided services on common terms to any farmer who wished to take advantage of them. In the French islands, however, services provided to banana growers by the government agency SATEC were focused on growers on the estates that had been bought and subdivided by the government in the execution of the planned *réforme foncière*.

A similar dichotomy could be discerned in approaches to market protection. In the early 1960s, Commonwealth bananas were protected in the United Kingdom market by a tariff of £7.10.0 on non-Commonwealth bananas and the exclusion of bananas from all dollar-area sources. France also had a tariff barrier for fruit originating outside the franc zone, but in 1962, when the market was threatened with oversupply, President de Gaulle stepped in and decreed a three-way division in specific percentages between Martinique, Guadeloupe and franc-zone African producers. All this seemed to epitomise the French tradition of *dirigisme* contrasted with the far less interventionist, more laissez-faire approach characteristic of British colonial policy: direct versus indirect rule, according to patterns distinguished in other spheres of French and British colonial influence, notably Africa (Whittlesey 1937, 371; Tanner 1965, 205).

Another cultural distinction commonly drawn between peoples of British and French colonial affiliation was that the former were far more cooperatively minded, being heirs to a tradition that began with the Rochdale Pioneers in 1844. The difficulties experienced in Guadeloupe in forming a single, all-embracing banana growers' association, and the problems in both islands with persuading small farmers to abide by the rules of their local SICAS, were ascribed by my French informants (with, it must be said, a note of self-satisfaction) to French *individualisme*.

Twenty years later, it is much harder to sustain one's faith in the enduring influence of two very different traditions and philosophies of government. Indeed it is questionable to what extent these traditions and philosophies have endured even in the countries that spawned them. The distinction between plans in the French islands and schemes in the Commonwealth ones has turned out to be a transitory political difference rather than an innate cultural one. In 1978, all-island schemes to expand certain crops gave way in Dominica to "zoned project benefits", so that only farmers with land above 1000 feet were able to get free coffee plants, while coconuts were restricted to farmers in the north and northeast and plantains to those in the southeast and east-central districts (Bully 1988, personal communication). In St Lucia, the Model Farms Project in the Roseau Valley has much in common with the SATEC-monitored subdivision of large estates under the *réforme foncière* of the 1960s in the French islands: farmers were carefully selected according to predetermined criteria; there were restrictions on the crops to be grown; and there was close supervision by technical personnel and an obligation to follow prescribed methods.

Conversely, a government-funded scheme administered by the Crédit Agricole in Martinique and Guadeloupe in 1988 to encourage young people to take up farming had certain maximum age and minimum acreage qualifications, but was otherwise open on an island-wide basis and was not prescriptive about crops or methods of cultivation.

While quotas and licensing arrangements carefully regulated by government still controlled the import of bananas into metropolitan France, by the 1970s the organisation of the United Kingdom market was very similar. Quotas were prescribed for Jamaican and Windwards fruit, and special licensing arrangements were required for importing fruit from elsewhere when necessary (Cairncross and Morris 1973).

If the distinction between national traditions and philosophies has proved more ephemeral than one might have predicted in 1966, it is still worth asking whether, given that they have changed, the changes have been reflected in the character and activities of island banana growers' associations. The answer is not clear-cut; certainly, in Guadeloupe and to a lesser extent in Martinique the provision of services on a common basis has been greatly expanded. In the Commonwealth islands, however, the principle of servicing all growers regardless of disparities in the cost of providing such services is still upheld, although there have recently been suggestions by officers of the associations that farmers in areas where rainfall is marginal for bananas should refrain from growing them.

So far as the tradition of cooperation is concerned, the stereotypes still persist. It is hard to conceive of a schism like the splitting of GIPAM from SICABAM occurring in St Lucia or Dominica. One suspects, however, that the difference is due not to the more individualistic tendencies of French farmers, but to the fact that legislation setting up and regulating the growers' associations in the Commonwealth islands ensured from the start that they would be all-embracing and left no room for individual initiatives that might undermine them.

While a structuralist dichotomy based on innate French and British characteristics cannot be fully sustained, there remains the question of the influence of interisland cultural differences of more local origin. Lowenthal, speaking of 'how shared perspectives of whole cultures incorporate the past', quotes Lynch's remark that 'the landscape in general serves as a vast mnemonic system for the retention of group history and ideals' (Lowenthal 1961, 260; quoting Lynch 1960, 126). In the 1960s, those who sought to account for the relative ease with which a single banana growers' organisation had been established and made to function effectively in Martinique, in contrast with Guadeloupe, believed that the explanation lay in the residual effects of events of the late eighteenth and early nineteenth centuries.

During the French Revolution, both islands were occupied by Britain. The British were, however, swiftly driven out of Guadeloupe by a Revolutionary force, and members of the island's long-established white Creole plantocracy either fled or were guillotined. In 6 years, their numbers fell from over 13,000 to just over 1,000 (Lasserre 1961, 287). In 1802, under Napoleon, slavery was reimposed and the scattered remnants of the old Guadeloupean plantocracy were authorised to return and reestablish themselves. Their experiences had demoralised them, however. The briefly liberated slaves were hard to control, and when the sugar industry entered a period of crisis in the 1850s, most of the planters went bankrupt and were bought out by large metropolitan sugar companies. Martinique, on the other hand, had remained in British hands until the Treaty of Amiens in 1802 (Pouquet 1960, 25), and its planter class survived unscathed. When the crisis finally came following emancipation in 1848, they managed, through mutual support, to hold onto their land and weather the storm. To this day they are said to be a closely knit community and the dominant economic force in the island.

It was to the chance preservation of Martinique's plantocracy in the late eighteenth century that commentators in the 1960s attributed SICABAM's cohesiveness, its elitist character, and the extent to which some of its members had carried vertical integration: some groups of large Martiniquan growers had interests in ripening facilities in the *métropole*. Guadeloupeans, it was maintained, lacked the resources or perhaps the impetus for such enterprise, and lacked the sense of solidarity that had facilitated SICABAM's success.

This may well have been a valid explanation, or it may have been no more than a post hoc rationalisation. Certainly, the differing histories of the two islands left a lasting imprint on their social and agrarian structures, and the cultural ambiance of each island was quite distinctive. Nevertheless, a much more detailed study of the differences between the two islands and their potential causes would be necessary before a fair assessment could be made of the residual effect of late eighteenth century history. In fact, the resilience of the Martiniquan plantocracy and its traditional power to command the loyalty of a work force with which its relationship was still somewhat paternalistic were cited in 1988 as reasons why Black Power agitation in the 1970s never acquired the momentum in Martinique that it did in St Lucia and Dominica, and did not lead to the break-up of many of Martinique's big estates. However, even though its social structure is dissimilar, Guadeloupe also came through the 1970s without much fragmentation of its large holdings. It is at least possible that this owed more to high wages and a French military presence than to lingering traditional loyalties.

THE LONG-TERM INFLUENCE OF INSTITUTIONAL STRUCTURES ON LAND USE

An analysis of the activities of Eastern Caribbean banana growers' associations over the past twenty or thirty years has demonstrated that they may be a significant factor in land use. By pursuing strategies that discriminate in favour of one class or type of farmer or another, according to the policies laid down by the majority of growers, an elite oligarchy, or the government, they can control who grows bananas, where, and by what methods. While they are not in a position to control droughts or hurricanes, arbitrary government decisions, or social upheavals, they may take steps to mitigate the impact of any of these factors; or they may take decisions that exacerbate their potential for harm.

To illustrate the last point: banana growers' associations may address the threat of drought in a variety of ways. They may take steps to discourage banana production in areas of marginal rainfall by withdrawing services from these areas; they may subsidise irrigation schemes in dry areas; they may arrange drought insurance; or by employing a system of equalisation payments so that no grower is disadvantaged by producing a crop at a season of low market prices, they may encourage farmers in drier areas to produce most of their fruit during the wettest months, and viceversa.

Whether such a manipulation of seasonal production would be practical is uncertain. It would require a high degree of centralised planning and might still be thwarted by the banana's unaccommodating vegetative cycle, which varies from nine to eighteen months, and tendency to grow extremely slowly during the winter months at higher altitudes and to produce a harvest mainly in the second half of the year (*La Bananeraie Guadeloupéenne* 1984, 7). Furthermore, any manipulation of harvest periods in different regions would have to be undertaken with the greatest caution, presumably only after extensive pilot studies. In Martinique, exhortations to time peak production to coincide with the period of high prices in the spring were so effective that they were counter-productive; they caused a glut on the market that brought prices down and necessitated the imposition of strict quotas on growers' exports (SICABAM 1988, 8–9).

Inappropriate decisions may be disastrous for the industry. For the past 20 years the associations, anxious to reduce expenditure on labour and chemical inputs to a minimum, have increasingly favoured intensive rather than extensive cultivation. In the French islands, where labour costs are extremely high, there may be no alternative to applying the techniques of agribusiness and constantly seeking remedies for the resultant environmental problems, such as the loss of organic matter from the soil. In the Commonwealth islands, the wisdom of encouraging ever greater intensification is at least open to question; both the social and the environmental consequences might prove beyond the resources of these small islands to repair. While it is true that in the 1960s some farmers planted bananas on precipitous, erodible slopes that were unfit for any kind of cultivation, there were many others, often with only a hectare or less, who together produced thousands of tons of bananas, in mixed cultivation with food and tree crops, using only moderate quantities of chemical inputs and leaving the soil cover intact and productive.

The introduction of new packaging and transport technologies is another area in which the associations may have a chance to exert a major influence on land use. In St Lucia, for instance, the changes from a dense network of wrapping-shed buying points to a much sparser network of boxing plants, and then to field packing in the 1980s, each produced changes in the land use patterns. At some future date, decisions may have to be taken about containerisation or the introduction of alternative methods of conserving fruit. Associations may influence the location of banana cultivation even more directly by subsidising or at least putting pressure on governments to finance the construction of aerial cableways, which are already in use in parts of Guadeloupe, to improve accessibility and handling in areas where ground communications are difficult.

Within the islands, then, banana growers' assocations may exercise a considerable influence on where the crop is grown. Outside, they may be instrumental in determining whether their islands continue to produce export bananas at all. It might have been supposed that when faced with the common threat posed by the impending full implementation of the Treaty of Rome in 1992, the associations of the French and Commonwealth islands would have been in full consultation to develop a common strategy that would ensure the survival of their industry. In 1988, however, there were no apparent signs of this, although as early as 1967, the managing director of SICABAM remarked that his association was hoping Britain would become a member of the EEC because this would mean that they could look to WINBAN as an ally in their campaign to ensure that Eastern Caribbean bananas were not driven out of the European marketplace by the United Fruit Company's cheap Central American fruit. During the 1970s and 1980s, the three successive conventions of Lomé assured Eastern Caribbean producers of a continuing share in the Western European market, but with the establishment of a European Single Market, the industry's very survival depends on the success of WINBAN and the French associations in convincing all parties involved in negotiations that their members' interests deserve exceptional consideration.

Hitherto, growers' associations have involved themselves to a greater or lesser degree in various aspects of production and in promoting their cause in intergovernmental deliberations, but they have not played a conspicuous role in the manipulation of demand. In 1965, the French each consumed an average of 8.8 kilograms of bananas annually, the British 7.3 kilograms, and the Swiss, Americans and Canadians between 9 and 10 kilograms (*La Banane* 1967, 2:29). Neither price-cutting nor increasing prosperity seemed to raise per capita consumption above 10 kilograms annually, so this was assumed to be the ceiling. It was supposed, in the optimistic ethos of the time, that as Britain and France became more prosperous, their consumption would rise to meet this ceiling.

In France, consumption did rise until 1974, when it reached a peak of 9.3 kilograms, but thereafter it declined, sinking to the 1960s level of 8 kilograms by 1985 (SICABAM 1988, 25). In Britain, 1966 was the peak year for banana imports, and twenty years later, the average Briton was consuming only 6.1 kilograms of bananas a year (DBMC 1987, 2). In the Windwards, I encountered no one who suggested that this might be a reflection on British prosperity. Some of my informants in both the French and Commonwealth islands blamed the decline in demand on the failure of the Lesser Antilles to put sufficiently attractive, high-quality fruit on the market; they suggested that metropolitan consumers had become more discriminating after shipments of Central American fruit had been let in when hurricane damage had decimated exports from the Eastern Caribbean. Others suggested that the banana might have an "image problem": it was perhaps perceived as a cheap, low-status fruit and was therefore spurned by the upwardly mobile, or those who wished to appear so. The problem with this explanation was that in North America, where bananas retail for half the British price and where the enhancement of one's socioeconomic status is generally regarded as a legitimate goal in life, the average citizen now consumes 11.2 kilograms of bananas annually (WINBAN 1987, 35).

In any case, while banana imports declined from 372,000 tons to 320,000 tons a year in Britain, and from 493,000 to 420,000 tonnes a year in France, it was not until 1987 that CEAB commissioned a serious study of the changing market situation (SICABAM 1988, 9). (CEAB, the Comité Economique Agricole Bananier des Antilles

Francaises, had succeeded the Comité National Bananier Antillais (CNBA) in 1969 as the coordinating body for SICABAM and ASSOBAG). Rapidly expanding production in the Windwards and the threat of surpluses in the United Kingdom market also alerted WINBAN to the need for a critical examination of policy issues regarding production, marketing, and risk management (WINBAN 1987, 1), but not, apparently, of the even more fundamental issue of why British people were eating fewer bananas.

It seems likely that the pressure of rising production will force growers' associations to seek ways of increasing demand. More aggressive promotion of their product would seem to be the most promising solution. It may be that in the past they have accepted too readily criticisms of the deteriorating quality of their fruit, which to me looked very much the same on the greengrocer's shelf in the 1970s and 1980s as it did in the 1960s. In Bermuda, which is a highly discriminating market, local bananas sold for US$1.15 a pound in 1988, while Central American bananas were 40¢ a pound cheaper. Consumers nevertheless preferred the local bananas, even though they were small and often heavily scarred. There is no obvious reason why a campaign to convince British consumers that the Windwards banana conceals superior contents within its homely exterior should not succeed. If the growers' associations do not fight for the survival of the Windwards banana, no one will, and then it can expect to share the fate of Cox's Orange Pippin before the inexorable advance of the Golden Delicious apple.

ANALYSIS, EXPLANATION, AND PREDICTION

When I embarked on the project of this book, in the heyday of 1960s positivism, I had a two-stage goal: to ascertain the nature of the relationships between the structure of growers' organisations and their impact on the landscape, and to determine whether these relationships were consistent enough to be used as a basis for prediction. Might it be possible to foretell, on the one hand, the type of policies likely to be pursued by an association that was controlled by a particular interest group, and, on the other, the results that such policies were likely to achieve on the ground?

By the time I was finishing the study in the late 1980s, realism was the order of the day. It was conceded that one could explain without presuming to predict, so long as explanations were compatible with reality (Bhaskar 1975; Sarre 1987; Sayer 1984).

Since the explanations first arrived at from areal comparisons in the 1960s were now being subjected to the more dispassionate test of time, it was perhaps just as well that predictability was no longer considered an essential concomitant of explanation.

When I made the original comparisons, explaining distinctive land use characteristics as functions of institutional structures was not, in the Eastern Caribbean context, incompatible with reality. Twenty years later, it was still fair to say that land use patterns had a discernable relationship with institutional structures, and in general, changes in land use were consistent with what one would have expected from changes in institutions. As for prediction, however, while past experience might permit one to forecast the general character and direction of land use changes that would be likely to result from certain mutations in institutional structures, hindsight has demonstrated that the goal of accurate prediction, in situations of this complexity, remains elusive.

While those who ignore history may be condemned to relive it, those who are familiar with the past recognise that it seldom, if ever, provides a precise blueprint for the future. Both circumstances and attitudes change. In the 1950s, for instance, a development with major implications for the future of agricultural land use in the Commonwealth Caribbean was the accelerating rate of emigration, which had it continued might have led to rural depopulation of the kind that has emptied entire villages in parts of the Iberian Peninsula (Welch 1968, 230). However, the Commonwealth Immigration Act of 1962 sharply limited the outflow. Political movements originating in North America in the mid-1960s spread to the West Indies, inspiring social unrest and a rejection of estate labour as a worthy way of earning a living, so that by the mid-1970s, many of the largest estates, even those that had once been held up as models of agronomic efficiency, had been rendered unworkable. On the other hand, the apostles of Black Power, while hostile to export agriculture, were strong advocates of a diet rich in green vegetables, which was not part of the Caribbean tradition, and they succeeded in bringing about a minor revolution in eating habits that has naturally had repercussions on land use patterns.

Attitudes change toward specific crops, and also toward farming in general. In the 1950s and early 1960s, banana cultivation was regarded as far less demeaning than work in the canefields. Sugar was associated with slavery, and the labour was gruelling, but only seasonal. By the 1970s, at least in the Commonwealth islands, sugar had generally ceased to be a focus of resentment, and in many eyes bananas had come to replace cane as the symbol of neocolonialist exploitation. Price levels that had been attractive to subsistence farmers earning a meagre income from the sale of surplus ground provisions appeared derisory to those who had become accustomed to selling bananas for two or three cents a pound more than their production costs. In the 1950s, bananas at four cents a pound were green gold; in 1966, to many, a waste of effort.

Farming in general had a poor image in the 1960s and 1970s, certainly so far as the young were concerned. For some years, the average age of farmers increased by a year annually; this despite rising levels of youth unemployment and few alternative prospects. In 1988, however, agriculture seemed to be acquiring a new aura of respectability and was said to be attracting a number of young recruits.

If human circumstances and attitudes in the Lesser Antilles have been less than consistent, there can be few parts of the world where nature has proved more capricious. Since the 1960s, the islands have had to contend with hurricanes, volcanic eruptions, and the rise of new diseases. In 1988, an unprecedented invasion of North African locusts was reported, giving rise to fears of a catastrophe of biblical dimensions. Fortunately, the locusts proved unequal to the stress of their transatlantic journey, and soon expired; but events such as these are not conducive to the development of reliable formulae for prediction.

In the Lesser Antilles, there is nothing that cannot be grown – but there is nothing that cannot be grown more cheaply somewhere else. The only resources are the land and the people, and to compensate for the deficiencies of the land, the people have evolved a variety of institutions. Without an understanding of the role these have played, it would be impossible to explain the present character of the landscape. As for the future, that may well depend upon the ingenuity with which the inhabitants of these islands devise ever more sophisticated mechanisms to confront the obstacles raised in their path by those often heartless adversaries, nature and the forces of world economics.

11 Postcript, 1995: Butter Mountain, Wine Lake, Banana Reef?

BANANA POLITICS 1988–95

Nineteen ninety-two, widely anticipated as Doomsday for the banana industries of the Eastern Caribbean, has come and gone. The bananas, for the most part, are still there: a feat of cliffhanging which should be an inpiration to others who see themselves destined to become the inevitable victims of the Juggernaut of Free Trade. In 1988, when the concluding chapter of this book was originally written, there were two views on the future of bananas in the Commonwealth Windwards. Diehard optimists put their faith in Prime Minister Margaret Thatcher's declaration of the previous year that the United Kingdom government would continue to fight hard to make sure that Commonwealth Caribbean bananas continued to enjoy preferential arrangements under the Lomé Convention agreements. Others, even if they did not question her sincerity, rated the chances of success extremely low. Despite fairly widespread pessimism, however, production was on the rise.

The United Kingdom had several potential allies among other members of the European Community who had similar concerns about their obligations to former colonies that had traditionally supplied them with tropical produce at above world market prices. However, the most forceful proponents of special dispensations for bananas were those countries with a significant production of the fruit within their national territories. For decades, Germany had been contesting France's claim that French bananas grown in Martinique and Guadeloupe were a "European" fruit. The expansion of the EEC to include Spain, Portugal, and Greece brought useful reinforcements to the French side, since they supplied their home markets with fruit from the Canary Islands, Madeira, the Azores, Crete, and even the Greek mainland, incontestably European.

Strong backing for the German position that there would be no place for concessionary arrangements for "traditional" banana suppliers in the post-1992 Single Market came from the major banana-exporting republics of Central America. Honduras and Costa Rica, low-cost producers with an enormous potential for expansion, were poised to sweep the Windwards producers from the British market. A belief in the inevitability of this outcome was fostered by American-based multinationals such as Chiquita (United Brands) and Dole, which had long supplied West Germany and the Benelux countries.

In March 1990, the United Kingdom government put forward a discussion paper containing proposals for the future of the banana trade. It was suggested that European imports of Latin American "dollar" bananas be limited to a quota set at recent levels, but with provision for moderate annual increases. "Dollar" imports would be controlled by licensing, and would be subject to a common customs tariff of 10 percent or higher, provided the tariff could be defended in GATT. EC and ACP producers would be paid transitional and degressive subsidies.

The response of the Caribbean Banana Exporters' Association (CBEA) to these proposals was that if adopted, they would represent a virtual death warrant for the Eastern Caribbean industry. Their effect would be to decrease traditional suppliers' income by over 40 percent for fruit sold in the United Kingdom market, while for that sold in the wider European market, returns would be less than a third of their current figure. No potential improvements in efficiency could compensate for such losses, and as soon as the less efficient growers had been forced to quit, overall volumes would decrease to a level at which freight costs would dramatically rise. Subsidies were an unappealing solution providing no long-term guarantees; trade was always preferable to aid, and if subsidies were to compensate for the full drop in producer income, an annual sum of £54 million would be required for the United Kingdom's traditional suppliers alone. All things considered, the CBEA felt that the proposals were neither within the spirit nor the letter of either the banana protocol of Lomé IV or Margaret Thatcher's commitment of 1987. The proposals had evidently been communicated to Brussels without adequate prior consultation with the CBEA, and were presumably formulated by civil servants who did not fully understand or support the government's official position of defending the status quo for its traditional suppliers (CBEA Memorandum 1990).

The submission of the United Kingdom discussion paper was followed by months of intense lobbying in the European Community on behalf of the Eastern Caribbean producers. Geest and WINBAN were active in Brussels, while Windward Islands prime ministers visited Britain to plead the cause of their industry. A particularly active campaign was waged by Dame Eugenia Charles of Dominica, who visited a number of European countries in March 1991. She put it to government officials that the collapse of banana exporting in the Windwards would lead to economic, social, and political chaos, and hinted that under such circumstances, the only viable alternative crops would be drugs (Patullo,1994).

In March 1991, the French government proposed a regime that would incorporate a system of price regulation as well as quotas. WINBAN regarded this as a more promising initiative (Patullo 1994), and the fact that it was opposed by Germany and the Latin American producers no doubt reflected their fear that it might actually prove effective in defending the interests of the traditional suppliers. Nevertheless, Chiquita continued to invest heavily in the expansion of its Central American banana business on the assumption that opposition to an unprotected Single Market would be overcome. Even Geest, committed to Windwards suppliers alone for four decades, acquired 3000 hectares of pastureland in Costa Rica and converted it to banana plantations; the rationale for this was to give the company a low cost production source with which to make inroads into the European market (Geest PLC 1991).

It was not until December 1992, only days before the long-heralded European Single Market was supposed to come into existence, that agreement was finally reached between Community agriculture ministers on the limitation of Latin American banana imports and the protection of African, Caribbean, and Community producers. Latin American fruit was to be subject to a tariff of 20 percent on 2 million tonnes a year, about 400,000 tonnes less than the then current levels. Additional imports would be subject to a 170 percent duty. Fruit from African and Caribbean suppliers would enter the Community duty-free in amounts based on recent import levels. It was anticipated that these measures would result in higher prices in Germany and lower prices in Britain. The new regime was to be introduced in July 1993, but it was intended that until then cheap bananas were still to be largely excluded from Britain (Narborough 1992).

The new arrangements were pushed through by an alliance of France, Britain, and Spain (Pettifer 1993). The Latin Americans regarded them as quite unacceptable and threatened to challenge their legality under GATT. On the other hand, Geest and the CBEA felt that the regime, as ratified, was barely adequate for the survival of the banana industries of the Caribbean exporting nations and that it was clearly in line with the legal obligations of Community members to ACP producers under the Lomé Convention. Geest and the CBEA felt it was essential that the agreed quotas and tariffs should not be eroded further in response to the "loud and sometimes hysterical publicity campaign" being orchestrated by certain interests (Geest PLC 1992).

The new regime was introduced on 1 July 1993; but in the preceding three-month period, market conditions were chaotic. Latin American bananas were flooding in and prices were low throughout the EC. There was a brief period of stable prices after 1 July, but in the fourth quarter prices fell again as a result of a serious oversupply. The licences allocated to import "dollar" bananas in this period raised the supply of bananas significantly above demand (Geest PLC 1993). Notwithstanding the hardships the new regime had already inflicted on the Windwards, the European Commission decided to offer to increase the quota of Latin American producers by an extra 100,000 tonnes in 1994 and by a further 200,000 tonnes in 1995 (James 1993). However, no agreement was reached on this offer, and it was withdrawn in February 1994 (Geest PLC 1993). Why the offer was made at all is not clear, since it had no market rationale and would only have made a bad situation worse for traditional suppliers. Presumably it was intended as a gesture of goodwill, but it certainly cut little ice with the Latin Americans, who pursued their appeal to GATT. They sought a declaration that the EC's banana Regulation violated GATT's prohibition of import quotas and of discrimination between GATT members.

In February 1994, a GATT panel published a report maintaining that the Lomé Convention was incompatible with GATT rules (Hargreaves 1994), but in June the advocate-general of the European Court of Justice rejected this view and concluded that the Regulation had been legally enacted (Van Schijndel 1994). Having failed to gain their point in the courts, opponents of the Regulation employed various other tactics to attempt to render it unworkable. There were numerous assertions in the German and Dutch press that because prices were 40 to 60 percent higher than they had been the previous year, banana consumption in Germany and the Netherlands had plummetted – a claim regarded with some scepticism by WINBAN officials (DeBeauville 1994, personal communication). In August, German officials promoted the introduction of absurd rules stipulating a minimum length and maximum angle of curvature for bananas entering the EC, rules that could only affect bananas of the varieties grown by ACP producers.

Notwithstanding these attempts to derail the Regulation, for the first eight months of 1994 it worked satisfactorily and provided adequate returns for traditional suppliers (Geest PLC 1994). On 16–17 September, however, tropical storm Debbie hit St Lucia, destroying 58 percent of the banana crop. Damage was also sustained in Martinique and St Vincent. Eastern Caribbean exporters anticipated that the shortfall could be met by a quota transfer, which would permit them to use their quota to ship bananas from elsewhere to the EC until their own production was fully recovered. This would have allowed them to defray fixed costs and keep regular customers supplied, and it was in fact the usual method of dealing with such a crisis. But as late as mid-November, the proposal of the banana management committee of the European Commission for a quota transfer for the islands was being blocked by the German commissioners (Hargreaves 1994).

It was not only the Germans and the Latin American producer countries that maintained a continuing hostility to the EC's banana regulation of 1993. Early in 1995, the United States trade representative Mickey Kantor, scourge of Canadian marketing boards during the NAFTA negotiations, attacked the EC's banana regime. He claimed that sales to Europe by Chiquita Brands International and other American companies producing bananas in Latin America had been cut by half, causing losses of hundreds of millions of dollars, at a minimum. Kantor threatened retaliatory measures against a host of European exports if the EC did not liberalise access for dollar bananas (Nash 1995).

INSTITUTIONS: THEIR ROLE AND EVOLUTION

In the political manoeuvring to secure the future of Commonwealth Eastern Caribbean producers in the European market, the growers' associations of individual islands delegated the responsibility of representing their interests on a day-to-day basis to WINBAN, which maintained lobbyists in Brussels. As a member of the CBEA, WINBAN worked closely with Geest, which by 1991 imported 55 percent of the bananas consumed in Britain.

Relations between either WINBAN or the CBEA and the French producers' associations appeared not to be particularly close. Although the French were clearly supportive of safeguards for "traditional" ACP suppliers, their first concern was for their own "European" bananas from Guadeloupe and Martinique. While bananas from these two islands were sold in the United Kingdom, Geest had never been able in practice to sell Commonwealth Windwards bananas in France, although substantial quantities were sold in Italy. The failure of the French to accept Windwards bananas engendered a certain lack of confidence on the part of WINBAN (Slipper 1991, personal communication; Geest PLC 1993; DeBeauville 1994, personal communication).

WINBAN's other functions included negotiating the contract with Geest and maintaining economic and research and development divisions. It did not purchase bulk inputs in the early 1990s, but it did try to encourage some degree of diversification. While export bananas were a priority, since without them there would be no regular shipping service, it was felt that farmers might take advantage of the weekly banana boats to ship exports of ripe plantain and grapefruit. WINBAN operated an insurance scheme, WINCROP, but like earlier insurance schemes this one did not appear to be entirely satisfactory. By 1994, when Debbie struck, many growers' premiums had lapsed, so that their losses were for the most part not covered (DeBeauville 1994, personal communication).

Individual island associations retained responsibility for determining how more than 50 percent of the receipts for their island's banana production should be spent. By their decisions on what types of pesticides and fertilisers to purchase, how to exercise quality control, what level of reserves to build up, or when and to what level to institute price support schemes, they obviously still exercised considerable power over the way in which the industry developed in their island. In the period leading up to the establishment of the Single Market, two imperatives dominated the rhetoric of the boards that determined association policy: the need for greater efficiency and the need to improve quality. Farmers were endlessly exhorted to improve the quality of their fruit while reducing the cost of its production.

Much of the pressure for improved quality came from Geest, which foresaw problems in disposing of fruit that was less than perfect in appearance once alternatives became available. To bring pressure to bear on growers to upgrade their fruit, it was suggested in 1991 by the operations manager of the Dominica Banana Marketing Corporation that the time had come for monetary incentives or disincentives to be incorporated in the price structure, both in the price paid by the shipper to the Corporation and by the Corporation to the grower (Didier 1991). In November 1993, a SLBGA press release announced a price differential to growers: in future, they would receive 31¢ a pound for grade A fruit, 28¢ for grade B, and 26¢ for grade C. Such a scheme has only recently become feasible with the development of more sophisticated measures for checking the condition of individual growers' fruit both before and after shipment. It is probably too soon to say what effect this initiative has had on patterns of cultivation in the islands.

While it is obviously not in the interests of the Windwards industries to deliver fruit that will prove unsaleable when it reaches the market, it is not clear that there is necessarily any close correlation between quality and "efficiency," which is generally taken to mean achieving maximum yields at minimum cost. The impetus for greater efficiency would seem to come from island boards; it was certainly a major preoccupation of the chairman of the DBMC. In August 1991, he declared that the continuing viability of the industry was dependent on the elimination of inefficiencies, which, in effect, meant the elimination of inefficient growers. It was the smallest, least productive growers, who were responsible for only 11 percent of production, who owed 60 percent of the DBMC's outstanding debt. Thirteen inland buying stations and six input stores were operated mainly for the benefit of this group, at a yearly cost of more than EC$1 million. Since all available data indicated that a yield of 10 tons per acre per year (25 tons per hectare) was the minimum required for a "positive contribution to the industry," it was suggested that it would make sense commercially to "consolidate the industry on this group of positive contributors" (Charles 1991). It was implied that the future should be with the 28 percent of those selling bananas in 1990 who had supplied 71 percent of the fruit purchased.

The emphasis on efficiency and productivity seems somewhat paradoxical, since the Windwards' main case for special treatment in the European marketplace has been based on recognition of the fact that no matter what efforts they made, physical constraints would ensure that they remained uncompetitive. On the other hand, Windwards associations may have felt that their chances of securing special dispensations would be improved if they could convince the European Commission that such expedients would only be temporary and would help to tide them over until they could implement whatever unspecified reforms would make them competitive. As a strategy for postponing the evil hour of a true European Single Market in bananas, this argument has a solid precedent in West Germany's requesting and obtaining deferral of the imposition of a common external tariff of 20 percent on its banana imports. The deferral lasted for more than thirty years after the signing of the Treaty of Rome.

It might have been supposed that if it really was the policy of the DBMC to eliminate its most marginal growers, it would have permitted a period of low prices to accomplish this goal in an unbiased way: it would simply have refrained from offering price supports. In October 1993, however, when the price paid to growers fell below what was considered the break-even point, the DBMC joined the growers' associations of St Lucia and St Vincent in subsidising prices. Farmers' riots in St Lucia may have convinced them that such a course of action would be prudent. Only in Grenada, where banana growers numbered a mere 600 (compared with a total of over 24,000 in the other three islands), was there no price support. In consequence of the large sums disbursed for price support, the three associations incurred heavy debts; indeed, by October 1994, the SLBGA was in receivership, although it was still operating normally. While production was down in the first half of 1994, there were no reports of a major exodus from the industry (DeBeauville 1994, personal communication).

WINBAN itself was destined to undergo major restructuring in 1994. It was reported in late 1993 that it would be dissolved and replaced by two new companies, both to be jointly owned by the four Windwards governments and private business. The company replacing WINBAN would have a subsidiary that would be responsible for procuring inputs at lower cost and carrying out technical operations and extension services to improve fruit quality. This development was being promoted by the Dominican Prime Minister, Dame Eugenia Charles, who was not in favour of statutory boards and believed that the restructured WINBAN would be able to operate on more commercial lines and to strike a better bargain in contract negotiations with exporters (James 1993). In October 1994, the transformation of WINBAN into a marketing agency was in progress, as were negotiations with Geest for a new contract (DeBeauville 1994, personal communication). It was not clear whether any rival shippers were anxious to compete for a share of the Windwards trade; Fyffes, the second-largest importer of bananas into the United Kingdom, drew its supplies mainly from Belize and Surinam.

JANUARY 1996

A decade after transforming itself from a private family firm to a PLC (p.251, above), Geest has quit the banana business - a startling development provoked by its recent failure to yield satisfactory profits. Price instability and widespread hurricane damage in the Windwards in 1994 and 1995 were contributory factors, but a further setback arose from a scheme to provide Geest with a source of low-cost bananas to supplement its Windwards supplies and give it the volume necessary to become a major player in continental European markets. In 1991 the company bought 3,400 hectares of land in Costa Rica, on which it hoped to produce 180,000 tons of bananas annually; but, due in part to an outbreak of Black Sigatoka, the project cost almost twice as much as envisaged.

By autumn 1995 Geest's board had decided to sell its troubled banana division. Talks were begun with an Ecuadorean group, NOBOA but, presumably to forestall the risk of becoming dependent on a company that could easily replace their fruit with its own, the four Windwards governments and the banana growers' associations backed WIBDECO (Windward Islands Banana Development and Exporting Company, the heir to WINBAN) in a joint bid with Fyffes to acquire Geest's Banana Division. On 8 January 1996 Fyffes and WIBDECO committed £147.5 million to become joint owners of Geest's shipping, handling, and ripening facilities - and a banana plantation in Costa Rica.

SUPPLY MANAGEMENT: LUXURY OR NECESSITY?

In the mid-1990s, Eastern Caribbean banana industries are going through a period of such turbulence that to assess the precise impact of their various institutional structures in the last few years would be an almost hopeless task. It is, however, probably safe to say that without these structures, the survival of the industries in any form would have been most unlikely. The 1993 Banana Regulation agreed upon by the European Community and banana-producing countries of Africa and the Caribbean is a vast enterprise of supply management on whose success or failure depend the patterns of land use, perhaps for decades to come, in several tropical countries with extremely fragile economies.

In a planet of limited dimensions with an ever-expanding population that even now is inadequately fed, it is hard to understand how anyone could oppose some degree of supply management when the alternative is a system of laissez-faire that results in thousands of tons of produce going to waste. Labour and valuable resources, often nonrenewable, are invested in crops that mature in the wrong place, at the wrong time, or in the wrong amounts.

A graphic, if small-scale example is provided by the hothouse tomato industry in Quebec, which supplied local consumers during the winter months when vine-ripened tomatoes brought slightly higher prices than Florida imports. Recently, an autumn hurricane destroyed the Florida tomato plantations, and farmers, anxious to recoup their losses, all replanted immediately. The following January, there was a glut of tomatoes, prices plummetted, and Quebec hothouse producers were obliged to sell their tomatoes for less than the cost of production. Clearly no one will derive any long-term benefit from this fiasco. Quebec dairy producers, who are protected by a marketing board, do not have to confront such uncertainties. If average consumers, who are also taxpayers, have to pay slightly more for these items than do their neighbours in the United States, at least they are spared the burden of supporting thousands of farmers who might be deprived of a livelihood by the natural forces of the marketplace.

The affluent consumers of Germany and the Benelux countries could well afford to pay a price for their bananas that would guarantee Eastern Caribbean farmers a fair return for their labour. With future markets secure, it is even possible that this region could specialise in, for instance, organically grown bananas for which a certain proportion of consumers would be prepared to pay premium prices. Surely this would be preferable to a situation in which Eastern Caribbean farmers live with the constant spectre of ruin, while off the coasts of Central America, huge quantities of bananas grown on speculation must periodically be dumped into the sea?

European folklore deals harshly with those who are ruthless to others less well-off than themselves. There is a story, doubtless apocryphal, of a once-thriving Dutch port whose burghers ordered that a cargo of grain should be dumped into the harbour rather than distributed to the starving poor. There it sprouted, causing the harbour to silt up and the port and its burghers to be ruined. Climate and a vegetative mode of reproduction render such an outcome improbable, even if cargoes of short, crooked bananas were dumped off Hamburg by order of Brussels Eurocrats. Nevertheless, failure to develop appropriate means of supply management has given the European Community the embarrassment of the Butter Mountain and the Wine Lake. If the banana trade is not managed with greater skill and forethought, these might soon be joined by the great Banana Reef.

APPENDIX

Questionnaire Used in Farm Survey, Dominica, St Lucia, Martinique and Guadeloupe, 1966–67 and 1970

QUESTION TOPICS

1 Land (holding size, tenure, etc.)
2 Crops and Methods of Cultivation
3 Livestock
4 Disposal and Marketing of Produce
5 Labour and Other Occupations
6 Credit and Financing
7 Cooperative Arrangements
8 Problems (including pests and diseases)
9 Influences in Decision Making
10 Attitude to Change and Future Plans

1 Land

a) How much is owned? rented? under various forms of tenure?
- area? (in hectares, acres or carrés)
- number of pieces?
- value?
- any rented out to other people? why? what for?
- how long has the farmer had each piece? who held it before?

b) Characteristics of each piece
- distance from home, from road, from nearest banana pick-up point in miles/kilometres and hours?
- what year did holding become accessible by motor road?

- elevation, aspect, ruggedness and slope, erosion, soil type, stoniness?
- drainage, contouring, ditches, fences, windbreaks, shade, irrigation, surface cover, other conservation measures?

c) How much is farmed?

- in cultivation? in pasture? in forest? unusable?
- how much land formerly cultivated is now abandoned?
- how much does the farmer intend to bring into cultivation?
- is there any rotation system? fallow?

2 Crops

a) Tree crops: e.g., bananas, coconuts, limes, cacao, grapefruit, oranges, coffee, bay, vanilla, spices (cinnamon, nutmegs, cloves), mangoes, pears, plantain, tamarinds, pawpaw, barbadeen)

(*i*) Bananas

- which year did farmer start growing bananas?
- why?
- where were plants obtained?
- how far from a road was farmer's holding when s/he started growing bananas?
- number of mats: bearing? plant mats?
- acreage: purestand? mixed?
- number of stems harvested/year (or week or fortnight)?
- peak production season?
- what proportion of mats throw bunches? how many underweights are left in the field? are any left because they cannot be carried out?
- average bunch weight? has it improved or declined lately?
- yields: last year? improving or declining?
- effect of hurricanes and wind: recently? in past?
- nematodes?
- where bananas were mixed with other crops: how many per acre/hectare of each?
- wrapping shed: where is the nearest shed? whose is it?

(*ii*) Other crops

- number?
- acreage: mixed? pure? when were they planted? expected bearing age? yield? density of trees per acre/hectare?
- were any crops recently cut out or abandoned? why?
- are yields improving or declining? variable or steady?
- methods of land preparation?
- cost of clearing? how is planting done? intercropping? source of plants? weeding, mulching, pruning, spraying, reaping?

(*iii*) Fertiliser and manure

- amount used? how often? where from? cost? how applied?

- participation in fertiliser credit scheme? terms of scheme?

b) Non-Tree crops: ground provisions, e.g., dasheen, tannia, yams, sweet potatoes, Irish potatoes, cassava, *tous-les-mois*; other vegetables, e.g., tomatoes, carrots, cabbage, cucumbers, pumpkin, eggplant, peas and beans, maize, lettuce; pineapples, cane, cotton, tobacco, ginger, flowers
- amount or number of holes or acreage? planting and reaping seasons? yields: variable or steady? improving or declining?
- how is planting done? land prepared? tillage? crop rotation? intercropping? source of seeds or plants? weeding? fertiliser?
- why did farmer choose these crops? any changes planned?

c) Grass or pasture
- khus-khus, pangola, etc.?

3 Livestock

a) Work animals
- kind? number? value? use? source?

b) Others
- kind? number? feeding? breeding? diseases? housing?

4 Marketing and Disposal of Produce

a) Disposal
- how much consumed by farmer and family? sold locally? sold to hucksters or in market of main town? for export?

b) Organisation
- individual selling?
- marketing boards or co-ops?
- agents in town?

c) Transport
- how are crops transported from field to market? how far? cost of trucking or bus fare?
- bananas: field to wrapping shed, how? how far to wrapping shed, buying-point or dealer?

d) Prices for different crops
- variable? with season or other conditions?
- bananas: price differential between dealer, buying-point, weighbridge? *ramasseur*, SICA, exporter?
- does farmer receive incentive bonus?

e) Losses
- proportion not sold? wasted? stolen?

5 Labour

a) Farmer's other occupations
- fishing? forestry? other?
- time devoted to each?
- percentage of income derived from each?

b) Labour investment
- how many hours per week on own land?
- how many hours per week on other people's land?

c) Labour employed
- family help: how much? how often?
- exchange groups? *coups-de-main*?
- paid labour: how many? how often? e.g., in a given week?
- extras for carrying bananas? other special jobs?
- is labour hard to get?
- has it got harder or easier lately?

d) Wages
- how much per day? per task?
- how many hours per week?

e) Technology
- use of weedicides? other machinery?

f) Personal
- has farmer ever been abroad? where?

6 Credit and Financing

a) Sources
- what sources of finance available? made use of? from banks, penny banks, credit unions, '*sou-sous*', other loans; subsidies, e.g., for ditching, development schemes; cheap plants; fertiliser credit; hurricane insurance; other insurances; remittances; savings from here or abroad?

b) Adequacy
- are these sources of finance enough?
- problems with finance? what would farmer do if he had more?

7 Cooperative Arrangements
- what co-ops exist? which ones does farmer belong to?
- what facilities do they offer? pros and cons?
- position in Banana Growers' Association?
- opinions of BGA?

8 Problems

a) Relating to land tenure
- family land? Crown land?

b) Pests and diseases
- nematodes? borers? leafspot? vanilla and tomato fungus, etc.? countermeasures?

c) Marketing
- gluts? transport difficulties?

d) Weather
- drought? hurricanes?

e) Insurance
- adequacy and speed of assessment? payment?

9 Influences in Decision Making
- how does farmer decide what crops to grow? where? how much? (e.g., parents'/wife's advice? children's advice? neighbours? large estates? agricultural officer? radio? newspapers? trial and error? seeing others?)
- influence of various schemes?
- where did farmer learn about farming?
- are there any local clubs?
- new techniques: awareness? where heard about?

10 Future Plans
- any changes? when? what? why? why not sooner?
- if prices dropped to a level at which a crop was barely profitable, would you stop growing it, or carry on in the hope prices would improve?

Table Q
Questionnaire response data, tabulated according to holding-size group

	Holding size (ha)					
	0–	*1–*	*5–*	*10–*	*20–*	*50+*
DOMINICA						
Number of holdings	4	35	17	6	4	4
Mean size of holdings (ha)	?	2.56	6.54	11.3	28.9	207.3
Mean percentage of holding area cultivated	most	80	58	54	30	15
Mean distance from road (m)	300	2,150	840	733	1,000	300
Mean annual banana production (tons)	3.6	13.8	30	53	30	101
Fertiliser used (tons per ha)	0.25	2.00	1.28	1.26	0.45	0.71
Mean yield (tons per ha)	4.5	6.7	7.9	8.7	3.5	3.2
Farms with other export crops (%)	50	94	94	100	100	100
Farms with food crops (%)	100	83	65	67	50	50
Farms with livestock (%)	75	54	29	67	75	100
Mean number of labourers employed	0	0.8	2.7	3.3	8.5	26.3
ST LUCIA						
Number of holdings	2	19	4	4	6	11
Mean size of holdings in (ha)	0.9	2.9	8.4	10.5	34.0	227.0
Mean percentage of holding area cultivated	most	78	90	90	40	50
Mean distance from road (m)	800	733	800	866	1,080	400
Mean annual banana production (tons)	5	22	115	89	113	1,854
Fertiliser used (tons per ha)	0.25	0.67	0.26	1.14	0.85	2.5
Mean yield (tons per ha)	5.5	9.7	15.2	9.4	8.3	16.3
Farms with other export crops (%)	100	100	100	100	100	100
Farms with food crops (%)	100	90	75	75	66	64
Farms with livestock (%)	50	74	25	75	100	73
Mean number of labourers employed	0	2	5	5	12	37

Table Q
Questionnaire response data, tabulated according to holding-size group *(Continued)*

	Holding size (ha)					
	0–	*1–*	*5–*	*10–*	*20–*	*50+*
MARTINIQUE						
Number of holdings	0	3	2	4	5	7
Mean size of holdings in (ha)	-	2.6	7	11	34	186
Mean percentage of holding area cultivated	-	100	60	59	61	19
Mean distance from road	-	most holdings on or near road				
Mean annual banana production (tonnes)	-	-	-	450	570	-
Fertiliser used (tonnes per ha)	-	-	-	3.75	2.70	3.00
Mean yield (tonnes per ha)	-	-	-	45	35	-
Farms with other export crops (%)	-	33	50	50	60	43
Farms with food crops (%)	-	67	100	75	60	57
Farms with livestock (%)	-	100	50	75	100	86
Mean number of labourers employed	-	<1	?	5	19	45
GUADELOUPE						
Number of holdings	1	8	5	4	1	3
Mean size of holdings in (ha)	0.5	2.3	7.3	14.4	28.0	175.0
Mean percentage of holding area cultivated	100	85	45	most	?	?
Mean distance from road		most holdings on or near road				
Mean annual banana production (tonnes)	-	5	150	475	-	?
Fertiliser used (tonnes per ha)	-	1.1	2.5	4.0	-	?
Mean yield (tonnes per ha)	-	10	25	33	-	40
Farms with other export crops (%)	0	100	40	50	?	67
Farms with food crops (%)	100	63	40	50	0	33
Farms with livestock (%)	0	50	60	50	?	67
Mean number of labourers employed	1	0	10	8	?	?

Bibliography

Acosta, Y., and J. Casimir. 1985. "Social Origins of the Counter-Plantation System in St Lucia." In *Rural Development in the Caribbean*, ed. P.I. Gomes, 34–59. London: C. Hurst and Co.

Andic, F.M., and S. Andic. 1965. *Fiscal Survey of the French Caribbean.* Special Study no. 2. San Juan: Institute of Caribbean Studies, University of Puerto Rico.

Arhin, K. 1985. "The Ghanaian Cocoa Marketing Board and the Farmer." In *Marketing Boards in Tropical Africa*, ed. K. Arhin, P. Hesp, and L. van der Laan, 37–52. London: Routledge and Kegan Paul.

Arhin, K., P. Hesp, and L. van der Laan, eds. 1985. *Marketing Boards in Tropical Africa.* London: Routledge and Kegan Paul.

Arthur, H.B., P. Houck, and G. Beckford. 1968. *Tropical Agribusiness: Structures and Adjustments.* Cambridge, MA: Graduate School of Business Administration, Harvard University.

Atkinson, H. 1967. "Speech by the Chairman of the SLBGA." *Voice of St Lucia*, 12 August.

Baker, P.L. 1994. *Centring the Periphery: Chaos, Order and the Ethnohistory of Dominica.* Montreal: McGill-Queen's University Press.

"Banana Growers and Marketing Cooperatives and Associations in Guadeloupe." 1964. Conference paper, Banana Demonstration Tour, Guadeloupe, 17–25 February.

Baptistide, J.C., and M. Etna. 1983. Le Sud basse-terrien (Guadeloupe): Approche géographique. *Cahiers d'Outre-Mer* no. 141: 49–74.

Barbados. The Secretariat, Council of Ministers. 1964. *The Oils and Fats Agreement, 1963–66, between the Governments of Barbados, British Gui-*

ana, Dominica, Grenada, Montserrat (withdrew 31.12.63), St Lucia, St Vincent, and Trinidad and Tobago. Barbados.

Barry, T., B. Wood, and D. Preusch. 1983. *Dollars and Dictators: A guide to Central America*. New York: Grove Press.

Bauer, P.T. 1954. "Origins of the Statutory Export Monopolies of West Africa." In *Markets, Market Control and Marketing Reform*, ed. P.T. Bauer, and B.S. Yamey, 138–155. London: Weidenfeld and Nicholson.

Bauer, P.T., and B.S. Yamey, eds. 1968. *Markets, Market Control and Marketing Reform*. London: Weidenfeld and Nicholson.

Beckford, G.L., and H. Brown. 1966. "The Prospects for Canada-West Indies Trade in Bananas." Paper prepared for a meeting of the heads of government of the Commonwealth West Indies, Barbados, June.

Benoist, J. 1972. *L'Archipel inachevé*. Montreal: Université de Montréal.

Bhaskar, R. 1975. *A Realist Theory of Science*. York, England: Leeds Books.

Biggs, H.C., C.J.M. Bennett, and R. Leach. 1964. *Report of the Commission into the Banana Industry of St Lucia, 1963*. Castries, St Lucia.

Blandford, D. 1979. "West African Marketing Boards." In *Agricultural Marketing Boards: An International Perspective*, ed. S. Hoos, 121–49. Cambridge, MA: Ballinger.

Burac, M. 1975. *L'Economie rurale dans le centre-nord de la Martinique (Marigot, Ste Marie, Gros Morne, Trinité): Contribution à l'étude de la crise d'une économie de plantation*. Bordeaux: Travaux et Documents de Géographie Tropicale, no. 21.

Burton, R.D.E. 1978. *Assimilation or Independence? Prospects for Martinique*. Occasional Monograph Series, no. 13. Montreal: Centre for Developing Area Studies.

Cairncross, F., and R. Morris. 1973. "Go to War on a Banana." *Observer* (London), 14 January.

Caribbean Banana Exporters' Association (CBEA). 1990. "Joint Response of the Caribbean Banana Exporters' Association and Their Marketing Partners to the United Kingdom Government Proposals on Common Arrangements for Bananas based on a European Quota for Dollar Source Imports." May, London, mimeographed.

Caswell, N. 1985. "Peasants, Peanuts and Politics: State Marketing in Senegal, 1966–1980." In *Marketing Boards in Tropical Africa*, ed. K. Arhin, P. Hesp, and L. van der Laan, 79–119. London: Routledge and Kegan Paul.

Champion, J. 1964. "The Use of High-Density Plantings in Banana Cultivations." Conference paper, Banana Demonstration Tour, 17–25 February, Guadeloupe.

Charles, V.J. 1991. "Protecting the Industry's Future." *Banana Business: Newsletter of the Dominica Banana Marketing Corporation*, August.

Chemin Dupontes, P. 1909. *Les Petites Antilles: Etude sur leur evolution économique*. Paris: Librairie Orientale et Américaine.

Colmet-Daage, F., and J. Gautheyrou. 1974. "Soil Associations on Volcanic Material in Tropical America, with Special Reference to Martinique and Guadeloupe." *Tropical Agriculture* 51:121–8.

Colmet-Daage, F., and P. Lagache. 1965. Charactéristiques de quelques groupes de sols dérivés des roches volcaniques aux Antilles Françaises. *Cahiers ORSTOM : Pédologie* 3(2):91–121.

Commonwealth Economic Committee. 1926. *Report of the Imperial Economic Committee on Marketing and Preparing for Market of Foodstuffs produced in the Overseas Parts of the Empire. Third Report : Fruit.* London: HMSO.

Cools-Lartigue, C. 1969. "The Banana Industry in Dominica: A Geographical Appraisal." B.A. thesis, University of the West Indies.

Crang, P. 1986. "Post-Plantation Agriculture and Landownership in the Cul-de-Sac and Roseau Valleys of St Lucia." Part II dissertation, Department of Geography, University of Cambridge.

Dardet, Victor. 1939. "Etude sur l'économie agricole des Antilles franç aises." Ph.D. diss., Université d'Aix, Marseille.

Demacque, D.J. 1983. "Bananas and the Eastern Caribbean." War on Want, London. Typescript.

Didier, M. 1991. "An Examination of Fruit Quality Control in the Banana Industry." *Banana Business: Newsletter of the Dominica Banana Marketing Corporation*, August.

Doeuff, D. 1968. *La Réforme Foncière dans les départements d'outre mer: Bilan de la période 1958–1968.* Paris: Ministère d'Etat, Départements et Térritoires d'Outre-Mer; Secretariat Général des Départements d'Outre-Mer, Service des Affaires Economiques et des Investissements.

Dominica Banana Growers' Association (DBGA). 1964. "Agreement for Sale of Bananas between the Dominica Banana Growers' Association and Geest Industries (WI) Ltd."

– 1966. *Annual Report and Accounts for 1965.* Roseau, Dominica: DBGA

– 1969. *Annual Report and Accounts for 1968.* Roseau, Dominica and Barbados: DBGA

– 1969. "Introduction of Legislation Providing for Local Banana Insurance Scheme : Chronology of Preceding Events." Mimeographed.

Dominica Banana Marketing Corporation (DBMC). 1986. *Annual Report and Accounts, 1985.* Roseau, Dominica: DBMC.

– 1987. *Annual Report and Accounts, 1986.* Roseau, Dominica: DBMC.

– 1988. "List of Growers Classified by District, Poundage Sold in 1987, and Acreage." DBMC, Roseau, Dominica. Computer printout.

Dominica Census. 1971. Census Tables: Land Use, Tenure, Production. Photocopied typescript, Government of Dominica, Roseau.

Dominica. Colony of Dominica. 1934–59. *Annual Reports, Department of Agriculture.* Roseau, Dominica. Various years.

- Colony of Dominica. 1953-9. *Overseas Trade Reports*. Various years. Castries, St Lucia: Voice Publishing Company Ltd.
- Commonwealth of Dominica. 1984a. *Dominica Banana Marketing Corporation Act. Act 11 of 1984, Official Gazette*: 71–82.
- Commonwealth of Dominica. 1984b. *Dominica Banana Marketing Corporation Act. Act 12 of 1984, Official Gazette*: 83–92.
- Government of Dominica. 1960. *Development Programme, 1959–1964*. Castries, St Lucia: Voice Publishing Company, Ltd.
- Government of Dominica. 1969. *Dominica Banana Industry Insurance Act. Official Gazette.*
- Ministry of Trade and Industry. 1968. *CARIFTA: Protocol Laying Down Agricultural Marketing Arrangements Mentioned in Article 13 of the Agreement for the Establishment of the Caribbean Free Trade Association.* Roseau, Dominica: Ministry of Trade and Industry.
- State of Dominica. 1968. *Annual Overseas Trade Report, 1967*. Roseau, Dominica: Ministry of Finance.
- Treasury Department. 1960-65. *Annual Overseas Trade Reports*. Castries, St Lucia: Voice Publishing Company Ltd.

Durand, A. 1964. "Speech of the Director of Agricultural Services of Guadeloupe." Opening session of the Banana Demonstration Tour, Guadeloupe, February. Translation.

Edwards, D. 1961. *An Economic Study of Small Farming in Jamaica*. Mona, Jamaica: University of the West Indies, Institute of Social and Economic Research.

Eguchi, N. 1984. "Relative Wealth and Adaptive Strategy among Peasants in a Small Village Community of Dominica, West Indies. Ph.D. diss., University of North Carolina at Chapel Hill.

Ellis, F. 1975. An Institutional Approach to Tropical Commodity Trade: Case Study of Banana Exports from the Commonwealth Caribbean. Report for the Commonwealth Secretariat, Mimeographed.

Engledow, F.L. 1945. *Report on Agriculture, Forestry, Fisheries and Veterinary Matters*. West India Royal Commission, Cmnd. 6608. London, HMSO.

European Economic Community (EEC). "Council Regulation No. 404/93 of 13 February 1992 On the Common Organization of the Market in Bananas." *Official Journal of the European Communities* 25: (February).

Farrugia, L. 1977. *Soufrière 76*. Guadeloupe: Jeunes Antilles.

Fentem, A.D. 1960. *Commercial Geography of Dominica*. Technical Report no. 5. Bloomington, IN: Department of Geography, Indiana University.

Finkel, H.J. 1964. "Patterns of Land Tenure in the Leeward and Windward Islands and Their Relevance to Problems of Agricultural Development in the West Indies." *Economic Geography* 40: 163–172.

Food and Agriculture Organisation (FAO). 1986. *The World Banana Econ-*

omy, 1970–84: Structure, Performance and Prospects. FAO Economic and Social Development Paper no. 57. Rome: FAO Commodities and Trade Division.

Frampton, A. de K. 1952. *The Agricultural Development of St Lucia.* Bridgetown, Barbados.

France. Commissariat Général du Plan de l'Equipement et de la Productivité. 1959. *Rapport Général de la Commission de Modernisation et d'Equipement des Départements d'Outre-Mer (Guadeloupe, Guyane, Martinique, Réunion). Troisième Plan, 1958–61.* Paris: Imprimerie Nationale.

– Commissariat Général du Plan de l'Equipement et de la Productivité. 1966. *Rapport Général de la Commission Centrale des Départements d'Outre-Mer. Ve Plan, 1966–1970.* Paris: La Documentation Française.

– Département de la Martinique. 1958. *Plan d'equipement économique et social; bilan des investissements réalisés au cours de la période 1946–56; nouveau programme 1957–61.* Paris.

– Institut National de la Statistique et des Etudes Economiques. 1961. *Annuaires statistiques de la Guadeloupe et la Guyane, 1957–9.* Paris: Imprimerie Nationale.

– Institut National de la Statistique et des Etudes Economiques. 1967. *Statistiques du commerce extérieur des Départements d'Outre-Mer en 1966.* Paris: Imprimerie Nationale.

– Secretariat d'Etat aux Départements et Territoires d'Outre-Mer. 1986. *Cinq ans d'action pour l'outre-mer (Guadeloupe).* Paris.

Geest Industries. 1987. "Banana Exports from the Windward Islands and Jamaica, 1965–86, and estimated figures for 1987." Castries, St Lucia. Duplicated.

Geest PLC. 1989–93. *Annual Reports.* Spalding, England.

– 1994. *Interim Report.* Spalding, England.

Groupement d'Intérêt des Producteurs Agricoles de la Martinique (GIPAM). 1987a. "Data on Membership Structure." Manuscript, 1987.

– 1987b. "Prix de revient, bananes, 01/10/87." Mimeographed.

Graham, S. 1970. Le Lareinty: Un cas de réforme foncière. M.A. thesis, Université de Montréal.

Guadeloupe. 1964. "Banana Growers and Marketing Co-operatives and Associations in Guadeloupe." Banana Demonstration Tour, Guadeloupe.

– Département de la Guadeloupe. 1965. Commission Locale du Ve plan, Sous-Commission: Agriculture-Pêche-Forêts, Groupes de Travail. *Cultures traditionnelles, bananes; cultures vivrières et maraîchères; elevage; cultures complémentaires.*

– Département de la Guadeloupe. 1987. *Enquête utilisation du territoire: Résultats des enquêtes menées de 1985 à 1987.* Ministère de l'Agriculture, Direction de l'Agriculture et de la Forêt de la Guadeloupe, Service de Statistique Agricole, Basse-Terre.

- Direction Départementale de l'Agriculture. 1966. *Etude préliminaire de la Côte sous le Vent. Rapport.* Service de l'Aménagement Hydraulique, Forestier et Foncier, Basse-Terre.

Guérin, D. 1956. *Les Antilles décolonisées.* Paris: Présence Africaine.

Guye, A. 1966. "Field Days Held at the Banana Demonstration Plots." WINBAN *News,* April–June.

Hägerstrand, T. 1967. *Innovation Diffusion as a Spatial Process.* Translation and postscript by Allan Pred. Chicago: University of Chicago Press.

Haliar, A. 1965. *Dans les départements d'outre-mer: du Colbertisme au Gaullisme.* Paris: Soulanges.

Hargreaves, D. 1994. "Caribbean Slips up over EU's Banana Regime." *Financial Times* (London), 6 February.

- 1994. "Windwards Impatient over Delay to EU banana deal." *Financial Times* (London), 10 November.

Harrison, A.R. 1965. "The Transition from Sugar to Banana Growing in St Lucia, 1950–1964." Honours Essay, Cambridge University.

Hart, K. 1982. *The Political Economy of West African Agriculture.* Cambridge: Cambridge University Press.

Hoy, D.R. 1961. *Agricultural Land Use of Guadeloupe.* National Research Council Publication no. 884. Washington, DC: National Academy of Sciences.

- 1962. "The banana industry of Guadeloupe." *Social and Economic Studies* 11: 260–6.

Institut Français de Recherches Fruitières Outre-Mer (IFAC). 1965. *Rapport annuel, 1963–1964.* Paris: IFAC.

Institut de Recherches des Fruits et Agrumes (IRFA). 1987. *Guadeloupe: Rapport Annuel, 1986.* Guadeloupe: IRFA.

- 1987. "Prix de revient: bananes, 1/9/87." IRFA, Guadeloupe. Mimeographed.

Institute of Social and Economic Research (ISER). 1964. *An Abstract of Statistics of the Leeward Islands, Windward Islands, and Barbados.* Barbados: ISER (Eastern Caribbean), University of the West Indies.

Jamaican Weekly Gleaner. 1971. "The Secret Banana War," 10 February. Reprinted from *The Sunday Times* (London), 10 January, 1971.

James, C. 1993. "Windwards to Restructure Banana Industry." *Financial Times* (London), 31 December.

Jesse, C. 1956. *Outlines of St Lucia's History.* Castries, St Lucia Archaeological and Historical Society, 2d edition, 1963.

Jordan, P. 1985. *Schistosomiasis: The St Lucia Project.* Cambridge: Cambridge University Press.

Joubert, L. 1948. "Les conséquences géographiques de l'émancipation des noirs aux Antilles (1848)." *Cahiers d'Outre-Mer* 1: 105–18.

Kervégant, D. 1935. *Le bananier et son exploitation.* Paris: Société d'Education Géographique.

Kopp, A. 1929. "L'Agriculture à la Guadeloupe." *Annales de Géographie* 38: 480–500.

La Banane. 1967. Pt. 1, *Production de la France et de la Zone Franc; Le Marché français*; Pt. 2, *Le Marché Commun*. Paris: Le Service des Affaires Economiques et Investissements du Sécretariat Général aux Départements d'Outre-Mer, Ministère d'Etat Chargé des Départements et Territoires d'Outre-Mer.

La Bananeraie Guadeloupéenne. 1984. Paris: Editions Bres.

Lang, D.M. 1967. *Soil and Land Use Surveys*. No. 21, Dominica. Regional Research Centre, University of the West Indies, St Augustine, Trinidad.

Lasserre, G. 1961. *La Guadeloupe*. 2 vols. Bordeaux: Union Française d'Impression.

Leiris, M. 1955. *Contacts et civilisations en Martinique et en Guadeloupe*. Paris: UNESCO.

Loubat, B., and A. Pistolesi-Lafont. 1977. *La Soufrière. A qui la faute?* Paris: Presses de la Cité.

Lowenthal, D., ed. 1961. *The West Indies Federation*. New York: Columbia University Press.

Luu, P. 1985. *Etude de fonctionnement de quelques exploitations agricoles de Ste Lucie (West Indies) et essai de Typologie*. Paris: Institut National Agronomique, Paris-Grignon and Centre National d'Etudes Agronomiques des Régions Chaudes, Montpellier, France.

Lynch, K. 1960. *Image of the City*. Cambridge, MA: MIT Press.

McFarlane, D. 1964. "The Future of the Banana Industry in the West Indies. *Social and Economic Studies* 13(1):38–93.

McQuillan, D.A. 1968. "Estate Production and Transportation, Dominica." M.A. thesis, University of Alberta, Edmonton.

Maguire, R.E. 1975. "Coast or Interior? Changing Perceptions of Land Use in Dominica, WI, 1870:1970." M.A. thesis, University of Florida, Gainesville.

Marie, J.M. 1979. *Agricultural Diversification in a Small Economy: The Case for Dominica*. Occasional Papers, no. 10. Barbados: ISER.

Marieu, J. 1966. "La canne à sucre en Martinique." Typescript.

Marsh, James. 1988. "Saskatchewan Wheat Pool." In *The Canadian Encyclopedia*, 1939. Edmonton: Hurtig.

Martinique. 1956. *Plan d'équipement économique et social: Bilan des investissements réalisés au cours de la période 1946–1956; Nouveau programme, 1957–1961*. Fort-de-France: Département de la Martinique.

- 1961. *Plan d'équipement économique et social: Programme Quadriennal 1962–65 (IVe Plan)*. Fort-de-France, Martinique: Département de la Martinique.

- (Préfecture). 1964. *La Martinique*. Fort-de-France: Préfecture de la Martinique..

- 1965. *Vème Plan 1966–1970*. Vol. 1, *Rapport Général*; vol. 3, *Sous-*

Commission Agriculture, Pêche et Forêts; vol. 7, *Sous-Commission des Problèmes Démographiques et de l'Emploi*. Fort-de-France, Martinique: Département de la Martinique.

- 1965-66. *Bulletin de statistiques.*
- 1966. *Plan d'équipement économique et social: Bilan des investissements réalisés au titre du IIIe Plan Quadriennal, 1958-1961*. Fort-de-France, Martinique: Département de la Martinique.
- 1985. Direction Départementale des Services Agricoles. *Bilan de l'Agriculture Martiniquaise*. Fort-de-France, Martinique: Département de la Martinique.

Mathurin, D.C.E. 1967. "An Unfavourable System of Land Tenure: The Case of St Lucia, WI." Paper presented at the Second West Indies Agricultural Economics Conference, University of the West Indies, St Augustine, Trinidad, April. Typescript.

Menauge, J. 1974. *Planteurs et plantations de banane en Guadeloupe*. Travaux et Documents de Géographie Tropicale. Bordeaux: CNRS.

Mitchell, H. 1963. *Europe in the Caribbean: The Policies of Great Britain, France and the Netherlands towards Their West Indian Territories in the Twentieth Century*. London: Chambers

Momsen, J.D. 1969. *Report on a Banana Acreage Survey of the Windward Islands (1965-6)*. London: Ministry of Overseas Development.

- 1970. "The Geography of Land Use and Population in the Caribbean, with special reference to Barbados and the Windward Islands." Ph.D. diss., University of London.

Morgan, D.J. 1962. "Imperial Preference in the West Indies, 1929-1955." *Economic Journal* 72: 104-33.

Narbrough, C. 1992. "European Import Deal Zips up Great Banana Split." *Times* (London), 19 December.

Nash, N. 1995. "Banana Follies." *Montreal Gazette*, 4 February.

Nicholls, H.A.A. 1890. *The Cultivation of the Banana in Dominica*. Roseau, Dominica.

Office de la Recherche Scientifique et Technique Outre-Mer (ORSTOM). 1965. "La Guadeloupe." Mimeographed.

O'Loughlin, C. 1963. *A Survey of the Economic Potential and Capital Needs of the Leeward Islands, Windward Islands, and Barbados*. Department of Technical Co-operation Overseas Research Publication, no. 5. London: HMSO.

Organization of American States. (OAS. General Secretariat. 1984. *St. Lucia Development Atlas*. Washington, D.C.: Executive Secretariat for Economic and Social Affairs, Department of Regional Development, OAS.

Patullo, P. 1991. "West Indies Fear Banana Warfare." *Guardian* (London), 18 March.

Perryman, D.A. 1964. "Insurance of Bananas Against Wind Hazards." Conference paper, Banana Demonstration Tour, Guadeloupe, 17–25 February.

Persaud, B. 1965. *A Banana-Costing Survey in St Lucia: The First Report.* Agricultural Series no. 2. Barbados: ISER, University of the West Indies (Eastern Caribbean).

– 1966. *An Abstract of West Indian Banana Statistics, with Special Reference to the Windward Islands.* Barbados: ISER, University of the West Indies (Eastern Caribbean).

– 1967. *The Second Banana Costing Survey in St Lucia.* Agricultural Series, no. 5. Barbados: ISER, University of the West Indies (Eastern Caribbean).

Persaud, B., O. de Barry, P. Haynes, F.R. Hore, E. Mathurin, and E.R. Ward. 1966. *Enquiry into the Feasibility of Re-introducing the Sugar Industry in St Lucia.* Barbados: ISER, University of the West Indies (Eastern Caribbean).

Pettifer, J. 1993. "Going Bananas." *Guardian* (London), 23 March.

Pouquet, J. 1960. *Les Antilles françaises.* 2d ed. Paris: Presses Universitaires de France.

Présence Socialiste. 1963. "Les problèmes soulevés par la surproduction de la banane illustrent l'échec de l'économie agricole en régime colonialiste." (Fort-de-France, Martinique,) 30 September.

Reading, A. 1989. *An Integrated Approach to Rural Production: A Case Study for Dominica, WI.* Geographical Papers no. 101. Reading, England: University of Reading.

Revert, E. 1948. "L'Economie Martiniquaise." *Cahiers d'Outre-Mer* 1: 28–39.

– 1949. *La Martinique.* Paris: Nouvelles Editions Latines.

Robelin, M. and F. Colmet-Daage. 1957. "Aperçu sur les sols de la Guadeloupe." *Bulletin de l'Association Française pour l'Etude des Sols* 88: 785–9.

Robinson, W.A. 1969. "Land Tenure in the British Eastern Caribbean." M.A. thesis, University of Michigan, Ann Arbor.

Romalis, R.S. 1968. "The Rural Community and the Total Society during Economic Change in St Lucia: A Case Study." Ph.D. diss., McGill University, Montreal.

Sable, V. 1955. *La Transformation des isles d'Amérique en départements français.* Paris: Editions Larose.

St Lucia Banana Growers' Association, (SLBGA). 1953. "Memorandum and Articles of Association of the St Lucia Banana Growers' Association Limited." Castries, St Lucia. Mimeographed.

– 1964. *Agreement for the Sale of Bananas between the St Lucia Banana Growers' Association and Geest Industries Limited and Geest Industries (WI) Ltd.* Castries, St Lucia.

- 1966a. "Memorandum by the St Lucia Banana Growers' Association Limited, Prepared for the Economic Tripartite Commission." Castries, St Lucia. Mimeographed.
- 1966b. *Banana Export Figures, 1949–1965*. Castries, St Lucia: SLBGA.
- 1987a "List of Growers, Active and Non-Active, by District, End December 1986, with Production Totals for 1984, 1985, and 1986." SLBGA, Castries, St. Lucia. Computer printout.
- 1987b "List of Numbers of Large, Medium, Small and Eligible Growers, by District, 1986." SLBGA, Castries, St. Lucia. Computer printout.

St Lucia. 1967. *St Lucia Banana Growers' Association Act. No. 6 of 1967. Ordinances, Acts, Statutory Rules and Orders*, 1967: 49–79.
- 1979. *SLBGA (Amendment) Act. No. 13 of 1979. Acts and Statutory Instruments*, 1979, 285–7.
- Development Bank. 1986. "Production Costs for the Average Farmer, 16/4/86." Mimeographed.
- Ministry of Agriculture, Lands, Fisheries, and Co-operatives. 1987. *Final Report on the 1986 Census of Agriculture in St Lucia*. Castries, St Lucia.

Sarre, P. 1987. "Realism in Practice." *Area* 19: 3–10.

Sayer, R.A. 1984. *Method in Social Science: A Realist Approach*. London: Hutchinson.

Schaefer, F.K. 1953. "Exceptionalism in Geography: A Methodological Examination." *Annals of the Association of American Geographers* 43: 226–49.

Serbin, A. 1990. *Caribbean Geopolitics*. Boulder, CO and London: Lynne Rienner.

SICABAM (Société d'Intérèt Collectif Agricole Bananière de la Martinique). 1964. "Organisation and Trends in the Banana Industry in Martinique." Banana Demonstration Tour, Guadeloupe, 17–25 February.
- 1965. "Prix de revient." Fort-de-France, Martinique. Mimeographed.
- 1966. "Dossier de groupement de producteurs." Typescript.
- 1987. "Data on Structure of Membership." Fort-de-France, Martinique. Typescript.
- 1987a. "Prix de revient, 1 septembre, 1987." Fort-de-France, Martinique. Mimeographed.
- 1987b. "Répartition des frais départ, 19/2/87." Fort-de-France, Martinique. Mimeographed.
- 1988. *Rapport Annuel, Exercice 1986*. Fort-de-France, Martinique: SICABAM.

Simmonds, N.W. 1959. *Bananas*. London: Longmans.

Simpson, A. 1988. *Whose Gold? Geest and the Banana Trade*. London: Latin American Bureau.

Smith, G.W. 1961. *The Irrigation Needs of Dominica, WI*. Trinidad, WI: Soils Research and Survey Department, Regional Research Centre, ICTA.

Spector, J. 1964. "Banana Research Problems." Conference paper, Banana Demonstration Tour, Guadeloupe, 17–25 February.

Stark, J., P. Lajoie, and J.A. Green. 1966. *St Lucia*. Soil and Land Use Surveys, no. 20. Trinidad: University of the West Indies, Regional Research Centre.

Tanner, R.E.S. 1965. "The Belgian and British Administrations in Ruanda-Urundi and Tanganyika." *Journal of Local Administration* 4(3): 202–12.

Thomson, Robert. 1987. *Green Gold: Bananas and Dependency in the Eastern Caribbean*. London: Latin American Bureau.

Touche, Ross, Bailey and Smart. 1967. A Study of the Opportunities for Improving the Banana Industry in St Lucia." Unpublished report prepared for the Government of St Lucia, January.

Trouillot, M-R. 1988. *Peasants and Capital; Dominica in the World Economy*. Baltimore, MD: The Johns Hopkins University Press.

Twyford, I.T. 1964. "Banana Research: Windward Islands." Conference paper, Banana Demonstration Tour, Guadeloupe, 17–25 February.

United Kingdom. Colonial Office. 1952. *An Economic Survey of the Colonial Territories*. Vol. 7, *The Products of the Colonial Territories*. London: HMSO.

– Colonial Office. 1953. *An Economic Survey of the Colonial Territories, 1951*. Vol. 4, *The West Indian and American Territories*. London: HMSO.

– West India Commission. 1945. *Report*. London: HMSO.

Van Schijndel, A. 1994. "The Trouble with Bananas." *Financial Times* (London), 12 July.

Veeman, M.M. and T.S. Veeman. 1988. "Agricultural Marketing Boards." In *The Canadian Encyclopedia*, 30–1. Edmonton: Hurtig.

Welch, B.M. 1966. "The Development of Volcanic Landforms in the Windward and Leeward Islands." M.Sc. thesis, University of Cambridge.

– 1968. "Population Density and Emigration in Dominica." *Geographical Journal* 134: 227–35.

– 1987. "A Synthesis of Soil Classifications Used in the Central Lesser Antilles." *Soil Survey and Land Evaluation* 7(1): 1–11.

– 1989. "Institutional Structures as a Factor in Land Use Decisions: The Impact of Banana Growers' Associations in French and Commonwealth Islands in the Eastern Caribbean." Ph.D. diss., University of London.

West Indian Census, 1946. Part A (General Report); Part B (Census of Agriculture in Barbados, Leeward Islands, Windward Islands and Trinidad and Tobago); Part H (Census of the West Indies). 1950. Kingston, Jamaica: Government Printing Office.

West Indies Census of Agriculture, 1961; The Eastern Caribbean Territories. 1968. Bridgetown, Barbados: British Development Division in the Caribbean.

White, M.G. 1970. "The Introduction and Development of New Crops in Dominica." *Proceedings of the 5th West Indies Agricultural Economic*

Conference, edited by D. Maharaj and J. Strauss, 24–6. St. Augustine, Trinidad: University of the West Indies.

Whittlesey, D. 1937. "Colonial Techniques in West Africa." *Foreign Affairs* 15: 362–73.

Williams, H.D. 1975. *The Agricultural Sector Plan, 1976–80*. Roseau, Dominica: Department of Planning and Development, Premier's Office.

Windward Island Banana Growers' Association (WINBAN). 1966. "Report of General Meeting held in Grenada, November." St George's, Grenada. Typescript.

– 1986. *Banana Growers' Manual*. WINBAN Research and Development Division. Castries, St Lucia: Voice Publishing Company.

– 1987. *Annual Report*, 1986. Castries, St Lucia: WINBAN.

– 1988. *Annual Data Report: All Islands, No. 1, 02/05/88*. Castries, St Lucia: WINBAN.

MAPS CONSULTED

West Indies. Dominica, 1:25,000. United Kingdom. Ministry of Overseas Development. Directorate of Overseas Surveys. 1961.

Lesser Antilles. Dominica, 1:25,000. United Kingdom. Ministry of Overseas Development, Directorate of Overseas Surveys. 1978.

Dominica, 1:50,000. United Kingdom. Ministry of Overseas Development, Directorate of Overseas Surveys. 1963.

Dominica. Soil Map, 1:40,000. To accompany Lang (1967). Regional Research Centre, University of the West Indies, Trinidad.

Dominica. Banana Lands, 1:50,000. United Kingdom. To accompany Momsen (1969). Ministry of Overseas Development, Directorate of Overseas Surveys. 1969.

Carte du département de la Guadeloupe au 20,000e. Ministère des Travaux Publics et des Transports. Drawn and published by l'Institut Géographique National. 1956. Paris.

Carte du département de la Guadeloupe au 50,000e. Ministère des Travaux Publics et des Transports. Drawn and published by l'Institut Géographique National. 1958. Paris.

Guadeloupe. Carte Routière et Touristique au 100,000e. Ministère des Travaux Publics et des Transports. Drawn and published by l'Institut Gèographique National. 1958. Paris.

Guadeloupe. Carte Touristique au 100,000e. No. 510. Institut Géographique National. 1982.

Carte des sols des Antilles à 1/20,000e: Guadeloupe. ORSTOM, Centre des Antilles, Bureau des Sols.

Carte du département de la Martinique au 50,000e. Ministère des Travaux Publics et des Transports. Drawn and published by l'Institut Géographique National. 1958. Paris.

Carte des sols de la Martinique à 1/100,000e. ORSTOM, Centre des Antilles, Bureau des Sols. Direction: F. Colmet-Daage. n.d. (pre-1967).

Martinique. Carte des exploitations et des industries agricoles de la Martinique, 1956–1959, 1:50,000. By J. Benoist and C. Crabot. Fort-de-France, Martinique. Société d'Histoire de la Martinique. 1960.

Carte des cultures et d'occupation des terres de la Martinique à 1/100,000. ORSTOM, Centre des Antilles, Bureau des Sols. Direction: F. Colmet-Daage, n.d. (pre-1967).

Lesser Antilles. St Lucia, 1:25,000. United Kingdom. Ministry of Overseas Development, Directorate of Overseas Surveys. 1972.

St Lucia, 1:50,000. United Kingdom. Ministry of Overseas Development, Directorate of Overseas Surveys. 1963.

St Lucia. Soil Map, 1/25,000. To accompany Stark, Lajoie et al. (1966). Regional Research Centre, University of the West Indies, Trinidad.

St Lucia, 1:50,000. Banana Lands. To accompany Momsen (1969). United Kingdom. Ministry of Overseas Development, Directorate of Overseas Surveys. 1969.

St Lucia. 1:50,000. Geology; Life Zones; Rainfall and Drainage System; Land Capability; Land Use and Vegetation. Organization of American States, Department of Regional Development. 1984. Washington, DC.

PERSONAL COMMUNICATIONS

M. Arneaud (SATEC), Ministère des DOM, Paris, March 1969.

Mr Harry Atkinson, Chairman, SLBGA, 1967.

M. Bachou, Service d'Agronomie, Direction Départementale d'Agriculture, Basse-Terre, Guadeloupe, 1988.

M. Bordaz, farmer, St Joseph, Martinique, 1966.

Mr Alec Boyd, General Manager, DBGA, 1967.

Mr Colin Bully, Superintendent of Agriculture, Dominica, 1988.

Mr Charles Cadet, Superintendent of Agriculture, St Lucia, 1966–67 and WINBAN representative in the United Kingdom and Acting High Commissioner for the OECS, 1988.

M. Jacques Daudin, Specialist in Plant Disease Control, Martinique, 1966–67.

Ms. Deborah DeBeauville, Market Intelligence Officer, Windward Islands Banana Growers' Association, 1994.

Mr Michael Didier, Operations Manager, DBMC, 1988.

M. Daniel Doeuff, Ministère des DOM, Paris, March 1969.

Prof. David Edwards, Department of Agricultural Economics, University of West Indies, St. Augustine, Trinidad.
M. Paul Emélie, Service d'Agronomie, Direction Départementale d'Agriculture, Fort-de-France, Martinique, 1966–67 and 1988.
M. Joseph Hazaël-Massieux, Directeur, Service d'Agronomie, Direction Départementale d'Agriculture, Basse-Terre, Guadeloupe, 1966–67.
Mr Winston Higgins, Department of Agriculture, Dominica, 1967.
Mr Stanley Iton, Department of Geography, McGill University, Montreal.
M. Jacquemart, Direction Départementale d'Agriculture, Fort-de-France, Martinique, 1966.
M. Lamure, Direction Départementale d'Agriculture, Fort-de-France, Martinique, 1966.
M. Pierre Léobon, Directeur, SICABAM, Fort-de-France, Martinique, 1966–67.
Mr Francis Leonce, Department of Agriculture, St Lucia, 1967, and Managing Director, Geest (West Indies) Ltd, Castries, St Lucia, 1988.
M. Mariotti, Ingénieur agronome, Ministère des DOM, Paris, March 1969.
M. Mauréaux, Vice-Président, SICA-ASSOBAG, Basse-Terre, Guadeloupe, 1967.
Mr N. Moffat, farmer, Micoud, St Lucia, 1966.
Mr Kenneth Monplaisir, Chairman, SLBGA, 1966–67.
M. Joël Morlet, Directeur du Service Agro-Technique, SICABAM, Fort-de-France, Martinique, 1988.
M. Morue, IFAC, Neufchâteau, Guadeloupe, 1967.
Mr Henry Nathanial, Assistant Financial Controller, SLBGA, 1988.
M. Nelson, farmer, Baillif, Guadeloupe, 1966.
M. Parmentier, Direction Départementale d'Agriculture, Fort-de-France, Martinique, 1988.
M. Piloquet, Directeur, SICA-ASSOBAG, Basse-Terre, Guadeloupe, 1988.
M. Olivier de Pompignan, Directeur, GIPAM, Fort-de-France, Martinique, 1988.
Mr. René Raveneau, Chairman, St Lucia Agriculturalists' Association, 1967.
Mr Thomas St Hill, Field Operations Co-ordinator, SLBGA, 1988.
M. Scholastique, farmer, Rivière Pilote, Martinique, 1966, 1988.
Mr Jefferson Scotland, Executive Secretary, DBGA, 1988.
Mr Anthony Slipper, Managing Director, Banana Sector, Geest PLC, 1991.
Mr Mark Thomas, economist, WINBAN, Castries, St Lucia, 1988.
Mr Bethel Williams, farmer, Millet, St Lucia, 1966.
Mr Jan C. Vermeiren, OAS Department of Regional Development, St Lucia, 1988.
M. Zébus, farmer, Capesterre, Guadeloupe, 1967.

Index